TOWARD MODERNITY

TOWARD MODERNITY

The European Jewish Model

Edited by

JACOB KATZ

Transaction Books
New Brunswick (U.S.A.) and Oxford (U.K.)

Published by Transaction, Inc.

Library of Congress Catalog Number: 86-4319
ISBN: 0-88738-092-1
Printed in the United States of America

Library of Congress Cataloging in Publication Data
Toward modernity.
  Includes bibliographies and index.
  1. Jews—Cultural assimilation—Congresses.
2. Haskalah—Congresses. 3. Jews—History—1789–1945—
Congresses. I. Katz, Jacob, 1904–   .
DS148.T68 1986   909ʹ.04924   86-4319
ISBN 0-88738-092-1

Contents

Preface

Trailing the historical process of the modern metamorphosis of Jewry and Judaism in ten countries—the result of a symposium organized by the Leo Baeck Institute in the spring of 1983 in Haifa—may well throw light on one of the central problems of Jewish historiography, namely, how Jewry and Judaism survived the crisis of the break up of Jewish traditional society, the transition from the closed ghetto or ghetto-like existence into a more or less open environment. The process starting in eighteenth-century Germany gradually encompassed the whole Jewish world. The ten scholars, each an expert on the history of one country, inform us about the course of events in their respective domain, while the editor's introduction attempts to draw the lesson concerning the nature of Jewish modernity in general.

In editing this volume I have been greatly assisted by Gabriel Motzkin.

JACOB KATZ

Introduction

Jacob Katz

As indicated by the title of the book, its purpose is to compare the process of modernization in German Jewry with its counterparts in other countries, with the question in mind whether the German-Jewish development had any influence on what transpired elsewhere. The inquiry being historically relevant, it is hoped that the comparison between the different countries would also throw light on the nature of the modernization, clarifying what factors were involved in the process. Accordingly we have solicited papers on the history of Jewish modernization in Russia, Galicia, Vienna, Prague, Hungary, Holland, France, England, and the United States. An essay on Italy has been added by an author who had not participated in the conference.

The expectation of gaining the desired insight is based on the assumption that the development in the said countries, if it had not a common source, at least reveals a common denominator. We may then ask whether the essays presented here indeed suggest such a common thread. Though not made explicit in any of the essays, the common denominator was implied in the criterion by which the modern variation of Jewish communities could be differentiated from its predecessor, the traditional Jewish society. In the latter the observance of the Jewish tradition could and would be enforced by the organs of the Jewish community. The authority to do so was conferred on the Jewish community by the state, and constituted a part of the communal autonomy. There was also a measure of control over the spread of ideas; non-Orthodox ones, as for instance Sabbateanism, could and would be suppressed. The posttraditional Jewish community was denied the right to impose its will concerning thought and action on the individual. This limitation of the communal authority applied to all the countries under consideration here, including Russia, where not even the initial stages of emancipation had been introduced. Still, the community lost political authority over its members.

1

The control that could be exercised over the behavior of the individual was of a social and not political nature.

The right of enforcement was withdrawn from the Jewish communities as a result of the change in the state's self-conception. Under the impact of rationalization and enlightenment the state relinquished its claim to be directly responsible for the religious conduct of the population. In the extreme case, realized first in the United States, the state's disclaimer became absolute, leading to the separation of church and state. In the European states it amounted only to the loosening of ties between the two. Everywhere the individual gained a certain amount of freedom in evolving or absorbing ideas and determining his conduct accordingly. Jews also gained this leeway in their relation to the community and the traditional values represented by it.

What were the options implied in this development? It is well to remember Voltaire's prognosis for the future of the Jewish community. Envisaging a society in which religion would have no institutional footing, he predicted that the educated among the Jews would join the corresponding layers of society at large, while the uneducated masses would be absorbed by the lower strata of society, the scum of the earth.[1]

This prognosis was fulfilled only marginally. Absorption of Jews into the different layers of society did take place, but it affected only a small portion of Jewry. The absorption nowhere dissolved the core of the community. Though losing their formal existential basis grounded in the enforceability of the tradition, Jewish communities continued to tie their members together in one way or another. Why and how did this happen?

Here we have to differentiate between two disparate situations Jews confronted. In one the Jew was indeed free to dissociate himself from his community altogether, as in the United States and in England, where the authorities did not concern themselves with people's religious affiliations. The other situation existed in Europe, where at least during the nineteenth century the state obliged its citizens to declare their religious affiliation. Only in the two English-speaking countries was affiliation with the Jewish community voluntary, a feature not sufficiently stressed in the essays on these countries. Here a situation arose where Voltaire's prognosis seemed to have a chance to be realized. Todd M. Endelman's description of what transpired in England in the first phase of modernization presents a perfect testing ground for Voltaire's thesis. There seemed to be neither external impediments nor internal inhibitions for Jews to be absorbed by the Gentile majority. The result, however, was not the disappearance of English Jewry but rather its establishing itself amidst the non-Jewish society as a less cohesive group, but still as one that retained its social boundaries toward a majority society. The case is the same in North America. Obviously acculturation and even a certain measure of social integration does not necessarily lead to social dissolution. Despite the lessening of religious tradition, Jewish society retained enough cohesion and solidarity to continue its social existence. The non-Jewish society retained its reservations toward its Jewish minority more effectively than meets the eye, notwithstanding Endelman's assumption.

The experience of the English-speaking countries holds two important lessons for the understanding of the European situation. In Europe the state assisted the Jewish communities in maintaining their communal organizations, as for instance in the collection of taxes. This led contemporaries to believe that the survival of the communities depended upon the cooperation of the state authorities. The English experience also invalidates the charge voiced often by Orthodox Jewish opponents modernity, that the German-Jewish example is responsible for the undermining of Jewish tradition wherever it occurred. Modernization resulted from the transmutation in all societies. What singled out the German scene was that this process did not take effect in a perfunctory accommodation but was carried out, so to speak, in the light of ideological supervision. Both the educational reform that replaced the traditional institutions (the *cheder* and the *yeshiva*) by modern schools and rabbinical seminiaries as well as the religious reform that adapted the religious service to the pattern of contemporary conception and taste, were carried out with the participants being fully conscious of the significance of their actions. The same has to be said about neo-Orthodoxy's reconstruction of the religious tradition that was not simply a recovery of lost ground but a novel interpretation of the tradition. Once this peculiar procedure of ideologically sponsored transmutation occurred, it could not fail to serve as a paradigm for other Jewish communities.

Factual, nonreflective accommodation, as exemplified by the English experience, is by nature locale-bound. Studied and reasoned change is prone to be mobile, but this mobility does not mean the exact transplanting of the German growth into another soil. As all the essays in this volume testify, local conditions determined everywhere not only the time of absorption but also the extent of emulation, adapting it to the needs and possibilities of the locality. In the examples of England and the United States we have two extreme cases. English Jewry carried through its adaptation in its own nonreflective way, referring to the German example only marginally, though I would think with greater effect than suggested by Endelman, who is looking for ideological conformity in the two countries and fails to find it. But the impact may consist in the fact that the mere knowledge of the Reform being established in Germany encouraged the English reformers to proceed in their own way.

Contrary to the minimal influence in England, in the United States the German example was dominating. This was due as much to the German background of the immigrants as to the lack of stimuli coming from the immediate American environment. The first generation of the German-Jewish immigrants seemed to live in a social vacuum, allowing the adhesion to the ideas and ideals of the homeland. Once the immigrants made American society proper into their reference group, their orientation became American, and they left behind the German example. The result was not a reduction of the German Reform as in England, but on the contrary its radicalization, as described in Michael A. Meyer's essay.

The dependence of the German-Jewish impact on the prevailing conditions in its sphere of influence was also evident in the role it played in Holland and France, the two western neighbors of Germany where the political enfranchisement of Jews proceeded at a more rapid pace than in Germany. Once emancipated by the Revolution, French Jewry could have steered its internal development without outside political pressure. Still, French Jewry experienced the exposure to governmental scrutiny possibly more than any other Jewish group when Napoleon convened the Sanhedrin, demanding the abolition of salient elements of the Jewish tradition as a price for French citizenship. And even when in the post-Napoleonic era this condition was waived, the expectation of the administration and of public opinon that Jews conform in their cultural behavior to the prevailing French pattern was tangibly present in the consciousness of French Jews, especially in that of their leadership. Unlike in England, here the accommodation could not be left to chance and exigencies. Indeed, changes were introduced deliberately by the centralized Consistoire. Those responsible for the changes were naturally interested in precedents in the Jewish world, and that is why French Jewry followed closely the accommodation process in Germany, not always to emulate it but sometimes to take a different path explicitly. Still, German development served as a point of orientation, and in some respects French development was a kind of translation of the German pattern. The education of rabbis for instance was first entrusted to the Seminar in Metz, which was modeled on the institutions for training Catholic priests; when it was transferred to Paris in 1859 it became a French, diluted version of the Seminar in Breslau. Jewish modern scholarship in France was to all intents and purposes an extension of the Wissenschaft des Judentums, as pointed out by Michael Graetz in his essay.

Dutch Jewry had a smoother avenue to modern conditions than its French counterpart. Its emancipation was achieved under direct French influence, but once granted it remained intact and undisputed. The cultural accommodation could proceed undisturbed here, conditioned only by the particular social structure and stratification, as emphasized in Joseph Michman's essay. The stimuli that governed the French and German development being absent here, Dutch Jewry escaped both the centralized reglementation that took place in France as well as the radical transformation of the religious institutions that occurred in some places in Germany. But the tendency to reexamine Jewish tradition in light of the changing situation was not lacking in Holland either. In this endeavor the example of Germany, where this process assumed a special intensity, was naturally cited and discussed. Owing to the special conditions in Holland, the proponents of a radical solution there remained a small and socially inconsequential group. If Reform did not have a great appeal to Dutch Jewry, its sequel, neo-Orthodoxy, did, and naturally here the German example served as a paradigm. Despite the fact that Dutch Jewry was left to its own devices by the governmental agencies and the surrounding society, it did not go the way of decimation as predicted by Voltaire. It revealed on the contrary some rudiments of renovation, showing once again that the modern tendencies evident in Germany and elsewhere were not merely a response to external stimuli but the result of internal growth.

The Western countries we considered until now were situated outside of Germany. Vienna and Prague on the other hand were a part of Greater Germany. Indirectly, even the Jewish community in northern Italy, at that time under Austrian rule, has to be regarded as within the German perimeter. The Edict of Tolerance of the Emperor Joseph II (1782), the immediate occasion for the first public debate on educational modernization recommended from Berlin, concerned also those Italian communities. It was natural that Italian rabbis and educators should be involved in the debate. In addition its initiator from Berlin, Naftali Herz Wessely, directly addressed them, expecting to receive their support in his struggle with his conservative opponents in other places. This support was indeed forthcoming, though in guarded form and without the revolutionary enthusiasm characteristic of the German reformers. Having been accustomed to a combination of secular subjects with the religious ones in the school's curriculum, the new educational reform failed to awaken among Italian Jewry either positive or negative emotions, a peculiarity stressed and documented in Lois C. Dubin's essay.

Vienna and Prague being more closely related to Berlin, the respective repercussion of the Berlin Haskalah in the two places still represents individual variations. Of course the expansion of modernity within Germany itself and its diffusion from the center to the periphery would be a legitimate point of inquiry by itself, for there is a center for the rise of modernity, namely Berlin and the other two Prussian cities, Königsberg and Breslau. It is a shrewd observation of Hillel J. Kieval that the new cultural trend changed the hierarchy among the Jewish communities. While up to the last third of the eighteenth century, as long as talmudic learning and rabbinical authority defined the communities' position, Frankfurt and Prague occupied the highest rank among the communities, the shift in the scale of values and the emergence of novel ideas gave Berlin the preference. People in Prague listened to what reached them from Berlin and reacted to it.

Though only on the receiving end, Prague was not a passive participant in the process of modernization. First of all the introduction of the new ideas met in Prague with the opposition of the rabbinical leadership headed by Chief Rabbi Yeheskel Landau. But this opposition was directed toward Enlightenment only in so far as it posed a threat to the religious values on which the traditional society rested. Rabbi Landau suspected the Berlin school to be heading toward total secularization of education. Yet an appeal to reform Jewish education was also made by the Austrian government, and this was interpreted by the traditional rabbis as a mere technical preparation for earning a living and good citizenship. Landau agreed to the legitimacy of this demand. His conciliatory attitude is taken by Kieval as one of the main reasons why modernization was relatively smoothly absorbed in Prague but led finally to the erosion of the traditional values altogether. I will not quarrel with him on this point, for the impact of the towering figure of *noda be'Yehuda* may have had a crucial role in giving the development a decisive direction.

However, social and political considerations must be taken into account as well. In Prague as elsewhere, local conditions must have played a part. What set Prague apart from Berlin? It is I think what Kieval has only hinted at: that Prague lacked a non-Jewish counterpart, into which the Jewish *maskil* could aspire to be included. The *maskilim* dreamed of a society where harmony prevailed between Jews and non-Jews, but this was a rather abstract aspiration, void of a concrete social objective. No wonder that the literary output of the Prague *maskilim* was destined for Jews only. In this sense the Prague Haskalah was indeed national, as defined by Ruth Kestenberg-Gladstein. Kieval's criticism of this definition is, I think, a matter of semantics.

Turning to Vienna, we encounter an altogether different situation. If Prague was one of the oldest Jewish communities in Europe, Vienna had no community organization at all at the beginning of the modern era. A few Jewish families were privileged to live in the capital because of their wealth and economic usefulness. Others, members of the communities in Bohemia, Moravia, and Hungary stayed there more or less

temporarily. Out of these elements the ever-growing community constituted itself, first barely tolerated and then, some time after the 1848-49
Revolution, legalized.

Having no local tradition to defend, one would expect to find here a
fertile ground for radical experiments. The situation offered an opportunity
for individual approaches to one's Jewishness—on the one hand defection
by accepting formal baptism or, on the other, joining the democratic
revolutionaries in 1848-49. As far as the majority of the community,
who sought a modus vivendi by accommodating Judaism to modern
conditions, is concerned, the Viennese variation is characterized rather
by settling for a compromise. This applies to the moderate reform
introduced in the synagogue as well as to the fact that groups of differing
and conflicting attitudes—Orthodox, liberal, nationalists—lived side by
side in mutual toleration. The description of this variegated scenery in
its historical development is the theme of Robert S. Wistrich's essay.

In Hungary the same agencies of modernization were at work as in
Bohemia, but interestingly with altogether different results. The educational reform of Joseph II was imposed upon Hungary as well, and
ripples of the Haskalah movement reached Hungary, mainly through the
mediation of Vienna and Prague. The response to the governmental
reform was not unfriendly, even in rabbinical circles; if it failed to yield
much result it was because of the lack of interest in secular education.
Bound to the traditional role of Jews in a semifeudal economy, Hungarian
Jews saw in secular education no professional or other advantages. The
idea of Enlightenment on the other hand did catch up with certain
intellectuals, outstanding among them Aaron Chorin, an acting rabbi in
Arad in southern Hungary who drew some practical consequences from
its Mendelssohnian philosophy. He adapted the religious service of his
synagogue to what appeared to him to conform to contemporary conceptions and taste. A halachist of some importance, Chorin tried to
vindicate his decisions on the basis of halachah. Though not significant
in themselves, Chorin's changes alerted some of the traditionalists, first
and foremost among them Rabbi Moses Sofer, the *chatam sofer* from
Pressburg. Born in Frankfurt, and having witnessed the first clash between
the innovators and their opponents in his homeland, the *chatam sofer*
became highly sensitive toward any deviation from the tradition, even
if halachically of not much importance. Accordingly he evolved a full-
scale ideology of traditionalism, epitomized in this famous slogan *hadash
asur min Ha'Torah,* that is, whatever is an innovation falls under the
category of biblical prohibition.

It can be said that in Hungary, because of a mere coincidence depending
on the presence of two personalities, the ideological contest emerged

already before the actual conditions elicited it. Indeed, the clash between the two schools did not erupt in the wake of some local issue but in response to what happened in Germany when in 1819 colliding factions solicited the halachic opinion of the rabbis concerning the Reform worship in Hamburg and Berlin. When, in the following decades, in the wake of social and economic advancement in Hungary, the Jewish community gained economic ground, living space, and finally political rights, the conflict between the two schools of thought assumed an unheard-of actuality. The conflict was fought out with unprecedented vehemence, resulting in a veritable schism between the Orthodoxy and the Neologists. While the latter cannot be said to represent more than a shady reproduction of the German innovations, the former was a local creation, though not unconnected to the German background of its founder, the *chatam sofer*, who had been scared by the deterioration of tradition in his homeland.

Social and political factors also played a part in the development in Hungary, as Michael Silver states in his essay. Still, Silver agrees that the role of personalities, especially that of the *chatam sofer*, must be regarded as decisive. It would be intriguing to compare the *sofer's* role in Hungary with that of Yeheskel Landau in Prague. As the outstanding halachist of his generation, the *chatam sofer* can be said to have inherited the position of *noda be'Yehuda*. Yet in his involvement in the historical process of his time the *chatam sofer* represents a new type of person—the militant traditional Orthodox.

Galicia, being a part of the Austrian Empire, received the same stimuli as Bohemia and Hungary. But the intervention of the government, intending to reshape Galician Jewry economically and culturally, was more far-reaching than in other parts of the empire. The absorption of rationalistic ideas coming from Germany was also more in evidence. The *maskilim* here were a more militant and conspicuous group than elsewhere. The Jewish community, however, had an altogether different complexion and structure, and accordingly the intended changes had much less effect than in Bohemia and Hungary.

First, Galician Jewry occupied an altogether different place in Galician society than in Bohemia and Hungary. It was, as pointed out by Israel Bartal, the only incumbent of the position of the middle class, posited between the aristocracy and the peasants. The attempts to reform it by the fiat of governmental ordinances or by the persuasion of the *maskilim* was even quantitatively a much more ambitious enterprise than in Bohemia or Hungary. While in Bohemia there was at least a remote reference group for the Jewish enlightened, namely, the German middle class in the cities of the empire, and in Hungary the emerging Magyar nation which the Jews were invited to join by assimilation, in Galicia none of these existed. A transformation of Galician Jewry, as envisioned by the state authorities and the *maskilim,* would have meant revolutionizing it, which is, however, a process that can be prompted by internal forces only, not by external agencies. Then Galician Jewry had just gone through a kind of revolution, the concussion of Hassidism, which through its mystical nature made it impervious to rational influences. Contrary to Hungary, where Orthodoxy had to create its ideological and institutional weapons to ward off the impact of modernization, Galician Orthodoxy could rely upon the arsenal put at its disposal by Hassidism. The latter turned out to be much more effective. While in Hungary—and for that matter also in Germany—Orthodoxy became a minority, Galician Orthodoxy retained the allegiance of the majority. The *maskilim* and their modernizing followers remained a minority.

Emanuel Etkes's paper is exceptional in that it deals with the absorption of the ideas of the Haskalah, but only marginally with its political and social effects. This condition was dictated by the historical circumstances, for in Russia the political and social segregation of Jews by the government continued almost unimpaired well into the twentieth century. Limited in his assignment, Etkes on the other hand was able to trace the exact path of German-Jewish influence as against the reliance of the *maskilim* on internal Jewish elements coming down from the Middle Ages. Here we have representatives of the type which Silver in his own area of reference called *maskil torani* or *rav maskil.* The emergence of this type is much easier to explain in Central Europe than in the East. Still, I would dare to suggest that a faint reflection of the modern era evident in the whole of Europe reached even the remote corners of the Pale of Settlement. Thus, where the counterrevolution of mystical Hassidism did not block the way, a rationalistic approach could be adopted. The subjective reliance of the *maskilim* on the medieval sources does not exclude the possibility that the initial stimuli came from the climate of opinion of European rationalism.

Having surveyed the process of modernization in the countries where the impact of the German model converged with the influence of local factors, we may attempt to determine the particular character of the original German model. This problem should be tackled historically as well as sociologically.

Historically speaking, German Jewry, including that of Bohemia and Moravia, was exposed to the slow but steady influence of the rationally saturated atmosphere of the absolutistic states since the end of the seventeenth century. As is well known, Azriel Shohat surveyed the relevant sources of this pre-Mendelssohnian period and thought he found indications of a cultural and social rapprochement of Jews to the Gentile environment.[2] On the basis of these findings, Shohat wished to predate the turning point in Jewish history by half a century at least. As a turning point presupposes the conscious experience of contemporaries —and of this there is hardly any evidence—I do not think that this predating is justified. Tradition held its sway over the community uncontestedly. Whatever stimuli in the form of scientific information or bits and pieces of a rational world view reached the ghetto could still be easily incorporated into the system of Jewish tradition. However, the steady contact with the increasingly rationalized environment on different levels—the Court Jews in doing business with their economically minded masters, the community leaders with the rationally trained officials of the state, and the occasional glimpses of students into treatises of non-Jewish scholars—had their effect on Jewish mentality. I fully agree with Michael Silver's claim that a relative openness and inquisitiveness is to be found in the rabbinical culture of Central Europe preceding Haskalah proper. This and the other phenomena mentioned set Central Europe apart from the east, where such types were "rare birds" only. The incipient gap between East and West brought about a new situation, for until the eighteenth century Ashkenazic Jewry from the Ukraine to the Alsace was regarded as a relatively homogeneous society. The detachment of the two areas was most tellingly documented by the fact that the Hassidic movement, erupting in the mid–eighteenth century in Podolia, reached all parts of Eastern Europe but stopped at the borders of the Central European countries. The rationally tinged communities remained non-responsive to the mystical trend, even when outstanding Hassidic representatives arrived in their midst, as when Rabbi Pinchas Horowitz arrived in Frankfurt and his brother Schmelke in Nikolsburg. In sum, Central European communities can be said to have been historically tempered for their reception of the Haskalah, and when it arrived it met with only small opposition, even in rabbinical and otherwise traditional circles.

The sociological aspect of this phenomenon is characterized by the fact that in Germany the Enlightenment of Jews could aim at a well-defined social target: the possible inclusion into the emerging middle class. Endelman argues that Germany, in contrast to the Eastern countries, "lacked a nascent entrepreneurically minded, politically conscious bourgeoisie." True, but the idea of creating such a bourgeoisie is a central theme in the German Enlightenment. And just because this class was not yet ready-made and had as yet no clear-cut boundaries, the idea of including the Jewish outsiders into it was easily conceived and accepted. Indeed, the classic recommendation of Jewish integration, Christian Wilhelm Dohm's *Über die bürgerliche Verbesserung der Juden*,[3] explicitly combines the future emancipation of the Jews with the emergence of the civic society, "die bürgerliche Gesellschaft." This civic society was destined to replace the rigid structure of contemporary society based on the division of the estates. Then in the course of the liberal era, when the civic society indeed did come into being, the parallel process of Jewish social metamorphosis fed the illusion that a fusion between the two streams would be the end result. Contrary to other countries under consideration here, where no Gentile counterpart to the Jewish middle class existed—or where it existed but, as in America, seemed beyond the reach of the Jews—in Germany the middle class was in the making, and Jews hoped to become an integral part of it. That this turned out to be an illusion does not change its relevance as a key to its historical understanding.

For the first generation of the *maskilim* there was an even more concrete social target, what many years ago I called—following the definition of one of my teachers, Hans Weil[4]—the *Geisteselite*. The group of enlightened Christians to whom Moses Mendelssohn found access was such an elite group. It was characterized by the willingness to ignore religious differences and meet on the basis of a common humanity according to the prevailing philosophy of tolerance. The *Geisteselite* served first as a social medium for individuals coming from the different estates, aristocrats, bureaucrats, artists, and others. That a Jew could be found who could take part in the spiritual activity and contribute to its creation can be regarded as a mere coincidence, Moses Mendelssohn's involvement in the shaping of the new trend in Jewish history is as striking an instance of the role of personality in history as that of the *chatam sofer* operating in an opposite direction. Mendelssohn's contribution became of decisive importance; due to him Jewish aspirations to have access to non-Jewish society were not simply displayed in practice, as in England, but carried out under the cover of intellectual vindication. Jewish modernization in Germany turned articulate. Mendelssohn gave the example and others followed suit. The educational reform was in practice accepted by Austro-Hungarian Jewry out of the hands of the government, but its ideological exposition came from Berlin, from Naftali Herz Wessely.

By virtue of intellectual articulation the German-Jewish social experiment became mobile, and that is why we find its influence in all the countries where similar experiments became the order of the day. The later stages of modernization, leading up to Reform, Wissenschaft des Judentums, and neo-Orthodoxy, came then simply as a continuation of the initial process. They too excelled in seeking literary expression of their tendencies, and due to it they became exemplary, to be emulated by their adherents and shunned and rejected by their adversaries.

Notes

1. See Jacob Katz, "Religion as a Uniting and Dividing Force in Modern Jewish History," in idem, ed., *The Role of Religion in Modern Jewish History* (Cambridge, Mass.: Association for Jewish Studies, 1975), p. 1.
2. Azriel Shochat, *Beginning of the Haskalah among German Jews* (Hebrew) (Jerusalem: Bialik Institute, 1960).
3. 2 vols. (Berlin, 1781–1782).
4. Hans Weil, *Die Entstehung des deutschen Bildungsprinzips* (Frankfurt am Main: Droller, 1930). I referred to it in my doctoral dissertation *Die Entstehung der Judenassimilation in Deutschland und deren Ideologie* (Frankfurt am Main, 1934), p. 13ff. Reprinted in Jacob Katz, *Emancipation and Assimilation, Studies in Modern Jewish History* (Westmead, Farnborough: Gregg International 1972), and in idem, *Zur Assimilation und Emanzipation der Juden* (Darmstadt: Wissenschaftliche Buchgesellschaft, 1982).

1

Immanent Factors and External Influences in the Development of the Haskalah Movement in Russia

Emanuel Etkes

The dependence of the Jewish Russian Haskalah (Enlightenment) upon that of Berlin is well known. And yet it is important to consider the possibility that internal factors, independent of the influence of Berlin, might have operated in the development of the Russian Haskalah. If so, the question arises as to the relative significance of these factors.

To deal with this question it is necessary to focus on the change that took place in the intellectual life of the Jews of Poland and Lithuania in the second half of the eighteenth century. A new orientation began to appear in the writings and cultural activity of a number of individuals, many of whom belonged to the scholarly elite. In retrospect, this orientation can be seen as an inclination toward the Haskalah. It has been variously evaluated in the literature; while some historians have interpreted it as the beginning of the Haskalah movement in Russia,[1] most have more cautiously described these people as "pioneers," "first shoots," or "fore-runners" of the Haskalah.[2] This difference in evaluation may derive not from different interpretations of the facts but rather from the lack of an agreed-upon, clear-cut set of concepts concerning the Haskalah. Hence it is not surprising that historians employ the terms *Haskalah* or *maskilim* with widely divergent meanings.

My own definition of the Jewish Enlightenment, or the Haskalah movement, emphasizes its mature manifestations. My model is the Berlin Haskalah of the 1780s, which took a new spiritual and cultural position regarding both Judaism and the Jews as well as their relation to European society and culture.

Characteristics of the Haskalah

Theology

The Haskalah leaned toward a rationalistic interpretation of Judaism. That tendency took several forms: one finds attempts to formulate a general conception of the beliefs and opinions of Judaism besides attempts to interpret such sources, generally rabbinic literature, which appeared to be stumbling blocks from the point of view of rationalistic criticism. The effort to provide a rationalistic interpretation of Jewish theology was accompanied by a critical view of the antiquity and authority of the Kabbala.

Halachah

The Haskalah was increasingly conscious of the historical character of the process by which the *halachah* (rabbinic law) took shape. Although it did not adopt a critical attitude toward the authority of the corpus of the halachah, it did so toward some *minhagim* (customs), which it viewed as late accretions and the product of unnecessarily strict interpretations.

Talmud Torah

The traditional value placed upon the study of the Torah for its own sake and the social ideal of the *talmid hacham* were supplanted by a functional view that restricted specialization in halachic literature to those who were to assume some rabbinic post. In contrast to the centrality of the study of halachic literature that typified traditional society, emphasis was placed upon the Bible, which was conceived as an expression of universal human values, a guide to "success" in this world, and as an embodiment of aesthetic values. Along with these changes in areas of study and the significance attributed to them, a change in methodology also took place. Criticism was voiced against talmudic casuistry or *pilpul* in the study of halachah, and literal interpretations were sought instead. In Bible study, a sharper distinction was made between *drash* and *peshat,* homiletic and literal interpretation. Literal interpretation was preferred, assisted by knowledge drawn from new research methods in history, geography, and especially philology.

Hebrew Language

The functional approach, which treats Hebrew as a vehicle for prayer and Torah study, was replaced by the romantic attitude, which glorified that language, viewing it as the single invaluable remnant of a glorious past to be cherished and preserved. The romantic approach focused on Hebrew as an object of philological research. It also stimulated the enthusiasm and excitement that accompanied attempts to compose Hebrew poetry, inspired by the Bible, which was seen as an aesthetic model worthy of imitation. This new attitude, which viewed Hebrew both as a subject for research and as a vehicle for the creation of poetry with its own intrinsic value, decidedly expresses the tendency toward secularization that characterized the Haskalah.

The Relationship with European Society and Culture

The particularistic self-conception that had characterized the traditional attitude toward surrounding cultures was replaced by a humanistic outlook expressing the common human element in the Jew and in all mankind. That new outlook necessitated a reevaluation of the culture of the surrounding non-Jewish society which was no longer seen as an expression of an alien religious and national tradition but rather as the fruit of human creative powers and thus as part of a common universal heritage. Consequently, Jewish participation in European culture was not merely permissible but actually desirable.

The belief that humanism had become the guiding principle of the political leadership and educated classes of European society led to the conclusion that there could be a new basis for the relations between Jews and their surroundings. Jewish cultural, political, and social involvement in their surroundings now appeared to be a desirable and feasible goal. Its achievement seemed to depend not only on influencing ruling circles and enlightened public opinion but even more on the Jews' effort to adapt and become worthy of integration. To that end programs critical of traditional Jewish life were designed to reform Jewish society in education, economic activity, and community organization. To those who had absorbed and internalized the standards and attitudes then current in European society, traditional Jewish life had many flaws. Their correction was of the utmost urgency, for they placed a barrier between Jews and their surroundings and impeded the inclusion of the Jews in the general society.

An Intermediate Phase

The term the *Haskalah movement* is applied here to the men who adopted those attitudes and who worked together in order to reform Jewish society accordingly. Thus there was no Jewish Enlightenment movement in Russia before the 1820s and 1830s, when its outstanding spokesman was Yitzchak Behr Levinsohn, and the new trend in the spiritual life of the Jews of Poland and Lithuania in the second half of the eighteenth century does not belong to the Haskalah movement. Only a few Haskalah characteristics are applicable to most of the men at that time. Some were rather close to the Haskalah position but were isolated and did not join forces to form a movement. The new direction discernible during the second half of the eighteenth century was an intermediate phase between the traditional way of life and the mature Haskalah movement. This phase is extremely revealing when we enquire whether the development of the Haskalah movement in Russia was due to immanent factors independent of the influence of Berlin. I shall therefore examine several figures who may be considered as representative of this intermediate phase.

The first two are the Gaon of Vilna[3] and Rabbi Shlomo of Chelm.[4] They differed in several respects. Unlike the reclusive Gaon of Vilna, Rabbi Shlomo served as the rabbi of several communities and was involved in public affairs. The Gaon of Vilna's intellectual achievements and influence in Torah studies were far greater than those of Rabbi Shlomo. Nevertheless, both adopted similar positions on issues related to the present discussion.[5]

Both the Gaon of Vilna and Rabbi Shlomo of Chelm criticized the way in which the Torah was studied in their time. The basis of their criticism was rationalistic. They especially condemned *pilpul,* whose primary aim was to exhibit ingenuity for its own sake. Instead they sought to base study upon the literal meaning of the text, to reach a correct understanding of the words of the rabbis. They pointed to the necessity of studying the sciences as a means of clarifying halachic issues, and both actually studied science in that spirit and with that aim. Rabbi Shlomo went even further than the Gaon of Vilna and attributed another virtue to the study of science: the development of intellectual capacity.

In contrast to these affinities between them, the Gaon of Vilna and Rabbi Shlomo differed with respect to the rationalistic philosophy of the Middle Ages. Whereas the beliefs and opinions held by the Gaon of Vilna were anchored in the kabbala, and his attitude toward philosophy was reserved, Rabbi Shlomo took pride in his practice of studying Maimonides's *Guide for the Perplexed.*

At this point, the question arises as to the sources of the respective positions of the Gaon of Vilna and of Rabbi Shlomo. It seems clear that both drew their inspiration from within the Jewish heritage. Science and philosophy had been commonly studied in Spanish and Provençal circles during the Middle Ages and by Italian Jews during the Renaissance. The justification of science as an aid to Torah study derived from these circles, and likewise the claim that the Jews thereby fulfill the verse,

"For it is your wisdom and your understanding in the eyes of the nations," a claim made explicitly by Rabbi Shlomo and also attributed to the Gaon of Vilna. Criticism of *pilpul* and the demand for rationalization of Torah study also originated, at the very latest, with the Maharal of Prague during the sixteenth century.[6] On the other hand, neither in the writings of the Gaon nor of Rabbi Shlomo can we find any hint of a *direct and conscious* influence from trends and attitudes which were developing in Western and Central Europe during the eighteenth century. Both men should rather be seen as "innocent" bearers of elements intrinsic to the Jewish tradition of the Middle Ages and the Renaissance.

These views of the Gaon and of Rabbi Shlomo were not common among talmudic circles in Eastern Europe, but they were not completely out of the ordinary. Quite a few among the Ashkenazic scholarly elite during the late Middle Ages justified studying the sciences as auxiliaries to Torah study.[7] The criticism of methods of study voiced by the Maharal was taken up in succeeding generations.[8]

Yet if the Gaon of Vilna and Rabbi Shlomo of Chelm were "innocent" exponents of elements of the Jewish heritage and if their attitudes were acceptable to a certain stratum of the scholarly elite, then what linked such figures to the intermediate phase between the traditional way of life and the Haskalah movement? It appears that the answer depends on timing. Even though the Gaon, Rabbi Shlomo, and others like them did not deviate from traditional norms, the very fact that they expressed elements taken from the medieval-Renaissance heritage at their time and place made them serve as a bridge between that heritage and the new trends that had begun to develop in Poland and Lithuania. In other words, the Gaon of Vilna and Rabbi Shlomo of Chelm served as a kind of handhold for those who, on the basis of that very tradition, or at least out of a positive regard for it, did in fact deviate from traditional norms and moved toward the Haskalah. Two figures that represent this transition to the intermediate phase are Rabbi Yisrael Zamoscz and Rabbi Barukh of Shklov. However, I should like to turn first to the less known Rabbi Yehezkel Feivel, the author of *Sefer Toldot Adam,* who has not been discussed in the historiography of the Russian Haskalah.

Rabbi Yehezkel Feivel[9] was born in Palanga, Lithuania, in 1756 and died in Vilna in 1834. While still a young man he was a *maggid* (preacher) in the communities of Palanga and Deretschin. In the course of his wanderings he also preached in the communities of Lvov and Brod and lived for a period in Breslau. He maintained close ties with members of his family in Vilna, the prominent Yosef Ben-Eliahu and his brother Arieh Laib. It appears that thanks to them he was invited to the home of the Gaon of Vilna several times. In 1811 he was appointed the official preacher of Vilna and served for twenty-two years.

Rabbi Feivel expressed his views in his book *Sefer Toldot Adam,*[10] the first part of which was printed in 1801 and the second in 1809. It recounts the life and personality of Rabbi Solomon Zalman of Volozhin, the brother of Rabbi Haim of Volozhin and the Gaon of Vilna's favorite disciple who died prematurely. The book belongs to the genre of didactic biographies as various aspects of Rabbi Solomon's life and personality are presented as models worthy of imitation. The author also permits himself occasionally to digress. These associative discussions also possess a didactic character.

A study of *Sefer Toldot Adam* shows that Rabbi Yehezkel was well acquainted with medieval Jewish philosophy and even markedly influenced by it. In contrast to the Gaon of Vilna and Rabbi Shlomo of Chelm, however, an influence of the Western European Enlightenment is discernible in Rabbi Yehezkel's book. It is visible in his choice of didactic biography, a common genre in the Enlightenment literature. Moreover, in 1788 Yitshak Euchel's biography of Mendelssohn had been published in Berlin. A few years earlier Euchel had published an article in *Hame'asef* [11] concerning the value of biographies. It is quite possible that these works of Euchel were before Rabbi Yehezkel Feivel as *Sefer Toldot Adam* was taking shape.

Following Maimonides and other medieval Jewish philosophers, Rabbi Yehezkel justified the study of science as leading man to appreciate the creator's greatness and motivating him to love and worship God.[12] Rabbi Yehezkel's rationalistic justification went much further than those of the Gaon of Vilna or of Rabbi Shlomo of Chelm. Rabbi Yehezkel also discussed in detail the need for reforming traditional education.[13] The essence of his proposals was systematic study of all the books of the Bible, with emphasis upon grammar; the creation of a curriculum containing a gradual transition from Bible to Mishna, and from Mishna to Talmud according to the pupils' ability to absorb the material. Similarly, Rabbi Yehezkel condemned *pilpul,* the major purpose of which was to display sharp minds. He called for basing the study of halachah upon an effort to reach the truth.[14]

Rabbi Yehezkel's proposed educational reforms do not seem innovative, and did not differ essentially from those of the Maharal and his followers. Moreover, Rabbi Yehezkel expressed his views by means of citations and summaries from the writings of Rabbi Jacob Emden. Nevertheless, his presentation did contain a new element. Although he advocated giving more weight to the study of Bible and basing that study upon grammar, Rabbi Yehezkel voiced an important reservation: one must select teachers "whose hearts are one with the Lord and place their faith in His Torah," for whom "the clear literal meaning is joined to our trustworthy tradition, and not separated from it." On the other hand, one must be wary of teachers "who study the Bible and change the words of the Lord according to their own ideas and who neglect His commandments and throw off the yoke, openly subverting the truth in our streets." It would appear that this reservation could only be addressed to one threat: the *maskilim* of Berlin who had acquired the reputation of casting off the yoke of Torah. One gathers that Rabbi Yehezkel was aware of what was transpiring in the West and of the dangers that might accompany educational reform. He recommended reforms while warning against their dangers.

A rationalistic trend of thought marked by the influence of medieval philosophy is conspicuous in Rabbi Yehezkel's discussion of these rabbinical legends that seem to fly in the face of reason. Following Maimonides, Rashba, and other medieval sages, Rabbi Yehezkel attempted to interpret these legends so as to resolve their contradictions. Some of his remarks on this issue merely paraphrase Rabbi Azaria de Rossi's *Meor Einayim*.[15] This rationalism is also apparent in Rabbi Yehezkel's polemics against those who would deny the eternity of the soul.[16] The explicit basis of his argument here is *Ruah Hen* by Rabbi Yehuda Ibn-Tibbon, to which he also adds some logical "proofs" without indicating their source.

It seems that Rabbi Yehezkel's references to rationalistic interpretations of rabbinic legends and his polemics against those denying the eternity of the soul were provoked by Western ways of thinking. Rationalistic interpretations of rabbinical legends had been widespread in the philosophical literature of the Middle Ages and the Renaissance, but were atypical of the homiletics and thought of Eastern Europe at the end of the Middle Ages. The return to that literary and intellectual prototype was therefore innovative. Rabbi Yehezkel might well have been influenced by *Hame'asef,* which published such discussions. Rabbi Yehezkel's polemics regarding the eternity of the soul could hardly have been addressed to arguments current among Russian Jews at the end of the eighteenth century; it may be assumed that he was reacting to heretical opinions expressed in Western Europe. Rabbi Yehezkel may well have been responding directly or indirectly to two works written by Moses Mendelssohn, "Phaedon" and "The Soul."[17]

When we compare Rabbi Yehezkel Feivel's position to those of the Gaon of Vilna and Rabbi Shlomo of Chelm, his strong affinity with the rationalistic philosophy of the Middle Ages is quite apparent. The Gaon of Vilna had expressed reservations about medieval philosophy and Rabbi Shlomo of Chelm had only expressed moderate admiration for it. Rabbi

Yehezkel's thought was not only more rationalistic, it also revealed an encounter and a reciprocal influence between medieval and the Enlightenment ways of thinking; yet the medieval elements still predominated. His proximity to the spiritual and cultural attitudes of the Haskalah movement was rather limited. Rabbi Yehezkel Feivel still belonged culturally, socially, and institutionally to the scholarly elite of Lithuanian Jewry, while representing a new variety within traditional society which inclined slightly toward attitudes typical of the Haskalah.

A more significant step toward the Enlightenment can be found in the opinions and activities of Rabbi Yisrael Zamoscz and Rabbi Barukh Shklover, Torah scholars whose intellectual curiosity was not sated within the four walls of the Halachah. Those two men were innovative by not merely studying science and justifying it, but also were active in disseminating scientific knowledge among East European Jews.

Rabbi Yisrael Zamoscz[18] (1700–1772) was a scholar who supported himself by teaching in the local yeshiva. In addition to the study of Torah, Rabbi Yisrael was deeply interested in medieval Jewish philosophy, mathematics, and astronomy. He acquired knowledge of those sciences on his own with the help of Hebrew books. In 1741 he published *Netsah Yisrael,* in which he sought to demonstrate how one may overcome difficulties in the Talmud through knowledge of various sciences. Among his other published works were commentaries on the *Kuzari* by Rabbi Yehuda Halevi and on *The Duties of the Heart* by Rabbi Bahya Ibn-Paquda. Another book, devoted to astronomy and geometry, was never published.

Rabbi Yisrael's efforts to disseminate knowledge met with hostile reactions. Whether for that reason or not, he left Galicia and settled in Berlin for several years, where, during the mid-eighteenth century, young Jews sought to study philosophy and science with him. The young Moses Mendelssohn was one of his students at that time.[19] In Berlin, Rabbi Yisrael also became acquainted with other scholars, including non-Jews, impressing them with the breadth and depth of his knowledge.

In the introduction to *Netsah Yisrael,* Rabbi Yisrael expressed his view about the status of the sciences. Following Maimonides and other exponents of medieval Jewish philosophy, Rabbi Yisrael classified metaphysical speculations as a form of Torah study. As for the sciences, he claimed that some of them were vital for keeping the commandments. Thus, for example, it was not possible to determine the calendar without knowledge of astronomy and geometry. Other branches of knowledge were necessary in order to resolve certain difficulties in the Talmud. On that basis Rabbi Yisrael sketched an idealized portrait of a Jewish scholar combining Torah learning with science. Another topic which concerned

Rabbi Yisrael in the introduction to *Netsah Yisrael* was methods of study. He attacked *pilpul* and advocated basing Torah study instead upon the literal meaning of the text.

Rabbi Barukh Shklover[20] was born in 1740. After he was ordained as a rabbi and began to serve as a dayan, he was overcome by the desire for learning and therefore traveled to Western Europe. He studied medicine in London and then wandered through several European countries, spent some time in Berlin and befriended *maskilim* there. Upon returning to Eastern Europe he devoted himself to the dissemination of knowledge among the Jews. In 1777 he published a book on astronomy by the medieval scholar Rabbi Yitshak Yisraeli. In succeeding years Rabbi Barukh continued to publish books in the areas of anatomy and mathematics. Some he wrote himself and others he adapted and translated.

In the introductions to the books he published, Rabbi Barukh defended the legitimacy and necessity of spreading scientific knowledge among the Jews. He invoked the authority of the Gaon of Vilna concerning the necessity of the sciences as an auxiliary to the study of Torah.[21] However, his main argument was the need to renew the honor of Israel among the nations. Following those medieval scholars who had justified the study of science, Rabbi Barukh claimed that the wisdom and sciences of the Gentiles originated among the Jews and were propagated by them. The lack of scientific knowledge among the Jewish sages was attributable to the wanderings and sufferings of Jews in the Diaspora. Therefore the dissemination of scientific knowledge among the Jews would restore their ancient glory and raise their prestige in the eyes of the Gentiles.

Rabbi Yisrael Zamoscz and Rabbi Barukh Shklover differed in several respects. Aside from divergent character and spiritual inclinations, a difference in age of some forty years separated them. When Rabbi Barukh Shklover published his first book, Rabbi Yisrael was no longer alive. Despite these differences they shared a common resolve to propagate scientific knowledge among the Jews. In so doing they departed from the traditional norm and took a significant step toward an attitude typical of the Haskalah. Their justification of the need to study science was also similar. Both depended upon claims and justifications found in the medieval Jewish tradition. Neither departed from a particularistic self-image and neither made the transition to a humanistic outlook. In addition, while both did seek to bring about a change in Jewish spiritual life, they did not link the dissemination of scientific knowledge with a program or vision of a radical change in Jewish society and its relation to the surroundings.

When we examine the sources from which Rabbi Yisrael Zamoscz and Rabbi Barukh Shklover drew, we see that both were influenced by

Jewish heritage as well as European Enlightenment. However, the relative influence of those two currents in their thought was not the same. Rabbi Yisrael's intellectual world was anchored in the medieval rationalistic tradition. When he attempted to bequeath that legacy to his contemporaries he was bitterly disappointed and was forced to go to Berlin. In Berlin, not in Galicia, he found conditions that permitted him to express his aspirations freely and openly. Rabbi Barukh Shklover, in contrast, obtained most of his scientific education in Western Europe. It is quite likely that in his activities as a publisher he was also inspired by the Enlightenment in Western Europe. However, the medieval tradition continued to play a significant role in his thinking as well. His justification of the need to study science was based on assumptions and claims derived from that tradition.

In conclusion, the views and activities of Rabbi Israel Zamoscz and Rabbi Baruch Shklover were shaped by two traditions: medieval Jewish rationalism on the one hand, and Western Enlightenment on the other. The relative impact of these two factors differed according to the differences in personality and in historical circumstances. They shared a spiritual dependence on these two traditions.

I conclude this survey with Rabbi Menashe of Ilia and Rabbi Mendel Lefin. Rabbi Menashe[22] was born in 1767 near Vilna. In his youth he stood out as a talmudic prodigy and became one of the students of the Gaon of Vilna. He gained most of his philosophical and scientific knowledge on his own, from the Hebrew *haqira* literature of the Middle Ages. At the same time he came across certain scientific books in German and Polish and through them became acquainted with the attitudes of the European Enlightenment. Rabbi Menashe wished to go to Berlin to broaden his knowledge but was unable to do so. The style of his life and writings is marked by the traditional patterns of Jewish existence. However, his views deviated conspicuously from the opinions which were dominant in the traditional society. In his writings Rabbi Menashe presented knowledge drawn from many areas. His justification of the necessity of studying the sciences was quite different from that of his predecessors. He did not see the sciences as simply auxiliaries to the study of Torah nor a means of restoring the honor of the Jews among the nations, but above all as useful for life in this world. In a distinction that recalls Wessely's famous differentiation between the Torah of God and the Torah of man, Rabbi Menashe argued that whereas the Torah is meant to direct us in our service of the Lord, the sciences are intended to guide us in our worldly lives.[23] This recognition of the independent value of the sciences was a clear indication of a trend toward secularization.

The dominant characteristic of Rabbi Menashe's writings was his unshakable faith that the human intellect is meant to be the principle according to which individual and social life are to be organized. Rabbi Menashe's rationalism was not limited to the interpretation of biblical verses and the words of the Rabbis. With an ardour reminiscent of the eighteenth-century French *philosophes* he attacked the prejudices and mistaken notions which had taken root among the people. He criticized bitterly the widespread tendency to envelop certain subjects in a veil of mystery and remove them from the scope of intellectual scrutiny.[24]

The area in which Rabbi Menashe's rationalism was expressed most daringly concerned methods of study and halachic ruling. Following the Gaon of Vilna's authority, he sought to sharpen awareness of the difference between literal and homiletic interpretation. As a rationalist to whom the value of truth was greater than the honor of the sages, however, authoritative, Rabbi Menashe did not refrain from exposing what he considered to be the errors of Rashi and the *Tosafot* in their interpretations of talmudic passages. Moreover, he claimed that in some instances the Amoraim interpreted words of the Mishna in homiletic fashion, so that their interpretations should not be accepted as the literal meaning of the Mishna. Rabbi Menashe's thoroughgoing criticism was not limited to the theory of halachah but also extended to halachic rulings. He did not hesitate to challenge the authority of the *aharonim* when he found that their rulings were not solidly based on the Talmud. Rabbi Menashe argued that in certain cases the *aharonim* were influenced by a mistaken notion which was then current among the people and were unnecessarily strict.[25] In general he held that certain customs had taken root among the people in the course of time which were erroneous and in need of reform. He therefore proposed establishing a special rabbinical body which would have the authority to implement the necessary reforms.[26]

Rabbi Menashe's reservations with regard to the interpretations of Rashi and the *Tosafot* and his defiance of the authority of the *aharonim* aroused bitter criticism among the scholars of Lithuania. He was persecuted on account of his opinions, which friends suggested that he renounce. It might seem that Rabbi Menashe continued in the path marked out by the Gaon of Vilna, for the Gaon of Vilna did not spare the greatest halachists of earlier generations when he found them in error and in misunderstanding of the words of the Sages, and he also reformed certain unfounded customs. However, the freedom of maneuver accorded by traditional society to a charismatic figure such as the Gaon of Vilna was not accorded to a scholar such as Rabbi Menashe. Further, the Gaon of Vilna's criticism had been limited to methodology, whereas Rabbi Menashe expressed opinions that deviated from traditional norms in other areas. Opponents could view Rabbi Menashe's criticism of the halachah as defiance of the authority of the tradition in general. In addition, Rabbi Menashe expressed his views during the first quarter of the nineteenth century, when word of *maskilim* who had thrown off the yoke of Torah and of the first gropings toward reform had already reached Russia. In any case, it is noteworthy that Rabbi Menashe's criticism in the realm of halachah was not motivated by social or political viewpoints but was rather an extension of immanent methodological consideration.

During the last years of Rabbi Menashe's life the Haskalah movement began to appear in Russia. He died in 1831, three years after the publication of *Sefer Teuda BeYisrael,* by Rival (Yitshak Behr Levinsohn). However, in the traditional environment in which he lived and which he tried to influence, Rabbi Menashe remained solitary and alienated.

If Rabbi Menashe of Ilia was nearly a *maskil,* Rabbi Menachem Mendel Lefin[27] was one in the full sense of the word. He was born in Satanov, Podolia, in 1749, and received a traditional Torah education. Lefin made his way to the Haskalah in two stages. First he was exposed to the *haqira* literature of the Middle Ages and the Renaissance, from which he gained his first scientific knowledge, acquiring a rationalistic conception of Judaism. In the early 1780s he lived in Berlin for four years, learning German and French, reading widely in the natural sciences and philosophy, and forming close ties with Mendelssohn and his circle as well as with Christian scholars. Upon Lefin's return to Eastern Europe he embarked on wide-ranging literary activities. He translated the *Guide for the Perplexed* of Maimonides and published books containing information in the fields of natural science and medicine. His moral work, *Heshbon Hanefesh* (self-examination) gained wide circulation. In an apparently traditional style, overlaid with rabbinical quotations and concepts deriving from medieval Jewish moralist writing, Lefin proposed innovative methods of moral education based on the psychological theories which he had gleaned from eighteenth-century European literature.

In 1791, Lefin presented a brochure written in French to the Polish Sejm, containing a detailed program for the reform of Jewish social life. In its content and spirit it was no different from similar programs which had been composed in various centers of the Haskalah movement. Lefin proposed far-reaching reforms in education, economic life, and community organization. He recommended that the Polish Sejm repress Hassidism, in which he saw the root of evil in Jewish life.

Although Lefin was a thoroughgoing *maskil* both in his views and activities, he was not part of the Haskalah movement in Russia. During the years of his residence in Poland and Russia conditions were not yet ripe for the emergence of the Haskalah movement. Lefin was rather representative of others living in Russia at the end of the eighteenth and early nineteenth centuries, men whose views certainly belonged to the Enlightenment yet did not join to form a movement. Only after Lefin moved to Galicia in 1808 did he find himself in the midst of a rather close-knit circle of *maskilim,* in which he became a leader.

Thus far we have dealt with several figures representing the new orientation that began to appear in the spiritual and cultural life of Polish-Lithuanian Jewry. Certainly these personalities do not represent all the possible variations of this phenomenon; yet they stand for its principal manifestations. They were not representative of a broadly based social phenomenon but rather part of a cultural current characteristic of a very thin social stratum. The extent of this group has not yet been fully explored by historians, nor do we have a complete picture of the connections among those who belonged to it. Most historians have dealt with each figure separately, and one thus gains the impression that they were isolated individuals who acted independently. However, some of them did maintain contact with others who shared their views. Rabbi Yisrael Zamoscz, for example, was friendly with Rabbi Shlomo of Chelm. Rabbi Barukh Shklover visited the Gaon of Vilna and made use of his authority. Rabbi Yehezkel Feivel was supported by his wealthy relative, Yosef Ben-Eliahu of Vilna[28]—a man who corresponded with David Friedländer, admired Mendelssohn, and supported Rabbi Solomon Dubno's attempts to publish a commentary on the Torah in Lithuania after parting company with Mendelssohn. These are but a few examples of a wider phenomenon.

These figures constituted a new cultural trend emerging with the traditional society. From the point of view of a historian of the Haskalah movement, they may be viewed as forerunners of the Haskalah in Russia. My assumption in using a concept such as *forerunner* is that a given cultural and social phenomenon, before emerging in mature form, takes shape gradually over a long period of time. Hence between an old and a new reality an intermediate phase can be discerned which is distinct from the new but points toward it. Clearly, any discussion of *forerunner* is retrospective and becomes possible only after the new phenomenon has taken its place in our historical consciousness, when we seek to determine how it emerged.

In this discussion of several forerunners of the Haskalah I have attempted to point out those attitudes and views that deviated from the traditional norm, and tended toward Haskalah. A review of them in the order they have been discussed displays a sequence of stages in the transition from tradition to the Haskalah. The Gaon of Vilna justified the study of sciences as auxiliary to the study of the Torah. Rabbi Shlomo of Chelm added the value of the study of science in the development of intellectual powers. Rabbi Yisrael Zamoscz was not satisfied merely to justify the study of science but worked to disseminate it. Rabbi Barukh Shklover also disseminated scientific knowledge but added the essential justification that in so doing he was augmenting the honor of the Jews among the nations. Although the justification rooted in internal Jewish tradition, it also represents a typical characteristic of the Haskalah: sensitivity to the image of the Jews in the eyes of the Gentiles. Rabbi Menashe of Ilia disseminated scientific knowledge because of its value in this worldly life, explicitly acknowledging its intrinsic value. And Rabbi Mendel Lefin, the complete *maskil,* combined the study of science and its usefulness with a comprehensive program for changing Jewish society.

These forerunners of the Haskalah, except the Gaon of Vilna and Rabbi Shlomo of Chelm, were all influenced by two factors: the Jewish tradition contained in the philosophical and scientific literature of the Middle Ages and Renaissance and the European Enlightenment, whether in general manifestations or in its Jewish form in Berlin. The influence of those two factors were probably reciprocal. One who had been exposed to medieval Hebrew rationalistic philosophy and scientific writing was prepared to absorb the message of the Western Enlightenment. Conversely, one who had been exposed to the spirit and ideas of the European Enlightenment was impelled to seek points where these ideas could be derived from within the Jewish tradition. The relative weight of these intellectual traditions differed in every case. Naturally those who were more exposed to the influence of the Enlightenment adopted positions closer to those which typified the Jewish Enlightenment in its mature phase. However, the inner Jewish tradition played a very important part for them as well. In all cases the phenomenon of the forerunners of the Haskalah arose out of the encounter with both traditions.

I now turn to the Haskalah movement in Russia during the first decades of its existence, during the 1820s, 1830s, and 1840s. As noted, the strong bonds between the Haskalah in Russia and Berlin were unquestionable. But were the *maskilim* of Russia, like the forerunners of the Haskalah, also influenced by the medieval and Renaissance Jewish tradition, and if so to what extent? The answer requires an elucidation of the way in which the influence of Berlin was expressed.

The dependence of the *maskilim* of Russia upon the Haskalah of Berlin was most conspicuous in the realm of ideology. This dependence is evident in the writings of Rival,[29] who is considered the "father" of the Russian Haskalah movement. Following the example of the Berlin *maskilim,* Rival embraced the rationalism and humanism of the European

Enlightenment, adapting them to the specifically Jewish context.[30] Like Wiesel, Rival distinguished between the Torah of Israel, which is particularistic, and the universalistic sciences. He used this distinction to support the conclusion that the Jews as human beings must take an active part in the culture of European society, which he considered the common heritage of all humanity. In the spirit of rationalism, Rival believed in the possibility and the need of "reforming" Jewish society to allow for its inclusion in the surrounding society. To that end he proposed reforms in education, spiritual life and culture, economic activities, and community organization, which Rival believed would encourage a change in the attitude of Christian society toward the Jews. Like the *maskilim* of Berlin, he believed in the enlightened and humane character of the state and was therefore certain that common interest existed between the authorities and the *maskilim,* which would be realized by their cooperation. On the theological level, Rival was influenced by Mendelssohn's deistic interpretation of Judaism.

In estimating the influence of the Berlin Haskalah on Rival in particular and on the Russian *maskilim* in general, one must add two caveats. First, the Berlin Haskalah which influenced Rival was the moderate school represented by such figures as Mendelssohn and Wessely. Rival sharply rejected radical manifestations of the Berlin Haskalah that surfaced in the 1790s, such as throwing off the yoke of the *mitzvot* and contempt for the Talmud and rabbinic culture. In one instance, however, Rival was influenced by his contemporaries, heirs of the Berlin Haskalah. Following the example of the *Wissenschaft des Judentums,* Rival engaged in philological and historical research into Judaism. His research was characterized by the tension between scientific objectivity and the tendentious motives that lay at the foundation of that research, a tension Scholem has perceived in the *Wissenschaft des Judentums* itself. Second, although the *maskilim* of Russia, including Rival, were influenced directly by the Berlin Haskalah because they read its writings, the principal conduit for such influence upon Rival and other *maskilim* in southern Russia was the Haskalah center in Galicia. Ongoing personal contact with the Galician *maskilim* and the study of their writings played a crucial part in shaping the Haskalah consciousness for Rival,[31] Gottlober, and their colleagues. The emergent Haskalah in Russia drew from Galicia because of their geographical and chronological contiguity. However, the important part played by the Galician *maskilim* in transmitting the message of the Berlin Haskalah to their Russian contemporaries can be explained by two additional factors. First, Rival and his companions found a moderate form of Haskalah in Galicia, similar to that of Berlin during the 1780s, one with which they could identify. Second, the similarity between the demographic structure of Russian and Galician Jewry presented similar problems to the *maskilim* in both areas. Both for example were forced to confront the phenomenon of Hassidism. It is no coincidence that the Russian *maskilim* used strategies in dealing with Hassidism which had been conceived by the Galician *maskilim*.

The influence of Berlin Haskalah upon the Russian *maskilim* was not limited to ideology. The Berlin *maskilim* served as a model for imitation and a source of inspiration. They appeared to have succeeded in becoming what the Russian *maskilim* so longed to become, "men" at home in European culture and also Jews. Here the myth surrounding the figure of Mendelssohn was particularly powerful. Thus the stories Gottlober heard about Mendelssohn and his brave struggle with Lavater made a deep impression upon him as a youth.[32] The depth and extent of the Mendelssohn myth can also be sensed in the strong reactions Smolenskin encountered when he attempted to challenge it.[33]

An event which demonstrates the respect, almost awe, with which the Russian *maskilim* regarded the figure of the enlightened German Jew is the Russian journey of Max Lilienthal. Lilienthal was in his twenties when he was invited by the Russian minister of education to assist him in reforming Jewish education. Despite his age and lack of any signal distinction, Lilienthal received an enthusiastic welcome from the Russian *maskilim*. And that is not surprising. For Lilienthal in addition to his title of "rabbi" also held a doctorate and spoke pure German rather than Germanized Yiddish. Furthermore, his dress and manners bore witness to his country of origin. At first sight Lilienthal appeared to the Russian *maskilim* as a marvelous embodiment of the figure of the Jewish human being.[34]

The tendency of the Russian *maskilim* to see the stereotypical figure of the German Jewish *maskil* as an ideal embodiment of the Haskalah vision was connected to their German linguistic and cultural orientation. German language and literature served as the principal gateway for the Russian *maskilim* to enter the realm of European culture. Hence it is not surprising that many of them saw German culture as representative of European culture in general. A typical expression of the relation of the Russian *maskilim* to German culture can be found in a passage from a letter of Elazar Halberstam to Mordecai Aharon Ginzburg: "Your book, *Pi Ha-Hirot,* is worthy of its author. Its style of writing is thoroughly beautiful and pleasant. Hebrew and German taste are combined together in it, and have become one in your hands."[35] Finally, the Russian *maskilim* did not hesitate to call themselves "Berliners."[36]

The question this paper has posed is whether the Russian Haskalah, in addition to its dependence on the Berlin Haskalah, was also influenced by the philosophical and scientific heritage of the Middle Ages and the Renaissance. My answer is positive: this heritage filled three functions in the emergence of the Haskalah movement in Russia.

First, it served as a bridge between rabbinic culture in the form it had taken among Ashkenazic Jewry at the end of the Middle Ages, and the Haskalah. That is true not only of the forerunners of the Haskalah but also of many nineteenth-century Russian *maskilim*. The biographies of Maimon, Gottlober, Ginzburg, Fin, and Lilienblum show that their first critical steps toward Haskalah were inspired and guided by the philosophical and scientific literature of the Middle Ages and the Renaissance.

Second, elements from that tradition were included in the ideological complex of the Haskalah in its mature phase. For example, the demand for reform in methods of study and education of the Maharal and his followers was included in the Haskalah's educational program, along with elements derived from the European Enlightenment. Similarly, elements drawn from the Jewish philosophical literature of the Middle Ages performed an important task in the framework of beliefs and opinions of the nineteenth-century Russian *maskilim*. Even those influenced to some extent by deism or other modern doctrines did not wish to repudiate a vital bond with Saadia Gaon, Maimonides, and others like them. Nor could they do so, for the desire to formulate a rationalistic interpretation of the entire Jewish tradition was a deep spiritual and intellectual need among the *maskilim*. The Russian *maskilim* of the nineteenth century made significant and valuable use of medieval Jewish philosophy.

Third, the *maskilim* did not envision themselves breaking down barriers and throwing off the yoke of Torah. On the contrary, they saw themselves as renewing and reviving Judaism in its pure and unalloyed form. In their pursuit of this aim the philosophical and scientific heritage of the Middle Ages played a primary role for two reasons: (1) The medieval sages had already been forced to explain and justify their study of "external" fields of learning and alien literature. In their works the *maskilim* of the nineteenth century found ready-made justifications and explanations. (2) The very existence of a Jewish proto-Enlightenment during the Middle Ages was a precedent which lent its authority to the new Haskalah. This legitimization based on tradition was not meant only for external consumption, i.e., in order to convince opponents of Haskalah. The essential significance of this precedent lay in the authority it lent to the self-image of the *maskilim*.[37]

In conclusion, even though the Haskalah movement in general and that of Russia in particular was in many senses a branch of the European Enlightenment, and Russian Haskalah was an extension of Berlin Haskalah, it is hard to imagine the emergence of Russian Haskalah or the form it took, without taking account of the heritage of the Jewish philosophy and the Hebrew scientific literature of the Middle Ages and the Renaissance. We might add that the rationalistic tradition of the Middle Ages, which had lost its influence as a central factor in the spiritual life of the Jews after the expulsion from Spain, remained in existence as a kind of potential option during succeeding generations. The new conditions that arose in Western and Central Europe during the eighteenth century permitted that option to reemerge upon the stage of Jewish history, a reemergence accompanied by modifications that were necessitated by changed historical circumstances.

Notes

1. See Shumel Yosef Fin, *Safa Lane'emanim* (Vilna, [5641] 1881), pp. 133ff.; Jacob S. Raisin, *The Haskalah Movement in Russia* (Philadelphia: Jewish Publication Society of America, 1913), pp. 72–75; Ze'ev Yaabetz, *Toldot Yisrael* (Tel Aviv, 1960), vol. 13, pp. 230–36. Raisin and Yaabetz see the beginning of the Enlightenment in Russia in the Gaon of Vilna and in several of his disciples.
2. See Yisrael Zinberg, *Toldot Sifrut Yisrael* (Tel Aviv: Sifriat Hapoalim), vol. 3, sec. 2, chs. 6–7; Ben-Zion Katz, *Rabbanut Hassidot Haskalah* (Tel Aviv: Dvir, 1956), vol. 1, pp. 140ff; Raphael Mahler, *Divrei Yemei Yisrael* (Tel Aviv: Sifriat Hapoalim), vol. 4, pp. 14–68.
3. For detailed bibliography on the Gaon of Vilna see Yitshak Ya'akov Dienstag, "Rabeinu Eliahu MiVilna—Reshima Bibliografit," *Talpiot* 4, nos. 1–2 (1949).
4. On Rabbi Shlomo of Chelm see Zinberg, pp. 305–6; Mahler, pp. 25–27.
5. On the relation of the Gaon of Vilna to the Enlightenment see Emanuel Etkes, "HaGra Veha'Haskalah—Tadmit Umetsiut," in *Perakim Betoldot Hahevra Hayehudit Bimei-Habeinayim Uva'et Hahadasha Mukdashim Li-professor Jacob Katz* (Jerusalem: Magnes, 1980), pp. 192–217. The views of Rabbi Shlomo of Chelm, which I discuss below, were formulated in the introduction to his book *Merkavat HaMishna* (1751).
6. See Simha Assaf, *Mekorot Letoldot Hahinukh BeYisrael* (Tel Aviv: Dvir, 1954), vol. 1, pp. 45–52.
7. Among them were ReMa (Moses Ben-Yisrael Isserles), MaHaRal (Rabbi Yehuda Loew Ben-Bezalel) of Prague, Rabbi Yom Tov Lippman Heller, Rabbi Yair Bachrach, and Rabbi Yehonatan Eybeschuetz.
8. The most prominent among them were Rabbi Ephraim Luntschitz and the author of *Shnei Luhot Habrit,* Rabbi Isaiah Horwitz.
9. For biographical information about him see Shmuel Yosef Fin, *Kirya Ne'emana* (Vilna: Funk, [5675] 1915), pp. 241–44; Hillel Noah Magid Steinschneider, *Ir Vilna* (Vilna: Ram, [5660] 1900), pp. 87–88.
10. Yehezkel Feivel, *Sefer Toldot Adam* (Dehrenfürth, [5561–5569] 1801–1809).
11. (Tishri-Heshvan, [5544] 1784).
12. Feivel, *Toldot Adam,* p. 14.
13. Ibid, pp. 23–25.

14. Ibid, pp. 20–21.
15. The influence of *Maor Einayim* on Rabbi Yehezkel was pointed out by Steinschneider (*Ir Vilna*, p. 87) following writings on the subject by Matitiyahu Strashun. Steinschneider does not mention where that influence is expressed, and I was unable to locate Strashun's remarks through Steinschneider's reference. While comparing the two books I found that pages 95–104 of *Toldot Adam* were influenced by chapter 15, especially pages 201–4 of *Maor Einayim* (Vilna, [5623] 1863).
16. Feivel, *Toldot Adam*, pp. 8–10.
17. The Hebrew translation of *Phaedon* was published in Berlin in 1787. *The Soul* was also published in Berlin during that year.
18. See Zinberg, pp. 306–7; Mahler, pp. 26–30. On the relationship of Rabbi Yisrael toward medieval Jewish philosophy see Eliezer Schweid, *Toldot Hehagut Hayehudit* (Jerusalem: Keter, 1978, pp. 111–13.
19. See Alexander Altmann, *Moses Mendelssohn* (Philadelphia: The Jewish Publication Society of America, 1973), pp. 21–22.
20. See Zinberg, pp. 325–28; Ben-Zion Katz, pp. 134–37; Mahler, pp. 53–56.
21. See the introduction by Rabbi Barukh to *Oklidos* (Amsterdam, [5540] 1780).
22. See Mordecai Plongian, *Ben-Porat* (Vilna, [5618] 1858); Sh. Rosenfeld, "Rabbi Menashe Ilier," *Hatekufa* 18 (5678), p. 250; Ben-Zion Katz, pp. 187–203; Zinberg, pp. 153–61; Mahler, pp. 63–68.
23. See *Alfei Menashe* (Vilna, 1822), 68 verso.
24. See ibid., 56 verso, 57 verso.
25. See ibid., 57 verso, 58 recto.
26. See ibid., 75 recto.
27. On the life and activities of Lefin see Israel Weinlez, "Rabbi Menahem Lefin MiSatanov," *Ha'olam* 4, nos. 39–42 (1925); Yosef Klausner, *Historia shel Hasifrut Haivrit Hahadasha* (Jerusalem: Dvir, 1953), vol. 1, pp. 224–53; Zinberg, pp. 328–32; Mahler, pp. 71–88; Hillel Levin, *Menahem Mendel Lefin,* unpublished Ph.D. diss., Harvard University, 1974.
28. See Yisrael Kloizner, "Rabbi Yosef Ben-Eliahu, Krovo Hanaor shel HaGra MiVilna," *He'avar* 2 (1954):73–85.
29. For a detailed bibliography on Rival see Klausner, pp. 33–35; Zinberg, pp. 164–203.
30. The principal writings containing Rival's program for Enlightenment are *Te'uda BeYisrael* (Vilna & Horodna, [5588] 1828), and *Beit Yehuda* (Vilna, [5599] 1839).
31. The strong and continued connections between Rival and the *maskilim* of Galicia can be seen in the letters which he exchanged with them. See Dov Ber-Natansohn, *Sefer Hazikhronot* (Warsaw, [5636] 1876); Yitshak Ber-Levinsohn, *Beer Yitshak* (Warsaw, [5660] 1900).
32. See Avraham Ber-Gottlober, *Zihronot Umasaot* (Jerusalem, 1976), vol. 1, pp. 81–82.
33. On this matter I have learned a great deal from the work of Shmuel Fainer, a student in the History of the Jewish People at the Hebrew University, "Tadmito shel Moshe Mendelssohn Behaskalat Russia Bishnot Hashishim Vehashiv'im Lameah Ha'yod-teyt."
34. See Benyamin Mandelshtam, *Hazon Lamoed* (Vienna, [5637] 1877), pt. II, letters 3, 9.

35. The letter is in the Ginzburg Archives in the National Library in Jerusalem, call number 4°, 1281 A, file 17/4.
36. The use of the appellation in a positive sense can be inferred from the letters of the *maskilim* of Lithuania during the 1840s, preserved in the Ginzburg Archives (see note 35, above).
37. See Emanuel Etkes, "Te'uda BeYisrael—Between Change and Tradition," introduction to Yitshak Ber-Levinsohn, *Te'uda BeYisrael* (Jerusalem 1977).

2

"The Heavenly City of Germany" and Absolutism à la Mode d'Autriche: The Rise of the Haskalah in Galicia

Israel Bartal

When asked about the origins of the Haskalah movement in the regions which had been torn from the divided Polish Kingdom, *maskilim* of Eastern Europe almost always adduced the same geographic and cultural model: the movement had spread from Berlin to Galicia, and thence to Volhynia and new Russia. It even reached distant Lithuania, where it encountered the direct influence of nearby Prussia. A.S. Gottlober presented this model several times in various writings and linked it to the fact that the language of the land and culture of Galicia were, he claimed, German:

> The Haskalah reached the regions of Volhynia and Podolia by way of Austria and her minions, none other than the cities of Galicia, chiefly Brody and Lemberg. Those slender rays were gradually gathered together until they became a great light.[1]

The other side—the traditional society—which was crystallizing in anti-Haskalah orthodoxy, also viewed Galicia as the cradle of the new evil. Rabbi Leib Ben-Sarah fought an aggressive campaign against the penetration of German influence into Eastern Europe. According to legend he went to Vienna and plunged a dagger into the progenitor of all that evil, Joseph II:

> And Leib Ben-Sarah came unto the Emperor Joseph, to his very palace and seat of honor, riding upon an airy cloud and invisible. He placed his hand within his breast and drew forth a small dagger and cut the monarch's

flesh, saying: "If you remove your decree from Israel, it will be well, but if not, I shall give your flesh to be eaten by the birds of the heavens!" Joseph hardened his heart like Pharoah King of Egypt and refused to respond to him.[2]

However, the degree to which German influence was identical with the beginnings of the Haskalah movement in Eastern Europe, and the stages of its penetration into Galician Jewish society are not sufficiently clear and unequivocal. Although historians have generally accepted the picture presented both by the *maskilim* and by traditional Jews, many matters still remain to be clarified which can shed new light upon the connection between Germany and German culture in the actual life of the Jews of Galicia on the one hand, and the rise and spread of the Haskalah movement in Eastern Europe on the other.

It is certainly true that in Galicia we find the most extensive actual contact, the first of its kind, between Central European culture as transmitted by means of the centralized absolute regime's bureaucracy and the Jews of Eastern Europe. Moreover, there is no doubt that the Austrian mode as expressed in the acts of Joseph II in Galicia served as an example to the Russian authorities when they drafted their own legislation, since it was considered the most suitable for coping with the large Jewish population which had become a part of the Russian Empire after the partition of Poland. Galician Jewry was no different from the rest of East European Jewry. The Jews of Galicia performed the same function in the ethnic and class structure of the surrounding society as did the Jews elsewhere in divided Poland. They constituted a distinct social class with their own religion and economic role in an environment in which every ethnic group possessed its own distinguishing economic features. Within the feudal economy of Poland which persisted well into the Austrian period, the Jews of Galicia were the catalysts as merchants and lessees on every level of the estate and village economy, and as importers and exporters. Thus it is not surprising that in the early days of Austrian rule, the district administrator of Sambor wrote of them in words similar to those used by travellers in Poland to describe the Jews in every region of that country:

Were it not for them, it would be impossible to procure even a strand of cotton or silken thread in the cities for the price of a few pennies. The estate owners would not sell their grain and linen, the peasants would be unable to buy on credit and thus obtain their most vital commodities. In this land, which is so lacking in diligence, they are the ones who influence its economy with a breath of life and serving all classes of the population.[3]

After the annexation of Galicia in 1772, the acts of the Austrian authorities introduced a series of new factors into the economic and social order: a new, German-speaking administration; limitations upon the traditional areas of Jewish economic activity; drastic reduction of the autonomous authority of the Jewish community and later its abolition. After an 8-year transition period (1772–1780), during which changes were introduced in Galicia in the spirit of centralized absolutism, an Enlightenment ideology was grafted onto the reforms of Joseph II. Its significance for the Jews was the broad intervention of the authorities in the traditional culture and ways of life. The new political conceptions that had characterized the Prussian monarchy were applied throughout the Hapsburg Empire within a short period of time and a series of decrees, ordinances, and administrative measures brought about a sharp change in the relations between the Jews and the state. Joseph II's intentions were far-reaching, touching upon every possible area of life from Jewish names, education, and marital life to the minute details of their economic and social activities. Thus, for example, the Jews of Galicia were required to assume German surnames (1787), exchange their characteristic costume for "German clothing" (1791), and, even worse, submit to the obligation of military service (1780), alter radically their business activities so as to be of benefit to the state (1785), and abolish completely the autonomous activities of the community, leaving only religious matters and charity in its hands (1785–86).

The conjunction of administrative reform in the spirit of centralized absolutism and the ideas of the Enlightenment was expressed in the *Toleranzpatent* of 1781 in which several of the prohibitions and restrictions of the Polish period and the reign of Maria Theresa were rescinded, and the rights of the Jews extended in the areas of local government, economy, and personal freedom. The goal of Germanization reflected in that document aimed to bring the Jews closer to the status of the non-Jewish burgher class and transform them into useful subjects integrated within the political body of the centralized state. As with the Letters Patent concerning other areas of the empire, communal office holders, most of whose authority had already been abolished, were required to know German and keep their registers in that language. Teachers in the new German schools had to be graduates of German schools themselves (in order to remove the "pernicious" influence of the Talmud), and the Jews were granted the possibility of participating in municipal government in the cities where they lived.

The chances for the successful Germanization of the Galician Jews by such means appeared to be quite good. Although the *Toleranzpatent* did not grant them rights fully equal to the rest of the urban population, it did give the economically active elements of the urban population the opportunity of participating in the internal trade of Galicia and forced broad segments of the society into actual contact with the new political and social model. Nevertheless, historical, geographical, and social forces prevented in Galicia what had happened in Bohemia and Moravia, which were also under Austrian rule. Development in Galicia remained similar to that in the areas of Poland annexed to the Russian Empire, demonstrating the similarity of Galician Jews to the other Jews of Russia and Poland.

Traditional society developed a defense mechanism against changes that threatened its autonomous activities. No doubt the spread of Hassidism throughout Galicia, which took place at the same time as the official imposition of Germanization, served as a real social barrier to the anticipated social and cultural disintegration. Thus it is hardly surprising that the spheres of German influence did not, until a relatively later period, extend beyond the larger cities, where Jewish cooperation with the measures taken by the authorities was combined with consistent opposition to the spread of the new Hassidic movement. Conversely, Hassidism saw itself as a hindrance to the spread of Germanization and a rejection of cultural change, and was also seen in that light by the *maskilim*. Joseph Perl, a militant *maskil* in his relation to Hassidism, placed a "confession" in the mouth of a Galician Hassid regarding the German education received by his son-in-law in the government school: he had learned to read and write *Daytsh,* but had forgotten all that, thank God, so that he could not tell one letter from another.[4]

In place of the authority of the traditional community which in accordance with the Central European model was limited to matters of religion and charity and relegated to the synagogue, voluntary organizations were created which functioned without official recognition and carried out the old activities based on the charismatic authority of the *tsaddik* or those who did his bidding. In fact the Galician *maskilim* saw the political character of Hassidism quite clearly, and realized that it was hostile to the principle of the modern state with its centralized authority. Therefore they labored to convince the representatives of the government that the economic and cultural activities of the Hassidim were harmful to the state. For example, the Hassidim were depicted as people who diminished the wealth of the state by smuggling gold to other countries (meaning the money raised for the Jews of the Land of Israel).

Besides the resistance to Germanization, which the spread of Hassidism stimulated at the end of the eighteenth and during the early nineteenth centuries, the many internal contradictions inherent in official Germanization also played a role. First, the radical tendencies of Joseph II did not persist for more than a few years. To a great extent, his successors repudiated his intention of incorporating the Jews in the appropriate Gentile social classes. However, the Germanization laws had a dynamic of their own, and most of them continued in force until the revolutions of 1848. Yet what persisted in them was not the universalistic, enlightened content characteristic of the eighteenth century but rather a political interest in dissolving the corporate status of the Jews and placing them under effective supervision. Further, not all the officials of the Austrian government were of the same opinion regarding the goals of legislation concerning the Jews. In the time of Joseph II some officials had been convinced supporters of Enlightenment ideas, but others were motivated by personal interest and even retained traditional anti-Jewish views. As the drastic political consequences of the Enlightenment ideology—the French Revolution and its aftermath—grew clearer, both the central administration and the local bureaucracy gave up the aim of abolishing old social structures. Developments in Galicia resembled those across the border in Russia. In both countries the authorities and the traditional society concluded that the Enlightenment conception had identified the wrong enemy. The bond between absolutism and the Enlightenment was severed. Thus a short circuit was created between the *maskilim* and the authorities, one which typified the activities of the Galician *maskil* in the first half of the nineteenth century. Joseph Perl and his generation labored to convince the authorities that it was necessary to reform traditional society,[5] while the local and central authorities attempted to thwart and delay any action in that direction.

Probably the most important obstacle in the path of Germanizing traditional Galician Jewish society was Galicia's ethnic and social composition. As noted, Galicia's demographic character resembled the rest of the Polish-Russian area, and not at all Central Europe. The aim of incorporating the Jews in the burgher class was thoroughly unrealistic. In Eastern Europe the Jews had been the principal urban element for hundreds of years, whereas the Poles were primarily members of the nobility (outside the indigenous ethnic borders of Poland). In fact, except for the Jews no ethnic or cultural group could serve as a behavioral model or as an environment to which they could assimilate. Such an environment existed solely across the borders in the cities of Germany or the German communities in Central Europe. Anyone who identified with the policies of the Austrian authorities and wished to adopt the language and "the culture of the state" had only one social element in his immediate surroundings which he could approach, namely the government bureaucrats. In Joseph Perl's satires we find close social ties between the *maskilim* of the city and the functionaries of the *Kreis*.[6]

In the harsh and even violent struggle between the *maskilim* and the Hassidim in Galicia during the early nineteenth century, the minority that identified with the state, the authorities, and Imperial culture in fact depended on the local bureaucracy. However, because of the short circuit in mutual understanding, here too reality defeated wishful thinking and utopian expectations, for the authorities and their representatives had no interest in arousing the ire of the Jewish population. Furthermore, in contrast to Germany and certain cities in Central Europe, other cultures competed for the souls of those who wished to assimilate to their surroundings, since German was not the language of the culture but rather the language of the state, while in terms of their cultural level, the functionaries of the *Kreis* were not exactly close to Schiller and Goethe. Some of these functionaries still viewed Galicia as a backward, conquered area of Polish culture and the Jews as people of a lower order and alien culture. All contact with them took place in a patronizing and aloof manner. Their attitude can be discerned in their use of the services of a Central European *maskil,* Herz Homberg, who forced a German school-system entirely manned by teachers from Central Europe on the Galician Jewish community. The lack of interest displayed by the authorities in the details of that school system, and the assumption that importing a *maskil* and his assistants educated in Germany could "reform" the backward Galician Jews hardly differed from the attitudes that motivated the Russian authorities in the 1840s who brought a German Jew, Lilienthal, to establish government schools for the Jews. The project was carried out in Russia only in a different form and without the active participation of the German "expert." In Galicia these schools existed until 1806, when Homberg was suspected of revolutionary activities. Nevertheless neither in Galicia nor in Russia were these factors decisive in effecting a shift within Jewish society toward the adoption of the culture of the state.

In its first stages Galician Haskalah, as elsewhere in Eastern Europe, was universalistic and essentially supranational. It was not linked in its expectations or conceptions to any well-defined national group, for such groups did not exist in Eastern Europe at the end of the eighteenth century. The *maskilim* felt bound rather to the Enlightenment community, which was international in scope and encompassed all Europe. The early *maskilim* in Eastern Europe, including several prominent Galician *maskilim,* were linked to a sort of pan-European community which, although largely belonging to the region of German language and culture, was not congruent with it. This state of affairs began during the 1780s and 1790s and persisted in Eastern Europe until the second half of the nineteenth century. Only after the opposition between *national* and *state* culture emerged clearly did the Germanizing of the Haskalah in Eastern Europe became a real problem for the *maskilim*. There was no better demonstration of that opposition in Galicia than the case of those Jews who participated in Polish nationalist activities before the revolution of 1848, and wrote and spoke about it in German, the language and model of their culture.[7]

Joseph Perl, who was steeped in German culture and wrote some of his literary works in German, was able to continue his educational activities under a Russian government when his city Tarnopol was annexed by Russia at the close of the Napoleonic period. Later he collaborated with officials of Polish, Bohemian, and Moravian origin.[8] Mendel Lefin, who wandered from place to place and traversed the sections of partitioned Poland and also settled in Galicia for a time, is a good example of the persistence of that supranationalism which characterized the absolutist regimes of separate estates, such as Prussia, Russia, and Austria during the eighteenth century. Lefin's patron, Adam Czartoryski, was himself a Polish nobleman who made a place for himself in the Russian absolutist state. Thus Lefin took part in activities connected with the reform of Jewish life in Poland before the second partition, publishing to that end a booklet in French.[9] A few years later he participated in Jewish activity related to the Russian authorities' reform plans before the 1804 ordinances of Alexander I.[10] Finally he found himself in a region where he advocated similar activities on behalf of the Austrian government.[11]

The universalistic character of the early Galician Haskalah and its strong links to men and cultural centers beyond Galician borders paralleled the expansion of the centralized state along Prussian and Austrian lines. This was not completely coincidental. The German Haskalah had been less bound to Germanness than to the Enlightenment's rationalist-universalist message. This message could be absorbed in any Eastern European city in a purely Jewish context thanks to the rationalistic tradition of medieval Jewish thought.

For the first and second generations of Galician *maskilim,* Germany and her culture served as an abstract model which was close to their hearts but far from their eyes. Every Galician *maskil* began a certain stage in his intellectual formation by reading openly or in secret the works of Mendelssohn, Lessing, Kant, and Shlomo Maimon.[12]

The Galicians were all connected by correspondence or by the publication of books and articles with a circle of *maskilim* who read German.[13] Some of them even left their homeland for Torah centers in such cradles of German culture as Prague or Berlin and returned full of new concepts and ideas.

Moreover, just as Jews once had to leave Ashkenaz for Poland in order to study Torah, or import teachers from Poland to Germany, now there was a movement of teachers from Germany and areas of German culture outside Germany to Galicia. Germanization, however, depended upon *state* power and interest, not upon the concrete society surrounding them which was subject to the same acculturation. The *maskilim* recognized that alienation in the polarization which took place within the Jewish society of Galicia, and discerned the anti-German traits in the language, beliefs, and opinions of the anti-Haskalah society surrounding them. The great outcry of the Galician *maskilim* against the audacity of their teacher, Mendel Lefin, in translating the Book of Proverbs into Yiddish was apparently a protest against the surrounding barbarism and the possible submergence of the small German presence in the Galician cities by a flood of low culture.[14] The dependence of the *maskilim* on the Austrian state, which they idealized, seemed rather ludicrous at times, alongside the lukewarm attitudes taken by the state functionaries out of their reluctance to attenuate the fundamental loyalty of the traditional society. The *maskilim* of Galicia seemed to bear in their hearts the memory of the days of Joseph II, who had attempted to create a "heavenly city of Germany" in the reality of Eastern Europe, although by the first half of the nineteenth century little remained of his radical and universalistic concepts in social and political matters apart from a stodgy bureaucracy.

In that sense Galician Jewry was similar to Russian Jewry: despite the presence of representatives of the German part of Europe in Galicia, and even though Galicia was the first region to experience administrative reforms affecting the separate existence of Jewish society, until the mid–nineteenth century, Jewish spiritual life and social structure were obstacles to any real Germanization. In such a city as Brody the Jewish community was no more Germanized than many communities on the other side of the Russian border. In both cases the *maskilim* among the Jewish elite were immersed in German culture while large sectors of traditional society saw German influence as destructive and disruptive. In a utopian work by I.M. Dick, a Lithuanian *maskil,* the *maskilim* of the city speak, read, and write in German:

> All can speak very good Russian, and so they can write in it, and among themselves they speak a highly refined Jargon [Yiddish] which is close to pure German.

In *Katloyke* I liked the Jewish public library, which included a club and a study. This house consists of two big halls with some side rooms. Almost every Jewish book, from small to large, of any value, is found there, equally bound, and very well classified so it is very easy to find the book one needs. Besides, all Jewish newspapers in their complete yearly volumes are here, as well as Russian and foreign papers and also many Russian and German classics, the *Konversations-Lexikon,* and also some expensive manuscripts. Every educated person, Christian and Jew, comes here every winter night, especially on Saturdays and on holidays. They entertain each other in a very friendly manner, some read, some copy from books, some discuss religion, politics, physics, and some dispute (Halakha). Commercial matters are also negotiated and deals are made there; also quite often matches are contracted. There also is a counter with beer, cigars, Schnapps, herring, sausage, etc.

[And the Rabbi is] an authentic type of the Old German Rabbiner.[15]

The place was hundreds of kilometers away from the area of Austrian administration and the description written decades after Perl's educational activities. Until the second half of the nineteenth century, "Germanization" of the *maskilim* of Volhynia, Lithuania, and Central Poland was more pronounced than that of most of the Jews of Galicia.

Notes

1. A.B. Gottlober, "HaGizra Veha'Binya" in *Memoirs and Travels* (Jerusalem: Bialik Institute, 1976), 2, p. 71 (Hebrew).
2. A.B. Gottlober, "Zikhronot Miymey Neuray," in *Memoirs and Travels,* 1, p. 182.
3. R. Mahler, *A History of Modern Jewry, 1780–1815* (London: Vallentine, 1971), p. 318.
4. J. Perl, *Megale Tmirin* (Wien, 1819), p. 3b (Hebrew): "I took the book and showed it to my son-in-law who is from the *Kordon* [Galicia] and had learned there in the German schools. And although he had forgotten all that he had learned, thank God, he still knows the German letters."
5. J. Perl referred mainly to Rabbi Meir Baal Hanes's collection, which was highly developed in his area. Cf. A. Rubinstein, "The Booklet *Katit Lamaor* by Joseph Perl," *Alei Sefer* 3 (1976):140–51.
6. J. Perl, *Megale Tmirin,* p. 216.
7. P. Friedman, "Yehudey Galitsya Bemahapekhat Hashana" 1848, *Sefer Hashana Liyehudey Polanya* (Kraków, 1938), vol. 1, pp. 206–7, 211–12.
8. Cf. P. Friedman, "Yoysef Perl Vi a Bildungstuer un zayn Shul in Tarnopol" (YIVO Bleter 30, 1948), pp. 131–92 (Yiddish).
9. Cf. N.M. Gelber, *Mendl Lefin-Satanover's Proposals for the Improvement of Jewish Community Life Presented to the Great Polish Sejm (1788–1792),* The Abraham Weiss Jubilee Volume (New York [privately published], 1964), pp. 271–305.

10. Cf. I. Halpern, *Eastern European Jewry: Historical Studies* (Jerusalem: Magnes, 1968), pp. 340–47 (Hebrew).
11. After 1808 he lived in Brody and Tarnopol, where his influence on Galician *maskilim,* such as Perl and Krochmal, was considerable; cf. J. Klausner, *History of Modern Hebrew Literature* (Jerusalem, 1930), vol. 1, pp. 211–13.
12. Such were the stages in the intellectual biographies of Solomon Judah Rappoport (Shir), Nachman Krochmal, and Judah Leib Mieses.
13. When Shalom Hacohen (1772–1845), a Polish *maskil* who settled in Germany, published his history of the Jewish people *Kore Hadorot* in Warsaw (1838), many *maskilim* of Galician cities and towns paid for his book in advance. The list of subscribers (Prenumeranten) includes 46 from Brody, 42 from Lwów, and 4 from Żółkiew. Cf. B. Kagan, *Hebrew Subscription Lists* (New York: The library of the J.T.S., 1975), pp. 46, 109, 155 (Yiddish). The other subscribers were from Berlin, Hamburg, Breslau, Kraków, Warsaw, Lublin, and Wilna.
14. In such strong language Tobias Feder (1780–1817) described the possible outcome of the translation in his polemic work *Kol Mekhatsetsim* (Berdichev, 1816).
15. S. Niger, "The Utopia of a Maskil: Introduction to an Untitled Manuscript of I.M. Dick," (YIVO Bleter 36, 1952), pp. 157, 161, 166–67 (Yiddish).

3

The Modernization of Viennese Jewry: The Impact of German Culture in a Multi-Ethnic State

Robert S. Wistrich

Ever since the reforms of Emperor Joseph II, the Austrian model of modernization had signified the growing impact of German influence and culture for the Jews of the Habsburg Monarchy.[1] In the late eighteenth and early nineteenth centuries, the mode of transmission for this process of Germanization had been the centralized bureaucracy of Habsburg absolutism—enlightened under Joseph II and reactionary under his successors. The impact of this bureaucratic Austrian model of German-ization and its accompanying Enlightenment ideology on the traditional way of life of Habsburg Jewry was enormous, transforming the relation of Austrian Jews to both the state and the surrounding non-Jewish society. This influence was later to be particularly felt in Western Austria where there was no firmly rooted traditional Jewish society living in compact, densely populated settlements and the obstacles to social integration and the adoption of German culture were less acute. Moreover, the identi-fication of Western Austrian Jews with the Austro-Germans, at least until the closing decades of the nineteenth century, was less complicated by the kind of ethnic and demographic factors that operated in other parts of the monarchy. The intensity of this identification, both with German language and literature as a cultural model and the medium of education and enlightenment, as well as with the German people in Austria, was well described by one of its later opponents, the Austrian Zionist leader Isidor Schalit.

> Throughout the nineteenth century the (Austrian) Jews taken as a whole were German—they were German as a result of their education—for the German culture was dominant in the multilingual Empire. They taught

43

and were taught in German schools. The Austrian Jews were German because the German nationality in Austria was for them the symbol of freedom and progress. . . . the Jews remained not only bearers of German culture, they were the most conspicuous defenders of German policy.[2]

From the perspective of the twentieth century and the nationality problems that eventually led to the collapse of the Habsburg Monarchy, this organic link between modernization and Germanization, between the hegemony of German culture and the cause of social-political progress, which was articulated by so many Austrian (especially Viennese) Jews, seems not only naive but even dangerous and ultimately self-destructive. It appeared to overlook the distinction between a universalist enlightened cultural paradigm modelled on Goethe, Kant, Lessing, and Schiller and the very serious, long-term political implications of the fin-de-siècle Pan-German *Hetzpolitik* directed against the awakening Slav nationalities and ultimately against the Austrian Jews themselves.

For most Viennese (and West Austrian) Jews before the 1880s, such a differentiation between Germanness on the level of *Volk* and *Kultur* would not however have been particularly meaningful. As Adolf Jellinek, the man who was to become Vienna's most famous preacher (*Prediger*), put it in a famous article in 1848, the Jews of Austria demanded their emancipation as an integral part of the German people in the Habsburg Empire; as Germans they were the bearers of education, culture, commerce and industry: "To feel German means to feel free," since the German spirit was identical with the spirit of liberty and the salvation of the Jews "can only come from a liberal government."[3] As Jellinek argued in 1848 in the case of Moravian Jewry—that the centers of industry and science were German and that the Jews were a vital reinforcement of Germanism against the dangers of Czechomania, Pan-Slavism, and the law of the fist—so the leaders of Viennese Jewry were in later years to pledge support consistently for the German-Jewish alliance.

In July 1848, Jellinek had even stated that the Jews were Germans "not because of but in spite of the will of the German population" and praised German as against Czech nationalism for not seeking to impose itself on others; this was the mark of a civilized nation with a rich history and confidence in its own spiritual mission rather than in brute force and numbers.[4]

The ardent identification with the German nation in Austria as well as its culture that had crystallized during the "springtime of the peoples" was inextricably linked to both internal Jewish and wider, general historical factors. German culture, long before 1848, had become for Jewish *maskilim* in the Habsburg lands the normative expression of Europeanism and enlightenment; the Berlin Haskalah in the field of Jewish learning and culture was widely accepted as a model and an ideology to be imitated; moreover, the whole *Jüdische Moderne* in Austria, the transition from a traditional to a modern society and outlook, the passage from the narrow confines of the ghetto to wealth, status, learning and social acceptance in the non-Jewish world, was inevitably mediated through the gateway of Germanism.

In the case of Viennese Jewry the reasons for this development might appear to be self-evident. Vienna was after all a German city, itself a major center of German power and cultural influence which radiated outward to the most distant parts of the Habsburg lands. Technically, one cannot speak here of a transplantation or importation of either German or specifically German-Jewish patterns of modernization unless one is to regard Vienna as an alien environment or as fundamentally separate from the world of German-speaking culture—a proposition which is clearly untenable. On the other hand, as the capital city and hub of a multi-ethnic empire (*Nationalitätenstaat*) standing at the crossroads of East and West—geographically, ethnically, and culturally—Vienna was also the least German of all German cities. Moreover, the pre-1848 development of the Jewish community in Vienna was significantly different from the pattern in other German cities, and this differentiation was to increase with time. Thus Vienna constitutes something of a special case— both a periphery that absorbed, emulated, and adapted German-Jewish models to local conditions and the center in its own right of Austrian Jewry that left its imprint on Prague, Budapest, Cracow, Lemberg, Trieste, and outlying provinces of the monarchy.

This paradoxical situation was already apparent even in the early nineteenth century in Vienna, when the Jewish Community had no officially recognized existence and the Habsburg Monarchy existed more as a myth than a reality for the masses of potential Jewish immigrants in Hungary, Bohemia, Moravia, and Galicia, against whom the gates of the Habsburg capital were firmly shut. In terms of Jewish modernization, Vienna's most important function in this pre-März period was to serve as a publishing center for the Hebrew periodicals and literature of the Berlin Haskalah and a channel for moderate Reform Judaism, more conservative than its German predecessors and better adapted to the needs of the more "backward" Jewish communities of Hungary and Galicia. The tiny elite of wealthy Viennese Jewish families who were "tolerated" in the Habsburg Monarchy before 1848, patrician in character and some of them ennobled, had unavailingly sought a secure Jewish emancipation at the Congress of Vienna in 1815.[5] They themselves could purchase the right to reside in Vienna only on payment of a toleration tax. Although Austrian-Jews like Arnstein, Eskeles, Herz, Lämel, Wert-heimstein, and above all Solomon Rothschild were crucial to the finances of the Habsburg Monarchy, they still remained foreigners, excluded from the possession of landed property. Since the policy of the government was to restrict at all costs the number of Jews in Vienna, the children of the *Tolerierten* were not even allowed to marry in the capital, so that in this one regard, they enjoyed fewer rights than Jews elsewhere in the monarchy.[6] Toleration itself was officially restricted after 1821 to those merchants who could provide exceptional qualifications or services to the state.

Not only was the pre-März nucleus of a Jewish community in Vienna exceedingly small (it was barely 4,000 on the eve of the 1848 Revolution, even with the illegal immigration of Jews to the city[7]), lacking any official standing and structurally weak, but the draconian police surveillance, legislation, and humiliating taxes made its situation seem abject and desperate in comparison with other German communities. Yet even then, without the legal right of residence, the Jewish elite of Vienna was already of great importance for the economic life of the monarchy, and their social integration with upper-class Christian circles had proceeded apace.[8] Some of the wealthiest Jewish families (e.g. the Arnsteins) were enthusiastic followers of the Mendelssohnian enlightenment and it was from this Berlin circle that Fanny von Arnstein, the daughter of the Berlin Court-Jew Daniel Itzig, originated.[9] Her Prussianism, shaped by the spirit of Kant and Lessing, encouraged by the sympathetic attitude toward Jews of Prussian representatives at the Congress of Vienna like Wilhelm von Humboldt and Hardenberg and close family connections with Berlin, was reflected in the Jewish sphere by a diluted Reform Judaism reminiscent of her Berlin brother-in-law, David Friedländer. Such pro-Prussian sym-pathies are not surprising in view of the sharp contrast between the early nineteenth-century attitudes of enlightened Prussian officialdom and the anti-Jewish atmosphere in pre-1848 Austria, despite Metternich's efforts in 1815 on behalf of Jewish civil rights and his close ties with Solomon Rothschild.[10] In this context, it was only natural that the Berlin Haskalah should provide the main point of reference for the Viennese Jewish elite, vitally concerned as they were with obtaining elementary recognition of Judaism and its tradition from the Habsburg authorities. Rehabilitating the moral standing of Judaism and emphasizing its humane spirit were perceived as a necessary precondition for improving Jewish civil status.

The building of the First Temple in the Seitenstettengasse (1826) was an important step in this direction which would have been unthinkable without the initiative of the Imperial and Royal Wholesale Merchant (later Court-Jeweller), M.L. Biedermann, who had first been exposed to the new reform efforts in Hamburg and Berlin during business visits to Germany.[11] Biedermann was the driving force among the "tolerated" Viennese Jews in introducing the German innovations and in securing the preacher Isak Noah Mannheimer, Danish-born but trained in the Reform temples of Germany for the Jewish community of the Habsburg capital. Together with the musically gifted cantor Solomon Sulzer, Mannheimer was to set new standards for the Viennese *kehillah* in adapting Judaism to the spirit of modernity, raising the level of decorum, dignity, and ennoblement (*Veredelung*) in the synagogue and cultivating the aesthetic side of *Bildung*.[12] The German influence in what became known as the Wiener Ritus was clearly evident in the emphasis on the uplifting inspirational sermon in the German language, the use of the choir, and in the efforts to invigorate the historical consciousness of Judaism as a form of culture, to demonstrate the purity and sublimity of Judaism and to improve its image in the eyes of Gentiles.[13]

On the other hand, the Mannheimer rite was considerably more moderate than some of the radical German rites, in which innovations were introduced such as organ music, the abolition of Hebrew, and the omission of certain traditional prayers, especially those relating to messianic hopes for a Jewish restoration in Zion.[14] Mannheimer was prepared to provide cosmetic reforms to satisfy the craving for social status and respectability of the Viennese Jewish *Grossbürgertum* but not to tamper with the institutions of Judaism or to indulge in anything that smacked of religious nihilism. Thus it is not surprising that the Mannheimer rite could be easily accommodated by congregations ranging as far apart as Copenhagen, Amsterdam, Munich, Prague, Karlsruhe, Mayence to the West, Lemberg or Cracow to the North, or Budapest and Prossnitz to the East. A religious approach that was acceptable to German Orthodoxy, the Jewish oligarchy of Vienna, and to Hungarian Neology testifies not only to Mannheimer's personal qualities as mediator, preacher, organizer and pedagogue but also perhaps to the *genius loci* of Vienna itself. If Germany was the decisive model for religious innovation and for a systematic, "scientific" ideology of reform and modernization, Vienna, situated as it was between West and East, between liberalism and tradition, between the values of Germanism and East European Orthodoxy, was uniquely placed to mediate between opposing worlds and to soften the sharp edges of confrontation.

Thus although only sermons were delivered in German in Vienna, Mannheimer did not object on principle to the use of German in the prayerbooks of the Hamburg temple nor did he refrain from inviting its preacher, Dr. Salomon, to preach in the Seitenstettengasse synagogue.[15] This liberality did not in the least weaken his determination to preserve the historic traditions of Judaism, its "outward unity and well-organized consistency," which he contrasted with those who sought to reduce it to a mere docrtine of monotheism or "some metaphysical idea." In his defense of circumcision in 1843, then a matter of dispute in Frankfurt, Mannheimer emphasized that Judaism was an "indivisible unit like any organism, in which the body and soul are inseparable," an historical institution with a national character, unified by divine revelation, ancestral tradition, and filial piety, not by philosophical doctrine.[16] As the founder of the Viennese *Kultusgemeinde* (whose official existence dates from 1852), Mannheimer was particularly aware of the need to proceed with caution and to take into account the susceptibilities of a pious, traditionalist population in the outlying Habsburg lands, which would not take kindly to any tampering with historic Judaism. The fact that he did not "incline to rationalistic views in the matter of Messianic teachings about the Kingdom of God and the Redemption" undoubtedly held him in good stead with Polish and Hungarian Orthodoxy; on the other hand, as "a teacher and spiritual guide of one of the most important communities in Germany, which with all due respect to tradition and ritual, devotes its efforts to the improvement and refinement of the religious service among the Jews"[17] (as he wrote from Vienna in 1842 to the Haham Bernays in Germany), Mannheimer was no less opposed to inflexible, separatist, and schismatic Orthodox tendencies.

Thus far we have emphasized the unifying influence of Mannheimer's rite and the mediating role of Vienna, where, to use his words, "the Orient, with its hoary traditions of thousands of years, meets the Occident, with its modern views—rigid observance of the past, alongside of the searching and constructive spirit of the New Age."[18] From the late 1850s onward, however, as Vienna opened up to the mass immigration of Jews from Hungary, Galicia, Bohemia, and Moravia, the newly constituted *Kultusgemeinde* was faced with the unprecedented challenge of blending widely heterogeneous Jewish groups together; here, more than in any other German city, Westernized Viennese Jews assimilated to German culture, encountered immigrant Eastern Jews, who may have been strangers in social, cultural, or economic terms, but were also brothers-in-faith, and no less important, citizens of a common fatherland; here the encounter between German, Bohemian, Moravian, Galician, and Hungarian Jews, between orthodoxy, reform, and *Indifferentismus* among the new immigrants, took place in the unique context of a cosmopolitan city which was the capital of a multi-ethnic state. The rapidity and scale of the influx of Jews (by 1880 there were 72,588 Jews in Vienna, i.e., 10.29 percent of the total population, while two decades earlier there had been only 6,000, their heterogeneity, varying degrees of assimilation, and diversity of customs inevitably produced a social setting very different from anything in Germany.[19] Not even late nineteenth-century Berlin, which also experienced a spectacular influx of Jews from the eastern Prussian provinces, could compare with Vienna as a gateway for the absorption of Eastern Jews into German-speaking culture.[20]

This dramatic demographic change was accompanied by a tremendous political leap forward from the oppression of the pre-März period and clerical neoabsolutism in the 1850s to the era of *Hochliberalismus* and full Jewish emancipation in 1867. In the internal Jewish sphere, these changes were paralleled by the strengthening of reform tendencies and liberal, universalist trends that received backing and support from radical German reformers like Geiger, Phillipson, and Lazarus. The Viennese reformers, represented at the Augsburg Synod (1871) by Joseph Ritter von Wertheimer, Leopold Kompert, and Simon Szántó clearly favored the adaptation of Judaism to the new situation of equality before the law, freedom of the individual, equal rights and duties toward the state, and freedom of religious convictions. In this respect, the reformers were in tune with the new Jewish middle *Bürgertum,* consisting of self-made men stemming from the free professions who were beginning to challenge the conservative financial elite that dominated the community and its *Vorstand.*[21] Nevertheless, the liberals had a hard struggle in the 1860s against Orthodox separatist tendencies in Vienna, led by the Hungarian rabbis Ignaz Deutsch and Salomon Spitzer.

The liberal, pan-German orientation of the reformers had already been challenged in the neoabsolutist period of reaction of the 1850s by the *kaisertreue,* monarchical loyalism of Deutsch and his Orthodox followers who hoped to persuade the authorities of their right to a separate community.[22] The police-state nature of the Habsburg regime in the first years after the 1848 Revolution, the tendency of the authorities to identify negatively religious and political liberalism and the ascendency of the Catholic Church in administration and education (which had the impact of excluding Jews from public life) had encouraged the Orthodox Jewish leaders to engage in aggressive separatist intrigues. Nevertheless, though police reports indicate that Reform Jews were indeed suspected by the authorities of liberal-democratic, revolutionary, and *staatsgefährliche* tendencies, Orthodox separatism not only failed but discredited itself as a result of Deutsch's intrigues with a reactionary government against fellow Jews.[23] Though East European Orthodox polemics against the "frivolous travesty" of Reform Judaism and the plague of German neo-Orthodoxy continued, and though the number of traditional Orthodox synagogues in Vienna (and of Orthodox taxpayers in the *Gemeinde*) steadily grew with the immigration of petty traders and small businessmen from

Hungary and Galicia, there was no schism such as in Germany or Hungary. Mannheimer's legacy of *Einheit* was preserved. The Orthodox financier Baron Jonas von Konigswärter was quietly succeeded as president of the *Kultusgemeinde* in 1871 by Ignaz Kuranda, the spearhead of Jewish political liberalism in Austria and a leader who had devoted forty years to fighting for Germanism in general.[24] This kind of symbolic liberal victory over the *Altglaübige* provoked no dogmatic conflict or dramatic split as in Germany or Hungary, partly because, as Dubnow noted,

> There was no favorable soil for ultra-orthodoxy of the Hungarian or Galician variety in Vienna. At the same time Jewish Reform in Vienna lacked the aggressive character whch typified it in the Eastern provinces.[25]

The policy of half-measures, compromise between conflicting interests and "modifications" rather than reform on the radical German or Hungarian pattern was indeed characteristic of Viennese Jewry.[26] As Szántó put it, in 1862 the Viennese approach was restorative, based on the well-tested historical principle of conservatism rather than on philosophic doctrine;[27] social emancipation and respectability and not ideological consistency were the decisive considerations guiding the modernization of religious customs. It had been perfectly summed up by the young Adolf Jellinek as far back as April 1848:

> The religious services, the outer garb of Judaism, must be made contemporary and aesthetic, if the Jew, long enough despised and persecuted, is to achieve standing and respect in society.[28]

The Moravian-born Adolf Jellinek, who succeeded Mannheimer in 1865 as Vienna's foremost preacher (he had arrived in the city eight years earlier from Leipzig) epitomized more than any other individual the liberal trend in Viennese Judaism. Unconditional allegiance to German culture and centralized bureaucratic control in the Josephine tradition, loyalty to political liberalism, and anticlericalism went hand in hand with a scholarly approach to Jewish sources derived from the Wissenschaft des Judentums and considerable liberality in matters of ritual.[29] Already in the 1840s Jellinek had felt the impact of German-Jewish modernity in Prague, listening to the sermons of Dr. Michael Sachs, whose language and style owed much to the latter's teachers in Berlin, Hegel, and Schleiermacher.[30] Subsequently, in Leipzig, on the borders of the Slavic East, Jellinek had acquired, along with a knowledge of Oriental languages, philology, and his pioneering explorations of the kabbalah,[31] an intense, passionate commitment to German cultural nationalism. In Vienna during the 1860s, in the era of constitutional liberalism and German hegemony within a grandly conceived Austrian *Rechtsstaat* that granted full civic equality to Jews, Jellinek's faith appeared to be fully vindicated.[32] The *Grundrechte,* embodied in the liberal Habsburg constitution of 1867, which came to be regarded by Viennese Jews as their inalienable Bill of Rights, had been implemented by a strong, centralized power that stood beyond the "particularism of the nationalities." The *Grundrechte* bore witness to the victory of the principle of *Reichseinheit,* which transcended every form of national, religious, or provincial particularism. They signified the hegemony of the liberal Austro-German bourgeoisie and its triumph over the obscurantism of the Catholic Church and the forces of feudal separatism.

This dominant ideology of emancipated Viennese Jewry linked Austrian patriotism with the Enlightenment legacy of German culture and a cosmopolitan version of German national identification. Already in 1859 the Jewish lawyer and liberal politician Heinrich Jacques had expressed it well in his *Denkschrift über die Stellung der Juden in Österreich,* in which he argued that by excluding its Jews from freedom of enterprise, ownership of property, civil and political office, etc., "Austria allows a substantial part of its material and spiritual national capital to lie idle." Jacques asserted that the Austrian state could only benefit from recognizing that Austrian Jews were Austrians like any other citizens. Their civic and political equality would naturally lead to the disappearance of the Jewish nationality. At the same time, like most liberal Viennese Jews of his generation, he advocated the closest connection with Germany, for "all that Austria must attain in the briefest possible time is and always will be solely and exclusively the native product and flower of the true German spirit. Our pride and our comfort are that great store of German science and literature, Lessing and Schiller, Goethe and Alexander von Humboldt."[33]

This was also the view of Ignaz Kuranda, who in the 1840s had been a lecturer in German literature and history at the University of Brussels and publisher of *Die Grenzboten,* a symbol of the alliance between liberal constitutionalism and cultural Pan-Germanism in the struggle against Metternich's rule. A delegate from Vienna to the Frankfurt Parliament in 1848, subsequently publisher of the *Ostdeutsche Post,* then *Landtag,* and finally in 1867 *Reichsrat* deputy for the first district of Vienna, Kuranda led the German liberal party in Austria for two decades. Since he was also a leading figure in the Kultusgemeinde from 1860 (elected president, 1871–1884) and head of the Wiener Israelitische Allianz, Kuranda's political orientation had a representative significance for Viennese Jewry as a whole in the era of liberal modernization.[34] What

Adolf Jellinek represented in the religious sphere was paralleled in the general political arena by the uninhibited commitment of men like Kuranda to German ideals (understood as synonymous with a powerful Austria) and the loyalty of most Viennese Jews to the legacy of 1848 embodied in the German liberal *Verfassungspartei.* This fateful commitment, which came under increasing strain in the 1880s and 1890s with the rise of illiberal mass movements such as Christian socialism, social-democracy, racial Pan-Germanism, Czech nationalism, etc., was nonetheless maintained throughout the nineteenth century.[35] As late as 1879, on the eve of those very changes that were to make this commitment extremely problematic, Adolf Jellinek wrote in *Die Neuzeit:*

> In line with their most vital interests, the Jews of Austria must adhere to the constitution and the forces of liberalism. With regard to their background and education they are inclined to German nationality, they sympathize with a grandly conceived Austria based on a strong centralized government.[36]

There can be no doubt that the leaders of Viennese Jewry considered German nationality in Austria culturally far superior to the non-German peoples of the empire. They themselves were German by education and culture, even though among the leading personalities of the official Jewish community only Joseph Ritter von Wertheimer had actually been born in Vienna.[37] Despite the defeat of 1866 and Austria's expulsion from German affairs, Vienna was still a great German city, Franz Joseph was considered first and foremost a German prince, and the *Neue Freie Presse* was indubitably a German newspaper. Both at the center and the margins of the Viennese-Jewish community there was initially a great reluctance to accept that Austria had finally been separated from Germany, to recognize the implications of rising Slav nationalism and the retreat of German liberalism, or to grasp the significance of the new nationalistic and clerical reaction among the German lower-middle classes in the Austrian towns and countryside. The Jewish involvement in Germanism's fight against the Slavs, in the German Liberal party, and in the propagation of German culture (which even slid after 1866 into a pro-Prussian, pro-*Anshluss,* and anti-Habsburg direction in certain cases) was indeed to have fatal consequences, inviting the hatred of all the nationalities in the Monarchy.

This danger had been foreseen by the farsighted liberal revolutionary and hero of 1848, Adolf Fischof, a Hungarian Jew impregnated with the cosmopolitan ethos of early German nationalism, who subsequently arrived at a precocious understanding of the complexity of Austria's nationality problems. Though Fischof's belated efforts to organize a social reformist *Deutsche Volkspartei* aborted in 1882 (and were vehemently opposed by pro-Prussian, Pan-German Jews like Heinrich Friedjung),[38] his warning to the leading Jews of Vienna was to prove prophetic: either a reconciliation of the claims of the Austrian nationalities would be found or the peoples of Austria would turn anti-Semitic.[39]

Fischof's reflections on the specificity of the Habsburg *Vielvölkerstaat* in his classic pamphlet *Österreich und die Bürgschaften seines Bestandes* (1869) were an early recognition of the fundamentally different pattern provided by Austria as a multinational state as against the relatively homogeneous nation-state model of Western Europe. The implications for the general political orientation of Viennese Jewry of Fischof's skepticism with regard to the benefits of centralized government, his arguments for the recognition of the neglected Slav nationalities, his call for personal and territorial autonomy as a protection for minorities, and above all his opposition to asserting one-sidedly the supremacy of German culture were clearly disturbing. Fischof was accepted and admired by Vienna's Jews as a fighter for German liberties, as a liberal-bourgeois democrat and even as a symbol of Jewish emancipation in Austria, *not* as a spokesman for multi-ethnic pluralism and greater equality for the non-German peoples. The connection that Fischof drew between individual liberties and national self-determination, which is perhaps implicit in the liberal revolutionary tradition, appeared in the Austrian context to be undermining Jewish interests, as long as these were identified with Josephine centralism, German hegemony, and resistance to centrifugal particularisms whether religious, ethnic, provincial, or cultural.[40]

Liberal Viennese Jewry's unconditional identification with German culture had moreover been reinforced by the enormous impact that Germany had exercised on modern Jewish scholarship and research. During Adolf Jellinek's years in Leipzig (1845–1856) he had been greatly influenced by his patron Zacharias Frankel (the first director of the Breslau Theological Seminary) and by the glorification of the Jewish past in the writings of the German-Jewish historian Heinrich Graetz. Jellinek's pioneering esoteric studies in the kabbalah between 1844 and 1854 and his later reconstruction of midrashic literature in Vienna owed much to the methodological example of Zunz and Steinschneider.

Similarly, Jellinek's conservative contemporary in Vienna, Rabbi Moritz Güdemann, born in northwest Prussia and a product of the Breslau Jewish Theological Seminary, was a classic exponent of the Wissenschaft des Judentums and the positive, historical Judaism advocated by Zacharias Frankel.[41] Güdemann's most important scholarly achievements, his three volume social history of Jewish education *Geschichte des Erziehungswesens und der Cultur der abendländischen Juden* and his earlier work *Das jüdische Unterrichtswesen während der spanisch-arabischen Periode* (1873), were eloquent testimony to the importance of the concept of historical development worked out by Heinrich Graetz and the Breslau school;[42] they also testified to the value of university training in philosophy and Oriental languages which was an integral part of the legacy of nineteenth-century German-Jewish *Wissenschaft* and its conception of the scholar-rabbi.[43] The scientific methods of the German school also found expression in the more traditional field of Talmud studies, obtaining an institutional foothold with Jellinek's founding of the periodical *Beth Hamidrash* in Vienna in 1862. The Orthodox Lazar Horwitz (a pupil of the great Hungarian rabbi Moses Sofer), Jellinek himself, I.H. Weiss, author of *Dor Dor Vedoreshav,* and Meir Friedmann in his lectures on the Midrash, contributed to reviving Vienna's standing as a seat of traditional Jewish learning, now analyzed with the more sophisticated conceptual tools of German science.[44]

Nevertheless, though strongly influenced by German models (all three seminal figures in Viennese Judaism of the nineteenth century, Mannheimer, Jellinek, and Güdemann were arguably more German than Austrian), Viennese Jewry never produced feats of specifically Jewish scholarship that bear comparison with the works of Zunz, Geiger, Frankel, Steinschneider, Holdheim, S.R. Hirsch, or Graetz in Germany, not to mention the later generation of Hermann Cohen, Buber, and Rosenzweig. This is all the more striking since German-Austrian (and especially Viennese) Jewry in their contribution to general scholarship, the arts and sciences, etc. were in no sense inferior to Jews in the Second Reich after 1870.[45] The function of Vienna from the beginning of the nineteenth century was much more that of a crossroads and bridge by means of which the *neuzeitliche* German Judaism was transmitted eastward to the dark and dirty ghettoes of *Halbasien,* to backward Hungary and on to the teeming multitudes of Russian Jewry.

In the first half of the nineteenth century, the Haskalah movement in Vienna, which was basically an offshoot of Mendelssohn and his periodical *Hame'assef,* had already played this clearing-house role for the Jews of the monarchy as a whole. Vienna, more than any other German city, established itself as a center for publishing Hebrew books[46]— the Bible in various editions, Talmud, Midrash, Shulhan Aruch, prayer-books, but also Maimonides, Nahmanides, Rashba, Eybeschutz, Azariah dei Rossi, Wessely, and others as well as the periodicals *Bikkurei Haittim* (1820–1831) and *Kerem Hemed* (1833–1856).

The Hebrew printing press of the Imperial-Royal publisher Anton Edler von Schmid reached a wide Jewish market in the monarchy, with Hebraist scholars and poets from Prague, Lemberg, and Brody to Padua,

Trieste, and Gorz sending their manuscripts to Vienna for publication.[47] This Hebrew Enlightenment literature, directly inspired by the Berlin Haskalah but aimed at the Jews of the Habsburg lands rather than specifically at a Viennese Jewish public, was permeated with the cosmopolitanism of the German classics and also with the desire to awaken greater consciousness of the Jewish heritage and of the glorious Jewish past. Viennese Jews were found among its contributors along with Bohemian, Moravian, Silesian, and Italian Jews. The continuity of this Hebraist tradition underlined once again Vienna's special role as a crossroads between West and East European Judaism. In the 1860s Hebrew periodicals like *Beit Hamidrash,* published by Isaac Weiss and chiefly concerned with the Talmud, or Perets Smolenskin's Jewish nationalist *Haschachar* (begun in 1868) also flourished in Vienna, the latter bitterly opposed to the ideology of the Berlin Haskalah[48] and primarily directed at a readership in Russia and East Europe.

Thus if Vienna lacked top-flight original scholarship in the field of Judaica, it did nonetheless contribute substantially to its dissemination and modernization, and more than any other German city nurtured a Hebrew language culture. Among the Viennese *maskilim* of the early nineteenth century, the proof readers of the printing establishments, the Jewish private teachers and scholars, Hebrew remained a *lingua franca* of literary activity in a way that it rapidly ceased to be in Germany.[49] This tradition was actively encouraged by Mannheimer and Jellinek,[50] neither of whom regarded it as in any way standing in contradiction to the innovations of German *Wissenschaft* and European *Bildung* or the new style of *Predigt* fashionable in Vienna.

In a classic essay Alexander Altmann has drawn attention to the importance of the replacement of the traditional *Derasha,* with this new type of Jewish preaching, a development pioneered by nineteenth-century German Jewry which affected not only the sermon's outward form but also its substance.[51] This innovation, so characteristic of the integration of Jews into modern German culture, arguably reached its peak in Vienna in the eloquent sermons of Mannheimer and Jellinek. German *Bildung* and the selective imitation of Christian models were harnessed in Vienna as in other German cities into the service of reviving Judaism by providing it with a more edifying and elevated tone.[52] The enlightened ideals of *Humanität* were woven into a fabric of midrashic and aggadic texts which preserved a strong Jewish flavor, even as they revolutionized religious thinking and modified the theological concepts of Judaism. Jellinek in particular transformed this new style of preaching into a veritable art form, replete with rhetorical pathos, in which the rich sources of rabbinical Jewish literature were blended with the general culture of humanity. In his hands the Derashah was transformed and modernized without sacrificing the spiritual uniqueness of Jewish monotheism, without banishing the Midrash or avoiding Hebrew quotations. What Jellinek may have lacked in the field of pure scholarship was more than compensated for by the artistic effect of his impassioned sermons, full of Jewish learning, which particularly appealed to the Viennese Jewish public, nourished by a general culture in which theatrical and musical elements stood in the foreground.[53]

If the artistry of Jellinek's addresses and their Hebraic flavor clearly owed something to the *genius loci* of Vienna, so too did his synthesis of the universalistic nature of Judaism with the particularism embedded in Jewish life and law. For all Jellinek's liberalism in matters of ritual and the struggle he waged against religious coercion of East European Orthodoxy, he had a strong sense of Jewish ethnic-national identity (*Stammesbewusstsein*) which acted as a brake on the assimilatory tendencies implicit in Reform Judaism.

Altmann has suggested that some of Jellinek's sermons and in particular his ethnographic study *Der jüdische Stamm* (Vienna, 1869) reveal a kind of "pre-Zionist humanistic Zionism," a sense of Jewish nationalism blended with "the ideal of Humanität."[54] This would seem to be stretching a point, for Jellinek's *Stammesbegriff* was not so much national as rather a dialectical effort to harmonize Hebraic universalism with ethnic particularism in such a way that neither the continuity of tradition nor of Jewish identity in the modern age would be abandoned. For Jellinek the Jewish *Stamm* was a historical category rooted not in racial or unchanging natural characteristics but in the essence of Hebrew religiosity and the messianic idea of Judaism which was fully compatible with liberal aspirations for the universal progress of mankind.[55] While the Jewish national character was indeed a reality expressed in the medium of language, literature, religious genius, history, morality, and above all the character and ethos of the Jewish people, Jellinek was careful to distinguish between *national* and *Stammeseigentümlichkeiten*. As he put it in *Der Jüdische Stamm*:

> The Jews have no national characteristics as such, but only tribal peculiarities. Thanks to their universalism, they accept and adapt the characteristics of the nations in whose midst they have been born and educated.[56]

The gulf between this *Stammesbegriff* and modern Jewish nationalism was revealed when an anguished Leo Pinsker, traumatized by the Russian pogroms and the Stoecker agitation in Berlin, visited Jellinek in Vienna in the summer of 1882 and put forward his program of auto-emancipation.

Jellinek's reply anticipated by fifteen years the objections of his conservative neo-Orthodox colleague, later the Oberrabbiner of Vienna, Moritz Güdemann, to Herzl's *Judenstaat*. He told Pinsker:

> Have the Jews, since the time of Moses Mendelssohn and especially since the great world-historical transformation in France sent out their best men to fight for recognition and equality in the European countries? . . . have they engaged their spiritual energies on behalf of emancipation in countless pamphlets, from the pulpit and the platform, in order to give up their achievements in the year 1882, in order to declare themselves homeless aliens and vagabonds, and with staff in hand to seek out a problematic fatherland? No.[57]

Neither Jellinek nor Güdemann, any more than the leadership of the Viennese *Kultusgemeinde,* could countenance an ideology of auto-emancipation. This ideology, based on the principle of secular Jewish nationalism which already in the early 1880s had obtained a foothold in Vienna itself among the students (mainly from Eastern Europe) who founded the organization Akademische Verein Kadimah, had been formulated not only by Pinsker but more directly by the Russian *maskil,* Peretz Smolenskin.[58] His Hebrew periodical *Haschachar,* printed in Vienna since 1868, inspired young Viennese students like Nathan Birnbaum and the marginalized, immigrant Eastern Jews who could find no place in the official Jewish community of the Habsburg capital, to create the first Jewish nationalist students' organization in Europe. As university students they suffered directly from the anti-Semitic Pan-German agitation of the Austrian Burschenschaften in the late 1870s, which had begun excluding Jews from membership in the nationalist fraternities. This exclusive policy increasingly affected school associations, gymnastic clubs (*Turnvereine*), and German cultural associations in Austria. The sharpening national confrontation in the Habsburg Monarchy, accompanied by humiliating reminders of Jewish "racial inferiority," convinced the founders of Kadimah that the ideology of emancipation and Germanization preached by the leaders of Viennese Jewry had led into a cul-de-sac.

Their marginal position in Viennese Jewish society made the students more sensitive to the social conflicts generated by Jewish emancipation in an era of growing nationalism. Smolenskin's backlash against the Berlin Haskalah, and the self-dissolution of Jewish identity in Vienna as a factor exacerbating anti-Semitism, spoke to their marginal situation, which led them to experience social discrimination as a form of national oppression. Those who came from the heartland of the Jewish masses in Russia, Rumania, and Galicia where they had experienced the ethnic-traditional sense of Jewish peoplehood, found themselves existing in a kind of spiritual and socioeconomic vacuum in cosmopolitan Vienna. Having broken with the communal framework of Judaism, remaining outside the oligarchical structures of the Viennese *Kultusgemeinde,* and in transition between traditional and modern society, they found in Jewish nationalism a means of self-assertion and social integration.

The rise of political anti-Semitism in Austria after 1880 dramatically underlined their marginality and threw them back on their own resources. Secular Jewish nationalism provided them with a way back to their own people and resolution of their identity conflict. At the same time, they too had been exposed to Central European culture and to the rising nationalist ideologies in Austro-Hungary. The inculcation of values derived from German culture and *Bildung* led these young Jewish intellectuals to a critical view of Vienna's assimilated Jewish society, whose materialistic outlook they openly despised.[59] It is only against this background that we can understand the reevaluation of Jewish tradition in a modern, secular spirit by Nathan Birnbaum and his devastating assault on the assimilation of German-speaking Jewry in the Habsburg lands.[60] Birnbaum's *Kulturkritik,* with its sharp attack on the moneyed middle-classes of Viennese Jewry and the aping of Gentile manners, its denunciation of national self-dissolution and the worship of German culture, was itself an internalization of values he had absorbed in Vienna.[61] For those of his postemancipation generation in Vienna no longer satisfied with liberal pieties and optimistic visions of permanent progress, Jewish nationalism provided the solution to a serious modernizing dilemma, particularly acute in the Habsburg Monarchy: How to bridge the gap between a prosperous, developing Jewry in Western Austria and the rapidly deteriorating situation of the poverty-stricken Jewish masses in the East.[62]

The great migration to Vienna from the hinterlands of the Habsburg Monarchy after 1860 which decisively shaped the character and baroque diversity of its Jewish community gave this problem a pressing urgency more than in any other German city at that time. For approximately two decades before 1880 the cultural and social contradictions arising from the heterogeneity of the Jewish community and the multinational structure of the empire were admittedly contained. The cosmopolitan character of the *Weltstadt* and of the Habsburg dynasty itself, with its relatively benign attitude toward the Jews, the seemingly unlimited prospects for social mobility and professional success in the liberal era, made integration appear a relatively painless process. By 1880, the Viennese-born element in the Jewish community already constituted 31 percent, as against 28 percent from Hungary, 25 percent from Bohemia and Moravia, and 18 percent of Galician-born Jews. The class divisions between the wealthy, sophisticated notables, and banking clans who dominated the *Kultusgemeinde,* the liberal Germanophile bourgeoisie, the lower-middle-class stratum of commercial employees and semiproletarianized stratum of immigrant Eastern Jews had not yet fully crystallized. The economic crisis that overtook the Viennese artisans and the gradual democratization of the franchise that contributed so much to making the Gentile middle classes in Vienna receptive to anti-Semitic demagogy, had yet to cast their shadow over the future.[63]

Nevertheless, by the end of the 1870s the stresses and strains that were an inevitable concomitant of the modernization of Vienna were already having their impact on the situation of the Jews. Not only Jewish immigrants from the *shtetlach* and *Judengassen* of the provinces but also Gentiles (especially Czechs) were streaming toward the Imperial capital, whose population leapt from 476,220 in 1857 to 726,105 in 1880 and 1,364,548 in 1890.[64] Vienna's character as a purely German city began to erode. Increasingly it reflected its post-1866 position as the capital of a polyglot state in which diverse nationalities were in constant competition and conflict. Within this ethnically pluralist environment the Jews remained a distinctive group, concentrated heavily in commerce and the free professions, socially mobile, and centered in the main in well-defined areas of the city such as the Innere Stadt, the Leopoldstadt, Brigittenau, and Alsergrund.[65] The pattern of Jewish immigration, residence, and socialization tended on the whole to work against a deep-seated structural assimilation, even before the rise of organized anti-Semitism, and to produce a greater sense of Jewish ethnic identity than was the case in other German cities.

Moreover, external factors related to the structure of the Habsburg polity in general reinforced the uniqueness of the Jewish position in Vienna. On the positive side, in contrast to the situation in the unified Prusso-German nation-state after 1870, the persistence of a specific Jewish identification was not perceived by the authorities as inimical to the process of integration. Since Habsburg officialdom had no interest in encouraging the development of Jewish national consciousness, the pluralistic political framework of the Austrian Monarchy eased the pressures for rigid conformity in Jewish self-definition. The role of the Jews in capitalist modernization was welcomed by the state as a centripetal factor holding together the threads of common economic interest between the contending nationalities. The extraterritorial character of the Jewish minority also posed no threat to a supranational dynasty that could count on its complete loyalty to the Austrian state.

However, the changing self-definition of the German population in Austria (by 1880 no more than 36.8 percent of the population in the Cisleithanian half of the Empire were German) did pose a serious and intractable dilemma for the Jews in Vienna. With the rise of an aggressive, racist *Volksdeutschtum* in Austria after 1880 which was illiberal, anti-Habsburg, and openly anti-Semitic in character, the one-sided love affair with German culture, which had been the foundation on which Viennese Jewry built its liberal dream, appeared increasingly problematic. That the new anti-Semitism was clearly inspired by German models derived from Berlin, that its prophets were Richard Wagner, Stoecker, Dühring, and Heinrich von Treitschke, was a particularly traumatic blow that could not be wholly repressed.[66] German *Wissenschaft* suddenly appeared in a new guise, not as a liberating guarantee of Jewish rights and access to European Enlightenment but as the rationalization for a brutal assault on the legitimacy of Jewish emancipation itself. In Austria, Georg von Schoenerer's Pan-German movement, enthusiastically supported by Viennese university students, led the way in redefining German culture so as to explicitly exclude the Jews.[67]

We have already noted the response of the Russian-born Peretz Smolenskin and a handful of Jewish students at the University of Vienna to this challenge. A Zionist-oriented Jewish nationalism which emphasized the necessity for a recovery of Jewish self-respect and a renaissance of Jewish cultural creativity was only one option among several that lay open to fin-de-siècle Viennese Jews. While the subsequent flowering of alternative directions such as Herzlian political Zionism, national autonomism, or calls for an independent Jewish state belong already to the early twentieth century, there was one option whose roots lay in the period of the 1880s that deserves brief consideration in our context. This specifically Austrian Jewish alternative, which recognized that the Habsburg Monarchy was fundamentally different from the German national model, was an outgrowth of Adolf Fischof's insight into the nationalities problem. Its prime exponent, the Galician-born Rabbi Dr. Joseph Samuel Bloch, was, however, unlike Fischof (who fought for Austrian ideals in general), devoted explicitly and exclusively to Jewish interests. Bloch developed Fischof's insight into the anachronistic nature of the German centralist model for fin-de-siècle Austria into the starting point for a new Jewish self-definition and political strategy.

Bloch's social background peculiarly fitted him for the historic role he was to play in the 1880s in galvanizing Viennese Jewry against the rising threat of Catholic and Pan-Germanist anti-Semitism from without and Jewish *Indifferentismus* from within. His crucial role in demolishing the anti-Semitic falsifications of the Catholic professor August Röhling need not detain us here, except insofar as it involved him in a direct clash with the communal leaders of Viennese Jewry. Bloch's insistence on militant, public opposition to anti-Semitic calumny went counter to the strategy of avoidance adopted by the *Kultusgemeinde* and the financial magnates of Viennese Jewry, for whom such Jewish self-assertiveness appeared as an alarming provocation. His determination to defend the Talmud in public against anti-Semitic demagogy, even to the extent of addressing social-democratic meetings in the Viennese working-class suburb of Florisdorf[68] (where he was rabbi), clearly embarrassed communal leaders, as did his emphasis on the living national content of Judaism. The spectacle of an outspoken Eastern Jew fiercely defending the talmudic Judaism of his native Galicia as a model of social justice for the exploited Gentile working classes of Vienna provoked the revealing reproach of the president of the Israelitische Allianz zu Wien, Josef von Wertheimer: "You defend the Talmud far too much; we don't know it and don't want it anymore."[69]

Bloch's Jewish self-consciousness and his spontaneous Jewish nationalism was rooted in his Galician background and a rabbinical education, which went together with a remarkable mastery of the German language and the sources of modern European culture. However, his synthesis of East European Jewish Orthodoxy and secular Western learning led him, under the pressure of Austrian conditions in the 1880s, to a full-blooded Jewish national identification that was unequivocally loyal to the supranational Habsburg dynasty. In contrast to the Jews of Vienna and Western Austria who still considered themselves Germans, Bloch argued:

We are neither Germans nor Slavs, but Austrian Jews or Jewish Austrians.[70]

The cult of *Österreichertum,* which Bloch consistently defended in his militant weekly *Österreichische Wochenschrift* (a title deliberately chosen to highlight his opposition to Heinrich Friedjung's pro-Prussian and Pan-German *Deutsche Wochenschrift*),[71] was based on a shrewd assessment of changing political realities in the monarchy. Since 1879 Count Taafe's government in Austro-Hungary had been built on a Slav-clerical alliance and a policy of reconciliation of the nationalities in the monarchy at the expense of German claims to hegemony. Bloch was convinced that it was in the best interests of Viennese and Austrian Jewry to back this policy and dissociate themselves both from supporting the liberal German *Verfassungspartei* and Pan-German efforts to dominate the Slavs. The mounting anti-Semitic agitation of the Pan-Germans underlined the threat from this quarter to Jewish civic equality. If the Jews allowed themselves to be harnessed to the German cart or that of any other national group, the results were likely to be disastrous. German or Slav nationalism in Austria could only disintegrate the structure of the state. The Jews, however, could find their salvation in regarding themselves as Austrians *tout court*[72] (as many Galician Jews already did) and helping to build a purely Austrian party devoted to the interests of the supranational state and not to the egoistic concerns of the nationalities. As a member of the *Polenklub* from 1883, representing the Galician Jewish constituency of Kolomea, Bloch consistently pursued this strategy which had the support of the Orthodox, *kaisertreue* Jewish masses in the monarchy. It was no less congenial to the interests of the Taafe administration itself and to the pro-Habsburg Polish aristocracy.

Bloch's *Wochenschrift,* with the original synthesis of Jewish Orthodox populism, Habsburg loyalism (a kind of late Jewish version of Palacky's Austro-Slavism), and the militant defense of specifically Jewish interests remained anathema to most communal leaders of Viennese Jewry. Liberal Germanophile Jews in Vienna and Western Austria recoiled from some of Bloch's strictures against identification with Germanism, his assault on assimilation as a form of "Semitic anti-Semitism," his populist appeal to the Jewish masses and his insistence on challenging the anti-Semites in public controversy. His concept of the Jews as the bedrock of a specifically "Austrian nationality" and his identification with Slavic (especially Polish) rather than German aspirations contradicted too sharply the cultural and political orientation of most Viennese Jews. The so-phisticated Jewish notables, the business and intellectual elites of Viennese Jewry, probably felt closer to their Gentile German neighbors than to unassimilated Orthodox Jews from Hungary or Galicia, the working-men of Florisdorf or Slavic immigrants from Bohemia.

Most liberal Viennese Jews resented the specifically Jewish identification that Bloch stressed, preferring the diluted humanitarian version of Judaism that severed the religious cult from its national roots. Joseph Bloch argued for a united religious and cultural organization with common goals based on consciousness of a common ancestry and *Schicksalsgemeinschaft* that stood beyond the old divisions between orthodox and reform. Viennese Jews, faced with a common enemy that threatened their civic rights, would have to organize under a united umbrella organization that overlooked the religious, cultural, and class divisions in their ranks. This indeed was the ideology that inspired the creation of the Österreichisch-Israelitische Union in 1886, the first Jewish civic defense organization in Europe.[73] The Union not only promoted Jewish culture and scholarship but also organized protest meetings against anti-Semitism and defended the political rights of Jews. The scope of its activities lies beyond our present concern. What is significant for our purposes is that this initiative, the first step toward organized, autonomous Jewish politics in Vienna initially encountered considerable resistance from the leaders of the Kultusgemeinde and the Jewish financial magnates. Similarly, when the government sought to appoint Bloch to a professional chair in Jewish Antiquities at the University of Vienna (which would have granted academic recognition to the study of the Talmud), Jellinek and the communal leaders blocked the initiative.[74] Bloch's embattled Jewish nationalism, rooted in a synthesis of tradition, Orthodoxy, and East European populism was initially more than they could stomach, in spite of its non-Zionist character.

Nevertheless, the establishment of the Union and Bloch's militant stance against the anti-Semites was to lead in the last decade of the nineteenth century to a significant reorientation in the attitudes of Viennese Jewry, confronted with the collapse of political liberalism under the onslaught of Karl Lueger's Christian-social cohorts. The irrefutable evidence that the great mass of the Gentile lower-middle classes had been won over to an anti-Semitic program and the German liberals were impotent to prevent this defection, could not be swept under the carpet. The vision of harmonious social integration slowly but surely began to crumble in the postliberal climate of nationalism, class struggle, and populist demagogy. Already in 1890 Jellinek, for example, had mellowed his opposition to Bloch's candidacy for the *Reichsrat* and concluded that a united front was necessary to secure the status of Austrian Jewry.[75] Disillusionment with the consequences of a one-sided commitment to Germanism and a growing emphasis on Jewish self-defense and independence began to make headway even among the German-oriented leaders of the Jewish community. Traditional loyalties and perceptions remained generally dominant among the Jews of Vienna, formed as they had been by German culture and the ethos of Austrian liberalism to reject any notions of religious or political separatism. Nevertheless, the dialectic of the modernization process in the Habsburg lands had led by the end of the century to an affirmation of ethnic identity among an ever-increasing number of Viennese Jews.

Notes

1. See Paul P. Bernard, "Joseph II and the Jews: the Origins of the Toleration Patent of 1782," *Austrian History Yearbook* 4-5 (1970), pp. 101–19; Max Grunwald, *Vienna* (Philadelphia: The Jewish Publication Society of America, 1936), pp. 145–65; Eduard Goldstuecker, "Jews between Czechs and Germans around 1848," *Leo Baeck Institute Year Book* 17 (1972), pp. 62–66; and Wolfgang Häusler, *Das galizische Judentum in der Habsburgermonarchie* (Wien: Oldenbourg, 1979), pp. 18–46.
2. *Festschrift des Kadimah 1883–1933. Zur Feier des 100. Semesters der akademischen Verbindung Kadimah* (Wien [privately published], 1933), p. 50.

3. Adolf Jellinek, "Die Juden in Österreich," *Der Orient* 17, 22 April 1848; "Die Freiheit der Juden ist zugleich die Freiheit des Deutschtums," Ibid. 20, 13 May 1848, p. 153.

4. Ibid, 28, 8 July 1848, pp. 217–18.

5. Grunwald, pp. 190–204; N.M. Gelber, *Aktenstücke zur Judenfrage am Wiener Kongress* (Wien: Verlag des Esra, 1920), pp. 4–20; Salo Baron, *Die Judenfrage auf dem Wiener Kongress* (Wien: Löwit, 1920), pp. 91, 138–44, 174–77.

6. Hans Tietze, *Die Juden Wiens* (Leipzig: Tal, 1933), pp. 140ff., Grunwald, pp. 209–13.

7. There were only 450 Jews in Vienna in 1752, under the protection of 12 tolerated heads of families. By 1830 the figure had risen slightly to 903 Jews. In 1847-48 there were officially a mere 179 "tolerated families" in Vienna, though many more had in fact illegally entered the city and set up businesses. I. Jeiteles, *Die Kultusgemeinde der Israeliten in Wien* (Wien, 1873), p. 42, estimated the number at 1,600; other estimates are closer to 4,000 on the eve of the revolution. See Sigmund Mayer, *Ein jüdischer Kaufmann* (Leipzig: Duncker & Humblot, 1911), pp. 107–11, and Tietze, ibid, pp. 138–39.

8. Sigmund Mayer, *Die Wiener Juden. Kommerz, Kultur, Politik 1700–1900,* (Wien: Löwit, 1918); Grunwald, pp. 306–9.

9. See Hilde Spiel, *Fanny von Arnstein oder die Emanzipation. Ein Frauenleben an der Zeitwende, 1758–1818* (Frankfurt: Fischer, 1962). Also Jacob Allerhand, "Die Rabbiner des Stadttempels von J.N. Mannheimer bis Z.P. Chajes," *Studia Judaica Austriaca* VI (Eisenstadt, 1978), p. 9, who describes the Arnstein-Eskeles circle as "das nach Wien verpflanzte Stück Berlinertum." In contrast to Berlin, where there were not only "gebildete Männer und Philosophen sowie eine Gemeinde, der jener Rationalismus eine geistige Richtung wies," in Vienna "gab es weder eine Jüdische Gemeinde noch geistige Führer, die ihren Weg hätten bestimmen können."

10. Grunwald, pp. 194–95, 209–13.

11. M. Rosenmann, *I.N. Mannheimer. Sein Leben und Wirken* (Wien: Löwit, 1922), p. 35. Biedermann first heard Mannheimer preach at one of the Leipzig fairs. For the semi-official history of the Temple and its communal role see Gerson Wolf, *Vom ersten bis zum zweiten Tempel. Geschichte der israelitischen Kultusgemeinde in Wien, 1820–1860* (Wien, 1861).

12. On the philosophy behind Mannheimer's sermons see Alexander Altmann, "The New Style of Preaching in Nineteenth-Century German Jewry," in A. Altmann, ed., *Studies in Nineteenth-Century Jewish Intellectual History* (Harvard, 1964), pp. 72, 79, 100–102.

13. On the Jewish Reform movement in Germany and its impact see M. Wiener, *Jüdische Religion im Zeitalter der Emanzipation* (Berlin: Philo-Verlag, 1933).

14. M. Rosenmann, *I.N. Mannheimer*, pp. 74–75, emphasizes his resistance to Geiger's radical reform proposals in the mid-1840s. He refused to call into question the inadmissibility of mixed marriages, the binding character of the Sabbath laws or belief in a personal Messiah. Jellinek inherited the method of harmonizing orthodoxy and "reform" from Mannheimer, though he was personally more liberal in manner and outlook. See his *Predigten,* III, (Wien, 1866), p. 113.

15. Grunwald, p. 347.

16. Ibid., pp. 347–48. Also David Philipson, *The Reform Movement in Judaism,* rev. ed. (New York: Ktav, 1967), pp. 87, 135.

17. Grunwald, pp. 346–47.
18. Gerson Wolf, *Isak Noah Mannheimer* (Wien: Knöpflmacher, 1863), p. 43.
19. I. Jeiteles, pp. 40 ff.; and Gustav Schlimmer, *Die Juden in Österreich nach der Zählung vom 31. Dezember 1880* (Wien, 1881), pp. 4–7. From 1857 to 1869 the Jewish population in Vienna rose from 6,217 to 40,230—a rate of growth considerably more rapid than that of the non-Jewish population. On the social and occupational structure of Viennese Jewry (more "modern" than that of Gentiles) on the eve of the great influx see Peter Schmidtbauer, "Zur sozialen Situation der Wiener Juden im Jahre 1857," in *Studia Judaica Austriaca* VI (1978), pp. 57–89.
20. On the demography and regional background to the influx of *Ostjuden* into Vienna see Anson Rabinbach, "The Migration of Galician Jews to Vienna, 1857–1880," *Austrian History Yearbook* 11 (1975), pp. 45–54; and the critical comments of Scott Eddie, ibid., pp. 59–63.
21. See Wolfgang Häusler, "Orthodoxie und Reform im Wiener Judentum in der Epoche des Hochliberalismus," *Studia Judaica Austriaca* VI (1978), p. 49, on the class background.
22. I. Oehler, "Geschichte des 'Leopoldstadter Tempels' in Wien," in H. Gold, ed., *Zeitschrift für die Geschichte der Juden* I (Tel Aviv, 1964), pp. 22–24; Tietze, pp. 217–20. Despite the proliferation of orthodox *Bethäuser* among Hungarian, Polish, and other *Altgläubige* who rejected the services in the first Temple as anathema, Deutsch's efforts to mobilize them into a common political front came to nothing.
23. For a stinging, contemporary response to Deutsch's intrigues see Gerson Wolf (under the pen-name, Israel Levi Kohn), *Beitrag zur Geschichte jüdischer Tartuffe* (Leipzig, 1864). Häusler, "Orthodoxie und Reform," p. 35, includes material from an 1855 police report on the Jews of Vienna, warning against the "liberal" tendencies and contrasting them unfavorably with the *Kaisertreue* of the orthodox.
24. See A. Kohut, *Allgemeine Zeitung des Judentums* 76 (1912): pp. 273–75, 282–84, 292–94; Grunwald, pp. 365–71.
25. Simon Dubnow, *Weltgeschichte des jüdischen Volkes,* vol. 9 (Berlin: Jüdischer Verlag, 1929), p. 387.
26. Jellinek, who epitomized this policy, regarded the terminology of *orthodoxy* and *reform* as inherently divisive and irrelevant to Vienna. *Aus der Wiener israelitischen Kultusgemeinde. Sieben Predigten* (Wien, 1863), p. 45.
27. Simon Szántó, "Staat und Synagoge in Österreich," *Jahrbuch für Israeliten* (Wien, 1862), p. 220.
28. "Die Juden in Österreich," *Der Orient,* 22 April 1848, p. 129. Aesthetic preoccupations, concern for decorum in the service and for "eine Religion des Geistes" derived from Jellinek's years in Germany, where he came to see the preeminence of modern Judaism as revealed in its striving for beauty. See *Zwei Kanzel-Vorträge in der Synagoge zu Ungarisch-Brod* (Leipzig, 1847).
29. M. Rosenmann, *Dr. Adolf Jellinek. Sein Leben und Schaffen* (Wien: Schlesinger, 1931), pp. 121, 124, 129, 194.
30. Alexander Altmann, pp. 84–86.
31. Rosenmann, pp. 36ff., 119.
32. "The Constitution [of 1867] was the crowning work of centuries; it was a victory for the Jews of Vienna after their long-continued struggles," Grunwald, p. 407.

66   Toward Modernity: The European Jewish Model

33. Ibid., p. 398.
34. Ibid., pp. 366–71.
35. For a class and cultural analysis of why Viennese Jews remained loyal to a crumbling Austro-liberalism see Carl E. Schorske, *Fin-de-Siècle Vienna: Politics and Culture* ([New York: Knopf, 1980], pp. 148–49), who argues that they "merely shared the prevalent values, holding them more intensely" of the liberal, urban middle class which was upwardly mobile and aspired to assimilation through the acquisition of higher culture. Jewish assimilation and liberalism becomes here nothing more than a "a special case" of bourgeois upward mobility; the impact of German culture in a multiethnic environment, the nationality problem and the internal dynamics of Jewish society are ignored.
36. A.J. "Zur Wahlkampagne," *Die Neuzeit,* 6 June 1879. See also ibid., 22 August 1884, for the continuing identification with liberalism in the face of German and Slavic anti-Semitism.
37. Joseph Wertheimer was more of an Austrian than a *grossdeutscher* patriot, and favorably contrasted the access enjoyed by postemancipation Austrian Jews to the army, upper echelons of the bureaucracy, and universities with the discrimination still practiced in the Second Reich. See his *Zur Emancipation unserer Glaubensgenossen* (Wien, 1882), p. 3.
38. On Friedjung's early career, especially the romantic, *völkisch* and Wagnerian influences, see William J. McGrath, *Dionysian Art and Populist Politics in Austria* (New Haven: Yale University Press, 1974), pp. 74–77, 198–207, 310ff. Also A.J.P. Taylor's introduction to his own translation of Friedjung's classic *The Struggle for Mastery in Germany* (New York: Russell & Russell, 1966), p. iv, where he describes the Jewish-born historian as "a German by adoption" who tended "to expect a similar subconscious recognition of German superiority from the other races and could not understand the reluctance of the Czechs, the Slovaks or the Croats to follow his example."
39. *Festschrift des Kadimah,* p. 51. See also Richard Charmatz, *Adolf Fischof. Das Lebensbild eines österreichischen Politikers* (Stuttgart: Cotta, 1910) which, as its title suggests, largely ignores the Jewish dimension; Werner J. Cahnmann, "Adolf Fischof and his Jewish Followers," *Leo Baeck Institute Year Book* IV (1959), pp. 111–38, which somewhat exaggerates it.
40. Apart from the liberal, *grossdeutsch,* pro-Habsburg orientation of mainstream communal leaders, there was also a radical, pan-German, illiberal and anti-Habsburg current that developed among marginalized, younger Jews in the 1870s; already alienated from Judaism and repelled by Catholicism, they could briefly play a central role in the German nationalist movement in Austria. This was the case of the group around Heinrich Friedjung and Victor Adler. See my *Revolutionary Jews from Marx to Trotsky* (London: Harrap, 1976), and the memoirs of the Marxist Karl Kautsky, *Erinnerungen und Erörterungen* (The Hague: Mouton, 1960), p. 530, dealing with "the intense German nationalism" of the Adler circle in Vienna: "While wanting to have nothing to do with the Habsburgs, they were all the more enthusiastic about the Hohenzollerns. The Jews of Austria were at that time the most passionate advocates of the *Anshluss* which Bismarck decisively rejected."
41. J. Allerhand, p. 19. See also Josef Fraenkel, "The Chief Rabbi and the Visionary," in his collection of essays, *The Jews of Austria* (London: Vallentine, 1967), p. 113. Ironically, the dominance of reform Judaism in Berlin had

prevented Güdemann's appointment there, but "his conservative outlook . . . was a point in his favour in Vienna." Under Orthodox pressure in the mid-1860s, the communal leaders of Viennese Jewry saw in Güdemann a valuable neo-Orthodox counterweight to the more liberal Jellinek.

42. Ismar Schorsch, "Moritz Güdemann: Rabbi, Historian, Apologist," *Leo Baeck Institute Year Book* XI (1966), pp. 42–66.

43. Allerhand, p. 19; Fraenkel, p. 112.

44. Lazar Horwitz had obtained the prior consent of the head of Hungarian Orthodox Jewry, Rabbi Moses Sofer, to work together with Mannheimer and guide him on matters of ritual. His conciliatory influence helped prevent a split in Viennese Jewry despite the tensions in the 1850s, and 1860s between *daytsch yidn,* Polish and Hungarian Jews. On Horwitz and Meir Friedmann (Ish Shalom) see Grunwald, pp. 247, 375–78, 383–84. The influence of the Breslau seminary and "Science of Judaism" was very clear in Eizik Hirsch Weiss's *Dor Dor Vedoreshav* (1871–1891), and its approach to the history of the Oral Law, as it was in the Hebrew publication, *Beit Hamidrash,* founded in Vienna in 1865.

45. N.H. Tur-Sinai, "Viennese Jewry," in *The Jews of Austria* (1967), p. 314: "Jewish Vienna, cultured Vienna, educated Vienna, was not really interested in rabbis or Judaism at all. Viennese Jews were interested—and extremely active and prominent—in general culture, not Jewish culture."

46. *Bikkurei Haittim,* the first modern Hebrew periodical in the Austrian Empire, was launched by the Galician-born Shalom Ben-Jacob Cohen, who arrived in Vienna in 1810. A central figure in early modern Hebrew poetry after Naftali Hartwig Wessely, he had previously been a member of the latter's Berlin circle, and edited and published the last three volumes of *Hame'asef.* Cohen is thus a key link between the Berlin and Viennese Haskalah. See Eisig Silberschlag, "Parapoetic Attitudes and Values in Early Nineteenth-Century Hebrew Poetry," in A. Altmann, ed., pp. 122–24. *Kerem Hemed,* the Hebrew annual of the Galician Haskalah, also published in Vienna, reflected all its diverse aspects: humanistic and scientific studies, revival of the Hebrew language, opposition to Hassidism and Jewish mysticism. Among the writers it published were S.D. Luzzato, Nahman Krochmal, Josef Perl, Solomon Judah Rappoport, and later, Zunz and Geiger. Other Hebrew journals published in Vienna included *Ozar Nehmad* (1856–1863) and *Kokhevei Yizhak* (1845–1873), ed. M.E. Stern.

47. On Anton von Schmid, A. Mayer's *Wiens Buchdruckergeschichte 1482–1882,* II, (Wien, 1887); on the Hebrew language printing industry and especially on *Bikkurei Haittim* see B. Wachstein, *Die hebräische Publizistik in Wien* (Wien: Historische Kommission der Israelitischen Kultusgemeinde, 1930), pp. xiii–xl.

48. *Selbstemanzipation* (Vienna), 17 March 1886, p. 8, observed that in all Smolenskin's works, even in the novels and stories, "erscheint eine Tendenz und diese Tendenz ist der Kampf gegen die 'haskalah berlinith,' die 'Berliner Aufklärung,' gegen die Mendelssohn'sche Schule, gegen diejenige Richtung, die dem Judenthum als Volk Vernichtung geschworen hat." The confrontation of the Russian *maskil,* like that of his East European followers, with the reality of German culture and Jewish self-dissolution in cities like Vienna, helped forge the consciousness of modern Jewish nationalism as a reaction *against* the Enlightenment.

49. Meir Henisch "Galician Jews in Vienna," *The Jews of Austria*, p. 362. The importance of the Galician Jewish presence in Vienna since the early nineteenth century and even more, after the post-1860 influx, was that it acted as a counterweight to assimilation and the otherwise complete domination of German culture and language. Many Galician immigrants had deep roots in Hebrew culture and Jewish national-religious life. In contrast to the Jews of Germany, Galician Jews in Vienna "worked towards a synthesis of historical Judaism and the new sciences, thus creating a basis for the revival of the Hebrew language and Hebrew literature."

50. Grunwald, p. 251, suggests that Mannheimer and Jellinek "deserve the credit for spreading the love of Hebrew culture." See, however, Jellinek's *Die hebräische Sprache* (Wien, 1881) where he dismisses efforts to revive Hebrew as a living, *spoken* language "wie man dies in jüdischen Schulen in Jerusalem versuchen will," ibid., p. 4.

51. Altmann, "The New Style of Preaching," pp. 65–116.

52. Ibid. Also Häusler, "Orthodoxie und Reform," pp. 42–43.

53. Tietze, *Die Juden Wiens,* p. 215, notes that the "colourful style" of Jellinek's preaching, its pathos and vividness were an adaptation to the cultural climate of Vienna rather than something he brought with him from Leipzig. Tur-Sinai, "Viennese Jewry," suggests that those Vienna Jews who went to sermons were primarily interested in the theatrical performance.

54. Altmann, p. 87. Also Jellinek, *Predigten,* II (Wien, 1863), pp. 155ff., 167ff.

55. Adolf Jellinek, *Der jüdische Stamm* (Wien, 1869), pp. 10–11. Also A.J., *Schma Jisrael! Fünf Reden über das israelitische Gottesbekenntnis* (Wien, 1869).

56. Jellinek, *Der jüdische Stamm,* pp. 47–48.

57. On the Jellinek-Pinsker encounter see N.M. Gelber, *Aus zwei Jahrhunderten* (Leipzig: Löwit, 1924), p. 199. Güdemann's original response to Zionism in the 1890s was not hostile, see Fraenkel, "The Chief Rabbi," though he could not understand why an assimilated Viennese Jew like Herzl who had received a German education wished to "uproot himself from his native soil." For Güdemann's later anti-Zionist position see his *Nationaljudentum* (Wien, 1897).

58. Most of the founders of Kadimah (except for Birnbaum, who was born in Vienna, though of Galician Jewish parents) were *Östler,* i.e. from Rumania, Galicia, and Bukovina. For this reason, Smolenskin's call for a struggle on two fronts, i.e. against the "counterfeit" assimilationism of the West and the fossilized orthodoxy of the East, fitted their own modernizing dilemma perfectly. See *Selbstemanzipation,* 17 March 1886, pp. 8–9; *Festschrift des Kadimah,* pp. 15, 30, 33, 35.

59. See *Selbstemanzipation,* 1 June 1893, p. 1, for a harsh critique of the materialistic aridity and lack of idealism in Viennese bourgeois Jewry, which remained "im allgemeinen geistigen ideellen Bestrebungen viel abgeneigter als in Deutschland." Jewish nationalist students in Vienna did identify themselves with the Austro-German student revolutionary traditions of 1848. Kadimah saw itself, for example, as continuing the tradition "des deutschen Studententums" and as being rooted in German *Kultur.* As Schalit put it in *Festschrift des Kadimah,* p. 81, "Unser Ideal war der 48 Legionär."

60. Nathan Birnbaum, *"Die Assimilationssucht. Ein Wort an die sogennanten Deutschen, Slaven, Magyaren mosaischer Confession* (Wien, 1884). In a number of subsequent articles, Birnbaum put forward a Jewish *völkisch* parallel to pan-German arguments concerning the chasm between the Jewish and German

Volksgeist. His critique of assimilation increasingly relied on racial concepts derived from positivistic models, from biology and vitalistic naturalism. E.g. "Nationalität und Sprache," *Selbstemanzipation,* 16 February 1886, and 16 April 1890, p. 1.

61. *Festschrift des Kadimah,* p. 40. See also Joachim Doron, "Social Concepts Prevalent in German Zionism: 1883–1914," *Studies in Zionism* 5 (Tel Aviv, April 1982): 1–31, on the general social and ideological background.

62. See Robert S. Wistrich, *Socialism and the Jews: the Dilemmas of Assimilation in Germany and Austria-Hungary* (London and East Brunswick, N.J.: Associated University Presses, 1982), for a more detailed discussion of this problem.

63. Ibid., pp. 187–203. See also John W. Boyer, *Political Radicalism in Late Imperial Vienna. Origins of the Christian Social Movement, 1848–1897* (Chicago: University of Chicago Press, 1981), pp. 67–121, for the most recent evaluation of anti-Semitism in the Viennese artisan class.

64. On the Czech immigration to Vienna, which provides an interesting comparative model in terms of modernizing dilemmas, assimilation, ethnic identity and national consciousness in a metropolitan environment, see Monika Glettler's massive study, *Die Wiener Tschechen um 1900* (Wien: Oldenbourg, 1972). My impression, on the basis of Glettler's work and my own research into Viennese Jewry, is that more Jews retained a collective sense of separate ethnic identity than did Czech migrants at the turn of the century.

65. For detailed quantitative data on the patterns of immigration, occupational and social structure of fin-de-siècle Viennese Jewry, see Marsha Rozenblit, *Assimilation and Identity: The Urbanization of the Jews of Vienna, 1880–1914,* Columbia University, Ph.D. Diss., 1980.

66. See for example A. Jellinek, "Antisemitisch-antiösterreichisch," *Die Neuzeit,* 20 October 1882, where Jellinek describes the term *anti-Semitism* as "die neueste Errungenschaft des Berliner sprachbildenden Genius," and Prussia as "das Vaterland des Antisemitismus." For the Austrian pan-German anti-Semites (as indeed for the more radical *grossdeutsch* Viennese Jews a decade earlier), Germany was their fatherland, Bismarck their political idol, and Berlin their capital. "Sie fühlen sich," Jellinek observed, "nicht als Österreicher, sondern als Söhne Germaniens." The unexpected development of pan-German racism increasingly obliged liberal Austrian Jews to stress their Habsburg-Austrian loyalty at the expense of *Deutschtum* if they were to differentiate themselves from the anti-Semites.

67. See Paul Molisch, *Geschichte der deutschnationalen Bewegung in Österreich* (Jena: Fischer, 1926), p. 143; E. Pichl, *Georg von Schoenerer und die Entwicklung des Alldeutschtums in der Ostmark* (Oldenburg: Stalling, 1938), vol. 2, p. 320; William J. McGrath, "Student Radicalism in Vienna," *Journal of Contemporary History* 2 (July 1967): 183–201; Robert S. Wistrich, "Georg von Schoenerer and the Genesis of Modern Austrian Antisemitism," *The Wiener Library Bulletin* 29 (1976): pp. 20–29.

68. Joseph S. Bloch, *Aus der Vergangenheit für die Gegenwart* (Wien, 1886), pp. 13–23. Also the autobiographical *My Reminiscences* (Wien: Löwit, 1923), p. 33.

69. *Festschrift des Kadimah,* p. 53.

70. Joseph S. Bloch, *Dar nationale Zwist und die Juden in Österreich* (Wien, 1886), pp. 40, 45–53.

71. For an example of Friedjung's assimilationism, see *Deutsche Wochenschrift* 43, 25 October 1885: "The only compromise lies . . . in the complete abandonment of the special status which the Jews frequently adopt, in the radical assimilation with the modern nations (i.e. with the Germans) among whom they live. For they have already completed the world-historical task which was assigned to them." For Bloch's attacks on Friedjung's Germanism as a form of "Semitic anti-Semitism" see *Österreichische Wochenschrift*, 16 January 1885, 16 July 1885, 14 November 1885.
72. Bloch, *My Reminiscences*, p. 182. *Österreichische Wochenschrift*, 30 April 1886, pp. 193–94.
73. For the motivations behind founding the *Union* see *Österreichische Wochenschrift*, 15 October 1884, pp. 1–3, and 10 April 1885, p. 1.
74. Bloch, *My Reminiscences*, pp. 155–56. Also *Festschrift des Kadimah*, p. 54. "Die Ernennung des Dr. Bloch, eines Mitgliedes des Polenklubs, zum Professor für hebräische Altertümer an der Wiener Universität wäre eine Provocation der Wiener Juden." This statement, drawn up by Jellinek and Emmanuel Baumgarten, a member of the *Kultusgemeinde* board, speaks for itself. Bloch's Polish orientation expressed itself in numerous speeches where he favorably contrasted the treatment of Jews by Poles and Czechs with the *urdeutsch* cry of "Hepp! Hepp!!" which modern German anti-Semitism had revived.
75. *Die Neuzeit*, 13 February 1891.

4

Caution's Progress: The Modernization of Jewish Life in Prague, 1780–1830

Hillel J. Kieval

To Franklin L. Ford, on the occasion of his sixty-fifth birthday.

Political economists today speak of a fundamental cleavage between North and South—First World and Third World—in the areas of economic and social development. Before the end of the nineteenth century, however, the basic division in comparative development was that which existed between East and West. As Robin Okey reminds us, the countries of East Central Europe (the part of the Continent which lies between the Rhine, the Vistula, and the Danube) comprised the first area outside of the advanced tip of Western Europe to attempt the social, economic, and cultural transformations to which the term *modernization* commonly refers.[1]

Compared with the two great commercial giants of the mid–eighteenth century, England and the Netherlands, both Prussia and the Hapsburg Monarchy—not to mention Russia—suffered from economic backwardness and underdevelopment. They possessed none of the prerequisites for industrialization and economic expansion such as capital formation, an advanced state of urbanization, or an international trading network. Yet it was to these lands that the West first directed the twin challenges of industrial development and political liberalism. While they could not hope to replicate the West, monarchs and government officials in East Central Europe could try to mold reasonable facsimiles. Taking advantage of their wealth in human and natural resources, and applying fiscal incentives to areas targeted for development, the "East" European governments could set about the task of accomplishing their own modernization.

Although the states east of the Rhine often tried to emulate Western patterns of economic and even cultural development, the process of adaptation was never complete. The absolutist monarchs, though at times "enlightened," were not prepared to allow the political and social underpinnings of a free market economy to coexist alongside more narrowly conceived inducements to economic growth and national consolidation. More often than not, government officials simply grafted an eclectic assortment of economic and social reforms onto a largely hierarchical and corporatist social structure. The lack of ethnic homogeneity in East Central Europe created both a more complicated demographic picture than in the West and an ever-growing potential for social conflict based on linguistic and cultural divisions. As a result, once these states did commit themselves, however uneasily, to "catching up" with the West, a new and uniquely East European set of problems emerged, prominent among which were intense national rivalries largely unknown in the West.[2]

Just as the transition from medieval to modern society in East Central Europe followed its own rather than a preconceived model, so too did the transformation of Jewish society in these regions. There is nothing self-evident about this statement, however. Modernization in Jewish history consisted of factors both intrinsic to Jewish culture, and hence present over a wide range of local circumstances, and extrinsic to the normal functioning of the local community. The second group of factors consisted primarily of changes imposed on Jewish life from without, often at the instigation of central governments, but resulting from general social and economic developments as well. It was in this area of change that the process of Jewish modernization depended most strongly on local political, social, and economic conditions. Thus one can point to no single model of development which would be applicable to all situations. Rather, a comparison of similar processes of change in different contexts reveals a more complicated pattern in which a small number of universal characteristics of Jewish "modernity" are intertwined with a much larger set of unique circumstances, varied timetables, and end results.

For Jewish communities in Germany, Austria, and Hungary the interplay of intrinsic and extrinsic factors usually took the form of a two-sided erosion of traditional Jewish existence. On the one hand, the independence, cohesiveness, and authority of the autonomous Jewish community broke down under the onslaught of governmental intrusion into its affairs and the steady curtailment of many of its legal functions and prerogatives. At the same time, proponents of the Jewish Enlightenment (Haskalah), patterned after the European intellectual movement of the eighteenth century, agitated for cultural and educational change within the community according to the standards of Western rationalism. Both sets of changes worked together in a variety of combinations to produce some of the basic features of modern Jewish history: the elimination of the independent, corporate status of the community; the weakening of rabbinic law (halachah) as a norm for individual and group behavior; the emerging legal status of the individual Jew as citizen of the state: and the elaboration of extensive areas of Jewish and Gentile interaction.

The question posed by this book, the influence of German Jewry on the modernization of Jewish communities elsewhere in Europe and North America, has particular relevance for Central and Eastern Europe. In some instances, change in these communities arose out of direct contact with German-Jewish culture. For example, both the friends and the opponents of the Haskalah in Austria, Galicia, Hungary, and Russia acknowledged the movement's German roots. To those Jews eager for a secular, rationalist orientation in Jewish culture, Berlin and Koenigsberg represented oases of intellectual creativity in a desert of medieval formalism and popular superstition. To those who, on the contrary, feared the caustic effects of manifestos such as Naphtali Herz Wessely's *Words of Peace and Truth,* the same names conjured up the spectre of reckless cultural assimilation and religious indifference.[3] One could well argue that it was the dissemination of Haskalah ideology to communities east and south of Germany which inaugurated the historic split between modernists and traditionalists—indeed between West European and East European Judaism—of the last century.

However, if we understand the question of *influence* to be that of providing a compelling model for change and development, then the question of the relationship between the Jewish communities of Germany and those of East Central Europe becomes more difficult. Prussia, after all, is part of East Central Europe. Therefore we must first determine in which circumstances German Jewry constituted an avant garde and in which circumstances it shared the characteristics of the region as a whole. We also must address the correlative question of whether the Jewish communities of Prague, Lvov, or Pest, for example, in the course of their respective modernizations, were following cues set by German Jewry or their own unique cadences. Finally, did the interplay of external and internal factors in the countries of East Central Europe produce a particular prescription for Jewish modernization that applied to the region as a whole and that was not necessarily indebted to the German example?

My goal in this essay is to address some of these questions while focusing on the major cultural and social changes that were occurring in the Jewish communities of Prague and Bohemia during the late eighteenth and early nineteenth centuries. I first place the general evolution of Bohemian Jewish society in the context of Hapsburg and Bohemian policy with regard to Jews and to the promotion of social and economic development. This part concludes with an examination of the major external catalysts of change in Bohemian Jewish life, the reforms of the 1780s and 1790s. The second section of the essay looks at the redirection of Jewish cultural concerns in Prague under the impact of the Haskalah. It deals primarily with the reception of the Haskalah in Prague, the contribution of Prague Jews to the program of the Haskalah, and the overall impact of the so-called Berlin school in the determination of both the tenor and the content of the Prague Haskalah. In the last section I examine the practical application of one of the major cultural reforms of the period: the establishment of a secular Jewish school system. A joint government and community venture, the new Jewish schools of Bohemia succeeded in winning the support of a wide spectrum of opinion within the Jewish community. Not only did they play an important part in the acculturation and socialization of Bohemian Jewry from 1782 to 1850, but they also provide the historian with an excellent view of the operation of Enlightenment values in a community and of the process of cultural transformation.

Bohemian Jewry and the Hapsburg Monarchy: The Effects of Partial Modernization

For urban Jews in Central Europe the fifteenth century spelled the beginning of a long period of economic decline punctuated by expulsion and migration. The major demographic consequence of this decline was the virtual elimination of Jews from the larger cities and towns in the region. In Germany, every major locality, with the exception of Frankfurt am Main and Worms, threw out its Jewish population at some point during the century. The six royal cities of Moravia succeeded in ridding themselves of their Jews between 1454 and 1514. Vienna expelled them in 1421 and again in 1670.[4] Yet for reasons that have never been sufficiently examined, Prague and Bohemia for a while stood out as islands of refuge in this storm of hatred and struggle. Bohemia in fact attracted large numbers of those Jews who were migrating eastward from the German parts of the Holy Roman Empire. And although in Bohemia as well as in much of Central Europe, the fifteenth century had been marked by continual battles between the royal government and both the towns and the landed nobility over claims to the exclusive control of the Jewish communities, there was reason to hope after 1526—when the Czech lands became part of the Hapsburg domains—that the Jews would be the beneficiaries of renewed political stability.[5]

This hope proved to be yet one more chimera of exilic existence. The Bohemian *Landtag,* encouraged by the prospect of the removal of Jewish economic competition, and undeterred by royal threats that the urban estates would have to make up the loss of Jewish tax monies from their own pockets, pushed for the expulsion of the Jews in 1540 and 1541. Ferdinand I acceded to the wishes of the royal cities of Bohemia and granted the expulsion of the Jews in 1541, ordering at the same time that the Jews of Prague would have to leave as well.[6] At this point it looked as though Bohemia would follow the pattern of the rest of Central Europe, ridding its cities and large towns of Jews and leaving only the small towns and rural domains of the nobility for Jewish settlement. That such was not ultimately to be the case, however, proved to be of enormous consequence in Czech Jewish history. The expulsion order for the royal cities remained in effect until the Revolution of 1848, but the government lifted the ban on Jewish settlement in Prague four years after it had been announced and only two years after it had gone into effect. Another, temporary expulsion followed in 1557, but both decrees in the end represented exceptions to the basic pattern, for Jewish life in the Bohemian capital, despite of all the upheaval going on around it, was to flourish throughout the early modern period.

The survival of Prague as a Jewish center bequeathed to Bohemian Jewry, if nothing else, a demographic configuration all its own. Unlike Germany (which by the end of the sixteenth century had only scattered Jewish settlements of relatively small size), unlike Moravia and Poland (where Jews lived by and large in compact settlements in medium-size towns as well as in some villages), and unlike Hungary (where down to the end of the eighteenth century the vast majority of the Jews were *Dorfjuden,* living in small clusters of families in isolated villages), no less than half of the Jewish population of Bohemia lived in a dense concentration at the center. The rest were dispersed in small villages and market towns, few of which contained enough families to support Jewish institutions of their own.[7] In Prague the number of Jews grew from about 6,000 at the start of the seventeenth century to 7,800 in 1636, and finally to about 10,000 or 11,000 by the beginning of the eighteenth century, making this Jewish community the largest in the world.[8] Meanwhile, the Jewish population in the countryside was also experiencing unprecedented growth. In 1635 the government indicated that there were some 14,000 Jewish "taxpayers" in Bohemia living outside of Prague, but unfortunately it did not explain whether a taxpayer was the same as the head of a household. Indeed, the first real census of Bohemian Jewry was not taken until 1724, at which time the number of Jews living in the Bohemian countryside was given to be approximately 30,000.[9]

That this "take-off" coincided with the devastation of the population and the economy of the country in the wake of the Thirty Years War did not go unnoticed. Representatives of the Bohemian Estates in Prague as well as government officials in Vienna began to express fears of an uncontrolled growth in the size of the Bohemian Jewish community, and both parties agreed that the situation called for some type of response. In 1650 the Bohemian Diet took the first step in what was to be a— largely unsuccessful—200-year campaign to limit both the number of Jews residing in the country and their places of residence. It combined a steady stream of restrictive legislation with frequent demands for higher Jewish taxation and even induced the crown to appoint a *Judenreduktionskommission,* whose special task it was to find ways to reduce the Jewish population of Prague.[10] The *Landtag*'s flurry of activity did little more than create a mood of desperation in Vienna. In the early eighteenth century when central government agencies inherited the task of "doing something" about the growth of Jewish population in Bohemia, they set about the task in a more systematic fashion and produced results which, if strictly followed, would have stifled Jewish life in the region.[11]

The long-term effects of the government's newly inspired anti-Jewish policies were spelled out in the so-called *Familiantengesetz* of 1726; disruptions of shorter duration occurred as a result of the temporary expulsion of the Jews from Prague between 1745 and 1748. Both measures worked to intensify the skewed demographic configuration of Bohemian Jewry. Intent upon freezing the number of Jewish residents in the kingdom at 8,541 families (the figure arrived at in the census of 1724), the framers of the *Familiantengesetz* decreed that only the eldest son in a household had the right to marry and settle in the locality where his family resided. Further Jewish expansion into areas that had not been allowed prior to 1724 was outlawed.[12] The legislation played havoc with Jewish family life in Bohemia and Moravia down to the middle of the nineteenth century. Most of the younger sons accepted the verdict that they emigrate, usually to Hungary or southern Poland, occasionally to Germany. However, many Jews chose instead to enter into illegal, or "garret" marriages. Still others, hoping to evade the watchful eye of the government, sought the protection of the nobility in villages even more isolated than the ones that their families may have inhabited.[13]

The expulsion order concerning Prague resulted in a further spilling over of Jewish population into the countryside. Maria Theresa's decree, issued in the aftermath of Austria's defeat at the hands of Prussia during the War of the Austrian Succession, was never applied to the rest of Bohemia. To tidy up business affairs, Jews were allowed to tarry in Bohemian villages on the way to their ultimate destinations. In 1748 the order was rescinded and Jews were once more permitted to reside in the capital. Many of those Jews who had already left the country did not come back. An unknown number, having found themselves in the Bohemian countryside in 1748, undoubtedly remained where they were. Most of the former Jewish residents of Prague chose to return.[14]

A government census of 1754 revealed that the Jewish population of Bohemia stood at just under 30,000, one-third of which was now concentrated in the capital.[15] Over the course of the next century the Jewish population would continue both to grow and to disperse. A Jewish-commissioned census of 1849 would detail no fewer than 1,921 localities outside of Prague in which Jews resided. Only 207 of these formed actual communities of more than 10 families with a formal synagogue; 148 others managed to assemble a *Betstube* on Sabbaths and holidays by drawing on the resources of neighboring villages.[16] Clearly, the laws which had been designed to limit the size and scope of the Jewish population did not have the desired effects. Growth tempered by rural dispersion emerged the ultimate victor. On the eve of Bohemia's post-1850 industrial expansion Prague maintained its position of preeminence among the Jewish communities, but the real potential for explosive growth lay in the countryside.

If the political and economic decline of the Czech lands following the Thirty Years War resulted in a worsening of the material conditions of Jewish life, it was also to call into play some of the very processes that would lead to Jewish modernization in the region. The depopulation of the cities and the abandonment of rural landholdings resulted in a shift in economic power from the cities to the countryside and from small freeholders to the landed nobility. At the precise moment that urban-based market economies were developing in Western countries such as England and the Netherlands, feudalism was enjoying a second wind in Central and East Europe. The loss of population in the countryside induced the Bohemian nobility to increase the labor obligations of the peasantry and to make it more difficult than previously to leave the land. The decline in urban domestic markets left rural landlords intent on building up large stockpiles of raw materials to sell in Germany, England, and the Netherlands. Nearly all finished products had to be imported. What small-time production did take place was based in the countryside rather than the city and involved a complicated network of merchant suppliers and domestic producers based on the "putting-out" system.[17] To make matters worse, foreign capital—primarily English— had penetrated the Bohemian linen industry by the end of the seventeenth century, and it was an English firm that succeeded in establishing the first large-scale linen factory in Bohemia in the first half of the eighteenth century.[18]

In the eyes of Austrian economic advisors, the country lagged visibly behind the West in economic development and, more important, had placed itself in a dangerously weak international position. Cameralist theory of the age held that national wealth and military strength were inextricably tied, that the key sources of a country's wealth lay in its population and its natural resources, and that commodities ought not to be sold outside of the country until they had become more costly finished products.[19] Proponents of mercantilism had periodically urged the government in Vienna to institute economic reforms along these lines as early as the late seventeenth century. But it was not until the second half of the eighteenth century (particularly in the last third) that such policies were applied with any consistency. At this point the state intervened directly to promote industry, limit foreign investment, and check the flow of natural resources from the country. It encouraged the growth of industry by offering subsidies and tax exemptions, by removing the newer economic sectors from the purview of the guilds, and by easing discriminatory restrictions toward Protestants and members of other religious minorities who were willing to establish new ventures. The state similarly sought to modernize transportation systems, abolish internal tariffs, and promote a unified customs policy.[20]

Much of this activity proceeded in a social and economic vacuum. No ready-made work force in the form of a large urban population existed. No international trading centers or investment banks were ready to lend financial support and commercial contacts. Nor had Austro-Bohemian culture produced the kind of individual entrepreneurial spirit that had emerged in some of the Protestant countries to the west and had been responsible in large part for the private economic initiatives that had accompanied the beginnings of industrialization. At the same time, the government did not engage in any sweeping overhaul of traditional forms of social organization or methods of economic production. Ancient privileged orders continued to defend their prerogatives in the Diets and at the Court. Government officials often worked at cross purposes to one another, defending privilege in one instance, promoting rationalization and uniformity in another. As a result, government-sponsored modernization never received an unambiguous mandate and appeared to move, when it did so, at half-speed.

The results of this partial modernization were likewise half-hearted. Aristocratic and middle-class *Fabrikanten* were recruited, internal tariffs within the two separate halves of the monarchy were abolished, and textile manufacturing became a vital part of the Bohemian-Moravian economy.

But Austria still found it difficult to create a vibrant group of middle-class producers; the customs division between Austria and Hungary remained in effect until 1851, and the extent of industrial production in the country remained far below that of England. The picture in Prussia and other German states did not differ markedly. German cities had been more actively engaged in international trade than almost any Austrian city. German ports were busier, their lines of transport and communication more efficient. However, with the exception of Saxony and Silesia, industrial production in the two regions proceeded at about the same pace. Only after 1830, and especially after 1850, did the economic development of Germany break off from that of Austria. In the second half of the nineteenth century—during Germany's industrial revolution—the Hapsburg Monarchy made considerable progress of its own but could not match her northern neighbor in any of the key areas of output, number of plants, or technological sophistication.[21]

Half-heartedness notwithstanding, Hapsburg efforts to catch up with the West while promoting national strength were to have a major impact on the course of Jewish life at the turn of the eighteenth and nineteenth centuries. Government recruitment of entrepreneurial talent, the easing of religious and social restrictions for those engaged in economic development, the promotion of universal education, and periodic assaults on the autonomy of medieval corporations loomed large as agents in this transformation. Yet, as with the secular course of change, Jewish modernization was to proceed in an artificial context, spurred on by government initiative and Jewish visions of social integration and advancement, but deprived of wider social and cultural supports. As with general modernization, government policies concerning the Jews were often contradictory and self-defeating; supporters of feudal privilege clashed head-on with advocates of sweeping change; both punitive restrictions and the promise of social acceptance were dangled before the eyes of the Jewish population.

Joseph II, who ruled with his mother Maria Theresa as coregent from 1765 to 1780 and then alone for the final ten years of his life, came to exemplify more than anyone else the enlightened monarch, acting on rational principles to transform state and society. The nineteenth century Jewish apologist Joseph von Wertheimer referred to his namesake as "a despot, like the Spring, which breaks apart the Winter's ice."[22] Joseph II had put in motion a number of political and economic reforms while his mother was still alive, but he stayed clear of direct involvement in Jewish affairs until he enjoyed complete control over the direction of government policy. Beginning in 1780 he began to act, and with his famous *Toleranzpatent,* issued for Bohemia in October 1781, he ushered in an era of conscious social, economic, and cultural reform.[23] The edict represented but one small part of a much larger package of reforming measures, among which also stood the application of religious tolerance to Austrian Protestants, the partial liberation of the peasantry from ties to the feudal domain, and the institution of compulsory elementary education. Joseph II's goal was to break down traditional societal privileges and remove barriers to economic growth, not to bequeath special privileges to the Jews, not even to end the population and settlement restrictions under which they had been living since the early part of the century.[24] The emperor expressed his intentions from the outset in quite practical terms: "To make the numerous members of the Jewish nation in my hereditary lands more useful to the state." He set out to transform the cultural outlook, social patterns and occupational distribution of the Jews, better to serve the interests of the developing state, without altering the legal status of the Jewish corporation and without encouraging any further growth of the Jewish population.[25]

In the economic sphere, the *Toleranzpatent* actually proved to be a major disappointment. Since its framers did not have a good idea about what the current occupational distribution of the Jewish community was, much energy was spent encouraging the Jews to abandon their traditional profession of money lending and to engage instead in commerce, industry, and agriculture. Apparently unaware of Prague's Jewish craft guilds, which had existed already for two centuries or more, Joseph II and his advisors gave the Jews permission to learn the crafts and manual trades from Christian masters, apprentice themselves to Christians, or work as journeymen. Because the emperor was unwilling truly to challenge the status quo in either the artisan shop or the countryside, he continued to bar Jews from attaining the degree of mastership or citizenship as well as from owning plots of land.[26]

The overall impact of these economic provisions appears to have been slight. Individual Jews did take advantage of the new mercantilism of the state and established industrial enterprises in the late eighteenth and early nineteenth century. However, the occupational distribution of the Bohemian Jewish community remained fairly stable between the 1770s and the 1830s. No radical reshaping of the economic structure of the community occurred as a result of the edict. In the areas of communal autonomy, education, and popular culture however, the Jewish legislation which poured from Vienna in the 1780s and 1790s did create immediate and lasting results. The *Toleranzpatent* erased overnight the use of Hebrew and Yiddish in public records and business transactions. It encouraged Jewish communities to establish German-language, or "normal" elementary schools with state-approved teachers and curricula. In areas where the Jewish community was too small to support a school of its own, Jewish children were welcomed to attend Christian primary and secondary schools. The universities of the monarchy, which had been removed from Jesuit control in 1773 and completely secularized in 1782, were declared open to Jewish attendance.[27]

Subsequent edicts bolstered the cultural provisions of the early Josephine reform and further transformed the social and legal character of the community. The judicial autonomy of the Jewish community in civil and criminal matters was suspended in 1784. An ordinance of 1786 made the granting of marriage certificates to Jews dependent on the parties' ability to demonstrate that they had attended a *Normalschule*. Legislation the following year made mandatory the adoption of German personal and family names. In 1788 Jews were required to serve in the Austrian army. Finally, in 1797—in a law that was never completely enforced—the state required that all rabbis and cantors to be appointed by the Jewish community produce a degree in philosophy from one of the monarchy's institutions of higher learning.[28]

Government policy by the beginning of the nineteenth century had made important strides toward altering the traditional complexion of Jewish life within the realm. It had declared its vested interest in the education, political loyalties, and economic contributions of its Jewish subjects. As yet, however, it was content to destroy the medieval autonomy of the Jewish community without incorporating the Jews into the social fabric of the state. Political reforms could raze the cultural defenses of the Jewish community but they left intact the ghetto walls.

Modernization and Jewish Culture:
The Reception of the Haskalah in Prague

No amount of government interference could, by itself, effect a reorientation in cultural outlook. Significant changes in religious practice and belief, group attitudes, shared knowledge, and in values, require an extended period of time in which to evolve. They may owe as much to subtle redirections that occur within a society as to any articulated program for change. Hence that the reform measures of Hapsburg officials coincided with the beginnings of a movement toward cultural readjustment on the part of Prague and Bohemian Jewry may simply have been the result of moderate but steady social and economic progress. We have noted, however, that the economic and social structure in Central and East Europe generally failed to provide the kinds of support that had allowed for thoroughgoing changes in the West. In a similar vein, traditional Jewish institutions in East Europe were not about to buckle under the weight of collective indifference or unarticulated dissent. Rather, cultural pioneers, like reformist bureaucrats, were likely to stand alone, conscious of their isolated position in society and determined to articulate explicit programs for the new order. The Haskalah movement in Prague found adherents at first only within a small group among the ranks of the wealthy and educated members of the community. The Haskalah in this context was not a by-product of increased economic opportunity and social mobility but rather a prescription for such developments: not an indicator of social transformation, but an instrument for change in its own right.[29]

If we were to divide the Prague Haskalah, as Ruth Kestenberg-Gladstein does in her opus on the subject, into a succession of four stages, we would begin by remarking that in its earliest phase the movement took the form of a received ideology.[30] The decade of the 1780s saw a handful of Prague Jewish figures reacting to impulses whose origin lay outside of their own community: following with interest developments within the Mendelssohnian circle in Berlin such as the appearance of the *Biur,* the translation of the Pentateuch into literary German and the accompanying Hebrew commentary, subscribing to German-Jewish publications, and even making original contributions to the mouthpiece of the German Haskalah, *Hame'asef.* But participation in the Jewish Enlightenment at that point was limited by and large to the reception of signals sent from abroad and the application of their messages to the context at home.[31] During the 1790s Prague still seemed to be taking the cue from Berlin. Now, however, Prague's home-grown *maskilim* (followers of the Haskalah) were beginning to react negatively to a number of aspects of the German movement including its open hostility toward Jewish law and traditions and, significantly, the mocking disrespect which *Hame'asef* editors had displayed toward the late Chief Rabbi Ezekiel Landau.[32]

During the later two stages of the Haskalah movement in Prague (approximately 1800 to 1830), the city's *maskilim* appear to have succeeded in striking out on their own and in making some truly original contributions.[33] Yet something of a paradox was at work here. If Prague Jews were not directly imbibing the dictates of taste or the cultural innovations emanating from Germany, they were reacting to them nonetheless. They may have been striving to achieve a style and vision of their own, but the point of reference in the definition of this new position remained the German model. Thus, while the Berlin Haskalah put forward a program of radical religious and educational reform, while it displayed indifference to the role of halachah in Jewish life, the Prague Haskalah insisted upon the sanctity of law and tradition. Prague's *maskilim* confidently pursued a policy of accommodation, weaving together European rationalism, respect for religious sensitivities, and loyalty to Jewish traditions. While *maskilim* in Berlin sought to further the prospects for political emancipation by eliminating national and ethnic components from Jewish culture, their Prague counterparts appeared to be remarkably free of such self-imposed burdens. Bolstered, perhaps, by the multinational quality of the Hapsburg Monarchy, Prague's *maskilim* proved to be more sensitive to the national realities which underpinned Jewish existence and did not hesitate to portray their community as one nation among others.[34]

The tone of moderation and traditionalism, so characteristic of the Prague *maskilim,* was not necessarily unique to this one city. However, the notion of a conservative Haskalah with quasi-national overtones may indeed have comprised the essence of Prague's contribution to the Jewish Enlightenment.[35] The sources of this conservatism lay in the areas of institutional leadership and what might be termed "cultural geography." Prague's rabbinate, under the direction of Ezekiel Landau and Eleazar Fleckeles, enjoyed tremendous prestige both at home and abroad. It is safe to assume that they possessed a greater ability than their counterparts in Western Europe either to thwart or to approve measures which could affect the nature of Jewish life in their community. Hence the attitude of such personalities to the spread of the Haskalah as well as to the growing interest of the central government in Jewish affairs may have been crucial to the fortunes of change in Jewish Prague.

Ezekiel Landau entertained serious reservations about the social and political effects of Joseph's toleration patent and condemned all efforts to upset the balance in traditional Jewish education. Yet (as will become clear in the section on the *Normalschule*) he determined from the beginning to exert his influence on the course of change rather than simply condemn it out of hand. Landau's critical views on the Haskalah emerged clearly in his sermons to the community. On the occasion of *Shabbat hagadol* 1782, which fell between the issuance of the *Toleranzpatent* and the opening of the Prague *Normalschule,* Landau made direct reference to the major events of the day. He lavished praise on the salutory intentions of the emperor; in the same breath he also warned his congregants not to alter their political conceptions, not to be overcome with pride and cease to treat with respect "the people of the state who own the land, for we are but strangers."[36] Having recently read Wessely's program for educational reform in the Hebrew pamphlet *Divrei Shalom Ve'emet,* Landau remarked: "I have seen a world turned upside down. . . . A wicked and arrogant man has arisen from our nation for whom the

Torah is not worth anything, for whom profane subjects are better than the study of Torah."[37]

Landau was willing to accommodate unavoidable changes in the political sphere and even to appropriate the technical expertise of western culture, but no innovation in politics or education could be allowed to threaten the foundations of Jewish faith.

> In truth the substance of the thing—to improve manners and to know the grammar of the language of the Gentiles [*dikduk halashon ha'amim*]—I too, praise highly. And how good it is (for us) that the government has taken upon itself to accustom us to speak properly. . . . For he who fears the Lord, he truly understands [*'einav berosho*]; he is able to hold fast to both matters [sacred and profane]; but Torah is central. And nevertheless, he learns this language [and] the correct manners to guide a person along the right way. Any [sacred] learning that does not include practical employment leads to idleness; indeed the essence of our activity is commerce, hence one needs to know language and writing.[38]

"The core is faith," Landau exhorted. It had to be protected from the incursions of reason and scientific inquiry.

In his summation, Landau charged the Jews of Prague to submit both to God and the king but to keep clear of all who would change the nature of Jewish belief and practice. The challenge of the age, he was convinced, was to educate oneself in western science and language, but to resist the temptation to apply the tools of the Enlightenment to the sacred body of revealed truths.[39]

For Landau the entire question of Haskalah revolved around the distinction between technical and substantive change, and it was according to this overriding criterion that he decided which programs to support and which to oppose. The educational provisions of the *Toleranzpatent* received his approval primarily because he was able to insure that the new schools would exist only as supplementary institutions, whose curriculum did not threaten the integrity of the traditional talmudic education. But he vehemently opposed programs such as Wessely's which sought to transform the nature of Jewish education. He also disapproved of such ostensibly neutral enterprises as Mendelssohn's translation and commentary of the Pentateuch (the *Biur,* 1780–1783). In a 1786 communication Landau explained that he had withheld approbation of the work precisely because Mendelssohn's translation had surpassed the bounds of what was necessary for a plain understanding of the Hebrew text:

> I refused because in the work printed at the time the holy [biblical text] and the profane [Mendelssohn's German translation] were joined together.

. . . We fear that this foreign element will prove a stumbling block to Jewish children and lead to the neglect of the study of Torah. . . . The translator deeply immersed himself in the language using as he did an extremely difficult German that presupposes expertise in its grammar. . . . It induces the young to spend their time reading Gentile books in order to become sufficiently familiar with refined German to be able to understand this translation. Our Torah is thereby reduced to the role of a maidservant to the German tongue.[40]

The strong positions taken by conservatives such as Landau may have engendered tension between the leadership of the Prague community and the early *maskilim*. Evidence of mild generational conflict, for example, does exist.[41] However, the remarkable thing about Prague is that fathers and sons on the whole did not divide. In fact, from 1790 to 1810 Prague *maskilim* stood out as staunch defenders of the rabbinic leadership. Baruch Jeitteles (1762–1813) submitted a eulogy for Landau to *Hame'asef* following his death in 1793. He then reacted with a bitter attack on the periodical when it ridiculed the eulogy and its object of praise. Later, Jeitteles joined forces with Rabbi Eleazar Fleckeles in denouncing the influence of Frankists within the Prague Jewish community.[42] Israel Landau, the late chief rabbi's youngest son, dominated the Haskalah publishing in Prague during the last decade of the century with works not only in philology and geography but also in popular halachic education.[43]

Bohemia's proximity to the traditional societies of Poland, Hungary, and, to some extent, Moravia also contributed to its conservative complexion. And the effects of the *Familiantengesetz* intensified whatever ties geography alone may have produced. A network of intimate family connections extended from Bohemia to the East and North wherever the younger branches were able to establish themselves. Ezekiel Landau's immediate family provides some interesting examples of such crosscommunal ties. His eldest son, Jacob, an ordained rabbi in his own right who made his living as a merchant, settled in Brody, where his father had once served as *dayan*. There he apparently maintained cordial relations with representatives of the Galician Haskalah.[44] Israel Landau, though born and raised in Prague, married a Polish Jew who bore him two sons. She became alarmed at the "liberal" spirit of Jewish life in the city and pleaded with her husband to leave Prague and return with her and their children to Poland. Landau demurred; his wife demanded and received a bill of divorce (*get*). She settled with the two boys in Poland, and her husband set out to find a new wife. This time he chose someone from a progressive, Dutch-Jewish family.[45] Meanwhile, one of the sons from the first marriage became a rabbi in Brody; Moses (M.I.) Landau, a son from the second marriage, established himself as a printer and publisher in Prague, producing works in Hebrew and German, including several volumes of the periodical *Kerem Hemed*.[46]

Even when the *Familiantengesetz* played no obvious role, Poland's proximity loomed large. It was to Jampol, Podolia—after all—that the community turned to fill the vacant position of chief rabbi in 1754. In the following decades, students from Poland as well as Central Europe flocked to Prague to attend Landau's yeshivah. As late as 1840, Prague continued to look to Poland to fill its highest rabbinical post. In this year the Galician scholar Solomon Judah Rappoport was called to Prague from Tarnopol; he served the community for the next twenty-seven years.

It would be incorrect to conclude that the Prague Haskalah in its search for a "third way" between radicalism and traditionalism set off on a course completely different from that of the German Haskalah. German Haskalah itself was a multidimensional phenomenon, not all of whose features were either radical or anti-halachic. More important, Prague's *maskilim* had neither the size nor the independence to maintain a distinct movement with its own publications. Only during one brief period, in 1802, did Prague's *maskilim* manage to create their own organization, the Gesellschaft der jungen Hebraeer, and produce their own journal, the *Juedisch-deutsche Monatschrift*. Even then the enterprise lasted only for six months.[47] Thereafter, as in the 1780s and 1790s, the *maskilim* in Prague had to rely on outside publications both for reading materials and as vehicles for the dissemination of their own writing.

Fortunately they found one such outlet in 1806 which proved to be quite compatible with their conception of moderation in change. The periodical in question, *Sulamith*, published in Dessau by Joseph Wolf and David Fraenkel, served as the principal sounding-board for Prague Jewish figures such as Ignaz Jeitteles, Peter Beer, M.I. Landau, and S. Leowisohn well into the second decade of the nineteenth century.[48] The editors of *Sulamith* intended for it to serve the role of mediator both within the Jewish community—reconciling Enlightenment to the mainstream of Judaism—and between Jews and the outside world. *Sulamith's* task, in the words of Joseph Wolf, was to step forth "out of the midst of an oppressed nation" and act as "peacemaker between this nation and its opponents."[49] Dessau may have been in Anhalt and not Prussia; nevertheless, it was a German enterprise that eventually provided the enlightened members of the Prague Jewish community with a sympathetic ear and a ready press.

In Kestenberg-Gladstein's view, the truly distinctive aspect of the Prague Haskalah—and that which most completely separated it from the western movement—was its national orientation.[50] The *maskilim* of

Bohemia, according to this argument, revealed a genuine appreciation not only for the multi-ethnic character of the Hapsburg realms but also for the unique, national qualities of Jewish existence. They peppered their treatises with German and Hebrew words such as *Nation, 'am, 'amei ha'arez,* and *'amei ha'olam,* all of which rang clear—to the contemporary ear at least—with the resonance of national spirit. When members of the Gesellschaft der jungen Hebraeer published historical studies in the *Monatschrift,* they raised preexisting ethnic sensibilities to the level of national pride and endeavored to awaken in the hearts of their readers a sense of belonging to *"ihrer verachteten Nation."*[51]

One could easily be tempted to read into the writings of the Prague Haskalah more than was actually there. After all, what better place than Prague, neatly situated between Western Enlightenment and Eastern traditionalism, to bring forth a unique brand of modern Jewish culture. Such a version would not only tiptoe cautiously around the domain of the sacred in Judaism but also retain cognizance of that essentially national dimension which alone was to survive the subsequent revolution from ghetto life to Zionism. Such a reading, unfortunately, is fraught with dangers not the least of which is anachronism. Terms of speech that in the second half of the nineteenth century betokened an anticosmopolitan view of group affinities usually had no such connotation either before or during the Haskalah.[52] The autobiographical introduction appended to Israel Landau's 1793 edition of *Iggeret Orhot Olam* (Epistle of the ways of the world), by Abraham Farissol, provides a good case in point.

Landau's ostensible purpose in composing the introduction was to describe how he went about the task of issuing a critical edition of this Renaissance work and to thank the people and institutions that aided him along the way. The university libraries of Prague and Vienna had made a particularly strong impression. Landau was grateful to have been allowed to drink from the well-springs of knowledge together with the non-Jewish subjects of the monarchy, and, in language borrowed from biblical and rabbinic literature, he prophesied about the future cooperation and peaceful coexistence of the peoples of the land:

> There many from among the nations of the land meet; and permission is given to the Jews as well to turn here and there. To their questions they will find an answer. There the waters of strife will be calmed. There fellowship and love will reign. From all the nations, they sit together around the table, secure and serene, like fresh, young olive seedlings.[53]

Israel Landau drew upon ancient terminology such as *'amei ha'arez* (peoples of the land), in order to subvert its pre-Haskalah meaning. What he meant to convey was that the experience of secular intellectual endeavor broke down divisions among groups. A common fellowship was achieved at the library; the universal, if ancient, ideals of peace, serenity, and love were realized. Hence, in this instance as in others, his sentiments coincided neatly with the social vision of the German Haskalah.

Thus one cannot speak of nationalism in the modern sense of the word in reference to the thought of the Prague *maskilim*. When they were not speaking in traditional categories, they were invoking the basic ideals of the Haskalah. Self-improvement through education and the cultivation of the eighteenth-century ideal of virtue dominated the themes of Jewish writing in Prague. The practical bent of the Prague movement led to an emphasis on "Volkserziehung," but the ultimate purpose of national education was not to accentuate feelings of Jewish distinctiveness. What mattered was *Bildung*, and tactics such as reaching out to the masses in their everyday language aimed at bringing Jews closer to the aesthetic considerations and social values of the European Enlightenment. One might even invoke *gedolei 'am yisrael* (great figures of the Jewish people), but one did so simply to demonstrate that models of "virtue" could be found in the Jewish past. These works stopped short of expressly articulating the conviction that Jews of the proper educational and moral standing were worthy of inclusion in the polite society of Enlightened Europe. But the message lay very close to the surface.[54]

In the end, an essential identity of interests linked the cultural programs of Berlin and Prague. The Haskalah in Bohemia did possess unique features born of the political environment of the Hapsburg Monarchy and both a physical and spiritual closeness to the Jewish culture of East Europe. Indeed, when interest in *Sulamith* waned after 1820, those *maskilim* who could still write in Hebrew found an outlet in the Vienna publications of the Galician Haskalah. However, on the question of the overall purposes of the Haskalah, Prague and Berlin displayed a common front. Prague's representatives may have preferred to show more respect and deference to normative Jewish practice and beliefs, but this was a question of tone more than of substance. At least with regard to the Haskalah, the German model exerted an inescapable influence. The Gesellschaft der jungen Hebraeer paid homage to Berlin in unambiguous terms when it chose to introduce its own publication with the motto of the *Gesellschaft der Freunde*, a quotation from Mendelssohn:

> We are called upon and dedicated by our ancestors to be righteous, and, in our righteousness, happy; called upon and dedicated to strive for *truth*, to love *beauty*, to will what is *good*, and to do one's *best*; called upon and dedicated to worship and to do good deeds.[55]

Ensuring Sociocultural Change:
The Role of Educational Reform

The point at which government interference in Jewish affairs and the ideology of the Haskalah most neatly coincided was in the area of educational policy. The promise of directing the scope and content of Jewish education for generations to come, of being able to mold attitudes and behavior, loyalties and beliefs, captured the imaginations of both Jewish illuminati and the Gentile authorities. Central European *maskilim* were quick to pick up on Joseph II's call for the Jewish communities of Austria either to establish state-supervised elementary schools of their own or else send their children to existing non-Jewish schools. The *maskilim* recognized in this call an invitation not only to alter the world view of traditional Judaism but also to create a new kind of Jewish individual, educated in Western science and languages, committed to the use of reason in determining questions of truth and value, loyal to king and to country, and loving of his fellow citizen.[56]

The educational reforms, which were directed at the Jewish community after 1781, grew out of a general educational program that had already been set in motion during the reign of Maria Theresa. In 1774 a commission led by Johann Ignaz Felbiger established a new system of elementary education for the hereditary lands, and in the following year the ordinance was applied to Bohemia. Felbiger's *Allgemeine Schulordnung* called for the establishment of a *Trivialschule* ("common-" school) in every village and market town in the countryside, at least one *Hauptschule* in every administrative district, and a *Normalschule* (teachers' training school) in every province.[57] The centerpiece of the new educational system in Bohemia was to be the "Imperial and Royal *Normalschule*" of Prague, opened in November 1775 at the site of a former Jesuit Gymnasium on the city's *Kleinseite (Malá strana)*.[58]

The Viennese government made a tentative move to include the Jews of Bohemia in the new educational policy as early as 1776. Maria Theresa suggested to the Governor's Office that Jewish schools, too, be established "nach dem Normallehrplane." Jewish leaders at the time opposed the idea, arguing that the children needed all of the hours of the day for religious study and prayer.[59] By 1782, however, not only had the Jewish community ceased to oppose calls for educational reform, it now appeared genuinely to welcome them. A number of events had intervened in the meantime. Joseph II had succeeded his mother as sole ruler of the kingdom; in 1781 he issued a decree for compulsory elementary education throughout the realm, and that same year he bestowed his Edict of Toleration on the Jews of Bohemia.

Much of the credit for the success of the program lay in the wise choice of supervisory personnel. Ferdinand Kindermann von Schulstein (1750–1801), a liberal-minded priest and educator, had been called to Vienna in 1774 to supervise the establishment of the new German schools of Bohemia. A tireless traveler who easily conveyed the depths of his own enthusiasm and commitment, Kindermann enjoyed wide-ranging success both in the Bohemian countryside and in Prague. In 1782 Joseph II chose him to oversee the establishment of the new Jewish schools as well. Kindermann approached his new role with no less determination than he had shown in the past and added a diplomatic skill that allowed him to disarm even the most wary of conservatives.[60]

Almost from the start, Jewish lay leaders and notables scrambled over one another to demonstrate their readiness to accommodate the new decree. The Prague community began construction on a new building for its German school even before the government had resolved where the necessary monies were to come from. *Hauslehrer* (private tutors) selected to serve in the new teaching corps hurriedly learned the proper pedagogical methods at the Kleinseite *Normalschule*. And on 2 May 1782 the new school opened amidst great celebration. Morning services on this day included special psalms and prayers in honor of the monarch; a *Festgottesdienst* took place at the Meiselsynagoge, where a prayer in verse, composed by the chief rabbi, was sung by a renowned Jewish vocalist from Mannheim. From the synagogue a ceremonial procession made its way to the new school building, where opening ceremonies were conducted. The president of the royal *Schulkommission,* Count Karl Clary, Deacon Kindermann, and the school director Schindler occupied places of honor, surrounded by dignitaries of the Prague Jewish community, including Ezekiel Landau, the *Stadtprimator* Israel Simon Frankel, members of the rabbinical court, and communal elders. Speeches and laudatory addresses highlighted the occasion. Fireworks closed the day's celebrations.[61]

Not to be outdone, the *Landesjudenschaft,* represented by its president Joachim Popper and the *Landesdeputierten,* met with Kindermann during the winter semester 1781-82 and easily resolved to carry out the reforms with dispatch. The Jewish leaders agreed that in places where the local community could not manage to build a new school building, German topics could be taught in the synagogue school at times when "religious instruction" (*Religionsunterricht*) was not going on. In general, the larger communities were to construct new schools. Those of middle size could contract with teachers in the Christian schools to teach Jewish children after hours. Families who lived in isolated villages would either have to make do with home tutors or send their children to the local schools. The rural communities chose to erect thirty-four new establishments as a first step in the new educational venture.[62]

In part, the enthusiasm of Prague and Bohemian Jewish leaders can be explained in terms of political lessons drawn from centuries of experience. Joseph II had sent signals that he intended to see the implementation of universal elementary education through to completion. The only prudent path for Jewish leaders to take was to show the willingness to comply. Some had already begun to show an interest in the educational and political programs of the Haskalah. Encouraged by the *Toleranzpatent,* they saw in its educational provisions an opportunity not to be squandered. However, neither of these factors is sufficient to explain the near unanimity of support given the school project in Bohemia. Indeed, the incursion of Haskalah attitudes into the community had the potential of engendering open conflict. The absence of public controversy over the schools distinguished Prague from communities in Galicia and Hungary. The extension of rabbinical acquiesence to actual participation in the project made Prague unique in all of Central Europe.

For Ezekiel Landau to have concluded that the German-Jewish schools would pose no direct threat to the traditional sources of moral authority within the community was in itself a remarkable achievement. It could only have resulted from the careful diplomacy of Ferdinand Kindermann, from his ability to make potentially transformative reforms ride safely on a sea of moderation. Kindermann had resolved from the start to include the chief rabbi in his advisory council, to clear with him all details concerning the new curriculum, and to agree in common on the structural features of the new institution.[63] Subsequent negotiations between government officials and the rabbinic leadership produced results that could only have relieved traditionalists within the community. The German school was to include four classes, and students would generally not enter before their tenth birthday, thus providing time for them to receive a grounding in Torah before they came into contact with secular subjects. The hours of instruction were kept at a minimum: four hours during the summer months—daily with the exception of Saturday—and only two hours during the winter. The remaining time was reserved for religious instruction and prayer in the synagogue schools (*hadarim*), which continued to function alongside the *Normalschulen.* The government succeeded in establishing as a minimum requirement that students remain in attendance at the normal schools until they had mastered the prescribed curriculum in reading, writing, arithmetic, and ethics.[64]

No differences existed between Jewish and non-Jewish curricula in the technical subjects such as grammar, arithmetic, physical science, and geography. In fact, the same textbooks were used in each school. However, the commonly used German language readers contained moral lessons drawn from Christian teachings and employed Christian religious imagery. At the start of the reforms, then, Kindermann faced the enormous task of adapting existing texts—with offensive passages excised—for use in the Jewish schools.[65] The effort proved to be quite trying and Kindermann may finally have provoked the disapproval of rabbinical authorities. He alluded to this fact with some exasperation in a letter to Moses Mendelssohn:

> What caused us some embarrassment at the time was the fact that the work was attacked the moment it was started. . . . The principal purpose in modeling the reader on part two of our own was to instruct Jewish youths in the social virtues and to guide them toward this end in community with others. . . . This surely is the great purpose: to make this nation more refined in manners and more sociable toward us, having hitherto been at such a distance.

> We, therefore, tried to eliminate . . . everything that was peculiar to the Christian religion. We inserted after every moral chapter . . . a moral story by some highly reputed author, and we did this not only in order to make the tuition more concrete, entertaining, and comprehensible to the Jewish children, but also because . . . the Jewish nation is descended from people who were fond of instruction by imagery and parable.

> Altogether, our endeavor in the reader and in the entire constitution of this work of school reform was to start the thing in a manner suited to the spirit, mental capacity, and present needs as well as future destiny of this nation.[66]

The difficulties which Kindermann's efforts encountered were never completely resolved. Moses Wiener, who was hired to teach German grammar and composition, produced his own *Lesebuch fuer juedische Kinder* in 1784, but it, too, apparently contained passages said to be "contrary to religion." It may have been of some consolation that Mendelssohn bestowed the work with his own approbation, and it never faced any serious challenge from the community. Wiener's *Lesebuch* remained the principal vehicle for linguistic and moralistic instruction until it was replaced by a new text in 1813.[67]

Some Jewish communities within the Hapsburg Monarchy did not prove to be as willing as Prague to enact the educational provisions of Joseph II's edict. Vienna and Pressburg (Bratislava) provide interesting contrasts, the former as an example of a progressive but structurally weak community, the latter from representing steadfast traditionalism. Leaders of the Pressburg community apparently informed the emperor in 1784 that they found it difficult to reconcile themselves to the new school system.[68] In Vienna Jews reacted with resentment, not because of their ties to traditional religious values but rather as an expression of their political impatience. Since the seventeenth-century expulsion, Viennese Jews had been denied the right to establish a legal community or even to erect a synagogue, and now they were being asked to establish schools at their own expense. Hence they responded coolly and ultimately refused. A statement from community leaders cited a number of interesting reasons for their refusal, in which they made the following points: (1) Well-to-do Jews already employed private tutors for their children (apparently for secular as well as traditional subjects), and (2) the children of less wealthy Jews were simply attending German *Normalschulen* and had already been provided with the Prague reader for the primary schools.[69] By refusing to establish their own schools the Viennese Jews may have hoped to exert leverage for the attainment of a legal corporate status. They may also have felt that separate Jewish schools would only act as an impediment to their ultimate aim of full integration into Viennese culture and society.

Finally, Trieste—Austria's port city on the Adriatic—reflected the broad cultural outlook of Italian Jewry. Its Jewish community demonstrated just as much enthusiasm as that of Prague, with none of the latter's conservatism. Trieste's Jewish leaders, with the blessing of the Chief Rabbi, Isacco Formiggini, informed the governor of the province, Count Zinzendorf, of its readiness to establish a primary school and asked his advice on the procurement of textbooks "for religious and moral instruction."[70] Later the Jews of Trieste as well as a number of Italian rabbis proved to be important supporters of Naphtali Herz Wessely and his educational manifesto.

Having acknowledged the fanfare and celebration that accompanied the opening of the Jewish schools in Bohemia, one would do well to sit back and consider the practical effect of these institutions on Jewish society. Ludvík Singer, the Czechoslovak Jewish historian of the 1930s, may have been overly optimistic when he characterized the new venture as "auffaellig und segensreich" ("triumphant and blessed").[71] Ruth Kestenberg-Gladstein, for one, has argued that neither Enlightenment reforms generally nor the German-Jewish schools in particular made great inroads in Prague before the 1820s.[72] She points out that the Prague school, unlike those of *maskilim* circles in northern Germany, did not become a vehicle for the diffusion of Haskalah, but maintained throughout its connection to the Orthodox Jewish establishment and pursued a narrow course of study in the technical arts and sciences. Traditional Jewish topics—Bible, Mishnah, Talmud, and Codes—were cut off from the *Normalschule* curriculum and shielded from the potentially negative effects of Haskalah rationalism. The school's Board of Overseers, even when it included moderate enlighteners such as M.I. Landau and Juda Jeitteles, represented the traditional social and cultural elite of the community. It fought successfully to prevent the administration of the school from falling into the hands of radicals such as Peter Beer and Herz Homberg, preferring instead to hire Christian headmasters who would not attempt to influence the handling of Jewish subjects or impose the values of the more radical elements of the Berlin Haskalah.[73]

Equally as important as the conservatism of the new schools was the fact that they did not stand alone as the sole vehicles for an education (Jewish or otherwise) within the community. A Jewish family in Prague could choose from at least three different paths in the education of its children: traditional study in the *heder* and yeshivah; private tutoring in the home (a favorite choice of the wealthy); the Jewish *Normalschule,* followed perhaps by a public, i.e. Christian, Gymnasium; or combinations of the above. Finally, there remained an untold number of children who refrained from attending any type of school. The first and last methods were not likely to produce the kinds of results desired either by *maskilim* or government ministers, although a ready pool of *maskilim* and educators emerged from the ranks of the yeshivah-educated in the 1770s and 1780s. Many of these people had been earning their living as private tutors when the provisions of the *Toleranzpatent* were announced. They quickly entered the teacher-training institute associated with the *Normalschule,* eager to be sent to small towns throughout the Hapsburg Monarchy to inculcate Jewish children in the new learning.[74] These private tutors could just as easily have transmitted Haskalah attitudes and taught Western languages and science in the context of their former employment, and many undoubtedly did. We probably will never know whether private tutoring or communal education had the greater impact on the cultural transformation of Central European Jewry during this time; neither figures nor adequate biographical material is available to make a judgment on education in the home. But we can speak with some precision about the new community schools.

How popular was the *Normalschule*? What percentage of Jewish children did it educate? To answer these questions we must make use of scattered printed sources that detail Jewish school attendance with varying degrees of completeness. Singer cites a semiofficial pamphlet of 1784 as well as a section of J.A. Riegger's *Materialien zur alten und neuen Statistik von Boehmen.*[75] Kestenberg-Gladstein bases her analysis on Johann Wanniczek's 1832 history of the school which contained a *Schulbesuchkalender* for the years 1790 to 1831.[76] The statistical information still needs to be carefully studied and compared before any definitive statement on Jewish attendance can be offered, but it is necessary to attempt to explain discrepancies that exist in the published figures as well as the apparently steep, short-term fluctuations that periodically creep into the curve.

The 1784 report, for example, sets the number of Jewish students at the Prague *Normalschule* at 347, and those in the Bohemian *Trivialschulen* at 584.[77] Government statistics for 1787 claim that 559 students were in attendance at 25 rural Jewish schools; in 56 additional localities, 278 Jewish children attended Christian schools. The first figure is said to represent an increase of 25 percent in one year, the second a jump of over 100 percent.[78] On the other hand, Wanniczek recounts that the Prague institution in 1790—which at this time also included a girls' school—attracted only 215 boys and 63 girls; over the next eight years, the number of students tended to drop and rise precipitously from one semester to the next.[79]

Some of the fluctuations might be explained as the outcome of periodic government interventions designed to hasten the success of the program. After 1786, Jews who wished to acquire a marriage certificate had to demonstrate that they had attended a *Normalschule;* predictably, the schools were considerably more filled the following year than they had been in the recent past. Herz Klaber relates that attendance fell off once again between 1796 and 1811, and only the concerted efforts of the Board of Overseers in tandem with more stringent government regulations succeeded in assuring the long-term health of the school.[80] In 1813 the government instituted a new and more rigorous examination for the marriage license, based on Herz Homberg's newly published reader, *Bnie Zion,* which also became a mandatory text in all of the Jewish schools of the monarchy.[81] This measure, together with an influx of new blood in the areas of community supervision, school administration, and teaching appear to have done the trick.

During the next decade, the attendance curve rose and was stabilized. The school was enlarged in 1812, when an "Elementarklasse" was added to the four existing "Knabenklassen." According to one source, in 1816 attendance hit a peak of 800 boys and girls.[82] In the same year, the community added a 2-class *Trivialschule* in the enlarged school building. In 1818, the 1st-year class in the *Maedchenschule* grew to over 200 and had to be divided into two groups. Attendance in general grew so large in 1822, particularly in the lower classes, that the administration was forced to institute double sessions.[83] All in all, some 17,800 Jewish children received an education in the Prague *Normalschule* between 1790 and 1831, an average of 424 per year.[84]

Contrary to the opinion of Kestenberg-Gladstein on this matter, I do not think that the Jewish attendance figures in Prague were particularly small. The rate of Jewish participation in the *Normalschule* in Prague may have been higher than Jewish attendance in comparable schools in Berlin and Frankfurt. Again, only a systematic comparison of the several cities will yield compelling results. We do know, however, that as late as 1812 Berlin sent 215 students, out of a school-age population of 900, to its Jewish school, while Frankfurt sent 120 from a population of 558.[85] The figures in both cases represented 20–25 percent of the pool of school-age children. On the other hand, one can argue justifiably that the yearly average of 424 students in attendance at the Prague institution comprised as much as 40 percent of the eligible Jewish children in that city.[86] Clearly, the majority of Prague's Jewish children did not attend the community school, but neither did the vast majority of those in Berlin or Frankfurt. Throughout this period wealthier families preferred to hire private tutors to teach in their homes; public education remained in large part the domain of the poor and the dispossessed.[87]

Attendance, of course, is but one of a variety of factors one would want to consider in judging the role of the new schools in the process of social and cultural modernization. Other issues that need to be addressed are: Did the focus of the new school remain as narrow as it had been at its conception, or did it broaden to include new areas of instruction? If so, with what consequences? How long did the traditional *heder* and yeshivah continue to operate alongside, but independently of the *Normalschule*? When did Jewish students begin to abandon the former in favor of an exclusive concentration on secular education? Finally, at what point did Jewish youth begin to attend gymnasia and universities in large numbers, and where did such students receive their elementary education?

I know of no study which focuses on these questions. As a result, only partial answers and suggestions can be offered in many cases. By the third decade of operation, the Prague school appears to have passed the turning point of its fortunes. From 1810 onwards, higher numbers were matched by significant changes in both the personnel and the curriculum of the institution. For the first time members of the community who themselves had been educated at the *Normalschule* began to assume administrative and teaching positions. Pinkas Kollin, who had been "Lehrer an der Moral" since the school's founding in 1782, died in 1810. He was replaced by a former private tutor turned provincial teacher, Peter Beer. A year later two new overseers were named, Samuel Dormitzer, who also served as "Imperial and Royal" director of taxes and Simon Hock, businessman and amateur historian, who had graduated from the *Normalschule* and had subsequently gone on to receive a Doctor of Laws degree.[88] When Dormitzer stepped down in 1815 he was replaced by another graduate of the institution, the printer-scholar M.I. Landau, future head of the Prague Jewish community and grandson of Ezekiel Landau. In 1818, the radical *maskil* Herz Homberg, having already served the emperor in teaching positions in Trieste and Galicia, was named instructor in "religious ethics" for Prague gymnasia students and Jewish private tutors, a sure indication of the breadth of Enlightenment indoctrination in the capital as well as of the greater participation of Jewish students in non-Jewish establishments.[89]

As for the expansion of the *Normalschule* curriculum and the encroachment of secular studies on traditional Jewish education, I can attempt only tentative conclusions based on a scanty amount of information. I have found no indication that the new school system ever sought to compete directly with the *heder* and yeshivah by teaching traditional subjects according to the Haskalah approach. Thus Ezekiel Landau's fears in this regard never materialized. The progressive members of the community appear to have been content to let the traditional educational tract wither of its own accord as it attracted fewer and fewer students over the decades. Indications of "benign neglect," coupled with moderate increases in the Jewish component of the curriculum, appear during the early nineteenth century. In 1809, for example, the Board of Overseers succeeded in having Hebrew taught at the school after hours and "under certain [unspecified] conditions."[90] With the publication the following year of Peter Beer's *Toldot Yisrael* (History of Israel), Jewish school children throughout the kingdom were fed a steady diet of biblical and ancient Jewish history. The text of the work was in Hebrew, but it was accompanied by a Hebrew-lettered German translation and notes by the author in the same language.[91] Finally, in 1815 the school day (which up until now had been relegated to the late afternoon) was divided into two parts extending from eight A.M. to four P.M. Such a move could greatly have reduced the stature of the *heder* as an equal partner in the education of the young. But it may also simply have reflected a decline in the *heder* long since in evidence.[92]

Whatever the actual chain of events, by the time Solomon Judah Rappaport was appointed Chief Rabbi in 1840, Prague's once famous yeshivah had sunk into obscurity. The decline in traditional Jewish education ran its course in little over half a century. Prague's rabbis in the 1780s and 1790s had taken great pains to warn Jewish parents that they must resist the temptation to reduce the amount of time devoted to the study of sacred matters in order to introduce their children to the new secular sciences. By 1870, a Jewish gymnasium student in Prague who supplemented his general studies with classes at the Talmud Torah had become a rarity.[93]

An obvious interpretation would link the successes and shortcomings of Jewish modernization in Prague to the fitful efforts of the Hapsburg regime to achieve economic and military parity with Western Europe. According to this argument, government programs which were designed to promote Austrian industry and create an educated and productive citizenry were doomed to fall short of English, French, and even German achievements because of the semifeudal nature of Austrian society and the lack of adequate institutional and cultural supports. Political determination alone could not achieve social and economic transformation. Similarly, the absence of what Jacob Katz has called "semineutral society"—areas in which Jews and Gentiles could establish new social relationships on the basis of common interests and shared values—rendered the process of Jewish modernization in Bohemia incomplete, if not tenuous, throughout much of the nineteenth century. London, with its liberal Protestant spirit and highly developed economy; Paris, the home of European rationalism and political democracy; and even Berlin, with its literary salons and progressive bureaucratic corps—all offered Jews the opportunity to participate in meaningful ways in the larger society of the Gentile world. Prague did not. Here political and cultural reforms went adrift, unable to drop anchor in a receptive environment.

Such an answer fails to satisfy completely. The Hapsburg Monarchy did, after all, enjoy its own industrial revolution. It never managed to pull even to the West (and eventually slipped far behind Germany) but nevertheless achieved a respectable position between the highly developed and underdeveloped countries of Europe. The transformations which occurred within Bohemian Jewish society, compared favorably to developments in the West. The political élan of revolutionary France may have eluded Prague; the pace of change may have been more gradual, its leading advocates more circumspect, than in Berlin. However, the fact remains that beginning with the 1780s Bohemian Jewish society began a transition from which there was to be no return. The dismantling of communal autonomy left a political vacuum that could only be filled by the state. The new educational structure combined with the widening of economic opportunities to overhaul both the civic horizons and the social aspirations of Bohemian Jews. As in most Central European communities, acculturation preceded political emancipation by a half century or more. But civic emancipation, true to its role as handmaiden of economic advancement, was achieved during the early stages of Austrian industrialization only gradually—as Hapsburg culture would have it—between 1848 and 1859.[94]

If Prague failed before 1848 to provide avenues for Jewish and Gentile social interaction comparable to what had developed in Germany, it nevertheless offered alternatives that better fitted the Austrian context. Bohemian Jews looked to the agents of change themselves—the state, the schools, and the economic world—as domains outside of the traditional community where they might participate and be received as individuals. The social clubs of the Prague bourgeoisie eventually opened their doors as well. Beginning in the 1850s, Jews constituted a large and crucial element in such civic institutions as the German casino. Seven decades of Germanization had made them indispensible allies in the politics of ethnic defense.[95] Later, in the postemancipatory period, growing national strife in Bohemia together with the massive immigration of Czech-speaking Jews from the countryside would alter the face of the community once more.

Notes

1. Robin Okey, *Eastern Europe, 1740–1980: Feudalism to Communism* (Minneapolis: University of Minnesota Press, 1982), pp. 9–11.
2. For a general discussion of the problems of modernization in East Central Europe see N.T. Gross, "The Hapsburg Monarchy, 1750–1914," in Carlo M. Cipolla, ed., *Fontana Economic History of Europe* (New York: Fontana, 1976), "The Emergence of Industrial Societies," pt. 1, vol. 4, pp. 228–78; and Okey, *Eastern Europe, passim.*
3. *Divrei Shalom Ve'emet* (Berlin, 1782). For the reaction of traditionalists to the pamphlet, see Alexander Altmann, *Moses Mendelssohn: A Biographical Study* (Philadelphia: (JPS) Jewish Publication Society of America, and Alabama: University of Alabama Press, 1973), pp. 474–89. Among the rabbis who openly condemned the dangers of the Haskalah following the appearance of Wessely's work were Ezekiel Landau of Prague, David Tevele of Lissa, Joseph Hazaddik of Posen, and Pinhas Halevi Horowitz of Frankfurt am Main.
4. On the century of expulsions see Salo Baron, *A Social and Religious History of the Jews,* 2nd ed., vol. 11 (New York: Columbia University Press, 1967), pp. 192–283. The Jewish exodus from the Moravian cities is pinpointed in Alfred Engel, "Die Ausweisung der Juden aus den koeniglichen Staedten Maehrens und ihre Folgen," *Jahrbuch der Gesellschaft fuer Geschichte der Juden in der Čechoslovakischen Republik* (hereafter JGGJČR) 2 (1930): 50–96.
5. For Jewish life in Bohemia at the end of the Middle Ages see Anton Blaschka, "Die juedische Gemeinde zu Ausgang des Mittelalters," in *Die Juden in Prag* (Prague: B'nei B'rith, 1927), pp. 58–87; and J. Čelakovský, *Příspěvky k dějinám židů v době Jagěllonské* (Contributions to the History of the Jews during the Jagiellon Dynasty, [Prague, 1898]).

6. See the illuminating article by Samuel Steinherz, "Gerush Hayehudim Mibeim Bishnat 1541" (The expulsion of the Jews from Bohemia in 1541), *Zion* 15 (1950): 70–92; also Jan Heřman, "The Conflict between Jewish and non-Jewish Population in Bohemia before the 1541 Banishment," *Judaica Bohemiae* 6 (1970): 39–54.

7. *Encyclopaedia Judaica,* vol. 4, col. 1177; Ruth Kestenberg-Gladstein, *Neuere Geschichte der Juden in den boehmischen Laendern, Erster Teil: Das Zeitalter der Aufklaerung, 1780–1830* (Tuebingen: Mohr, 1969), pp. 1–4. On the demographic configuration of German Jewry in the eighteenth century see A. Shohet, *'Im Hilufei Tekufot* (beginnings of the Haskalah among German Jewry [Jerusalem: Bialik Institute, 1960]), pp. 20–21. For Hungary, see chapter 6 in this volume, by Michael Silber. In contrast to the some 800 localities in Bohemia in which Jews lived in the early eighteenth century, Moravian Jewry was distributed among 52 communities of "medium" size (Kestenberg-Gladstein, "Mifkad Yehudei Beim Shemihuz LePrag Bishnat 1724" [Census of nonmetropolitan Jews in Bohemia in 1724], *Zion* 9 [1944]: 1–26).

8. J. Prokeš, "Der Antisemitismus der Behoerden und das Prager Ghetto in nachweissenbergischer Zeit," *JGGJČR* 1 (1929):42–43; Kestenberg-Gladstein, *Neuere Geschichte,* pp. 29–30.

9. *Encyclopaedia Judaica,* vol. 4, col. 1177; Kestenberg-Gladstein, "Mifkad Yehudei Beim."

10. Prokeš, "Antisemitismus der Behoerden," pp. 49–110, 149–235; K. Spiegel, "Die Prager Juden zur Zeit des dreissigjaehrigen Krieges," in *Die Juden in Prag* (Prague, 1927), pp. 107–86. Anita Franková, "Erfassung der juedischen Bevoelkerung in Boehmen im 18. und in der ersten Haelfte des 19. Jahrhunderts," *Judaica Bohemiae* 6 (1970): 55–69.

11. Franková, "Erfassung."

12. Kestenberg-Gladstein, *Neuere Geschichte,* pp. 1–2. Antonín Tokstein, *Židé v Čechách* (The Jews in the Czech lands [Prague: Beaufort, 1938]), p. 42.

13. The collusion of the landed estate in Jewish efforts to circumvent the effects of Vienna's restrictive legislation is a highly suggestive topic, but it has yet to be treated definitively. For literature that does exist on the subject see Josef von Wertheimer, *Die Juden in Oesterreich* (Leipzig, 1842), vol. 1, pp. 187–94; L. Singer, "Zur Geschichte der Toleranzpatente in den Sudetenlaendern," *JGGJČR* 5 (1933): 236–37; Karel Adámek, *Slovo o židech* (A word about the Jews [Chrudim, 1899]), pp. 5–8; and A. Stein, *Die Geschichte der Juden in Boehmen* (Brno: Jüdischer Buch und Kunst Verlag, 1904), pp. 86–90.

14. On the expulsion of 1745–1748 see J. Bergl, "Die Ausweisung der Juden aus Prag im Jahre 1744," in *Die Juden in Prag* (Prague, 1927), pp. 187–247; Paul P. Bernard, "Joseph II and the Jews: The Origins of the Toleration Patent of 1782," *Austrian History Yearbook* 4–5 (1968–69), pp. 101–19; L. Singer, "Zur Geschichte der Toleranzpatente," pp. 235–43; and B. Mevorakh, "Ma'aseh Hishtadlut Be'eiropah Lemeniyat Geirusham shel Yehudei Bohemia Umoravia" (Diplomatic efforts in Europe to prevent the expulsion of the Jews of Bohemia and Moravia), *Zion* 25 (1963): 125–64.

15. In addition to the works cited above see *Encyclopaedia Judaica,* 4, 1177; and Kestenberg-Gladstein, *Neuere Geschichte,* pp. 1–3, 8–12. Kestenberg-Gladstein feels that the Jewish population of Bohemia in 1754 stood closer to 40,000.

16. "Statistische Tabellen ueber alle israelitischen Gemeinden, Synagogen, Schulen und Rabbinate in Boehmen," in A. Kohn, ed., *Die Notablenversammlung der Israeliten Boehmens in Prag* (Vienna: Sommer, 1852), pp. 383–414.
17. A. Klíma, "Industrial Development in Bohemia, 1648–1781," *Past and Present* 11 (April 1957): 87–97; H. Freudenberger, "Industrialization in Bohemia and Moravia in the Eighteenth Century," *Journal of Central European Affairs* 19 (1960): 347–56.
18. Klíma, "Industrial Development," pp. 90–91.
19. A. Klíma, "Mercantilism in the Hapsburg Monarchy—With special reference to the Bohemian Lands," *Historica* 11 (1965): 95–119; Freudenberger, "Industrialization"; and N.T. Gross, "The Hapsburg Monarchy," pp. 228–78.
20. Klíma, "Mercantilism"; Gross, "Hapsburg Monarchy," pp. 237–61.
21. Gross, "Hapsburg Monarchy"; see also Knut Borchardt, "Germany 1700–1914," in Carlo M. Cipolla, ed., *The Fontana Economic History of Europe*, (New York: Fontana, 1976), vol. 4, "The Emergence of Industrial Societies," pt. 1, pp. 76–160.
22. Joseph von Wertheimer, *Die Juden in Oesterreich,* vol. 1 (Leipzig, 1842), p. 137: "Ein Despot wie der Fruehling, der des Winters Eis zerbricht."
23. Bernard, "Joseph II and the Jews"; Jacob Katz, *Out of the Ghetto* (Cambridge, Mass.: Harvard University Press, 1973), pp. 161–67. See also R.J. Kerner, *Bohemia in the Eighteenth Century* (New York: A.M.S. Press, 1969, 1932), *passim.*
24. In a *Resolution* distributed by the Emperor on 1 October 1781, he assured the *Staatsrat*: "Meine Absicht gehet keineswegs dahin, die Juedische Nation in den Erblanden mehr auszubreiten oder da, wo sie nicht toleriert ist, neu einzufuehren, sondern nur, da wo sie ist und in der Maass, wie sie als tolerirt bestehet, dem Staate nuetzlich zu machen" (A. F. Pribram, ed., *Urkunden und Akten zur Geschichte der Juden in Wien,* vol. 1 [Wien: Braumüller, 1918], p. 137).
25. Letter of Joseph II to Count Bluemegen, 13 May 1781 (Pribram, *Urkunden,* p. 440). Concerning both Joseph's original intentions and the ultimate effects of the law, see Singer, "Toleranzpatent"; Bernard, "Joseph II and the Jews"; and Katz, *Out of the Ghetto,* pp. 161–67. A text of the Edict for the Austrian hereditary lands is found in Pribram, vol. 1, pp. 494–500.
26. Pribram, *Urkunden,* pp. 494–500; Katz, *Out of the Ghetto,* pp. 161–64. The census of 1724 and 1729, dealing with the Jews of Bohemia and of Prague respectively, indicated that over 27 percent of Prague Jews and 19 percent of Bohemian Jews worked as artisans; some 50 percent of Prague Jews and 52 percent of Bohemian Jews were listed as being involved in trade (Kestenberg-Gladstein, *Neuere Geschichte,* p. 12).
27. Kestenberg-Gladstein, *Neuere Geschichte,* pp. 96–105; Pribram, *Urkunden,* pp. 494–97; Singer, "Toleranzpatent," pp. 258–61.
28. Kestenberg-Gladstein, *Neuere Geschichte,* pp. 66–85; L. Singer, "Zur Geschichte der Juden in Boehmen in den letzten Jahren Josefs II," *JGGJČR* 6 (1934): 197–99.
29. Kestenberg-Gladstein's magisterial work *Neuere Geschichte der Juden in Boehmen* stands as the only study to date of the Prague Haskalah. Outside of this there are the primary sources themselves: the works of such figures as Baruch Jeitteles, Juda Jeitteles. Israel Landau, M.I. Landau, Solomon

Loewisohn, Peter Beer, Herz Homberg, and Solomon Judah Rapoport as well as the sermonic writings of Ezekiel Landau and Eleazar Fleckeles.

30. See Kestenberg-Gladstein, *Neuere Geschichte,* pp. 115–331. The four phases divide chronologically as follows: (1) 1780s; (2) 1790s; (3) 1800–1820; and (4) 1820s.

31. The major Bohemian contributor to *Hame'asef* during this period was Baruch Jeitteles (1762–1813), son of the physician and proto-*maskil* Jonas Jeitteles (1735–1806). Subscribers to the *Biur* from Austria and Bohemia following the publication of Mendelssohn's 1778 *Prospectus* numbered fifty-seven (Altmann, *Mendelssohn,* p. 377).

32. For the specific incident over which the two groups split, see below.

33. The clearest sign of Prague's original course arose in 1802 with the establishment of the *Gesellschaft der jungen Hebraeer* and the publication of the *Jeudisch-deutsche Monatschrift.* Chief among the contributors to the third and fourth stages of the Prague Haskalah were Ignaz and Juda Jeitteles, M.I. Landau, and S. Loewisohn.

34. Kestenberg-Gladstein, *Neuere Geschichte,* pp. 146–69, 191–236. See also, Kestenberg-Gladstein, "Ofiyah Hale'umi shel Haskalat Prag" (The national character of the Prague Haskalah), *Molad* 23 (1965): 221–33.

35. This, for example, is Kestenberg-Gladstein's view. She stresses throughout the national and conservative character of the Prague Haskalah and at one point states bluntly, "Die Eigentuemlichkeit des Prager Weges ist also der *nationale* Aspekt" (*Neuere Geschichte,* p. 200, emphasis in the original).

36. Ezekiel Landau, *Derushei Hazelah* (Warsaw, 1886), fols. 53a–54a.

37. Ibid., fol. 53a.

38. Ibid.

39. Ibid., fol. 53b.

40. From the *Haskama* to Sussmann Glogau's Pentateuch translation, reproduced in *Hame'asef* (1786), pp. 142–44; and in English translation in Altmann, *Mendelssohn,* pp. 382–83. A number of Prague *maskilim,* including Avigdor Levi and Juda Jeitteles, testified that Landau resisted clamorings for legal action against Mendelssohn and for the issuance of a ban against the *Biur.* He did, nevertheless, rule that Mendelssohn's Pentateuch could not be introduced into the curriculum of the Prague Jewish School (Altmann, *Mendelssohn,* pp. 396–98).

41. Baruch Jeitteles, who had been educated at Landau's Yeshivah, apparently ran away to Berlin at some point in his young adult life, only to return and achieve a reconciliation with both father and teacher. (This point is alluded to in Juda Jeitteles' biography of his father, Jonas, *B'nei Hane'urim* [Prague, 1821], pp. 1–86). Similarly, Ezekiel Landau may have been inclined not to issue a formal ban on Mendelssohn's work because at least one of Landau's sons, Samuel, was a subscriber to the *Biur* as well as, later, *Hame'asef.*

42. See Kestenberg-Gladstein, *Neuere Geschichte,* pp. 133–46, 173–91. Jeitteles' retort to *Hame'asef* appeared in the work *Ha'orev* (The one who lies in wait [Salonika, 1795]), published under the pseudonym Pinhas Hananya Argosi de Silva. His attack on the Prague Frankists appeared in 1800 in the piece *Siha Bein Shenat 5560 Uvein 5561* (Dialogue between the years 5560 and 5561). Apparently the autumn of 1800 had seen a number of open conflicts between Frankists and their adversaries in Prague culminating in the brief imprisonment of Eleazar Fleckeles and Samuel Landau.

43. In 1793 Israel Landau issued a critical edition, with commentary, of Abraham Farissol (ca. 1451–1525), *Iggeret Orhot Olam* (Epistle on the ways of the world). He attempted to further the cause of popular education in the fundamentals of Judaism with his 1798 work, *Hok LeYisrael* (A law unto Israel), a compilation of the positive and negative commandments of the Hebrew Bible translated into the German-Jewish dialect of Bohemia.
44. *Encyclopaedia Judaica,* vol. 10, pp. 1389–90.
45. Kestenberg-Gladstein, *Neuere Geschichte,* p. 126.
46. *Encyclopaedia Judaica,* vol. 10, p. 1391 (on Eliezer Landau [1778–1831]). On M.I. Landau (1788–1852) see Kestenberg-Gladstein, *Neuere Geschichte,* pp. 249–53, 315–16.
47. The *Juedisch-deutsche Monatschrift* published six issues during the winter, spring, and summer of 1802 (Adar through Tamuz), totalling less than 200 pages.
48. *Sulamith: Eine Zeitschrift zur Befoerderung der Kultur und Humanitaet unter der juedischen Nation,* ed. D. Fraenkel and Wolf (Leipzig, 1806; Dessau, 1807 etc.).
49. *Sulamith* (1806), p. 164 (quoted in M. Meyer, *The Origins of the Modern Jew* [Detroit: Wayne State University Press, 1967], p. 120).
50. See note 35, above.
51. Kestenberg-Gladstein, *Neuere Geschichte,* pp. 195–209, 222–34.
52. Both Jewish and non-Jewish sources from medieval time down to the end of the eighteenth century employ terminology that today rings with nationalist overtones. For example, the universities of medieval Europe were divided into many "nations," and rabbinic literature continually distinguished between the "nation of Israel" and the "nations of the world." Moreover, most government authorities, whatever their relationship to Enlightenment, quite simply held the Jews to be a nation and referred to them as such down to the end of the century.
53. ("Shalmei todah" [Offerings of thanks], the second foreword to the Farissol edition; printed in Kestenberg-Gladstein, *Neuere Geschichte,* p. 151).
54. The historical entries of the *Juedisch-deutsche Monatschrift* were included under the general heading "Biographien grosser Maenner unserer Nation," but this turns out to be a direct borrowing of phraseology found in 1784 in *Hame'asef* (Kestenberg-Gladstein, *Neuere Geschichte,* p. 208). In these essays the *gedolei 'am Yisrael* were invoked simply to demonstrate that models of "virtue" could be found in the Jewish past. Contributions like Ignaz Jeitteles' "Die Macht der Tugend," *Sulamith* (1806), and the biography of Josephus Flavius which appeared in the second number of the *Monatschrift,* served essentially the same purpose: to demonstrate that both the sources of Judaism and the history of the Jews could produce example of virtue, beauty, and truth worthy of any classical or enlightened standard.
55. Quoted in Kestenberg-Gladstein, *Neuere Geschichte,* p. 196, emphasis in the original.
56. Naftali Herz Wesseley is an often cited example of this phenomenon. His pamphlet *Divrei Shalom Ve'emet* appeared shortly after the issuance of the "Toleranzpatent" and included a plea for the Jewish communities of the monarchy to put the provisions of Joseph's educational reforms into place. See Jacob Katz, *Out of the Ghetto,* pp. 66–69.

57. Wenzel Hammer, *Geschichte der Volksschule Boehmens von der aeltesten Zeit bis zum Jahre 1870* (Warnsdorf: Commissions-Verlag von A. Opitz, 1904), pp. 79–81.

58. Hammer, p. 82; also Eduard Winter, *Ferdinand Kindermann Ritter von Schulstein* (Augsburg: Stauda, 1926), pp. 43–44. On general educational reform during the period of enlightened absolutism see Eduard Winter, *Barock, Absolutismus und Aufklaerung in der Donaumonarchie* (Vienna: Europa Verlag, 1971), pp. 171–77, 202–10.

59. Singer, "Toleranzpatent," pp. 264–65; see also Moses Wiener, *Nachricht von dem Ursprunge und Fortgange der deutschen juedischen Hauptschule zu Prag* (Prague, 1785).

60. Altmann, *Mendelssohn*, p. 475; Winter, *Kindermann, passim;* and Winter, *Barock*, pp. 202–10.

61. Singer, "Toleranzpatent," pp. 267–68.

62. Winter, *Kindermann*, p. 132; Singer, "Toleranzpatent," pp. 264–66, 269–70.

63. Singer, "Toleranzpatent," p. 267; Wiener, *Nachricht.*

64. Singer, "Toleranzpatent," p. 267; Kestenberg-Gladstein, *Neuere Geschichte*, pp. 46–52.

65. Altmann, *Mendelssohn*, pp. 474–76; Singer, "Toleranzpatent," p. 267.

66. Ferdinand Kindermann to Moses Mendelssohn, 5 January 1783 (Depositum Robert von Mendelssohn, C II, no. 34), translated and published in Altmann, *Mendelssohn*, pp. 475–76.

67. Altmann, *Mendelssohn*, p. 488; Kestenberg-Gladstein, *Neuere Geschichte*, pp. 54–56.

68. Information relayed in a letter of Kindermann to Oberamtsverwalter J. Braum in Schurz (undated, August/September 1784 or 1785); reproduced in Winter, *Kindermann*, pp. 166–68. Joseph II is reported to have replied to the Jewish leaders of Pressburg, "Gehts nur nach Prag; dort bin ich recht wohl mit der Schule zufrieden" (p. 167).

69. Altmann, *Mendelssohn*, pp. 476–77.

70. Ibid., pp. 477–78.

71. Singer, "Toleranzpatent," p. 264.

72. Kestenberg-Gladstein, *Neuere Geschichte*, pp. 34–65, *passim.*

73. Kestenberg-Gladstein, *Neuere Geschichte*, pp. 62–65. From 1814 to 1838 two men, both Christians, occupied the position of headmaster: Anton Raaz and Johann Wanniczek.

74. Singer, "Toleranzpatent," p. 267; Winter, *Barock*, pp. 204–5. The *maskil* Peter Beer (ca. 1758–1838), who had attended the Prague and Pressburg yeshivot, was one of the first Jews to be trained as a teacher under the new program. He taught at his native Nový Bidžov from 1785 until his call to Prague in 1811.

75. I. Boehm, *Historische Nachricht von der Enstehungsart und der Verbreitung des Normalinstituts in Boehmen* (Prague, 1784); J.A. Riegger, *Materialien zur alten und neuen Statistik von Boehmen*, vol. 7: *Zustand der Normal- Buerger- und Landschulen in Boehmen* (1787), pp. 43ff., in Singer, "Toleranzpatent," pp. 269–70.

76. Wanniczek, *Geschichte der Prager Haupt- Trivial- und Maedchenschule der Israeliten* (Prague, 1832).

77. Singer, "Toleranzpatent," p. 269.

78. Ibid., p. 270.

79. Kestenberg-Gladstein, *Neuere Geschichte*, pp. 47–49.
80. Herz Klaber, *Beschreibung der am 30. Mai 1832 gehaltenen fuenfzigjaehrigen Jubelfeyer der israel. deutschen Hauptschule in Prag, nebst einer Geschichte dieser Schule* (Prague, 1833), pp. 63ff. I am indebted to Michael Silber of the Hebrew University in Jerusalem for making a copy of Klaber's report available to me.
81. *Bnie Zion: ein religioes-moralisches Lehrbuch fuer die Jugend israelitischer Nation* (Vienna, 1812). See Kestenberg-Gladstein, *Neuere Geschichte*, pp. 47–48; and Klaber, *Beschreibung*, pp. 65–67.
82. Klaber, *Beschreibung*, p. 69.
83. Ibid., pp. 71–75.
84. Kestenberg-Gladstein, *Neuere Geschichte*, p. 48.
85. Figures provided by ibid., p. 49.
86. If one assumes that the 10,000 Jews in the city divided roughly among 2,000 families, and that each family had school age children for approximately ten years, then in any given year only one-quarter of the families (i.e. 500) contributed to the pool of potential students (Wanniczek's tables extended over a period of forty years). Moreover, in any given year each family would have had no more than two children of school age. Thus the total pool could not have been much higher than 1,000 per year. (Again, my thanks to Michael Silber for discussing these figures with me.)
87. See Kestenberg-Gladstein, *Neuere Geschichte*, pp. 49–50; Altmann, *Mendelssohn*, p. 477.
88. Klaber, *Beschreibung*, p. 64.
89. Ibid., pp. 68–72.
90. Ibid., p. 64.
91. Peter Beer, *Sefer Toledot Yisrael, Kolel Sippur Kol Hakorot asher Karu . . . 'im Rimzei Midot Tovot Umusar Haskel . . . leto'elet Hinukh Benei Yisrael* (History of Israel, including the story of all that happened . . . with allusions to virtue and morality . . . for the education of Jewish children [Vienna, 1810]).
92. Klaber, *Beschreibung*, p. 68.
93. See for example Ezekiel Landau's sermon of the Ten Days of Repentance 1782 or 1783, in *Derushei Hazelah,* fol. 42a–42b. On Jewish education in turn-of-the-century Prague see Shmuel Hugo Bergman, "Petah Davar" (Foreword), in *Yahadut Czechoslovakia* (Czechoslovak Jewry [Jerusalem: Ministry of Education, 1969]), pp. 7–10.
94. The legal validity of the ghetto was formally abolished in 1848, and Jews were permitted to reside in all areas of the Crown Lands. Franz Josef's Constitutional Edict of 1849 granted Jews equal status to Christians under law. After 1859, the last barriers to free economic activity and association were torn down and the government also confirmed the right of Jews to own land. Full political emancipation was proclaimed only in 1867. See Wolfdieter Bihl, "Die Juden," in Wandruszka and Urbanitsch, eds., *Die Hapsburgermonarchie, 1848–1918,* vol. 3 (Eisenstadt: Edition Roetzer, 1980), pp. 890–96.
95. On the Jewish role in German ethnic politics and social life in Prague see Gary B. Cohen, *The Politics of Ethnic Survival: Germans in Prague, 1861–1914* (Princeton: Princeton University Press, 1981).

5

The Historical Experience of German Jewry and Its Impact on Haskalah and Reform in Hungary

Michael Silber

To my mentor, Professor Jacob Katz, on his eightieth birthday

Recalling in 1839 the profound impression created by the appearance of Mendelssohn's Bible translation almost sixty years before, the *maskil* Peter Beer wrote, "A light dawned in me that to understand this Book of Books it was not enough to rely upon old, often contradictory legends, but rather it was through grammar, knowledge of the past, religious and moral reflection that head and heart could be brought closer together." That at the time he was a private tutor in a remote village in Hungary is just one indication of the rapid, if not extensive, dissemination of the German Haskalah to this country as early as 1780.[1] This reception of German Haskalah was all the more remarkable since Hungarian Jewry was all but cut off from Germany: trade between the two countries was negligible and in consequence, direct communication rare.[2] In contrast to Eastern Europe, for example, there was a near total absence of subscribers from Hungary to the two most representative and significant projects of the Haskalah, the journal *Hame'assef* and Mendelssohn's Bible translation with commentary, *Netivot Hashalom*.[3] To cap it off, state censorship and bothersome restrictions on the import of foreign books further enforced the already insular character of Hungarian Jews.[4] And yet, if direct ties with Germany were lacking, they were compensated for to a great extent by the close family and business connections Hungarian Jews enjoyed with Vienna and Prague Jewries. Both communities served, first, in the 1780s and early 1790s, as conduits of books printed in

Germany and at a later stage, from the mid-1790s, as publishing centers reissuing along with the short-lived Brünn press a good deal of the literature of the Berlin Haskalah.[5]

To gauge the influence of German Jewry it is not enough to note the simple spread of ideas. Once the Haskalah, and as we shall see Reform, reached Hungary, it did not assume the same historic role it had played in Germany; several factors, both social and cultural, intervened to modify its actual impact on Hungarian Jewry. In this essay I identify these factors and discuss how they affected the Hungarian reception of German ideologies, thus illuminating the question of what specific weight should be attributed to the German experience in Hungarian developments.

The ideology of the Berlin Haskalah was transplanted here into a social context markedly divergent from the cultivated, wealthy urban setting of its origin. First, the social composition of Hungarian Jewry was different: in the 1780s, over 60 percent of Hungary's 80,000 Jews lived scattered about the countryside in settlements varying from one or two families of *Dorfjuden* to a village, isolated from communal life for the greater part of the year. No more than 15 percent of Hungarian Jews lived in organized Jewish communities of more than 500 people.[6] Only three communities—Pressburg, Alt Ofen (Obuda) and Eisenstadt—were relatively well-off, but their wealth was in no comparison to that of the Jews of Berlin. The truly wealthy were rapidly siphoned off, abandoning the country to settle in Vienna.[7] As a result, the strength of those groups that were the natural carriers of Haskalah ideology—the very wealthy and their intellectual protégés—was relatively very weak in Hungary. Hungary could not compete not only with Germany, but even with the other Habsburg provinces in patronage, which played such a crucial role in determining and sustaining Haskalah centers. Consequently, Hungary seldom attracted foreign *maskilim* and was not always successful, as in the case of Shlomo Löwisohn and Moritz Gottlieb Saphir, in retaining its own homegrown talent.

The dissimilarity between Hungarian and German Jewries paralleled the very different structures of their two host societies. Hungary was primarily an agrarian society. The timid urban population, weak both numerically and politically, was largely composed of non-Magyar ethnic groups. The Hungarian nobility, on the other hand, was one of the most numerous and powerful in Europe.[8] Stubborn, unyielding in their centuries-old struggle against the encroachments of the absolutist state, by the end of the eighteenth century they were probably unique among the nobles of Europe in having successfully defended and preserved much of their medieval corporate privileges.

It was from the nobility, specifically from the middle nobility, the gentry, that the carriers of the Enlightenment in Hungary were largely drawn.[9] Ideas of religious toleration found favorable reception among the gentry in particular, because the choice of religious affiliation had been one of the most zealously guarded privileges of the noble Estates since the sixteenth century and many of its members indeed belonged to religious minorities.[10] A Roman Catholic cleric could write in 1790, "It is stupid to give privileges to anyone in Hungary on the basis of his religious affiliation. . . . The constitutional people of Hungary [i.e., those with political rights] are neither Roman Catholic nor the Orthodox Catholics, but the Hungarian nobility."[11] In contrast to the relative religious toleration obtained within the nobility, social relations with other classes, even between the various strata of the nobility, were considerably strained if not entirely unheard of.[12] As a result, the occasional voice urging the integration of the Jews such as János Nagyváthy's frequently cited pamphlet of 1790, *A tizenkilenczedik században élt igaz magyar hazafinak örömórái* (A nineteenth-century true Hungarian patriot's hours of happiness)—"We have no reasons to exclude the Jewish people from society," he wrote—remained largely a dead letter with no possible social implications.[13] Though some of the intellectual preconditions of a "neutral" or "semineutral society" such as religious tolerance may have been met in Hungary, its social preconditions were not. No neutral society emerged in Hungary. On the one hand, no wealthy or intellectual stratum among Hungarian Jewry as yet sought social satisfaction outside the boundaries of traditional Jewish society, and on the other, given the rigid social divisions of Hungarian society, it was inconceivable that even its enlightened elements would welcome Jews as their social equals.[14] Take for example Ignác Martinovics, the leader of the Jacobin conspiracy in Hungary who raised the argument against the institution of the nobility by noting that nowadays even rich Jews, along with other dregs of society, could aspire to ennoblement. He wrote in his political cathecism, composed for the revolutionary Society of Liberty and Equality in 1794: "What is the origin of this institution? . . . The world in past times thought it a great merit to kill people in a knightly fashion, [therefore] only soldiers could become nobles. Nowadays, the usurer merchant, money-changer, rich Jew, useful spy, wealthy beer-brewer and the majestic, imperial and apostolic whorehouse owner can become one too."[15] The absurdity of a Jew attaining social equality as a nobleman was so patent that it served as a clinching argument for the abolition of this much degraded institution. The Haskalah in Hungary was thus not provided with a concrete reality of social rapprochement upon which its ideology of social change could be based; hence the double significance of German Jewry as both the source of ideas and as a point of reference of an alternative social reality for the Jews in Hungary.

In the absence of a "neutral society," its function was partially filled in Hungary, as elsewhere in the Habsburg Empire, by a political surrogate, the state. Under Joseph II, it was the state and its bureaucracy who now became the standard bearers of the Enlightenment;[16] here, unlike in Prussia, legislation preceded and initiated social change among the Jews with far-reaching implications in determining the actual impact of the German Haskalah in Hungary.

Given the limited resources of the Haskalah in Hungary, the intervention of the state must have been seen as heaven-sent to a *maskil* such as Peter Beer. For instance, by 1790 he could have noted with satisfaction that in the past decade almost in every sizable *kehillah*— and often even in remarkably small communities, some with less than 200 Jews—Jewish *Normalschulen* had been created and that more Jewish children during this time had received secular education in "backward" Hungary (about 2,000 according to one estimate) than in the heartland of the Haskalah, Germany.[17]

On the other hand, it was the vision of the state, not of the Haskalah, which was being implemented. In effect, the state coopted *maskilim* into its bureaucratic apparatus—mainly as school teachers—neutralized them and substituted for the Haskalah its own program of change in its stead. This is apparent from the different reception accorded to the two programs by representatives of traditional society. Rabbi Ezekiel Landau and Rabbi David Tevele of Lissa vilified the educational platform of the Haskalah as embodied in Naftali Herz Wessely's *Divrei Shalom Ve'emet*. They perceived it correctly as a threat to traditional education; the curriculum of the state's *Normalschule*, on the other hand, was clearly something which could be accommodated.

> How great are his [the Emperor's] works—exclaimed R. Tevele—and how precious is his kindness, for indeed all parents wish to provide their children with an education in every type of wisdom, science and craft. . . . Our children shall study the sciences as an adornment. . . . [Wessely] has interpreted the thoughts of his mighty and wise Majesty, the Emperor, in light of his own schemes.[18]

It is ironical that although the *maskilim* were probably correct in their assessment that the strategy of the state was more or less in line with their own aims to bring about a thorough transformation of traditional society, the specific tactics of the state in the early years of the 1780s actually favored the traditionalist interpretation. I will give two examples.

First, the nature of the curriculum. Joseph II's notoriously skeptical attitude toward the usefulness of higher education and his emphasis on the utilitarian aspects of elementary instruction were much more in harmony with the instrumental bent of Rabbi Tevele and Rabbi Ezekiel Landau than with the ambitious course of study outlined by Wessely. The Josephinian elementary school system aimed primarily at imparting very basic skills, essentially no more than the three *r*'s: reading (both German and Latin characters), writing, and arithmetic which were taught only nine hours weekly in the first year and fifteen during the second.[19]

The second example concerns the sequence of the study. Wessely and other *maskilim* favored teaching the child secular subjects first and only later religious studies. This point struck at the very foundations of traditional educational values and both rabbis fiercely attacked it in the sermons. The chief inspector of the Bohemian school-system, Ferdinand Schulstein, reporting on the talks he had with Rabbi Ezekiel Landau and the heads of Bohemian Jewry in the fall of 1781, noted:

> They believe that because small Jewish children must study their religion before attending German schools, that Jewish youth are not ready to attend the German schools before reaching their tenth year.[20]

The rabbi's request was met at the recommendation of Schulstein. The Prague school served as the model for the Hungarian Jewish school system and it was probably for this reason that the inauguration of the school in Pressburg was marked by public celebrations and a sermon of thanksgiving by the rabbi—much the same as it had in Prague.[21]

However, the enactment of the 1789 *Judenpatent* for Galicia, which reflected the radical turn Joseph II's policy had taken toward the second half of his reign, dissolved the traditionalists' illusions about the state's intentions; it was clear that the Habsburg state was bent on carrying out a far-reaching program of social change inimical to the values of traditional society.[22] With reference to the question of the order of study, paragraph 12 of the Galician Patent stated:

> No young person will be allowed to study Talmud unless he can produce a certificate from the German school teacher that he has properly attended the German school and has profited from its instruction.

Small wonder that the third point of Galician Jewry's petition of grievances to Leopold in 1790 objected to the early age at which children were obligated to commence their secular studies, leaving no time for Jewish learning. The Galician Jews argued that secular schooling should start only at the age of ten.[23]

The 1789 Galician Patent was slated for extension to the other Habsburg provinces as well,[24] and only Joseph II's untimely death in 1790 prevented its application. Of all the Jewries of the empire, Hungarian Jewry was especially spared further interference in its internal affairs thanks to the regained autonomy of the Hungarian Estates. Faced with the Hungarian nobility's threat of rebellion over his cavalier disregard of their traditional liberties, Joseph II rescinded on his deathbed all but three pieces of legislation concerning Hungary and had promised to curtail his "unconstitutional" meddling in the country's affairs.[25] With the withdrawal of state intervention, most of the Josephinian reforms in Hungary disappeared overnight. Without state coercion the Jewish school system collapsed. Only a generation later, in the teens of the nineteenth century, could the Hungarian Haskalah muster the resources necessary to reestablish schools once again in Pressburg and Pest, the two largest communities in Hungary.[26]

The collapse of the Josephinian schools, it must be stressed, was not due to any traditionalist *ideological* opposition to secular education.[27] As noted, the German Haskalah program was moderated by the state, and unlike in Galicia, the school system never achieved an autonomous status: supervision remained in the hands of the communal lay leadership and of the rabbinate. To ensure the acceptance of the schools, Schulstein wrote: "We do not press upon the Jews [any matter] before first convincing through joint deliberations the elders and the rabbis of its worthiness and kind intentions. They themselves are permitted to take part in the matter and to discuss it." The contrast with the thinly veiled threats which Herz Homberg, the supervisor of the Jewish schools in Galicia, levelled at the rabbis and communal leaders in his open circular of 1788 is noteworthy.[28] The primary cause of the breakdown of the school system in Hungary was probably due to the mundane fact that in the absence of effective state coercion, the schools proved to be a financial burden too cumbersome to shoulder voluntarily.[29]

The attitude of the rabbinate and lay leadership alike to the Haskalah was quite favorable, especially once its challenging programmatic sting had been removed, first by the state and later by the lack of resources. This cooptation by traditional elites of an emasculated variety of the German Haskalah—what Raphael Mahler sneeringly dismissed as no more than a belated "Hebrew humanism"—characterized Hungary and the Bohemian Lands. Members of the Jeitteles and Landau families in Prague, the Rosenthal family in Moór and Pest (in Galicia, the Kalir and Landau families in Brody), are good examples of wealthy, learned communal heads who almost all stemmed from rabbinic families and patronized the Haskalah. For example, David Wertheimer (1739–1817) of Vienna, a grandson of the Court Jew Samson Wertheimer, belonged to the elite of European Jewry. He was one of the founders of the Viennese *Chevra Kadisha* in 1763 and a *Vertreter* of the Viennese Jews from 1791. He is listed on the subscription lists of the 1783 *Biur* and Avigdor Glogau's *Chotem Tochnit* (Vienna, 1797) as well as for six copies of Homberg's *Ben-Jakir* (Vienna, 1814). The Viennese *maskil* Meir Obernik, who was a tutor in his house between 1787–1794, dedicated to Wertheimer his commentary and translation of *Joshua* and *Judges* (Vienna, 1792). Wertheimer's reputation as both a pious talmudic scholar and as one versed in the sciences is attested by Homberg's fulsome dedication to the second edition of *Imre Shefer* (Vienna, 1815).[30] The typical carriers of the Haskalah in these provinces form a continuous spectrum of social types from the *maskil hatorani* to his patron, the wealthy *lamdan*, to the *rav hamaskil hechacham hakollel*, who willingly grants his approbation to Haskalah works. The boundaries between rabbinic and Haskalah cultures were not sharply defined in Hungary and the Bohemian provinces. Significantly in these lands the Haskalah was welcomed without abandoning appreciation for traditional rabbinic culture—indeed, several *maskilim* tried their hand at writing responsa and novellae.[31] Criticism of the rabbinate in these areas was tempered with respect, in part probably because of the relative openness of rabbinic culture to extra-talmudic interests, a phenomenon that was certainly apparent by the middle of the eighteenth century.[32] One would be hard pressed to come up with a Bohemian, Moravian, or Western Hungarian rabbi at the turn of the century who did not display an intellectual curiosity concerning "external studies," be it medieval Jewish philosophy, grammar, the sciences, in fact all the shibboleths so dear to the radical Haskalah's criticism of rabbinic culture.

Take for example the rabbis of Obuda and Pest and the members of their rabbinic courts at the turn of the century. Rabbi Moses Münz of Brody (ca. 1750–1831), elected rabbi of Obuda in 1789, gave approbations to, among others, the 1818 edition of the *Biur* and to Aaron Chorin's *Emek Hashaveh* (1803). Not only did he also approve Eliah Hurwitz's encyclopaedic *Sefer Habrit* (1797), he was one of the book's distributors as well. Rabbi Wolf Boskowitz (1740–1818), briefly rabbi in Pest from 1795 to 1796, was one of the most acute talmudic scholars of his time and the head of some of the larger yeshivot in Moravia and Hungary. He had gained some familiarity with secular studies to the extent that he even instructed some of the pupils of his yeshiva in the natural sciences. One of them, Rabbi Shimon Oppenheimer (1751–1851), who

himself later became a member of the Pest rabbinic court, composed a
book on astronomy, *Amud Hashachar* (Prague, 1789), expressly attributing
his knowledge of the sciences to studies with Rabbi Wolf, his master.
Rabbi Israel Wahrmann (1755–1826), rabbi of Pest since 1799, was one
of the moving forces behind the establishment of a communal school
along German lines. He corresponded with David Frankel of Cassel, the
editor of *Sulamith,* for advice on the school curriculum, recalling the
seventeenth-century critique of Rabbi Horowitz of the traditional Ashkenazic educational system. Rabbi Azriel Brill (1778–1853) served as a
teacher in the Obuda *Normalschule* before becoming a member of the
Pest rabbinic court. He composed, among others, a brief work on
Hungarian geography *Ein Ha'aretz* (Buda, 1821), and a descriptive historic
essay on the Second Temple in his *Hadrat Kodesh* (Buda, 1827). Rabbi
Moses Kunitzer (1774–1837), member of the Pest rabbinic court and
rabbi of the small community of Buda, was the most remarkable of this
group; he typified the uncertain demarcation between rabbinic culture
at its most open and the Haskalah. He composed the first Hebrew play
in Hungary, *Beit-Rabbi* (Vienna, 1805). His preface, a historic biography
of Rabbi Judah Hannasi; his *Ben Jochai* (Vienna, 1815), a magisterial
study in defense of the traditional authorship of the *Zohar;* and his
unusual collection of responsa, *Hamazref,* 2 vols. (Vienna, 1820–Prag,
1857) are all works which earn him a niche among the pioneers of
Wissenschaft des Judenthums.[33]

Men such as Eleasar Fleckles, Samuel Landau, and Samuel Leib
Kauders in Bohemia; Mordechai Banet, Joachim Deutschmann, and
Nechemiah Trebitsch in Moravia; Moses Münz, Wolf Boskowitz, and
Moses Perls in Hungary, all prominent rabbis and heads of talmudic
academies, are illustrative of this tendency which I am tempted to label
a sort of "rabbinic haskalah," with a small *h*.[34] These rabbis were almost
all sympathetic toward moderate Haskalah. I endorse Moshe Samet's
claim that with a handful of notable exceptions, it would be unusual to
find a rabbi in these lands in the first decades of the nineteenth century
who did not show appreciation of the *Biur;* and this applied even to
disciples of its most vigorous opponent, Rabbi Moses Sofer.[35]

Perhaps the fact that this was the one region where yeshivot still
flourished during this crucial transition period[36] played an important
role in muting the potential conflict. Yeshivot played the unforeseen role
of Haskalah centers par excellence—when and where else did the cream
of Jewish youth have the opportunity to encounter each other so intensively
and to devote their time exclusively to intellectual pursuits? At the same
time, future *maskilim* were exposed here to the best traditional rabbinic
culture had to offer. Isaac Mayer Wise's description of the open culture

of these yeshivot in the 1820s and 1830s is also relevant to the previous generation, and despite his contrary claim, to some of the more important Hungarian yeshivot such as those headed by Rabbi Wolf Boskowitz and Rabbi Moses Perls:

> There was not in a Bohemian Yeshibah that bigotry, as in Hungary and elsewhere, that the students were prohibited from reading belletristical works, or that it was considered a crime to know Ibn Ezra's Commentary to the Bible, or Maimonides' *Moreh Nebuchim.* On the contrary, it was considered an accomplishment to have read Schiller's, Goethe's, Lessing's, or Wieland's works, and the young man spent considerable time in philosophic theological books, such as *Kusari, Moreh, Chobath,* etc. We remember distinctly that we had formed a secret club for the study of *Cabalah,* and we met for this purpose three times a week from nine to twelve P.M., but when our old master found out the secret of our club, he earnestly exhorted us not to spend our time with such impracticable study, calculated to make young men bigots and phantasts. He said it would be better for us to read Moses Mendelssohn's, Arbarbanel's, or De Rossi's works.[37]

This harmonizing tendency so characteristic of the Haskalah in this region is captured in the title page etching of a 1793 eulogy on Rabbi Ezekiel Landau by the *maskil* Joseph Ephrati of Troplowitz. The revered rabbi is depicted in the world to come, rushing into the welcoming arms of none other than Moses Mendelssohn![38]

One last point concerns the tone of the Hungarian Haskalah. Its moderate tone was in no small part due to the lack of a dynamic opposition movement such as Hassidism in Galicia. (The clash with Rabbi Moses Sofer in Pressburg [see below] took place only after 1810 and at least for a decade had a contained, local character.) In Hungary neither the shrill, embattled voice of Galicia nor the radical content of the German Haskalah prevailed. It was to Bohemia and Moravia that the Hungarian *maskil* turned, especially to Prague, which served to mediate and moderate the militancy of Berlin.[39] While direct contact with Berlin as we have seen was very unusual, at one time or another almost every Hungarian *maskil* of note maintained correspondence with or visited Baruch Jeitteles, the undisputed leader of the Prague Haskalah (and typically, the head of a yeshiva as well).[40] In the Bohemian Lands, thanks to the survival of the Josephinian school system up until 1848, the aspirations of the Haskalah and actual developments moved apace— there was no frustrating gap to spur on a crusade. In Hungary, the absence of these schools created conditions that left much to be desired from the point of view of the Haskalah. Nevertheless, because of the power of Prague to serve as a center and a point of reference for the Haskalah in Hungary, Hungarian *maskilim* were content to adopt its

וילך ויפגשהו בהר אלהים וישק לו

בשבעה עשר לחורש אייר ואני על נהר מאָלוי, היתה עלי
יד ה׳ וארא והנה נפש אדונינו יחזקאל הלוי מרחפת
אל מזל פתח גן עדן, ונפש בן מנחם הופיעה לקראתה, ויהי כי
הכירה נפש הרב אותה, ותפול על צוארה ותחבקנה ותאמר :

פה ידיד ה׳ וידידי ! פה, במקום אשר לא תשורני עין בער וחסר
לב, פה אחבקך ואשקך בכל אות נפשי · — אהה, עד אן
תכבד עין ישראל !

כה דברה נפש הרב, ותאוחז ביד בן מנחם, ותלכנה יחדיו
מושיהות אשה את רעיתה, בין צבאות מלאכי מעל, עד
בואנה עד מטמון רב טוב, מנת כל תום דרך ·

איכונוגרפיה של ההשכלה ההרמוני־זאטורית: משה מנדלסון ור׳ יחזקאל לנדאו נפגשים
בעולם הבא. רמז לפגישת אהרן ומשה בשמות ד: כז, ומעניין שרי לנדאו מזוהה כאן עם
אהרן, איש רודף שלום.

המקור: יוסף אפרתי מטרופלוביץ, אלון בכות, וינה תקנ״ג, השער.

sanguine tone. Instead of referring to their own dismal reality and developing their own specific style and ideology, Hungarian *maskilim* failed to develop an independent cultural center. Hungary, despite its much larger Jewish population, remained but a satellite of the neighboring Bohemian lands.

The role of mediator between Germany and Hungary played by Prague in the diffusion of the Haskalah, was assumed by Vienna in the spread of Reform.[41] Not that Vienna was the only channel whereby Reform reached Hungary. Aside from the curious case of Marcus Nissa Weiss,[42] a former *Normalschule* teacher in Ungvár who had advocated religious reform as early as 1802, it should be recalled that three Hungarians— Aaron Chorin, rabbi of Arad, Moshe Kunitz, the future *dayan* of Pest and rabbi of Buda, and the mysterious Eliezer Liebermann, apparently the former *dayan* in the northern community of Hummene all played key roles in the Berlin and Hamburg temple controversies. In the history of Hungarian Jewry they are significant not so much in determining the future of Reform in Hungary—and this applies even to the indefatigable Chorin—as in serving as rallying symbols of heresy for the Orthodox and perhaps as reminders of that deadend in the historic development of the Reform movement, the halachically justified innovation.[43] Not Hungarian, but German stimuli bestirred them to activity and German conditions provided the fertile soil for the realization of their ideas.

If not in laying the ideologic foundations of Hungarian Reform, Chorin did play an important pioneering role in the dissemination of German Reform in Hungary. Already in 1811, quite soon after the Westphalian consistory issued its *Synagogenordnungen,* a Hungarian correspondent proudly reported in *Sulamith*:

> In our land, too, there are many Israelites who have a sense and feeling for good and for betterment and who can properly appreciate the institutions of the Westphalian Consistory. A few weeks ago, for instance, R. Aaron Churiner, rabbi of Arad, performed the marriage ceremony for an Israelite couple *within* the synagogue after he had first held on the previous Sabbath a very appropriate public speech in which he fittingly explained the beauty and the usefulness of the Consistory's directives.[44]

Despite these autochthonous carriers, developments in Vienna were even more important in channeling German currents to Hungary. Direct commercial relations between Hungary and Germany were nearly nonexistent in the first third of the nineteenth century, thus enhancing the function of Vienna as economic and cultural mediator between the two countries. A glance at the composition of Hungary's trading partners in

TABLE 1
The Composition of Hungary's Foreign Trade, 1819–1828

Hungary's Trading Partners

Habsburg Hereditary Lands	Imports %	Exports %
Lower Austria (Vienna)	43.00	56.00
Moravia	26.80	21.00
Bohemia	0.00	0.50
Galicia	7.70	3.40
Brody	0.00	0.05
Other Habsburg lands	5.90	10.40
	83.40	91.35
Germany		
Prussia	0.50	1.10
Saxony	0.24	0.60
Southern Germany	0.60	1.00
	1.34	2.70
Other Countries		
Ottoman Empire	15.10	4.00
Poland and Russia	0.05	1.10
Cracow	0.02	0.30
Italian lands	0.60	0.50
	15.77	5.90
Total	100.50	99.50

Source: Gyula Mérei, "A magyar királyság külkereskedelme, 1815–1848" [Hungarian monarchy's foreign trade, 1815–1848], in *Magyarország története,* 10 vols. (Budapest, 1980), vol. 5, pp. 252–53, table 3.

the decade of 1819–1828 (see Table 1) illustrates the extent to which Hungary was cut off from the German lands.

The total volume of trade in this decade came to about 79 million fl. C.M.—38.2 million fl. imports and 40.8 million fl. exports. The largest share by far, roughly half the total, was garnered by Vienna. Moravia, with almost a quarter of the Hungarian market, and the Ottoman Empire with its impressive transit trade (ca. 10 percent of the total) came next as Hungary's strongest trading partners. Trade with Galicia (5.5 percent of the total volume) and Bohemia (almost nil) was surprisingly weak. As to Germany, only 2.7 percent of Hungary's exports and less than 1.4 percent of its imports were conducted with Prussia, Saxony, and the southern German lands.

TABLE 2
Number of Jewish Merchants Attending the Leipzig Fairs in 1821, by Country of Origin

	New Year's Fair	Easter Fair	Michaelis Fair
Vienna, Bohemia, Moravia	54	84	76
Galicia and Brody	44	90	92
Poland	68	173	116
Russia	4	4	29
Hungary	0	1	0
Others (mainly Germany)	635	1,307	992
Total	805	1,659	1,305

Source: Richard Markgraf, *Zur Geschichte der Juden auf den Messen in Leipzig von 1664-1839* (Bischofswerda, 1894), pp. 21-35.

In the absence of economic ties between the two countries, one of the primary channels of cultural diffusion was effectively blocked off. Personal commercial contacts between East European Jewry and Germany, especially at the Leipzig fairs, played a crucial role in the eastward dissemination of modern German trends. As repeatedly emphasized in Jewish historiography, it was at these fairs that Russian and Galician merchants were first exposed to the Haskalah—Nachman Krochmal's father is a frequently cited case[45]—and later, to Reform. Hungarian Jews, on the other hand, ceased to attend the German fairs from the latter half of the eighteenth century.[46] Direct trading ties between Germany and Hungary were severed in the mid-1750s as a result of Maria Theresa's tariff war against Prussia and to a lesser extent Saxony, and of her punitive domestic economic policy aimed at the recalcitrant Hungarian Estates.[47] Trade flowed through Vienna, which became Hungary's economic bottleneck. In 1789 alone, some 10,500 Jews from the entire monarchy came to Vienna on business,[48] of whom, in contrast to the Leipzig fairs, many were Hungarians.

Not only economically but culturally as well, Vienna increasingly assumed the role of prime mediator between Hungary and Germany. And it was in Vienna, in the early teens of the nineteenth century that an aggressive campaign for educational and religious reforms was launched which was rapidly to spill over into the neighboring Hungarian communities.

The guiding spirit behind this offensive was the energetic *Vertreter* of Viennese Jewry, the wealthy wholesale merchant Michael Lazar Biedermann.[49] He was spurred on by his bookkeeper, the *maskil* Leopold Harzfeld, who significantly also served as the Viennese Hebrew book censor. Harzfeld was Biedermann's link with Jewish intellectual circles in Berlin as a police agent with a nose for conspiracy reported. "During his stay in Berlin, the [Reform] society had assured itself of [the services] of the bookkeeper of Herr Biedermann, Harzfield, as its most active agent in Vienna through considerable payments; he knew how to win over even his very Orthodox boss."[50] Harzfeld was in close contact with Chorin and later supplied the German translation to Chorin's trilingual pamphlet, *Ein Wort zu Seiner Zeit* (Vienna, 1820).[51] Biedermann too had at one time planned to have Chorin installed as rabbi of Vienna and had sought to introduce reforms along Westphalian lines. Later, burning with enthusiasm for the new Reform services he had attended at the Leipzig fair, he urged that a separate temple on the model of Hamburg and Berlin be erected.[52]

Biedermann became the primary conduit of German innovations, rapidly assuming the role of patron saint not only of Viennese Reform, but also of Pressburg and perhaps Pest reforms as well. Urging the establishment of a modern school in Pressburg, one hopeful wrote: "By the way, I also count on the charitable and generous contributions of many Viennese and Pest inhabitants who possess the Pressburg *incolat* [right of residency]" expressly naming Hermann Biedermann, Michael Lazar's brother and partner.[53] The close family and business ties which intimately linked the economic elites of all three communities and the oligarchic nature of the *kehillot,* greatly facilitated the diffusion and imposition of change. The Breisach family, for example, originally from Eisenstadt, moved first to Pressburg in the last third of the eighteenth century and then branched out to Pest and Vienna. In the 1820s, members of this family occupied leading positions in all three communities and played important roles in advocating reforms. Salomon Breisach (1775–1835), for instance, was one of the *Vertreters* of Viennese Jewry from 1816 to 1828; his cousin Isaac (1758–1835), who had been a member of the Pressburg *Vorstand* from 1781 to 1795, moved to Pest, and served as one of the heads of the Pest community for over twenty-seven years (1806–1833). Isaac's son-in-law, Hermann Biedermann (1774–1816), played an energetic role in the affairs of the Viennese, Pressburg, and Pest communities and felt equally attached to all three as the philantrophic provisions of his last will and testament indicate. Isaac's son, Wolf (d. 1827), headed the Pressburg community at least from 1820 until 1827 and as we shall see, almost succeeded in suppressing the yeshiva and imposing reforms from above. The family probably reached the height of its influence in 1826, when father and son were members of the 8-man delegation representing Hungarian Jewry at the 1825-26 Diet.[54]

Pest was a bloodless victory for the reformers. As early as 1810, a correspondent from Pest reported in *Sulamith* on plans of Rabbi Israel Wahrmann and the heads of the community to establish a school in accordance with the *Zeitgeist*. The community *pinkas* noted that the curriculum was to be entrusted in care of Wahrmann, who was to contact "Berlin or other large communities with well-ordered schools" and present a proposal before the communal representatives. As already noted, Rabbi Wahrmann did correspond on the subject of the projected school with David Fränkel, the editor of *Sulamith* and consistory-secretary at Cassel. The school was inaugurated in 1814 amidst public festivities and was honored by the presence of a number of non-Jewish officials and notables.[55] Religious reforms were not far off.

In Pressburg, the fight was bitter. From about 1810 until 1826 Rabbi Moses Sofer, the champion of Hungarian Orthodoxy, was fighting a losing battle against the *maskilim* in his own community. Especially around the time of the *Hamburg Tempelstreit* he was forced to yield to his opponents step by step. Wolf Breisach, the head of the Reform camp, captured the leadership of the *kehillah* at about this time, and with the moral and financial support of Biedermann immediately applied himself to implementing a radical Haskalah program: a *Primärschule* was created despite the vehement opposition of the rabbi in 1820; a society for productivization followed in 1821 (although apparently this project did receive the blessing of the rabbi); and the crowning achievement, the yeshiva, the largest in Europe at the time, was shut down in 1826. There were clear indications that religious reforms were in the offing: Chorin came to Pressburg to lend his professional advice and a certain S— [Skreinka?] even preached modern sermons to a congregation of Reform sympathizers.[56] The Reform camp perhaps would have triumphed had not a droll act of fate intervened and saved the day for the Orthodox.[57]

For the course that the Reform movement was to take in Hungary, however, the decisive step was the invitation of Isaac Noah Mannheimer to Vienna. Mannheimer had served his apprenticeship as a preacher in the Reform temples of Copenhagen, Berlin, Hamburg and Leipzig. While he had already given a sermon on a brief stay in Vienna as early as 1821, his summons to the post of *Prediger* came only in 1824.[58] In the impressive new synagogue in Seitenstettengasse, however, Mannheimer made a conscious decision to tone down the more radical aspects of German Reform.[59] In effect, what came to be known as the Viennese rite was little different from the Westphalian reforms of the previous generation. Its most characteristic features—the new type of uplifting sermon in pure German, a choir, *chupa* in the synagogue, the *bima* up front, stress on decorum, etc.—were, unlike the more radical Berlin and Hamburg reforms, readily reconcilable with the *Shulchan Aruch*.[60]

Mannheimer's moderating influence on the direction of Viennese Reform can best be appreciated by noting that for several years prior to his coming plans had been afoot to set up a temple with services modelled along the lines of Hamburg and Berlin Reform. Elieser Liebermann, in his prolonged sojourn in Vienna in 1819, certainly had this purpose in mind. Around February 1819 he began a sweeping tour of various communities in Bohemia, Moravia, and Hungary, stirring up along the way a hornet's nest of activity among the Orthodox. His destination was Vienna, where he stayed about a half a year, returning to Berlin only in August 1819. A police report noted that he had spent several years in northern Germany and was now traveling about the monarchy as an "emissary of the Reform party," with the intention of founding a journal, *Siona,* to propagate his views.[61]

Whatever contribution Liebermann may have actually made toward the introduction of Reform in Vienna, by 7 January 1820 the *Vertreter,* among them Biedermann and Salomon Breisach, submitted a petition to the Lower Austrian government, stating that Viennese Jewry requested "to introduce religious services after the example of their religious brethren in several cities in Germany, namely Berlin, Hamburg, etc., where [reforms] had been felt similarly necessary." German prayers, choir singing accompanied by an organ, reading the Torah without chanting, an uplifting sermon delivered in pure German, decorum, etc., all hallmarks of the new German temples, were to be instituted in a separate synagogue erected for this purpose. Appropriate prayerbooks and songbooks were available from the Hamburg and Berlin Reform societies.[62] A prompt— by Austrian terms a very prompt—response came from none other than the emperor. Two weeks later, in a decree issued on 22 January 1820, Franz ordered that henceforth no rabbi was to be installed unless he could display a "well-grounded knowledge of the philosophical sciences," and that "the prayers, religious exercises and instructions in the syngogue," should be held "in German or in the national tongue."[63] Thus several years later, Mannheimer in his moderation was swimming headlong against not one but two currents: government policy and mainstream Reform. Furthermore, he not only abandoned the model of the Hamburg services as too radical, but also succeeded in prevailing upon the Viennese not to establish a separate Reform temple, thereby preserving the unity of his community.[64] In time, the Viennese *Chortempel* became, as Gotthold Salomon had predicted in a letter to Mannheimer, the norm . . . for several countries.[65] It was this moderate version of Reform which was adopted in rapid succession by Pest (1827), Prossnitz (1832), Prague (1832), Lemberg (1846), Cracow, and Odessa.[66] Its diffusion to these regional centers and in turn to the smaller communities took place in much the same textbook fashion as Reform had spread from Leipzig to Vienna.

> The local Temple here is surely a child of the Viennese [reported a correspondent from Lundenburg, Moravia]; the constant traffic of local merchants with the Austrian capital has brought about the acceptance of the new mode of religious services by the local Jewry.[67]

It was Gabriel Ullmann who brought the Viennese rite to Pest. Enchanted by the newly inaugurated services in Vienna, this dynamic young leader of the community became the driving force behind establishing of a *Chorschule* in Pest. With like-minded youths he set up in 1827 the Chessed Neurim Verein, with services conducted in a separate synagogue. Upon his election to the Pest *Vorstand* on May 1830, he immediately raised the status of the synagogue of the youth society to a *Gemeindesynagoge,* and simultaneously, in a move characteristic of the arrogance of his paternalistic caste, he worked energetically to stamp out all rival, independent *minyanim.*[68]

The Pest *Chorschule,* the first to be modelled on Vienna, was initially a close imitation of the mother temple. Mannheimer's advice was sought on the choice of a *Prediger* and a *chazan;* Joseph Bach and Eduard Denhoff, both local men, were installed in the respective posts. Bach, who officiated as *Prediger* of the Chessed Neurim Verein for the next quarter of a century, slavishly imitated Mannheimer's, Salomon's, and Kley's sermons. The rather inflated title of his first sermon says it all:

> Homiletische Erstlinge, als Muster einiger religiös-moralisches Vorträge zur Erbauung und Veredlung des sittlichen Gefühls vor einer angesehen Versammlung mosaischen Confession in der, nach dem gegenwärtig in der k.k. Residenzstadt Wien bestehendcn mosaischen Ritus, umgestalteten Chessed-Neurim Synagoge (Pest, 1827).[69]

With the arrival in 1836 of Löw Schwab to occupy the Pest rabbinate, an interesting departure from the Viennese model took place. In his negotiations with Salomon Rosenthal defining the spheres of his authority and the extent of his rabbinic duties, Schwab referred expressly to the state of affairs in Vienna and dismissed the possibility that the office be confined to the restricted functions of "the rabbi in Vienna" (Eleasar Horowitz). He insisted that in Pest the office retain its traditional integrity and not have its functions split between a *Prediger* and a sort of *shatz-*

matz—a tendency then at its height in Germany and Vienna.[70] Schwab further demanded that both the traditional and Reform synagogues be placed under his authority and that he retain the prerogative to preach on a regular basis at the *Chorschule*. His German sermons, he cautioned Rosenthal, were not modelled on Mannheimer's or Salomon's style:

> Accordingly, my religious-moral lectures do not at all follow the rules of the *Kanzelrhetorik* styled speeches which comply perfectly with strict aesthetic demands. Rather they weave together explanations of many Biblical and Talmudic passages and yet are nevertheless clearly connected without being deformed by over-subtle exegesis. They are as far from benighted pietism as from lax worldly morals, yet appropriately considerate of the well-educated audience.

Nor would he preach every Sabbath, since not only was he a "talmudic rabbi" who consecrated most of his time to the study of Talmud and *Poskim,* but he also intended to devote himself to public affairs and "in consequence, I cannot burden myself with more than one monthly sermon."

Rosenthal hastened to allay his fears, reassuring Schwab first, that blissful harmony obtained among the devotees of both synagogues—"so what if there are two synagogues?"—second, that his sphere of authority would extend to the *Chorschule* with the stipulation that the *Prediger* Bach be allowed to continue to preach after his own fashion, and third, that he need deliver a sermon only once a month alternating between the two congregations. "And as to the *drasha* that you will preach at the old synagogue," the Orthodox Rosenthal added, "we neither request nor desire to hear it in German, rather begin by expounding on a topic of *halachah be'pilpul,* by resolving some problem, and afterwards go on to a deliver a moral exhortation couched in a mixed Yiddish and German language according to our preference." The pure German sermon is to be reserved for the new synagogue, where "many Christians, learned men and clergy" drop in to visit.[71]

Despite this divergence from the Viennese norm it was clear that Mannheimer's deliberately modified reforms were decisive in determining the course of what became known as *Neology* in Hungary. "The Reform communities in Hungary," wrote Leopold Löw summing up the progress of Reform in 1867, "follow the Viennese rite; they are about ten in number."[72] The impact of the second generation of Reform thinkers, men like Geiger whose ideology was an outgrowth of the *Wissenschaft des Judenthums,* was truly negligible. Certainly the handful of "progressive rabbis"—Leopold Löw being the most outstanding example—read with enthusiasm and even contributed to the growing body of Reform literature, but their relative weight in Hungarian neology both in numbers and influence was nowhere near that of their German colleagues. It was laymen, in this case the wealthy merchants who in an oligarchic fashion dominated their communities, who were instrumental in implementing the Viennese innovations, quite satisfied by what was contempuously dismissed by the ideologues as mere "cosmetic reforms."

The German rabbinic conferences of the 1840s, for instance, found little sympathetic hearing in Hungary. The laymen were as a rule uninterested, the rabbis, even those with Reform tendencies, too conservative. For example, when Zvi Hirsch Lehren of Amsterdam and Rabbi Jakob Ettlinger of Altona mounted the Orthodox counteroffensive to the rabbinic conferences, the rabbi of Pressburg, the *ktav sofer,* could suggest to Ettlinger in January 1845 that he approach Schwab to solicit an anti-Reform responsa for the forthcoming collection, *Torat Hakanaut.* Samuel Enoch, Ettlinger's right-hand man did indeed write Schwab about two months later, requesting his signature on the forthcoming circular protesting the Reform assemblies.[73] Leopold Löw, probably the most dogmatic of Hungarian reformers in *Vormärz,* clearly aligned himself with the conservative wing of the Reform movement. In the summer of 1845, for example, he wrote S.L. Rappaport (ShIR) asking his opinion on the playing of the organ on the Sabbath by a Jew: "Even though in theory, to my mind it is clearly permissible, I would not wish to permit it in practice if . . . you should disagree with my opinion. And you should know . . . that I present my query only before two great men of our generation: to you . . . and to the great rabbi, R. Zacharias Frankel." Indeed, Löw's name is to be found among those who proposed to join Frankel's aborted *Theologen Versammlung* to be held in Dresden as a counterweight to the more radical rabbinic assemblies.[74]

The conservatism of Hungarian Reform did not escape German observers. "There, culture has not yet reached the stage which has been attained in Germany"; wrote one reviewer in 1845, commenting on the work of one of Hungary's more energetic lay reformers, "It is still as it was by us at the beginning of the century."[75] It must have come as a surprise, when a scant three years later, during the heady days of the Hungarian Revolution of 1848, radical reforms along the lines of the Frankfurt *Reformfreunde* and the Berlin *Reformverein* were introduced in rapid succession in breakaway congregations not only in Pest but in several provincial towns such as Arad, Pécs, Nagy Becskerek, Lugos, and Nagy Várad as well.[76] Now it was to Samuel Holdheim, one of the most radical men of German Reform, that the Arad group turned to obtain confirmation for their far-reaching reforms abolishing the Sabbath, *kashrut, mila,* etc., and again it was to Holdheim that the Pest Reform association sent Ignatz Einhorn in the fall of 1848 to study and bring back the very latest in Reform fashions. When the revolution collapsed in the summer of 1849 and Einhorn had to flee Hungary, his equally radical namesake, David Einhorn, *Landesrabbiner* of Mecklenburg-Schwerin, was called on to lead the short-lived Pest *Reformgenossenschaft.* (It was shut down by the order of the government in 1852.)[77]

In contrast to the religious turbulence which had marked the decade of the 1840s as one of the most exciting in the nineteenth century, the next two decades were a period of relative tranquility for German Reform. Probably the most important German contribution in these twenty years to Hungarian Reform was the establishment of the Breslau rabbinic seminary. During this time, an increasing number of Breslau graduates, men such as Alexander Kohut, became a much sought after commodity by Reform-minded congregations and came to fill important rabbinic positions. Even more important, until 1876, the year the Budapest seminary was inaugurated, Breslau served as a model for the Reform camp in its campaign to erect a similar, native institution which would turn out modern, academically trained rabbis. The establishment of a rabbinic seminary whether along the lines of Breslau or in antithesis to it, became in many ways the central issue in the violent confrontations of the 1860s in Hungary, not only between Neologues and the Orthodoxy, but among the Orthodox camp itself.[78]

Charting the diffusion of Reform from Germany raises the question of the role played by the time lag between the two Jewries. Clearly, German Jewry served as both model and precedent for Hungarian Jews. The German precedent, significantly narrowed and widened at the same time the range of choice open to Hungarian Jewry. It grew broader because German Jewry's historic experience of trial and error was available to Hungarian Jews to adopt or discard. The differentiation of the German Reform, a result of constant polemics both within and without the movement, had introduced a broad spectrum of opinion with subtle shadings and nuances. Hence the early Pest reformers could decide to adopt the more moderate Viennese rite and reject the Hamburg and Berlin models; the radical reformers in 1848, on the other hand, could opt for the extreme end of the spectrum and bridge a gap of what one observer pronounced as not less than fifty years in a mere three. The same selectivity applied to Reform institutions such as the new type of German sermon and the substitution of the *Prediger* for the rabbi. But Germany also narrowed Hungary's choices. By the time of Reform's dissemination, that same chaotic, groping process that marked the early history of the Reform movement had largely disappeared with its increasing institutionalization. Thus, once certain innovations—which from a historic perspective seem to have come about in a totally random fashion—

became identified in Germany as symbols of the Reform movement, they were judged no longer either by reformers or by the Orthodoxy in purely objective terms. How else are we to explain why precisely such an arbitrary innovation as the placement of the *bima* in the front of the synagogue came to assume in Hungary a role totally disproportionate of its aesthetic significance?[79]

Germany played the role of a trailblazer; it also made its more developed resources available to Hungary. Although German rabbis were rarely imported—David Einhorn, Wolf Meisels, and Esriel Hildesheimer were notable exceptions—their authority was invoked by Hungarian reformers in several key controversies.[80] Since polemic literature and *Wissenschaft* were scarce local products, Germany often provided the ideological rationale for Hungarian reforms whenever it was called for. But the most important asset of German Jewish life that Hungarian Reform could draw on was undoubtedly the German-Jewish press.

By around 1880, Hungarian Jewry was probably the largest German-speaking Jewish community in Europe. By this time Hungarian Jewry had both overtaken German Jewry in population—the Jewish population of Greater Hungary (including Transylvania and Croatia) stood at 638,310, that of Germany at 562,610—and was in addition sufficiently acculturated that German was certainly understood and spoken by a large sector of the population. Of course, there were regions in Hungary where the mother tongue was already Magyar, while in others it was still Yiddish and literacy in non-Hebrew characters was still very low. Only about one-third (223,450) of Hungarian Jewry in 1880 declared German to be their mother tongue, while as high as 57.5 percent declared it to be Magyar. Nonetheless, German was prevalent as a second language. As late as 1900, after several decades of intensive Magyarization, only 25 percent of Hungarian Jews stated that they knew no other language but Magyar; for the previous decades this percentage must have been much lower. If we recall that the urban population of Hungary had a sizable German community, and that German was spoken and read by every educated Hungarian, then it is easy to see why bi- and trilingualism was the rule.[81]

In the absence of a language barrier, the German Jewish press could and did play a crucial role in acquainting the Hungarian public not only with foreign developments but also with communal controversies at home. The oppressive isolation was now lifted as an enthusiast noted in his 1842 description of the impact of the *Allgemeine Zeitung des Judenthums* in Hungary:

> The Jew in Hungary [living] at times in far corners of the countryside found few opportunities to get to know his own element. The journal gives

a summary of the condition of the Jews in every known part of the world, wherever they may exist; out of it develop conceptions of a totality. Whereas previously the Jew hardly knew if he had a coreligionist in the next province, he learns today not only of his presence all over the world, but also of his condition, the level of his civilisation and his culture, as well as the manner in which he has begun to go forward and how he does from here on. Whereas previously everything was diffused so that one did not know about the other, Herr Phillipson joined it all into a whole, into a genuine Jewry.[82]

Indeed, just little over a decade and a half before, in 1826, Mannheimer could plead with Zunz to keep him informed, because "the state of Jewish affairs in Germany and without Germany is so distant that I myself have agreed to ask more than once *vesheeino yodeia lishol ata p'tach lo,* that is 'open for me' what news has stirred up in the last one and a half years, old which has become new, fresh which has become stale, the bud which was nipped, the living which has died."[83] Mannheimer's predicament was indicative of the tenuous nature of communications, largely restricted to personal correspondence in the decades prior to the advent of the German-Jewish press in the late 1830s. If someone as well connected as Mannheimer, residing in a metropolis like Vienna, could feel so cut off from German events, then certainly even in the larger Hungarian communities only a murky picture must have emerged of what was happening beyond the borders.

How widely read was the German-Jewish press in Hungary? German newspapers may not have always been available. The rabbi of Arad, Chorin, had written to Löw in 1841: "I do not get a chance to read the *Orient.*" And indeed, four years later, the journal was not readily found in the community. "The cultured folk of Arad have not even *one* copy of the *Orient?*" asked the incredulous editor in 1845. It should be recalled that the total circulation of the various German journals both within and outside Germany was not very high: *Der Israelit des neunzehnten Jahrhunderts* had 500 copies in 1848; *Der Orient,* 500 in 1850; *Allgemeine Zeitung des Judenthums, (AZdJ)* 700 in 1850. An official Austrian statistical publication placed the number of copies of *AZdJ* imported into the Habsburg Monarchy in 1841 as 32 for the first half of the year and 50 for the second.[84] Assuming that additional copies slipped by the censor's reach and that in time their number increased, at most a few hundred copies of all the Jewish newspapers combined could have reached Hungary. But as Jacob Toury has noted, there were surely more readers than the number of subscribers would lead us to believe. This was the era of reading societies which were formed precisely for the purpose of disseminating reading material to a wider public. Here, in the confines of the café or club, one copy could circulate among tens, if not hundreds of members.[85] Indeed, from the geographic spread of the Hungarian correspondents in the German journals it would seem that their diffusion in Hungary was quite extensive.

Orthodox Jews were aware early on of the importance and the influence of the German-Jewish press. In a petition to the government in 1850 Rabbi Meir Eisenstadt requested that immediate measures should be taken to prohibit the import of foreign Jewish publications and journals into Hungary. Journals such as the *AZdJ, Israelit des XIX. Jahrhunderts, Monatsschrift,* and countless other publications had inundated Hungary in "the last decade in hundreds of copies in a destructive torrent." They were the chief carriers of corruption, "sowing heresy and modernism" in the hearts of the young.[86]

The German press was often enlisted in local squabbles, the drawn out conflict in Pápa in the 1840s is a good example. Again the broad ideologic spectrum of the German-Jewish press ranging from radical Reform to Orthodox provided a wide variety of choice and helped Hungarian Jewry to establish boundaries and demarcate positions at home. With one notable exception it was not until the late 1850s that local newspapers began to appear, but even then the German journals continued to play an important part in the increasingly bitter struggle between the Orthodox and Neologs. That the language of the Hungarian-Jewish press remained largely German goes without saying.

A consequence of the availability of German precedent was that Hungarian Jewry did not necessarily have to replicate the exact historic experience of German Jewry: now stages could be skipped and sequences altered. Here I would like to return to the questions I raised with regard to the Haskalah: What happens when an ideology is transplanted into a different social setting? Is the meaning and significance of Reform the same in Hungary as in Germany? Does it fulfill the same historic function? And what is the specific weight of German Reform in the development of Neology, the Hungarian brand of Reform?

With Reform as with the Haskalah in Hungary the sequence of social reality and ideological response was out of joint. In Germany, Reform ideology and institutions were to a great extent the response to an already changing reality. In the 1830s and 1840s, but perhaps even in the teens, Reform appeared after a period of alienation and crisis had already set in. Leopold Zunz's description of the High Holiday services conducted at the Reform congregation in Berlin provides a vivid illustration:

> Yesterday or rather on Saturday I was at Jacobson's synagogue. People who in twenty years had nothing in common with Jews spent the entire day

there: men who believed that they had already been relieved of religious feeling, poured out tears of devotion; the majority of young people fasted.

In Vienna, too, estrangement from the traditional forms of worship motivated a desire for Reform services. As an 1820 memorandum to the government stated, "The majority participate only on the High Holidays, otherwise, however, they do not come to the synagogue, proof that they find no edification even there."[87] The epidemic of conversions in the vulnerable 1820s, and the oft-condemned phenomenon of religious indifference both pointed to the spiritual limbo in which German Jewry was suspended.

By the end of the 1830s the breakdown of traditional Jewish society in Germany was more or less a thing of the past. Key institutions—the autonomous *kehillah,* the rabbinate, the yeshivot, the *chadarim*—had been dramatically transformed. In Prussia, for instance, the state had begun to interfere with communal autonomy in the first half of the eighteenth century; the judicial powers of the rabbinate were severely curtailed already in the middle of the century.[88] Symptomatic of the decline of the traditional rabbinate in Germany was that the post of chief rabbi in the larger German communities in effect gradually "died out" along with their last incumbents around the turn of the century.[89] By 1840 most of the great German yeshivot had faded into oblivion.[90]

On the other hand, acculturation to the German environment, in admittedly its most elementary forms, was by then nearly complete. Although specific statistics on Jewish literacy around 1840 seem to be unavailable, from the high literacy of the still largely agrarian non-Jewish population (estimated by Carlo Cippola as over 70 percent before 1850 and close to 90 percent by 1860), one can infer that literacy among German Jews must have been very prevalent. For example, Posen Jewry, the most "backward" in Germany, had attained by 1871 about 78 percent literacy among the Jewish population over the age of ten.[91] In this region, secular schooling had become widespread if not universal by the 1840s. I estimate that in 1841 85-90 percent of school-age Jewish children attended school; by 1847, the ratio had risen to almost 94 percent. For the rest of Prussia the percentages approached 100 percent.[92] Posen's turning point had come when the government issued its 1833 Edict for the province—the last in a series, but this time most effective—demanding the suppression of the so-called *Winkelschulen* and the compulsory attendance of all Jewish children in elementary schools. Government intervention had been even more intensive earlier in the southern German states: compulsory education had been decreed in Baden in 1809, in the Grand Duchy of Hesse in 1815, in Bavaria in 1828, and in Würtemberg in 1828. By 1834 Würtemberg had already 38 functioning schools; Baden had 42 in 1842. In these regions where the proportion of Jews living in rural areas was very high, at times 80 percent and more, the state's educational reforms were not confined to the cities, but reached out to transform the countryside as well.[93]

Government intervention played an important role in the emergence of the modern rabbinate in almost all the German states with the notable exception of Prussia. Baden (1809), Bavaria (1813), Kurhessen (1823), Würtemberg (1828), and many other smaller principalities had in varying degrees stipulated academic studies and state examinations of some sort as prerequisites for rabbinic posts. These measures were remarkably effective in transforming the profile of the rabbinate in southern Germany: in 1847, 11 out of 44 rabbis in Bavaria and 6 out of 12 in Würtemberg had university degrees. The days of the traditional rabbi lacking any sort of formal secular education were numbered. In Würtemberg, for instance, 45 rabbis were dismissed in 1834 for failing to pass the new state examinations.

As Ismar Schorsch has shown, by 1847, 67 German rabbis and preachers had attained university degrees. This figure represented as much as 20 percent of the entire German rabbinate and doubtless an even higher proportion among the younger generation of rabbis. It should also be recalled that many others had also attended institutions of higher learning but without attaining the much-prized doctorate. That among these university-educated rabbis a handful were Orthodox is a strong indicator of the increasing discontent with the traditional training of the rabbinate even among Orthodox circles.[94]

In the last twenty years, there has been a tendency in German Jewish historiography to revise previous assessments of the rapid pace of modernization of German Jewry. The work of Jacob Toury and more recently of Steven Lowenstein as well as others has proved a useful corrective to undiscriminating generalizations about German Jewry. Emphasis has been placed on regional variations, on the rural character of much of German Jewry before 1870, on lingering traditional modes in the countryside. In *Vormärz,* much of the older generation still felt comfortable speaking Yiddish and reading and writing *jüdisch-deutsch,* German in Hebrew characters. Their sense of German national identity and their social integration into their German surroundings was proceeding at a slower rate than previously thought.[95]

While it is true that the cultural and socioeconomic profile of the German Jew had not yet merged with the stereotypic German patriot of Mosaic faith of a later era, the extent of the breakdown of traditional institutions in this admittedly transitional period should not be underestimated. I have already noted the changes which had taken place in education and the rabbinate. Further evidence can be marshalled from Jacob Toury's quantitative assessment of the extent of the abandonment of traditional religious observance and the relative strength of the Orthodoxy in German Jewry. Toury based his conclusions mainly on data from the end of the 1830s and the beginning of the 1840s; they can be taken, therefore, to reflect tendencies prevalent already by 1840. This is important, because the Reform movement in Germany moved into high gear in Germany after this date. Toury's figures, convincing on the whole, are eloquent proof of the widespread erosion of traditional observance. Slightly less than half of all German Jewry (45 percent, and outside of Posen, more than 55 percent) were no longer traditional.[96] If we recall that even in the overwhelmingly observant province of Posen literacy and secular education were well on the way to being universal, the progressive dissolution of traditional Jewish society in Germany should become readily apparent.

A comparison with the pace of modernization of Hungarian Jewry strengthens the impression that German Jewry had undergone far-reaching changes already before midcentury. In contrast, the social structure of Hungarian Jews favored the maintenance of a traditional society. Around 1840 a large proportion of the Jewish population—about one-third of the total—still lived in isolated clusters of one or two families in villages where the fabric of traditional life was left intact. Often even the towns were hardly touched by modern currents. Many had no communal secular educational institutions until well into the decade of the 1840s, and even by 1846, after several years of feverish Reform activity in Hungary, Leopold Löw could record no more than 29 communities with modern schools.[97] In terms of schooling and literacy, Jews in the most backward regions of Germany compared favorably with the most advanced sectors of Hungarian Jewry. As late as 1869, at most about 42 percent of Jewish children of school age attended school in Hungary, whereas attendance in Germany was nearly universal already in the previous generation.

The different level of acculturation attained by the two Jewries was also reflected in their rates of literacy. Even the Jews of Budapest, with one of the highest levels of literacy among Hungarian Jewry, registered in 1870 only 68.5 percent who could read and write in non-Hebrew characters, only slightly higher than the "backward" Jews of Posen. To gain the measure of a truly traditional society, one need only turn to Máramaros county in northeast Hungary, where as late as 1880 literacy was attained by only 15 percent of the Jewish population![98] That traditional cultural patterns were left undisturbed so long in Hungary was to no small degree the result of the lack of state interference in internal Jewish

affairs, a phenomenon close to unique in *Vormärz* Europe. Hungarian
Jews paid the central government in Vienna a fraction of the taxes
extracted from their brethren in the other Habsburg lands; they contributed
a much lower proportion of recruits to the army.[99] Hungary insisted on
its constitutional rights to be free of Viennese meddling and as a by-
product the Jewish community enjoyed a respite from government reform
plans. This was noted by Ignatz Jeitteles as early as 1811:

> For reasons which reside in its Constitution, Hungary has not kept in step
> especially in school affairs with the other lands of the Austrian Empire;
> Hungarian Jews have nearly no educational institutions.[100]

Traditional institutions, on the other hand, were experiencing a renaissance. In some communities much of the autonomy of the previous
century was successfully maintained thanks to this same absence of state
meddling; the rabbinate was in some respects more powerful than it had
been a hundred years before; the yeshivot flourished.[101]

It is true that a growing sense of religious indifference was noticeable
in the larger urban centers early in the century,[102] and there seems to
have been a steady trickle of conversions. But these developments did
not induce a sense of crisis which one found in Germany as the historic
background to Reform. Only in the third and fourth decades did reports
of public transgressions of the Sabbath begin to crop up. Even then most
of the violations—the *chatam sofer* could catalogue only scattered instances in an 1832 petition—were contained until the 1840s with the
aid of the local authorities. In a responsa dating probably from the 1820s,
the *chatam sofer* wrote to the community of Nagy Várad:

> And as to whether here in our community Pressburg there are those who
> would make light of the precepts, I am astonished at your inquiry! How
> could you even imagine that in a Jewish community there would be public
> violations of the Sabbath?! Heaven forbid! The like of this will not be in
> Israel, not only because thank God the Jewish leadership stands in the
> breach, but also because the county and municipal officials prohibit religious
> transgression.[103]

Bonaventura Mayer's *Die Juden unserer Zeit* (Regensburg, 1842) played
a key role in Jacob Toury's assessment of the state of tradition in
Germany; Mayer's survey of conditions in Hungary around 1840 in that
work makes it a unique source for a comparison of the two communities.
Mayer noted that in Arad and Szeged, both towns in the south of Hungary,
there remained little of traditional observance. These towns, however,

"have many qualities which set them apart from the other Jews." Turning to Buda-Pest, he writes:

> A third of the Jewish inhabitants of Pest adhere to the preacher Pasch [Bach] and these are not greatly troubled about celebrating the Sabbath, nor do they worry themselves about the laws the Bible prescribes concerning what is clean and unclean. . . . What we have said about Pest is also valid for Buda.[104]

Comparing Mayer's estimate of the state of affairs in Pest, two-thirds traditional, with his appraisals of some of the larger German communities—Frankfurt, one-fifteenth; Berlin, one-eighth; Breslau, one-fourth traditional—we find that only in Hamburg were conditions similar to those in the Hungarian capital. Since Pest Jewry clearly formed the vanguard of modern trends in Hungary, the proportion of traditional or Orthodox Jews in the country as a whole as certainly higher. Not for another generation, until the end of the 1860s, did a constellation of forces come about comparable to the near balance of power which obtained in 1840 Germany.

One of the results of the impact of German Jewry was that Hungarian Reform did not have to develop in an indigenous fashion. It could adopt from its very infancy a full-blown ideology, but one which had matured under quite different social and cultural conditions. Unlike in Germany, Reform in Hungary spread not in the wake of dramatic social and cultural changes, but rather coincided with the introduction of those selfsame changes. As a result, precisely because it was wed to processes as fundamental as acculturation, it had a wrenching effect on traditional society which was in many ways even more far-reaching than in Germany. This and the paradoxical fact that from the point of view of dogmatic and ritual innovations Hungarian Neology seemed like a watered-down version of German Reform, imbued it with its own peculiar stamp. The differences, however, between the two movements should not obscure the fact that Hungarian Reform was recognizably no more than a variation on the German theme.

There can be no doubt, therefore, that German Reform was crucial in defining much of the form and content of religious innovation in Hungary. As a causal factor in the development of Hungarian Neology, however, it did not operate in a vacuum. It was subject to a confluence of other historical forces that often proved to be decisive in setting the particular pace and direction of the movement in Hungary.

Already in Germany, Reform Judaism, primarily a religious movement, was shaped by other historical stimuli, social and intellectual forces in particular. Although the values promoted by these forces were originally external to Jewish society, they were rapidly internalized. *Wissenschaft des Judenthums* and Reform thought of the 1830s and early 1840s, for example, were both heavily indebted to contemporary intellectual currents, most important of these being German idealism. As a mode of thinking it not only pervaded German thought but also left its mark on every aspect of society; it was small wonder that Jews, too, whether university-trained rabbis or laymen, were caught by its spell. Martin Philippson could justifiably entitle a chapter of his work on modern Jewish history as "Idealism and the Striving for Reform in Germany."[105]

On the other hand, the place allocated to cultural concerns in general, and idealism in particular, was much smaller in both Jewish and non-Jewish society in Hungary. Furthermore, the strength of those social groups who were the natural carriers of such trends was much weaker here than in Germany. The rabbinate, numbering between 300 to 350 men, was still largely traditional. As late as 1851, one critic of its backward state could state, perhaps with exaggeration, that "hardly twenty are in command of pure German or Hungarian . . . with the exception of some talmudic knowledge, they are empty and deprived of any other wisdom and science!"[106] Even among the some half dozen rabbis in prerevolutionary Hungary who tended toward Reform few had formal university training, let alone a doctorate. (Leopold Löw, for instance, had never obtained one.) It is true that the number of university-trained professionals in Hungary was growing at an impressive rate, and that often these men were to be found in the vanguard of Reform. However, their education was mainly professional and confined to the medical faculty. In the first semester of 1851, for example, there were 90 Jews in a student body of 695 at the University of Pest. There were no Jews in the theology faculty; 7 Jews out of 115 (6 percent) in the law and political science faculty; 83 Jews out of 247 (33 percent) in the medical faculty; and no Jews among the 279 students studying in the philosophy faculty.[107] And although the total absence from philosophy may have been a fluke that year, nevertheless, the Hungarian situation was in sharp contrast to that in German universities. During the first half of the nineteenth century at Bonn, Heidelberg, and Tübingen, 41 percent of the Jewish academics attended the medical faculty, 31 percent law, and 28 percent philosophy. It seems that it was from the ranks of these last two faculties in particular that the type of alienated intellectual who numbered so prominently among the founders of the radical Reform societies in Frankfurt and Berlin was drawn.[108]

Reform in Germany was further fuelled by the striving for social integration. The sense of frustration at being excluded from non-Jewish society was particularly acute among economic and intellectual Jewish elites who felt that their educational and financial attainments entitled them to the social status of their non-Jewish peers. Social integration, whether successful or more frequently frustrated, proved a very real goad to religious reforms.[109]

In Hungary, political more than intellectual and social forces provided the external stimulus for Reform. The liberal, nationalist movement led by a politically savvy nobility held out the promise of a tantalizingly near emancipation, but expressly made it conditional on religious reforms. Here, a sort of "neutral polity" had emerged by the 1840s; religious differences increasingly receded into the background in the feverish excitement of nation-building. The rapprochement in the 1840s among the churches in Hungary—especially among the Protestants—against the background of a triumphant liberal nationalism was truly remarkable. Unlike in Germany, where similar tendencies remained confined to marginal groups, in Hungary proposals for a unified Protestant Church, for intermarriage, for submerging ritual and doctrinal differences in the interest of national unity were espoused by the liberal mainstream of both Protestant Churches.[110] Hungarian liberals naturally applied this model to their invitation to the Jews to join the nation.

The earliest linkage between religious reform and emancipation was raised by the Temes county assembly in its 26 March 1833 instruction to its two deputies to the national Diet. They were to propose the emancipation of the Jews at the Diet "on the condition that henceforth they will employ exclusively Hungarian characters and the Magyar tongue in their documents and will be compelled to observe their *Sabess* on Sunday."[111] In the next decade and a half, precisely during the period that in Germany "the liberal demand for reformation of Judaism receded into the background,"[112] the call for emancipation as being conditional to religious reform came increasingly to dominate Hungarian debates on the Jewish question. Although there were occasional democrats and left-wing liberals who were principled advocates of unconditional equality for Jews, they were a minority in their own camp. More representative of the thinking of most liberals was an editorial written on 5 May 1844 by Louis Kossuth, a statement that was to play a crucial role in molding liberal public opinion toward the Jews in Hungary.

Kossuth began his article by placing himself squarely in favor of legal emancipation. Legal emancipation, however, was only one side of the coin; even more important was to ensure the proper conditions for social emancipation, what he called a true social "fusion" (*egybeolvadás*). Hungarian society had legitimate reasons to question the efficacy of a purely legal step. Much depended on the nature of Jews and Judaism and the possibility of breaching the wall that maintained the Jews as a separate body in Hungarian society. To many it was clear that the Jews were not only a separate religion but more a nation apart. What troubled Kossuth was not that Jews were identifiably a distinct cutural and ethnic group (this he was willing to grant; after all there were many other so-called nationalities in multinational Hungary), but rather that they con-stituted a separate "political organism" within the state. It was this political manifestation of Judaism which could not be tolerated by Kossuth and Hungarian nationalists of his brand since they maintained that the political element, as opposed to say the linguistic or the ethnic, was the defining quality of Hungarian nationhood:

> If I were asked [Kossuth concluded] in what fashion could Jews prepare their full emancipation most effectively, I would reply, "With timely reforms." Let them establish a general Sanhedrin to place their religion under thorough scrutiny to determine what is genuine dogma and its appropriate ritual expression, and what, on the other hand, is a political institution in the trappings of religious commandment. It may indeed have been once wisely legislated by Moses the great statesman, but adherence to it in Christian states only serves to thwart amalgamation [egybeforrás] with other classes of the public—let them, therefore, excise it from their religious corpus. They should strive to become a separate denomination while ceasing to be a separate nation. In so doing, they lay a solid cornerstone of social amalgamation on which—despite defamation, hostility and persecution—the edifice of their complete political emancipation will be erected to the glory of the common deity of humanity and the holy freedom of conscience.[113]

Reverberations of Kossuth's article echoed in debates over the Jewish question during the 1848-49 Revolution. Although the heady March days of 1848 marked the triumph of the liberal opposition in Hungary, Jewish emancipation did not figure among the series of emancipatory measures legislated by the Diet to the chagrin of Hungarian Jews, especially the radical youth. An aborted proposal dating from 21 March would have postponed the final decision to the forthcoming National Assembly while urging much-needed reforms and validating mixed marriages.[114] When the issue was raised in the newly constituted Assembly on 3 August 1848, the majority declared that prior to granting emancipation, the government should contact the Jewish *intelligens* concerning the execution of desired reforms.[115] With these procrastinations, liberal Hungary became the last country in Central Europe to issue emancipation during the 1848-49 Revolutions. Not only did Hungary lag four months behind reactionary Vienna, but unlike other countries it was unique in including a clause calling for a Sanhedrin to deliberate religious reforms.[116]

The constant political pressure was not without effect. To be sure reformers of every stripe denied the linking of emancipation and reform. Nevertheless, evidence points to a disquieting proximity between peaks of public debate on Jewish legal status and spurts of activity on behalf of reform. In 1848, the oppressive climate of opinion drove many to despair, especially those whose hopes had been pinned highest on the triumph of liberalism in Hungary. Jonas Kunewalder, who as chairman of the Tolerance Tax Committee was the leading representative of Hungarian Jewry, is an outstanding example. Profoundly despondent at the Hungarian Diet's latest refusal to grant emancipation, he composed a circular on 22 March 1848 to all the Jewish communities urging them to exercise patience. "Meanwhile, let us provide the most public clarification of what was hitherto kept in the mysterious dark concerning our religious and communal constitution, so that we could at least . . . commence upon the most radical [leggyökeresebb] reforms."[117] Within a week, sensing the hopelessness of the situation, Kunewalder converted. The combination of pogroms, the government's willingness to yield to mob's demands, and its reluctance to grant emancipation drove other Jews, especially among the politically most radical, to make preparations to emigrate to America. In this climate of despair, radical reform societies mushroomed in Pest and several provincial centers. At times, members of these societies admitted with artless candor the influence of political pressure on their striving for religious reforms. The radical reformers of Arad wrote to Samuel Holdheim on 23 April 1848 that in light of the present, momentous times "useful reforms of institutions and external practices of the Jewish religion are desirable from a political and social viewpoint as well."[118] Later, the radicals repeatedly protested against the government policy of linking emancipation and reform and stressed that their own activities were not motivated by external forces. Their timing, however, led many, especially among the moderate reformers, to suspect otherwise. For example, the National Assembly renewed its call for reforms on August 3; the radicals issued a statement of intent to introduce Berlin-style reforms on August 4. Their disclaimer, which appeared the next day denying accusations that outside pressures had led to the reforms, left the moderate wing unconvinced. In a pamphlet written on August 11, Löw Schwab, the rabbi of Pest, condemned both the government and the *Centralreformvereine* for compromising reform by placing it in the service of emancipation. "Was emancipation linked to reform in Germany, France, England, Netherlands or Italy?" The policy of free Hungary could only be compared to that of despotic Russia. The reform society, on the other hand, in shifting the Sabbath to Sunday surpassed in its zeal even its Berlin model; Schwab declared that it could no longer be tolerated within the Jewish community.[119]

One need not present a crude argument for a causal relationship between reform and emancipation to note that the overall political climate had a definite effect. A glance at Germany during the revolution can provide a useful comparison. As one astute correspondent of the radical *Israelit des neunzehnten Jahrhunderts* noted:

> We find it only natural in Germany that movements in the ecclesiastic-religious sphere which had outpaced the political by a significant stretch, have receded now into the background as political life comes awake in a most powerful fashion. Elsewhere, for instance in Hungary, where spiritual movements of every tendency were at a standstill, now, the religious [sphere] has been stirred up by the political.[120]

Germany and Hungary differed in respect to reform in 1848 in two ways. First, in the resolution of Jewish legal status. In Hungary, the question of emancipation remained outstanding for the duration of the revolution and Hungarian Jews simply could not afford the leisure of devoting themselves to broader concerns. Jewish energies were directed into more parochial channels—at least during the first six months of the revolution. An illustration of this tendency is the founding of the first Hungarian Jewish journal—*Der ungarische Israelit*—by the very same radical elements who in Germany had decided that a specifically Jewish journal was no longer needed and therefore dismantled *Der Israelit des 19. Jahrhunderts.* Precisely because in Germany there existed a clearly perceived convergence of liberal and Jewish aims, activists could abandon the specific Jewish struggle with a clear conscience and fling themselves wholeheartedly into the general political arena.[121] In Hungary, on the other hand, from the very first week of the revolution it was patent that a victory for the liberal opposition did not necessarily signal the fulfillment of Jewish aspirations.

Second, the nature of Hungarian society precluded the type and extent of Jewish participation in revolutionary movements possible in Vienna and Germany. As noted above, the drive for social integration influenced the development of Reform in Germany. To a great extent this was also true of Hungary: there was a rather clear-cut correlation in the 1840s between members of mixed societies or casinos and advocates of reform. Nevertheless, in Hungary two obstacles barred the path to social integration. The religious barrier could eventually be breached as in Germany, but the second barrier, that of class was a different matter. Jews in Germany were aspiring for social integration into what was largely a bourgeois society, their aspirations were reasonable, hence all the more frustrating when met with rejection. German liberal middle-class society served not only as an identification reference group for German Jewry, but potentially, as a membership group as well. Hopes of integration were fuelled by ready examples of the salons and of close friendships between Germans and Jews. More than any other factor, the premium placed on *Bildung* in Germany provided Jews with a channel of access to society, and consequently, also to political power.

Indeed, viewed from the perspective of the Jewish experience in Hungary, the political prominence to which Jews rose in bourgeois liberal movements in Central Europe, especially in 1848, was quite remarkable, and sheds much light on the varying nature of social integration of Jews in different societies.

> Decisive influence [wrote Ignatz Einhorn in 1851 in his study on the Hungarian Revolution and the Jews] of the kind exercised, for instance, by Fischof and Goldmark in Vienna, by Jacoby in Berlin, by Crémieux in Paris, and by other Jews in smaller German states was at no time acquired by the Hungarian Jew. . . . In the National Assembly there was not one Jew.[122]

To a certain extent this was a reflection on the strength of different political cultures. Only in a city so lacking in a politically mature opposition as Vienna could a previous political unknown such as Fischof be catapulted to power virtually overnight. The social composition of the Frankfurt Parliament also reflected the peculiarities of German political culture. Only in Germany, where politics was associated with *Bildung* and political participation perceived in spiritual terms, could the *Intelligenz* garner close to half the parliamentary seats (professors and teachers, 15.4 percent; lawyers, 16.3 percent; physicians, 3.1 percent; writers and journalists, 4.5 percent; clergy, 5.6 percent; total, 43.9 percent). Less than 10 percent were landowners. In contrast, close to three-quarters of the representatives at the 1848 Hungarian National Assembly were noble landowners, almost all having participated at one time or another in the no-holds barred county politics which could not be characterized even remotely as a "spiritual" experience. At most, 18 percent belonged to the *Intelligenz*—two-thirds of these were lawyers, most of them probably also noblemen. While businessmen made up almost 10 percent of the German Parliament, in Hungary they constituted only 1 percent of the National Assembly. In Germany there was a sense that the *Mittelstand* was the true representative of society, that it was "das eigentliche Volk," the "real nation"; whereas in Hungary, with its German-speaking, reactionary *Spiessbürgertum* such claims would have been met with derision. It was the nobility, specifically the gentry, who were the carriers of liberalism and were identified with the interests of the "nation."[123]

Although the predominant tendency in both Hungary and Germany in the 1840s was liberal, clearly the social structure and social values of the two societies accorded different opportunities for Jewish integration. As noted at the beginning of this essay, social divisions were particularly rigid in Hungary and only partially attenuated in the half century since Joseph II. Ferencz Pulszky, one of most prominent Hungarian liberals, recalled that until the 1830s intermarriage between the noble and burgher classes was close to unheard of and was usually viewed as a social calamity. Moreover, "the gentry shut itself off, not only from below, but also from above." A noble who spent too much time in the company of his aristocratic betters was as likely to be the butt of ridicule as his fellow noble who married beneath himself.

> In other words, society was sharply divided into different classes which may have come into contact with each other, but never totally fused [*összeolvadni*]. It was to [Count Stephen] Széchenyi's credit to attempt this fusion through the establishment of the Pest casino [in the late 1820s]. Yet even this brought only the gentry county magistrates [*táblabirák*], the magnates and the higher officials into daily contact; the wholesale merchants in Pest, who did not feel at ease in this company, founded their own casino, whereas the real petit bourgeois [*nyárspolgárok; Spiessbürger*], however rich they might have been, frequented neither, but remained faithful to their cafés.[124]

As far as the Jews were concerned there was a marked improvement already in the 1830s. Increasingly Jews were accepted into mixed casinos and various societies formed with a patriotic purpose in mind. However, Kossuth's demand for full social integration, including mixed marriages, was cruel taunt considering the state of Hungarian society. It was against this bad faith that one of the more principled liberals, István Bezerédy, retorted in 1844: "These would first require that they [the Jews] integrate with us, unite with us; but does it enter the mind of the pariah to assimilate with the brahmin?"[125]

In fact, Kossuth's promised integration into Hungarian society did eventually come about, but in the absence of a significant middle class there was no segment of Hungarian society into which Jews could be absorbed. In Hungary Jews entered Hungarian society *en masse,* comfortably slipping into the social vacuum between the peasantry and the nobility. Since there was no conflict of interest with the nobility, and no illusory social expectations, the "integration" of the Jews took place with minimal social friction. They knew their place. To be sure, Jews and nobles met in the patriotic casinos formed at the time; yet here again, social contact took place with a political and especially a politically linked economic purpose in mind and not for its own sake. Within these societies, for instance in the Hungarian *Schutzvereine,* the division of labor between the gentry and the Jews—one dominating politics, the other the economy—so characteristic of Hungary at the turn of the twentieth century, was already visible. The head of the economic section of the society was inevitably a prosperous Jewish merchant, whereas the political head was always a nobleman.[126]

Such symbiotic relationships did little to blur social boundaries or induce the type of aspirations for social acceptance which would engender a deeply felt sense of relative deprivation. The tortured soul-searching characteristic of a generation of German Jews—whether they stood tantalizingly just beyond the pale of middle-class society or tentatively within it—frequently led to a profound internalization of the most critical assessments of Jews and Judaism. This type of social tension which derived from intimate contacts with non-Jewish society and which found in some cases an outlet in Reform was far more unusual in Hungary. Pressure for reforms derived from less subtle sources, mainly from the political sphere, and as a result, it seems to me, were internalized in a more superficial manner.

German Reform undeniably provided Hungarian Jewry with an ideology and a specific program of religious innovation. It served as an impetus for local reforms, but it was only one of a variety of factors. Although the forces which tugged at Reform in Hungary may have been similar to those which had operated in Germany, their vectors and valences were different: here, cultural concerns were minimal, social tensions not as intense, and political demands more salient. It was with these forces that German Reform combined to mold the unique character of Hungarian Neology.

To gauge the impact of German Jewry on Hungarian Jewry in the modern era I limited my presentation to a brief survey of Haskalah and Reform, two central themes in the history of modernization of Hungarian Jewry until 1870. Yet many of the issues raised in analysis of these two movements could have been applied to other topics of Hungarian Jewish history such as the Orthodox response to modernity or perceptions of Jewish identity.

Although the impact of German Jewry on Hungary was not as straightforward as one might have assumed, there is no denying that it was quite substantial. Because of its typical German obsession with articulating ideologies, German Jewry played a decisive role in giving meaning to the process of modernization. In the first century of modernization, in formulating the choices open to the modern Jew, it was the ideologies first put forth by German Jewry which were adopted to a greater or lesser extent by other Jewries; the variations were largely variations on a theme. This was certainly true for the Haskalah and Reform in Hungary, and although the Orthodoxy was an exception to this rule, developments in Germany were crucial to the emergence of this modern conservative ideology in Hungary.

To emulate or shun the German-Jewish model of modernization was an option which lay open to Hungarian Jewry; as a provocative precedent, however, the German experience could not be ignored—it was an ineluctable paradigm which of necessity compelled response.

Notes

I wish to thank Dr. Richard Cohen for his helpful suggestions.

1. Peter Beer, *Lebensgeschichte* (Prag, 1839), pp. 13–14. Some of the more important work on this period in Hungarian Jewish history are Joseph Ben-David, "The Emergence of a Modern Jewish Society in Hungary in the Beginning of the Nineteenth Century" (Hebrew), *Zion* 12 (1952): 101–28; Nathanel Katzburg, "Changes in Hungarian Jewry in the First Half of the Nineteenth Century" (Hebrew) *Bar-Ilan Annual* 2 (1964): 163–77; idem, "The History of Hungarian Jewry" (Hebrew), in *Pinkas Hakehillot: Hungary* (Jerusalem: Yad Vashem, 1976), pp. 14–36; Raphael Mahler, *A History of Modern Jewry* (New York: Schocken, 1971), pp. 268–78; and idem, *History of the Jewish People in Modern Times* (Hebrew) (Tel Aviv: Hakibbutz Hameuchad, 1976), vol. 6, pp. 230–70.

2. See tables 1 and 2, and note 48 below.

3. Although more than fifty names from Poland and Lithuania appear among the 500 odd *Praenumeranten* of the first Berlin edition of Mendelssohn's *Netivot Hashalom* (1780–1783), one searches in vain for a subscriber from Hungary. More surprising is that only four Hungarians are listed in the second edition (Vienna, 1795): being a local *schwartz-gelb* product a much higher participation would have been anticipated. A glance at the occasional subscription lists appearing in *Hame'assef* tells a similar story: no Hungarians among the 1785 subscribers; only two in 1788 (here, however, the privileged Viennese families, many of whom had close family ties with Pressburg, make their debut en masse); and finally, again only two—one being "Rabbi Aaron Choriner of Arrat"—in 1809.

4. Already the *Toleranzpatent* issued on 2 January 1782 for the Jews of Lower Austria placed restrictions on the import of foreign books. See A.F. Pribram, ed., *Urkunden und Akten zur Geschichte der Juden in Wien, 1526–1847 (1849)*, 2 vols. (Wien: Braumüller, 1918), vol. 1, p. 495. This decree was renewed on 14 July 1800 (ibid., vol. 2, p. 71). On censorship in general see Guido Kisch, "Die Zensur jüdische Bücher in Böhmen," *Jahrbuch der Gesellschaft für Geschichte der Juden in der Cechoslovakian Republik* (hereafter JGGJC) 2 (1930): 466–67.

5. Compare the publications of the Berlin *Jüdische Freischule* in Moritz Steinschneider, "Hebräische Buchdruckerei in Deutschland," *ZGJD* 5 (1892): 166–82, with Haskala works published in the Habsburg Monarchy in Peter Beer, "Ueber Literatur der Israeliten in den kaiserl. österreichischen Staaten im letzten Decenio des achtzehnten Jahrhunderts," *Sulamith* II, 1 (1808), 342–57, 421–26; II, 2 (1809), 42–61; and A. Freimann, "Die hebräischen Druckereien in Mähren," *Zeitschrift für Hebräische Bibliographie* 20 (1917): 40–43. Steinschneider (p. 176) notes that the founding in 1792 of the *Gesellschaft der Freunde* with its declared program of Germanization, sounded the deathknell for the Hebrew Haskalah press in Berlin. This no doubt added one more factor in the shift eastward of the Haskalah press, to Breslau, Prague, Brünn, and Vienna.

6. My analysis of the 1784–1787 census listing the population of nearly every settlement in Hungary, published by Dezsö Dányi and Zoltán Dávid, eds., *Az elsö Magyarországi népszámlalás (1784–1787)* (The first Hungarian census [Budapest, 1960]); and idem, "Potlás a józsefkori számláshoz" [Supplement to the Josephinian census], *Történeti statisztikai tanulmányok* [Studies in historical statistics] 2 (Budapest, 1975). For a graphic presentation based on my analysis see the maps "The Jewish Settlement in the Habsburg Empire in the Second Half of the Eighteenth Century," and "The Jewish Settlement in Austro-Hungary in the Beginning of the Twentieth Century," in Evyatar Friesel, *Carta Atlas for the History of the Jewish People in Modern Times* (Hebrew) (Jerusalem: Carta, 1983), pp. 28, 32.

7. For instance, the Leidesdorf family of Pressburg, the Liebenbergs of Temesvár, the Kanns of Stompfa, the Breisachs of Eisenstadt and Pressburg. See Bernard Wachstein, *Die Inschriften des Alten Judenfriedhofes in Wien,* 2 vols. (Wien: Braumüller, 1917), vol. 2, index for Pressburg, Eisenstadt, and other Hungarian towns.

8. According to the Josephinian census, there were about 300,000 nobles in Hungary proper, comprising close to 5 percent of the population. The urban population was roughly the same. Whereas the nobility of every one of the counties had two votes in the Lower House of the Diet, all fifty-odd royal free cities combined had only one. The ethnic composition of most of these cities was mainly German or Slovak. The size of the Hungarian nobility— some 75,000 families—can best be appreciated by comparing it with the 26,000 to 28,000 noble families in France in 1789, or to the 20,000 Junker families in Prussia. For the Habsburg provinces in 1837 the ratio of noble to commoner was 1:20 for Hungary; 1:68 for Galicia; 1:300 for Lombardy-Venice; 1:350 for the German provinces; 1:828 for the Bohemian lands. Elek Fényes, *Magyarország statistikája* [Statistics of Hungary], 3 vols. (Pest, 1842–1843), vol. 1, pp. 117–20; Henry Marczali, *Hungary in the Eighteenth Century* (Cambridge: Cambridge University Press, 1910), p. 104; and Bela K. Kiraly, *Hungary in the Late Eighteenth Century: The Decline of Enlightened Despotism* (New York: Columbia University Press, 1969), pp. 37–38.

9. Peter F. Sugar, "The Influence of the Enlightenment and the French Revolution in Eighteenth-Century Hungary," *Journal of Central European Affairs* 17 (1958): 333–55; R.R. Palmer and Peter Kenez, "Two Documents of the Hungarian Revolutionary Movement of 1794," *Journal of Central European Affairs* 20 (1961): 423–24.

10. Kiraly, pp. 114–25, 243.
11. See Ibid., p. 164. On religious tolerance see Géza Ballagi, *Politikai irodalom Magyarországon 1825-ig* (Political literature in Hungary until 1825 [Budapest, 1888]), pp. 169–99, 616–754; Elemér Mályusz, *A türelmi rendelet: II József és a magyar protestántizmus* (The Toleration Patent: Joseph II and Hungarian Protestantism [Budapest: Magyar Protestáns Irodalmi Társaság, 1939]); C.H. O'Brien, "Ideas of Religious Toleration at the Time of Joseph II," *Transactions of the American Philosophical Society*, n.s., vol. 59, pt. 7 (1969).
12. On social rigidity see note 125, below.
13. For an extensive quote in the Hungarian original see Mózes Richtmann, "A régi Magyarország zsidósága (1711–1825)" (The Jewry of Old Hungary) in *Magyar Zsidó Szemle [MZsSz]* 29 (1912): 302–4; Kiraly, p. 168, cites a paragraph in English translation. On the polemic literature on toleration of Jews see Ballagi, pp. 611–16.
14. For these analytical concepts see Jacob Katz, *Tradition and Crisis* (New York: Free Press, 1961), pp. 245–74; and idem, *Out of the Ghetto* (Cambridge, Mass.: Harvard University Press, 1973), pp. 42–56.
15. Palmer and Kenez, "Two Documents," p. 440.
16. On the complex relations between the Enlightenment and the state, see Ernst Wangermann, *From Joseph II to the Jacobin Trials: Government Policy and Public Opinion in the Habsburg Dominions in the Period of the French Revolution* (London: Oxford University Press, 1959); idem, *The Austrian Achievement, 1700–1800* (London: Thames & Hudson, 1973), esp. pp. 130–47; Paul P. Bernard, *Jesuits and Jacobins: Enlightenment and Enlightened Despotism in Austria* (Urbana: University of Illinois Press, 1971).
17. Beer served as a teacher in the newly opened Mattersdorf school from 1783. Bernhard Mandl, *Das jüdische Schulwesen in Ungarn unter Kaiser Josef II, 1780–1790* (Posen: Merzbach, 1903), pp. 32–36, lists 23 Jewish schools he was able to trace in the archives, but reasonably assumes that there must have been more which left no archival trace.
18. The sermons of both rabbis, preached on *Shabbat Hagadol* 1782, are extant. Ezekiel Landau, *Derushei Hazelach* (Jerusalem, 1966), sermon 39, fols. 53a–54a; and Louis Lewin, "Aus dem jüdischen Kulturkampfe," *JJLG* 12 (1918): 182–94. The translation is from Paul Mendes-Flohr and Jehuda Reinharz, eds., *The Jew in the Modern World: A Documentary History* (New York: Oxford University Press, 1980), p. 68.
19. For the curriculum see Mandl, pp. 21, 30. For Joseph's attitudes toward education, see Paul von Mitrofanov, *Joseph II. Seine politische und kulturelle Tätigkeit*, 2 vols. (Wien-Leipzig: Stern, 1910), vol. 2, pp. 802–19.
20. The talks took place on 19 November 1781. The report was written a year later and forwarded to Hungary to serve as a guideline for the establishment of Jewish schools there. *Magyar Országos Levéltár (MOL [Hungarian National Archives]) C43. Helytartótanácsi Levéltár. Acta Secundum Referentes. "Apponyi".* 1783 Nr. 55–9. See also Johann Wanniczek, *Geschichte der prager Haupt-, Trivial- und Mädchen- schule der Israeliten* (Prag, 1832), pp. 9–11; and Ruth Kestenberg-Gladstein, *Neuere Geschichte der Juden in den böhmischen Ländern, Ersten Theil: Das Zeitalter der Aufklärung, 1780–1830* (Tübingen: Mohr, 1969), pp. 44–45.
21. Although the Edict of Toleration for Hungarian Jewry issued on 31 March 1783 stated that mandatory schooling was to begin at six (paragraph V.k.4),

the Jewish communities of Buergenland expressed in their 3 June 1783 petition the hope that "as in Prague and other German Hereditary Lands, the age will set at ten." See *MZsSz* XIII (1896), 367-74 and MOL. C43 Acta "Apponyi". 1783 Nr. 55-22 ad V.k.4. For the Pressburg celebrations reported in the *Magyar Hirmondo* (13 August 1783), pp. 306-7, see Mandl, pp. 19-20. For the Prague celebrations, Moses Wiener, *Nachricht von dem Ursprunge und Fortgange der deutschen juedischen Hauptschule zu Prag* (Prague, 1785), pp. 32-34. (I wish to express my gratitude to Prof. Ruth Kestenberg-Gladstein for making both Wiener and Wanniczek's books available to me.) For Prague as the model for Hungary, see MOL. C29, Nr. 11, fol. 456, on the session of 13 March 1783 of the special commission set up for implementing the Edict of Toleration for the Jews of Hungary. An excerpt is cited by Ludwig Singer, "Zur Geschichte der Toleranzpatente in den Sudetenlaendern, *JGGJC* V (1933), 306-7, n. 83.

22. The Galician legislation appears in the German supplement to *Hame'assef* 6 (1790), and now in Josef Karniel, "Das Toleranzpatent Kaiser Josephs II. für die Juden Galiziens und Lodomeriens," *Jahrbuch des Instituts für Deutsche Geschichte,* vol. 9 (1982), pp. 75-89. Among other measures communal autonomy was abolished (para. 16), as were rabbinic courts (para. 44); traditional Jewish garb was to be restricted to rabbis only (para. 47); etc. Secular education was now made a prerequisite for marriage (para. 13), communal office and the rabbinate (para. 5).

23. Gerson Wolf, "Zur Geschichte des jüdischen Schulwesens in Galizien," *AZdJ* 51 (1887): 231.

24. Ludwig Singer, "Zur Geschichte der Juden in Böhmen in den letzten Jahren Josefs II. und unter Leopold II.," *JGGJC* 6 (1934): 204-12, 273, n. 20.

25. Joseph's resolution, written at the end of January is published in C.A. Macartney, ed., *The Habsburg and Hohenzollern Dynasties in the Seventeenth and Eighteenth Centuries* (New York: Harper & Row, 1970), p. 139.

26. Mandl, pp. 22, 40, n. 1, 48; Béla Vajda, *A zsidók története Abonyban* (The history of the Jews in Abony [Budapest, 1896]), p. 36; idem, "Az abonyi zsidók történetéhez" [To the history of the Abony Jews], *MZsSz* 14 (1897): 163.

27. I wish to emphasize that by this I do not mean to imply that there was no reluctance on the part of many Jews to send their children to these schools, which they may have seen as innovations potentially harmful to tradition. But this type of suspicious reaction to any innovation is a *psychological* response, a sort of knee-jerk conservatism bent on preserving the status quo. The behavior of Jewish parents, in this respect, differed but little from their non-Jewish neighbors. Unlike *ideological* conservatism which varies from society to society and can be transmitted culturally, this type of response is difficult to sustain—today's innovation rapidly becomes tomorrow's status quo. For these basic methodological distinctions see Mannheim's "Conservative Thought," in Kurt Wolff, *From Karl Mannheim* (New York: Oxford University Press, 1971), pp. 152-54; and Klaus Epstein, *The Genesis of German Conservatism* (Princeton: Princeton University Press, 1966), esp. pp. 7-11.

28. Supervision of the Hungarian schools was in the hands of Christian officials (Pressburg, Obuda, Nagy Várad, Miskolc, Nagy Károly), the *Judenrichter* (Trencsén, Baán, Sasvár) or the local rabbi (S.A. Ujhely, Abauj-Szántó,

Bodrogkeresztur, Lovasberény). Mandl, pp. 44–45. For Schulstein's report see note 16, above. See also Wiener, *Nachricht,* pp. 36, 55–56; and Simcha Assaf, ed., *Sources to the History of Jewish Education* (Hebrew), 4 vols. (Tel Aviv: Dvir, 1931–1954), vol. 1, pp. 252–56. Only in Galicia did a significant Jewish bureaucracy independent of the community and working in various capacities for the government develop.

29. Eduard Winter, *Ferdinand Kindermann, Ritter von Schulstein, 1740-1801* (Augsburg: Stauda, 1926), p. 167 appends an undated letter from Schulstein [ca. September 1786 is my guess] in which he remarks, "In Pressburg, wo die Juden sagten, als Er [Joseph II] ihre Schule besuchte, sie könnten sich nicht recht darein finden, sagte Er, gehts nur nach Prag; dort bin ich recht wohl mit der Schule zufrieden." However, from the various petitions cited by Mandl (p. 22, dated 31 August 1786, 22 December 1786, 1790, and 1791) it is clear that finances, not ideology, were involved. As early as 1782, in addressing themselves to a government questionnaire, Szabolcs county Jews repeatedly emphasize that it is their impoverished state which makes the prospect of establishing a school less than welcome. "Question: Are there any obstacles to [carrying out] these regulations, whether arising from their nature, or from conditions and the lack of means? Answer: There are no [other] reasons or obstacles to these regulations but the poverty of this community and the scattered [nature of the Jewish] settlements in this noble county." *MOL. C43. "Apponyi."* 1782 Nr. 3 II 24–6, fols. 501–3.

30. See Wachstein, *Inschriften,* vol. 2, pp. 416–18, 494.

31. Baruch Jeitteles, *Ta'am Hamelech,* commentary on Moses Isaac Nunes Belmonte, *Sha'ar Hamelech al Mishne Torah le-Rambam,* 3 vols. (Brünn, 1801–1803); Moses Kunitzer, *Hamazref,* 2 vols. (Wien, 1820–Prag, 1857); Bernard (Beer) Oppenheimer, *Mei Beer* (Wien, 1829).

32. See Azriel Shohet, *Im Chilufei Tekufot* (Jerusalem: Mossad Bialik, 1960), pp. 198–241. This openness was apparent on two levels: first, that legitimacy was accorded Jews to study extra-talmudic material within certain well-defined bounds; second, that an increasing number of Jews among them rabbis and talmudic scholars were expressing interest in these subjects. Rabbi Chaim Bacharach is a good early example, see his *Chavas Yair* (Frankfurt am Main, 1699), no. 219.

33. See Leopold Löw, "Abraham and Josef Flesch und ihre Zeit: Ein Beitrag zur neuern Geschichte der Jeschiboth und der jüdischen Studien," in his *Gesammelte Schriften,* 5 vols. (Szeged, 1890), vol. 2, pp. 219–49.

34. See Sándor Büchler, *A zsidók története Budapesten* (History of the Jews in Budapest [Budapest: Lampel R., 1900]), pp. 264ff., 307ff., 391ff.

35. Moseh Samet, "Mendelssohn, Wessely and the Rabbis of Their Time," (Hebrew) in *Studies in the History of the Jewish People and the Land of Israel in Memory of Zvi Avneri,* ed. A. Gilboa et al. (Haifa: University of Haifa, 1970), pp. 233–57, esp. pp. 255–57.

36. Zelig Margoliot writes in the introduction of his *Chiburei Likkutim* (Venice, 1715), "Because of our many sins the yeshivot have become extinct in the Land of Poland." See Aaron Jellinek, "Korot Seder ha-Limud," *Bikkurim* 2 (1866), p. 19. Jonathan Eibeschütz, in a 1749 sermon bemoans the sad fate of *bachurim* from his native Poland who now must wander to the West to attend yeshivot. *Ya'arot Dvash* (Jerusalem, 1972), fol. 117a. Although these accounts should probably be taken with a grain of salt, they nevertheless,

point to a shift in the center of gravity of these institutions. The brief
efflorescence of Central European yeshivot in the eighteenth century has yet
to be dealt with systematically.
37. Isaac Mayer Wise, "Recollections of Bohemia," *The Asmonean* 9 (1854),
nos. 22, 23, quoted in Max B. May, *Isaac Mayer Wise, the Founder of
American Judaism* (New York: Putnam, 1916), p. 14. The Jenikau yeshiva
in the 1820s and 1830s was the most important Bohemian yeshiva with
150 students (p. 29). See also Moritz Feitel, *Reminiscenzen aus meinem
Umgange mit Leopold Löw* (Pápa, 1885), pp. 5–6, on the Trebitsch and
Kolin yeshivot. That yeshivot served as Haskalah centers is probably behind
the interesting statement attributed by Rabbi Chaim Halberstamm to his
father-in-law, Rabbi Baruch Fränkel-Teomim, rabbi and head of yeshiva in
Leipnik, Moravia, at the beginning of the nineteenth century. "There are
no yeshivot in our land [Galicia]," writes R. Halberstamm to a Hungarian
rabbi in 1862, "for some very good reasons as I heard from my master
and father-in-law of Leipnik . . . rather they sit in the Beit-Hamidrash in
groups and study Torah. . . ." Assaf, vol. 4, p. 211. It should be noted that
yeshivot were also the breeding grounds of that other eighteenth-century
heterodoxy, "Sabbatianism." See Jacob Emden, *Sefer Hitavkut* (Lemberg,
1877), fols. 32b–41a.
38. Joseph Ephrati of Troplowitz, *Alon Bachut* (Wien, 1793), frontispice.
39. For the break of the Prague Haskalah with the radicals around *Hame'assef*
in 1794, see Kestenberg-Gladstein, pp. 133–46.
40. This is true of Salomon Rosenthal, Moses Kunitzer, Beer Oppenheimer,
Moses Samuel Neumann, Salomon Löwyson, and probably others. See Reuven
Fahn, *Pirkei Haskalah* (Stanislwow, 1937), pp. 65, 94, 173, 184.
41. Although Prague was still the largest Jewish community in Central Europe,
around the turn of the century it had clearly entered a period of decline.
For the next few decades it would live on the credit of its bygone glory.
42. His manuscript "Die Jude, wie er ist" (1802) was never published. He also
wrote *Der bedrängte Markus Nissa Weiss an die Menschen* (Wien, 1803),
and after his conversion, *Unpartheyische Betrachtungen über das grosse
jüdische Sanhedrin zu Paris* (Buda, 1807). See Sándor Büchler, "A zsidó
reform úttöröi Maygyarországon" (Pioneers of reform in Hungary), *MZsSz*
17 (1900), 107–9.
43. See Moshe Samet, "Halacha and Reform" (Hebrew; unpublished Ph.D.
dissertation, Hebrew University, Jerusalem, 1967).
44. The Westphalian *Synagogenordnung* is published in *Sulamith* III,1 (1810),
pp. 366–80; regulations concerning marriages to be conducted in the synagogue, *ibid.*, pp. 146–47, 294–96. On Chorin, *ibid.*, III,2 (1811), p. 426
(emphasis in the original).
45. Meir Letteris, *Zikaron Besefer. Memoiren: Ein Beitrag zur Literatur- und
Culturgeschichte im XIX. Jahrhundert. Erster Theil: 1800-1831* (Hebrew)
(Wien, 1869), pp. 37–38. Max Freudenthal, "Juden als Messgäste in Leipzig,"
*Aus Geschichte und Leben der Juden in Leipzig: Festschrift zum 75 jährigen
Bestehen der Leipziger Gemeindesynagoge* (Frankfurt-am-Main: Kauffmann,
1928), pp. 26–27. Jews from Brody were especially prominent at the fair.
See Wilhelm Harmelin, "Jew in the Leipzig Fur Industry," *LBIY* 9 (1964):
241–42. The influence of German Reform on Leipzig was powerful. The
Beth-Jacob Betschule, called at times the "Leipzig-Hamburger Tempel" or

"Leipzig-Berliner Synagoge," was inaugurated during the High Holidays of 1820. Music was composed for the occasion by Meyerbeer, sermons were held by Zunz and Wolfson. See Leopold Zunz and J. Wolfson, *Zwei Predigten, gehalten bei der Erweihung des in Leipzig, nach dem Gebrauche des Tempel-Vereins zu Hamburg . . . eingerichteten Betsaales Beth-Jacob. 30 September 1820* (Leipzig, 1820). Zunz's letter, dated 3 October 1820, describes the impact of his sermons on Eastern European merchants. Nahum N. Glatzer, ed., *Leopold and Adelheid Zunz: An Account in Letters, 1815–1885* (London: Published for the Leo Baeck Institute by the East and West Library, 1958), p. 19. See also Gustav Cohn, "Die Entwicklung des gottesdienstlichen Verhältnisse bis zum Einweihung der Synagoge," in *Aus Geschichte und Leben der Juden in Leipzig*, pp. 47–48.

46. Markgraf (see reference in table 2) gives sporadic data on the attendance of Hungarian Jews from 1756 to 1839. 1756: 4 Hungarian Jews; 1768: 1; 1775: 4; 1782: 0; 1789: 0: 1796: 0; 1806: 5; 1807: 5; 1811: 0; 1813: 0; 1817: 1; 1821: 1; 1832: 0; 1839: 0. Compare for the period prior to 1764 with the Hungarian merchants listed in Max Freudenthal, *Leipziger Messgäste: Die jüdischen Besucher der Leipziger Messe in den Jahren 1675–1764* (Frankfurt am Main: Kauffmann, 1928) and conveniently assembled by Bernát Mandl in *Magyar Zsidó Oklevéltár* (MZsO, [Hungarian Jewish archives]), 17 vols. to date (Budapest, 1903–1977), vol. 2, pp. 124–26.

47. Ferenc Eckhart, *A bécsi udvar gazdasági politikája Magyarországon Mária Terézia korában* (The Economic Policies of the Viennese Court in Hungary in the Era of Maria Theresa [Budapest: Budavari tudományos társáság, 1922]), pp. 44–66, 149–57, 313–44, 356–57.

48. Pribram, vol. 1, pp. 610, n. 17, 613–14, 648.

49. For bibliography on Biedermann, see Wachstein, *Inschriften*, vol. 2, 514–15, n. 4; and idem, *Die ersten Statuten des Bethauses in der Inneren Stadt* (Wien: Israelitische Kultusgemeinde, 1926), pp. 12–13. Biedermann's sympathy for German Reform was shared by members of his family. When Abraham Geiger visited Vienna in the early 1840s, it was Biedermann's two daughters, Babette von Kaulla and Regine von Biedermann, he writes, "die uns so freundlich in Wien entgegengetreten." It was through Biedermann that Geiger also met the leading lights of the Pressburg reform camp. See Abraham Geiger's letter to Jakob Auerbach in Vienna, 29 July 1841, in his *Nachgelassene Schriften*, 5 vols. (Berlin, 1875–1878), vol. 5, p. 157.

50. Gerson Wolf, *Geschichte der Juden in Wien*, pp. 132–33. On Harzfeld see Leopold Löw's note in *Ben Chananja* 3 (1860): 643–46; and Bernhard Wachstein, "Die Wiener Juden in Handel und Industrie nach den Protokollen des Nieder-österr. Merkantil- und Wechselgerichten," in *Nachträge zu . . . Quellen und Forschungen zur Geschichte der Juden in Österreich* (Wien, 1936), p. 315.

51. Leopold Löw, "Aron Chorin," in his *Gesammelte Schriften*, vol. 2, pp. 293–94.

52. Gerson Wolf, *Von ersten zum zweiten Tempel: Geschichte der israelitischen Cultusgemeinde in Wien (1820–1860)* (Breslau, 1885²), pp. 13–14; and Löw, "Aron Chorin," p. 293.

53. "Anrede eines Israeliten an seine Mitbrüder in Pressburg, um sie zur Verbesserung der Schulanstalten aufzumuntern," *Sulamith* III, 2 (1811), p. 290; the reference to Biedermann is on p. 298.

54. Sigmund Husserl, "Die israelitische Kultusgemeinde Wien," *Ost und West* 10 (1910): 514; Zsigmond Groszmann, "A pesti zsidóság vezetöi" (Leaders of Pest Jewry), *MZsSz* 56 (1939): 51; Bernhard Wachstein, *Urkunden und Akten zur Geschichte der Juden in Eisenstadt* (Wien: Braumüller, 1926), p. 717, n. 7; Löw, *Kongress*, pp. 83–87; Karl Blumberger, "Das Testament Herschel Biedermanns," *Jüdisches Archiv* 1, 3 (1927): 19–23. For family ties among the elites of the three cities see Pribram, vol. 2, pp. 531–44 for annual listings of marriages contracted between 1785 and 1846 in Vienna, with data on the origin of the brides and bridegrooms. For business ties see Bernhard Wachstein, "Die Wiener Juden in Handel und Industrie nach den Protokollen," *Urkunden*, pp. 265–355.

55. *Sulamith* III, 1 (1810), p. 360; Ignaz Reich, *Beth-El: Ehren-tempel verdienter ungarisches Israeliten*, 3 vols. (Budapest, 1878), vol. 1, p. 124; Bernát Mandl, "A pesti izr. hitközségi fiuiskola monográfiája" (Monograph of the Pest Israelite community's boys' school), in Jonás Barna and Fülöp Csukási, eds., *A magyar-zsidó felekezet elemi és polgári iskoláinak monográfiája* (Monograph of the Magyar-Jewish denomination's elementary and municipal schools), 2 vols. (Budapest, 1896), vol. 1, pp. 4–5.

56. See the productivization society's statutes dated 23 January 1820, signed by R. Moses Sofer in *Bikkurei Haitim* 2 (1822): 175–82; "Neue errichtete jüdische Lehranstalt in Pressburg" (in Hebrew characters), ibid., 3 (1823): 221–22, reproduces a report published in *Wiener Zeitung*, 7 July 1821; Shimon Sidon, *Shevet Shimon* (Pressburg, 1884), pt. 2, fol. 17b; Chizkia Feivel Plaut, *Likutei Chever Ben-Chaim*, 11 vols. (Pressburg, 1879), vol. 2, fols. 32b–33a; Akiva Yehosef Schlesinger, *Lev Haivri* (Lemberg, 1868), pt. 1, fol. 10b, n.; and J.J. Grunwald, "Stormy Periods in the Life of the Chatam Sofer" (Hebrew), in *Otzar Nechmad* (New York, 1942), pp. 69–77.

57. I refer to the mischievous stroke of fate which catapulted three impoverished Orthodox Jews—Bettleheim, Pappenheim, and Guttmann—to fortune and power. In 1822, their apostate brother-in-law, Anton Calman (né Kalman Wannefried) died, bequeathing them as sole heirs a legacy of several million florins. Room was immediately made for the new "millionaires" as they came to be known, on the Pressburg communal board. By chance—or by the hand of Providence, as the Orthodox perceived it—sudden death struck Wolf Breisach soon after his attempt to close down the yeshiva was foiled (8 August 1827; see Wachstein, *Eisenstadt*, p. 642, n. 2). This smoothed the way for a conservative takeover of the community leadership, especially since the growing exodus to Vienna effectively removed those wealthy elements who may have mounted a challenge to Orthodox rule. The Bettleheims and Pappenheims dominated the Pressburg Orthodox community (and ex officio Hungarian Orthodoxy) well into the twentieth century. See Paul J. Diamant, "Der Millionererbschaft in der Pressburger Judengasse," *Judaica* 2, nos. 11–12 (1935): 20–26.

58. Gerson Wolf, *Isak Noa Mannheimer* (Wien, 1863), p. 17; and Glatzer, ed., *Leopold Zunz: Jude-Deutscher-Europäer* (Tübingen: Mohr, 1964), p. 121, letter to Ehrenberg, 21 August 1821.

59. See his revealing correspondence in 1829 and 1830 with the rabbi of Copenhagen, A.A. Wolff, in "Zwei interessante Briefe Mannheimers," *MGWJ* 20 (1871): 276–83, 331–36.

60. For example, see on *chupa* within the synagogue the glosses of R. Moses Isserles to the *Shulchan Aruch, Yoreh De'ah,* 391, para. 3; and *Even Ha'ezer,* 61, para. 1. See also Z.H. Fassel, "Ueber Trauungen in der Synagoge," *Wissenschaftliche Zeitschrift für jüdische Theologie* 3 (1839): 36–39; and J.J. Grunwald, "Is It Proper to Marry in a Synagogue?" (Hebrew), in his *Otzar Nechmad,* pp. 47–54. Mannheimer himself wryly noted that in matters of worship "ich den *Schulchan Aruch* als Norm streng handhabe." "Zwei interessante Briefe," 280. For a description of the Viennese rite, see besides Mannheimer's letters to Wolff, also Wolf, *Von ersten zum zweiten Tempel,* pp. 24–39.

61. Moses Sofer, *Responsa of the Chatam Sofer,* vol. 6, nos. 91, 92, 94, 96; idem, "Liebermann Eliezer levele Rosenthal Salomonhoz. Berlin 1819 Decz. 6" [E.L.'s letter to S.R.], *MZsSz* 17 (1900): 184–85; Wolf, *Mannheimer,* p. 10, n.; Gerson Wolf, *Joseph Wertheimer* (Wien, 1868), pp. 168–69. On *Siona, ein encyclopädisches Wochenblatt für Israeliten,* which was scheduled to appear on February 1819 under the editorship of Ignatz Jeiteles, see *Jedidja* 2 (1818–19): 286.

62. Sigmund Husserl, *Gründungsgeschichte des Stadt-Tempels der Israel. Kultusgemeinde Wien* (Wien: Braumüller, 1906), pp. 80–82.

63. Pribram, vol. 2, pp. 305–6; also Glatzer, ed., *Leopold Zunz,* p. 108.

64. Wolf, *Von ersten zum zweiten Tempel,* pp. 14, 19.

65. M. Rosenmann, "Briefe Gotthold Salomons an Isak Noa Mannheimer," *JJGL* 22 (1919): 76.

66. Leopold Löw, *Der jüdische Kongress in Ungarn* (Pest, 1871), pp. 107–9; idem, "Das mährische Landesrabbinat seit hundert Jahren," in *Gesammelte Schriften,* vol. 2, pp. 205–7, 212, n. 2; Peter Beer, *Reminiscenzen: Bezüglich auf Reorganisation des öffentlichen Gottesdienstes bei den Israeliten* (Prag, 1837), pp. 24–28; Mayer Balaban, *Historia Lwowskiej Synagogi Postepowej* (Lwow, 1937); N.M. Gelber, "The Jews in the Republic of Cracow, 1815–1846" (Hebrew), in A. Bauminger et al., eds., *Cracow* (Jerusalem: Mossad Harav Kook, 1959), pp. 80–81; Joachim Tarnopol, *Notices historiques et caractéristiques sur les israelítes d'Odessa* (Odessa, 1855), pp. 104–5.

67. *Der Orient* 5 (1844): 46. See also *Sulamith* VII (1826), p. 297, for a report from Vienna: "The Polish Jews residing here . . . frequently attend . . . the religious services and fully approve of the adjustments that have been made."

68. Gabriel Ullmann (b. 1792) was born into a prominent German family which had first settled in Pressburg in the 1780s. He moved to Pest in 1809 to follow his older brother and father-in-law, Moritz. Moritz Ullmann (b. 1783) had made a fortune in tobacco, and was considered after Samuel Wodianer, his son's father-in-law, the second wealthiest Jew in Hungary. In 1825, Moritz got into a tiff with other members of the communal leadership, resigned the post he had occupied since 1806, converted and was promptly ennobled with the predicate Szitányi along with his six sons on 2 December 1825. (Antal Áldásy and Alfréd Czobor, *A magyar nemzeti múzeum könyvtárának címerslevelei,* only 2 vols. published (Budapest, 1941), vol. 7, pp. 538–40.) Gabriel, however, did not join his brother at the baptismal font. Until a debilitating illness forced him to retire from communal life in 1836, he was the driving force behind Pest reforms. See Löw, *Kongress,* pp. 107–8, and Groszmann, "A pesti zsidóság vezetöi," pp. 52, 57.

69. A report, "Einweihung des neuen Israelitischen Bethauses zu Wien am 9. April 1826," *Sulamith* VII (1826), p. 297, already notes, "The congregation in Pesth is reported to be willing to adopt for itself the adjustments made in religious services here . . . Baja, a congregation in deepest Hungary, is supposed to have expressed the same desire." See Gerson Wolf, "Zum 1. Oktober," *AZdJ* 29 (1865): 715–16, for Mannheimer's reply of 15 September 1827 to the *Vorsteher* of the *Chessed Neurim* society; Löw, *Kongress,* pp. 108–9, 111, 164–66.

70. Rosenmann, "Briefe Salomons an Mannheimer," p. 78. On the division of labor in Vienna see "Zwei interessante Briefe Mannheimers," pp. 279–80, 335; Mannheimer's letters to Zunz in 1835 on the limited sphere of activity the latter could expect in Prague, in M. Brann and M. Rosenmann, "Der Briefwechsel zwischen Isak Noa Mannheimer und Leopold Zunz," *MGWJ* 61 (1917): 309–17. See now Ismar Schorsch, "Emancipation and the Crisis of Religious Authority: The Emergence of the Modern Rabbinate," in Werner E. Mosse, Arnold Paucker, and Reinhard Rürup, eds., *Revolution and Evolution: 1848 in German-Jewish History* (Tübingen: Mohr, 1981), pp. 228–31.

71. M. N. Mehrer, "Letters between Salomon Rosenthal and R. Löw Schwab on his Appointment as Rabbi of Pest" (Hebrew), *Hatzofe* 15 (1931): 167–85, esp. p. 174. See also Alexander Altmann, "The New Style of Preaching in Nineteenth-Century German Jewry," in idem, ed., *Studies in Nineteenth-Century Jewish Intellectual History* (Cambridge, Harvard University Press, 1964), pp. 65–116.

72. See his "Gutachten" in Abraham Hochmuth, *Leopold Löw als Theologe, Historiker und Publizist* (Leipzig, 1871), Beilage 12, p. 246.

73. Shlomo Sofer, ed., *Iggerot Sofrim,* (Tel Aviv: Sinai, 1970), pt. III. p. 7; and Schorsch, "Modern Rabbinate," p. 218, n. 36.

74. Ben-Zion Dinaburg (Dinur), "From the Archives of ShIR" (Hebrew), *Kiryat Sepher* 1 (1924): 322, and *Der Orient* 7 (1846): 237. Solomon Marcus Schiller [-Szinessy], another Hungarian reformer preaching in Eperjes, also attacked the rabbinic assemblies. See his *Die zweite Rabbiner-Versammlung zu Frankfurt am Main* (Leipzig, 1845), and *Die Versammlung deutschen Rabbiner* (Leipzig, 1846).

75. *Der Israelit des neunzehnten Jahrhunderts* 6 (1845): 303, in a review of Moritz Feitel's *Meshivat Nefesh: Hauspostille zur Belehrung und Erbauung für Israeliten* (Wien, 1842; 2nd. ed. 1845).

76. Béla Bernstein, "Reformmozgalmak a magyar zsidóságban" (Reform movements among Hungarian Jewry), *Izraelita Magyar Irodalmi Társaság Évkönyve* (IMIT) (1898): 251–65.

77. David Philipson, *The Reform Movement in Judaism* (New York: Ktav, 1967), pp. 276–82.

78. Marcus Brann, *Geschichte des jüdisch-theologischen Seminars in Breslau: Festschrift zum fünfzigjährigen Jubiläum der Anstalt* (Breslau, 1904), pp. 134–207, *passim* for Hungarian graduates.

79. Leopold Löw, "Die Almemorfrage," *Ben Chananja* 8 (1865): 681–88. Reformers apparently insisted that the *bima* be moved up front in order to afford an unobstructed view of the preacher. On the other hand, one Orthodox rabbinic candidate from Würzburg, restricting himself to aesthetic and rational arguments, contended that the central location of the *bima* was essential so

that all could conveniently hear the Torah reading. See S. Adler, "Ueber die Zweckmässigkeit des in der Mitte der Synagoge erbauten Almemor," *TZW* 2 (1846): 99–100. An anonymous correspondent from Hamburg, "Das Ritus der portugiesischen Synagoge," *AZdJ* 2 (1838): 53, writes: "Is imitation of the Portuguese the source of this, as of other aesthetic reforms?"

80. See for instance the collection of responsa published by the reform camp of Pápa, *Zulässigkeit und Dringlichkeit der Synagogen-Reformen* (Wien, 1845). Most of the respondents were from Germany.

81. *Magyar statisztikai közlemények,* n.s., 27 (1909), tables 28, 29, 33. Out of 265 Orthodox rabbis in 1900, 164 (62 percent) preached *exclusively* in German and another 34 (13 percent) in German and another language. It may well have been that some of the "German" sermons were actually in Yiddish; nonetheless, it should be noted that 54 (20 percent) rabbis did not hesitate to declare that they preached in "Hebrew" (Yiddish). In contrast, only 28 (49 percent) of the status quo and 33 (23 percent) of the neologue rabbis preached in German. *Magyar statisztikai évkönyv,* n.s., 7 (1899): 727.

82. Elias Oesterreicher, *Der Jude in Ungarn wie er war, wie er ist, und wie er seyn wird* (Pest, 1842), pp. 44–45.

83. Brann and Rosenmann, "Briefwechsel zwischen Mannheimer und Zunz," p. 299.

84. Joachim Kirchner, *Das deutsche Zeitschriftwesen seine Geschichte und seine Probleme* (Wiesbaden, Harrasowitz, 1962), vol. 2, p. 146 (I owe Ita Shedlitzky this reference.); *Tafeln zur Statistik der österreichischen Monarchie für das Jahr 1841* (Wien, 1844), table on "Zeitungwesen"; *Orient* 6 (1845): 296; and Löw, "Aron Chorin," p. 398.

85. Jacob Toury, *Turmoil and Confusion in the Revolution of 1848* (Hebrew), (Tel Aviv: Sifriat Hapoalim, 1968), pp. 17–23. His estimate of three or four readers per copy seems far too conservative to me. For reading circles in Pest and Liptó Szent Miklós see *AZdJ* 4 (1840): 4, 513; for Vág Ujhely, Trencsén, and Arad see *AZdJ* 6 (1842): 442, 701–2.

86. Löw, *Kongress,* pp. 218–19. See also the letter of R. David Löwinger to R. Pinchas Frieden in Miksa Weisz, "Adatok a Paksi Rabbigyüléshez" [Data on the Paks Rabbinic Assembly] *MZsSz* 25 (1908): 160. Another Orthodox rabbi recalled: "Thus when, in the beginning of the 1840s, the congregation in Miskolcz grew extensively by virtue of new arrivals and, along with this, stimulated by Philipsohn's then frequently read Jewish newspaper, the elements favoring reform grew stronger." Simon H. Fischmann, *Vier Nachrufe* (Budapest, 1875), p. 6. Fischmann, later rabbi in Kecskemét, was the son of the Miskolc rabbi.

87. Nahum N. Glatzer, ed., *Leopold and Adelheid Zunz* (London, 1958), p. 4; and Husserl, *Gründungsgeschichte,* p. 86. See also Nahum N. Glatzer, "On an Unpublished Letter of Isaak Markus Jost," *LBIY* 22 (1977): 129–37; Michael A. Meyer, "The Orthodox and the Enlightened: An Unpublished Contemporary Analysis of Berlin Jewry's Spiritual Condition in the Early Nineteenth Century," *LBIY* 25 (1980): 101–30, esp. p. 111, n. 25.

88. Selma Stern, *Der preussische Staat und die Juden,* 3 vols. (Tübingen: Mohr, 1962–1971), vol. 3, pp. 116–33, 265–317.

89. Schorsch, "Modern Rabbinate," p. 229, and Nachman Berlin, *Kadur Katan* ([Breslau?], 1819), fols. 10a–10b. Prague and Vilna can be added to Schorsch's list of communities without a chief rabbi.

90. David Friedländer, *Ueber die Verbesserung der Israeliten im Königreich Pohlen* (Berlin, 1819), pp. 10–11, and I.M. Jost, *Neuere Geschichte der Israeliten von 1815 bis 1845,* 2 vols. (Berlin, 1846), vol. 1, p. 132, on the fate of the Fürth yeshiva in the late 1820s. With the deaths of R. Abraham Bing (1752–1841) of Würzburg and R. Akiva Eger (1761–1837) of Posen, the fate of the yeshivot was sealed.

91. Carlo Cippola, *Literacy and Development in the West* (London: Penguin, 1969), pp. 113–14. The 1871 Posen figures are in A. Heppner and J. Herzberg, *Aus Vergangenheit und Gegenwart der Juden und der jüd. Gemeinden in den Posener Landen* (Koschmin-Bromberg: Selbstverlag, 1909), pp. 279–80, has 10,418 illiterates over the age of ten out of a total Jewish population of 61,982. For the over ten population, which I estimate at 75 percent of the total, about 77–78 percent were literate. Based on the figures for st, 1870 (see note 99, below) I assume that 30 percent under ten was literate, hence the percent of literacy for the entire population was around 65–66 percent.

92. For 1841, see *Denkschrift zu dem Entwurf einer Verornung die Verhältnisse der Juden betreffend* (Berlin, 1847), Anhang, pp. 54–55; for 1847, see A. Menes, "Zur Statistik des jüdische Schulwesens in Preussen um die Mitte des vorigen Jahrhunderts," *ZGJD*, n.s., 3 (1931): 204.

93. A. Warschauer, "Die Erziehung der Juden in der Provinz Posen durch das Elementarschulwesen," *ZGJD* 3 (1889): 54–63; Jost, *Neuere Geschichte,* vol. 1, pp. 132–33, 149–50, 160, 165, 169, 185, 207, 214, and 217, 228 for Kurhessen and Sachsen-Weimar-Eisenach. See also Jakob Toury, *Soziale und politische Geschichte der Juden in Deutschland 1847–1871* (Düsseldorf: Droste, 1977), pp. 166–67.

94. Jost, *Neuere Geschichte,* vol. 1, pp. 98, 132, 134, 165, 174–75, 182, 185, 216–17, etc.; Schorsch, "Modern Rabbinate," pp. 214–17, 245–47. My guess of 20 percent university-trained rabbis is based on an estimate of the size of the entire German rabbinate which I think Schorsch overestimates. A rule of thumb which I have found useful in calculating the ratio of rabbis to population for this period is roughly between 1:1000 to 1:1200 depending on the type and density of Jewish settlement. Since German Jewry numbered a little over 400,000 around 1848, between 330 to 400 rabbis in all of Germany seems a judicious guess, and in all probability much too high. Sixty-seven rabbis came to about 20 percent of the total, which only strengthens Schorsch's case for the growing importance of the modern rabbinate.

95. For example Jacob Toury, "'Deutsche Juden' im Vormärz," *LBIB* 8 (1965): 65–82, and Steven M. Lowenstein, "The Pace of Modernization of German Jewry in the Nineteenth Century," *LBIY* 21 (1976): 41–56.

96. Toury, "Deutsche Juden," p. 81.

97. Leopold Löw, "Statistik der Israeliten in Ungarn," *Kalender und Jahrbuch für Israeliten* 5 (1846): 55.

98. Bernát Alexander, "A magyar közoktatás állapota 1884/85-ben" (State of Hungarian education in 1884–85), *MZsSz* 3 (1886): 291, has in 1869, 34,777 out of 82,147 school-age Jewish children attending school. For Pest: 12,425 of 39,384 Jews were illiterate. To compare with Posen (see note 92): in the over ten population, 5,735 of 29,820 were illiterate (19.2 percent) about the same as in Pest. József Kőrösi, *Pest, szabad királyi város, az 1870-dik évben*

(Pest, Royal Free City, in the year 1870 [Pest, 1871]), pp. 225, 228. The national average for Jewish literacy in 1880 was 71 percent in Budapest, 71 percent in the cities, and 54 percent in the counties, with Máramaros county only 15 percent. *Magyar Statisztikai Közlemény* 27 (1909): 160–61.

99. I developed this theme in my master's thesis carried out under the supervision of Professor Istvan Deak, "Absolutism, Hungary and the Jews: A Comparative Study of Military Conscription of the Jews in the Habsburg Lands, 1788–1815" (Columbia University, 1977). The ratio of central government bureaucrats was the lowest in Hungary of all the Habsburg lands—about ⅓ the imperial average. Johann Springer, *Statistik des österreichischen Kaiserstaates,* 2 vols. (Wien, 1840), vol. 2, pp. 10–11.

100. Ignatz Jeitteles, "Ereignisse, die Israeliten in Ungarn betreffend," *Sulamith* III, 2 (1811), pp. 289–90.

101. On the survival of judicial autonomy: compare the 1694 Mattersdorf privilegium with the revised 1800 version which was valid at least until 1833. The absence of any meaningful change is remarkable. Fritz P. Hodik, "Geschichte der Juden in Mattersdorf," in Hugo Gold, ed., *Gedenkbuch der Untergangenen Judengemeinden des Burgenlandes* (Tel Aviv: Olamenu, 1970), pp. 94–96, 105–6 brings both texts. See esp. para. 11. The Pápa privilegium issued in 1748 granted judicial autonomy to the community and was renewed without change by the Counts Esterházy in 1755, 1801, and 1829. *MZsSz* 2 (1882): 623–24. Complaints about the authority of the Jewish courts were voiced often; see *Pressburger Zeitung* 79 (1842): 641, and Ferenc Kovács, *Az 1843/44. évi magyar országgyülési alsó tábla kerületi ülésének naplója* (The diary of the 1843–1844 Hungarian diet's circuit sessions), 6 vols. (Budapest, 1894), vol. 6, pp. 123–26. On the yeshivot: Abraham Fuchs, *Hungarian Yeshivot: From Grandeur to Holocaust* (Hebrew), (Jerusalem: Kiryat Sefer, 1978), and Shmuel HaCohen Weingarten, *The Yeshivot in Hungary: Their History and Problems* (Hebrew), (Jerusalem: Kiryat Sefer, 1976). I hope to elaborate on the rabbinate elsewhere.

102. Markus Jakob Weiss, *Unpartheyische Betrachtungen über das grosse jüdische Sanhedrin zu Paris* (Ofen, 1807), pp. 24–26. It is not clear whether Weiss is actually describing local Hungarian conditions.

103. Moses Sofer, *Responsa, Choshen Mishpat,* no. 195; Leopold Löw, *Der jüdische Kongress in Ungarn,* pp. 142, 153–54; Immánuel Löw and Zsigmond Kulinyi, *A szegedi zsidók 1785-töl 1885-ig* (The Jews of Szeged [Szeged, 1885]), pp. 164–67; Pribram, vol. 2, pp. 456–57; Wolf, *Joseph Wertheimer,* pp. 181–84.

104. Mayer, *Die Juden unserer Zeit,* pp. 38–39.

105. Martin Philippson, *Neueste Geschichte des jüdischen Volkes,* 3 vols. (Leipzig: Fock, 1907), vol. 1, pp. 146–95. Also Hajo Holborn, "German Idealism in the Light of Social History," in his *Germany and Europe: Historical Essays* (Garden City, N.Y.: Doubleday, 1970), pp. 1–32.

106. Jakob Kern, *Seiner Excellenz . . . Carl Freiherrn v. Geringer-Oedenberg . . .* (Pest, 1851), pp. 6–7.

107. *Tafeln zur Statistik der österreichischen Monarchie* (Wien, 1856), n.s., vol. 1, table on "Lehranstalten."

108. Monika Richarz, *Der Eintritt der Juden in die akademischen Berufe: Jüdische Studenten und Akademiker in Deutschland, 1678–1848* (Tübingen: Mohr, 1974), pp. 96, 105 no. 66, 106, 111, 115, 117, 122–23, 125, 127; Michael A. Meyer, "Alienated Intellectuals in the Camp of Religious Reform: The

Frankfurt Reformfreunde, 1842–45," *AJS Review* 6 (1981): 61–86, and Ismar Schorsch, "Ideology and History in the Age of Emancipation," in his edition of *Heinrich Graetz, The Structure of Jewish History* (New York: Jewish Theological Seminary of America, 1975), p. 22.

109. See for instance the example of the Frankfurt Jewish Freemasons in Jacob Katz, *Jews and Freemasons in Europe, 1723–1939* (Cambridge, Mass.: Harvard University Press, 1970), pp. 82–95.

110. Mihály Horváth, *Huszonöt év Magyarország történelméböl 1823-tól–1848-ig* (Twenty-five years of Hungary's history from 1823 until 1848), 2 vols. (Geneva, 1864), vol. 1, pp. 609–18, vol. 2, pp. 82–86, 204–5. For the proposals of Count Károly Zay on institutional merger of the Protestant Churches, see *Pesti Hírlap* 1 (1841): 159, 353, 511–12. Liberal laymen dominated both Churches. See *ibid.*, pp. 613–14.

111. Jakab Singer, "Temesmegye és a zsidók polgárosítása," (Temes county and the embourgeoisment of the Jews) *IMIT* (1907): 153–54.

112. Reinhard Rürup, "Jewish Emancipation and Bourgeois Society," *LBIY* 14 (1969): 80. Michael A. Meyer, *German Political Pressure and Jewish Religious Response in the Nineteenth Century. Leo Baeck Memorial Lecture 25* (New York: Leo Baeck Institute, 1981) argues against the importance of political pressure on Reform in Germany.

113. *Pesti Hirlap* 3 (1844): 300.

114. Jenö Zsoldos, ed., *1848–1849 a Magyar zsidóság életében* (1848–1849 in the life of Hungarian Jewry [Budapest, 1948]), p. 62, but without the date. The text appears in *Hetilap* 4 (1848): 389–90 in the 28 March issue, but reference to it can already be found on 24 March in *Marczius tizenötödike* 1 (1848): 23. Kunewalder's circular of 22 March (see below) is clearly in reaction to this proposal.

115. Árpád Zeller, ed., *A Magyar egyházpolitika 1847–1894* (Hungarian church politics, 1847–1894), 2 vols. (Budapest, 1894), vol. 1, p. 174.

116. Zsoldos, p. 219. Some of these points were stressed by Nathanel Katzburg, "The Public Debate Regarding Jewish Emancipation in Hungary" (Hebrew), *Bar-Ilan Annual* 1 (1963): 282–301, and Jacob Katz, *From Prejudice to Destruction: Anti-Semitism, 1700–1933* (Cambridge, Mass.: Harvard University Press, 1980), pp. 230–42, esp. pp. 235–36.

117. Zsoldos, p. 60. A German version is in *MZsSz* 6 (1889): 62.

118. *Der Israelit des neunzehnten Jahrhunderts* 9 (1848): 164.

119. Zeller, vol. 1, p. 174; Zsoldos, pp. 159–60; Johann Janotyckh von Adlerstein, *Archiv des ungarischen Ministeriums und Landesvertheidigungs-ausschusses,* 3 vols. (Altenburg, 1851), vol. 2, pp. 159–60; Löw Schwab, *Gutachten an den israelitischen Gemeinde-Vorstand zu Pesth, in Betreff der daselbst sich gebildeten, sogennanten Central-Reform-Genossenschaft* (Pest, 1848).

120. *Der Israelit des neunzehnten Jahrhunderts* 9 (1848): 164, 21 May issue.

121. Jakob Toury, "Die Revolution von 1848 als innerjüdische Wendepunkt," in Hans Liebeschütz and Arnold Paucker, eds., *Das Judentum in der Deutschen Umwelt 1800–1850* (Tübingen: Mohr, 1977), p. 370.

122. I[gnatz] Einhorn, *Die Revolution und die Juden in Ungarn* (Leipzig, 1851), p. 118. The translation is from Reinhard Rürup, "The European Revolutions of 1848 and Jewish Emancipation," in *Revolution and Evolution,* p. 29. On Jewish deputies and other political activists in Germany see Jakob Toury,

Die politische Orientierungen der Juden in Deutschland: Von Jena bis Weimar (Tübingen: Mohr, 1966), pp. 47–68.

123. James Sheehan, *German Liberalism in the Nineteenth Century* (Chicago: University of Chicago Press, 1978), pp. 14–17, 26–27, 57; János Beér, ed., *Az 1848/49 évi népképviseleti országgyülés* (The 1848–1849 popular representative assembly [Budapest: Akadémiai Kiado, 1954]), p. 17.

124. Ferencz Pulszky, *Életem és korom* (My life and times), 2 vols. (Budapest, 1880), vol. 1, pp. 46–48. Most of the translation is from George Barany, *Stephen Széchenyi and the Awakening of Hungarian Nationalism, 1791–1841* (Princeton: Princeton University Press, 1968), pp. 166–67.

125. Kovács, *1843/44. évi magyar országgyülés,* vol. 6, p. 13.

126. See the list of officers of the various provincial societies in *Hetilap* 1 (1845): 223.

6

The History of an Estrangement between Two Jewish Communities: German and French Jewry during the Nineteenth Century

Michael Graetz

When, after the Franco-Prussian War of 1870, the plenipotentiaries of the two countries convened in Versailles and bitterly disputed questions concerning the indemnity which France should pay to Germany and the German annexation of Alsace, two Jews were sitting near the negotiating table, Alphonse de Rothschild and Gerson Bleichröder. They were the heads of two Jewish banking houses, one in Paris and the other in Berlin, with a tradition of cooperation since 1828, when Gerson's father, Samuel, was chosen by the Rothschilds as their agent in Berlin. This tradition of business relations had passed from father to son, from James to Alphonse de Rothschild on the one side and from Samuel to Gerson Bleichröder on the other, and had practically never suffered from national boundaries that separated the two banking houses. Now, in Versailles in February 1871, an estrangement became manifest. Each banker felt himself the representative of a different government and of particular national interests. Bleichröder did his best to be loyal to the German cause and to justify the expectations of Bismarck, while his counterpart, Alphonse de Rothschild, called by Thiers to attend the meeting in Versailles, worked hard to improve the terms of the agreement imposed on a defeated France. Alphonse's loyalty to the French cause was persuasive and therefore provoked a furious reaction from Bismarck.[1]

Not only on the level of the economic elite but also among middle-class intellectuals the Franco-Prussian War was a major cause of estrangement. The following story is typical: Abraham Geiger and Joseph Derenbourg met first in Bonn. Together with others who later became well-known scholars and rabbis such as S.R. Hirsch, they belonged to a special circle of Jewish students who discussed common problems of Jewish life and religion in modern society. Out of this acquaintance grew a lifelong friendship between the two. Their exchange of letters continued for more than forty years, providing a precious historical source that demonstrates the existence of a "Jewish republic of intellectuals" during the main part of the nineteenth century.

At the University of Bonn Geiger and Derenbourg studied classical culture, philology, philosophy, and history. There they conceived far-reaching projects of research: the publication of a corpus of philosophical writings dedicated to medieval Jewish rational thought. This scientific work had never been fully realized, but the project in itself was a source of inspiration in their scholarly work even after each had gone in his own direction, Geiger to Wiesbaden and Breslau, Derenbourg to Paris. The fruits of their initial projects can be found in various periodicals such as the *Wissenschaftliche Zeitschrift für jüdische Theologie,* and in the edition of Rav Saadia Gaon's writings by Derenbourg toward the end of his days, representing the realization of a youthful vision.

Nothing could prevent the two scholars from remaining friends, but what time and geographic distance could not achieve was accomplished by a nationalistic war: the estrangement between two Jewish friends living each on another side of the Rhine. In the fall of 1870, a few months after the outbreak of the Franco-Prussian War, Derenbourg sent a letter to his German-Jewish friend in which he condemned in harsh words "the destruction caused intentionally by a cruel German soldiery." He criticized the patriotic blindness of the German Jews, who refused to acknowledge that France and not Germany meant freedom and equality for the Jews. Geiger wasted no time and reacted immediately: "Germany was forced against its will to engage the enemy and after France's aggression German Jews had no choice. In this conflict of two nations they had to defend the cause of the German people by word and by sword."[2]

This estrangement could also be felt on a purely institutional level. If before 1870 Jews living in Germany consented to join the Alliance Israélite Universelle, notwithstanding its Francocentrism, an opposition to such an affiliation developed after the Franco-Prussian War. Finally, after the foundation of the Hilfsverein in 1901, German Jews possessed an autonomous institution in pursuit of philanthropic aid for Jewish communities all over the world.

This evidence, focusing on the early 1870s as the turning point in the history of the relations between the two communities, should not mislead us. From 1770 to 1870 there existed a common basis broad enough to sustain a relationship. One such common ground was the result of the thin but persistent flow of immigrants from Germany to France, particularly to Paris.

It grew larger in times of political reaction such as after 1815 and 1848, but it never became a mass migration. Since the Revolution of 1789, France attracted Jews who felt there was more freedom there than in Germany. Not only Jewish radicals escaping Prussian repression such as Börne, Heine, Hess, or Marx regarded Paris as a haven and an inspiration and France as the threshold of a new world,[3] but even "bourgeois" newcomers like Rothschild, d'Eichthal, Halévy, Offenbach, or Mayerbeer and young followers of the Science of Judaism such as Salomon Munk or Joseph Derenbourg settled in France in the search for greater freedom.

Munk wrote to his family in Silesia after his arrival in Paris in 1828, "What a great difference between France and Prussia." He tried to illustrate his contention by comparing the reactions of two ministers, one French, the other German. Munk had solicited a job in government administration in Prussia only to be hurt by a biting answer from Alterstein, the Prussian minister: "As long as you adhere to your Mosaic faith, there is no reason why we should cede to your supplication." When Munk submitted a similar request to the French minister after settling in Paris, the latter did not react negatively. As soon as a position became vacant in the National Library Munk was put to work in the department of manuscripts, even before he had been naturalized. This afforded him an opportunity to penetrate the library's sealed treasures of Hebrew documents, embarking him on his scholarly exploration of medieval Jewish literature.[4]

The flow of immigrants reveals the attraction France had for German Jews. Although the migration was small, it influenced French Jewry's path to modernization, giving a serious impetus to the Science of Judaism during the first half of the nineteenth century.

Intellectuals like Munk and Derenbourg arrived in France after studying at German universities such as Berlin and Bonn. They brought with them not only classical erudition and modern methods of research but also a new approach to the Jewish past. The first articles published by Munk were "On the Cult of the Hebrews Compared with the Cult of Other Peoples in the Ancient World's Introduction to Leviticus" (1833), and "Two Chapters of the Guide for the Perplexed—Part III" (1834).[5] These two papers were the precursors of further, more extensive scholarly work—including a book *Palestine* (1845)—describing the people's life in the ancient land and based on a wide spectrum of Jewish as well as non-Jewish sources. Munk fully exploited his profound knowledge of

Semitic philology in publishing the remaining parts of Maimonides's *Guide* (1856–1861), which he translated from the original Arabic text discovered in the Bodleian Library in Oxford. In 1857 Munk edited a selection of Jewish and Arabic philosophical writings of the Middle Ages. He included a French translation of "Fons Vitae" from a Hebrew version which he identified as a work of Shlomo Ibn-Gabirol (1845). The repercussions of Munk's achievements were immediate. In 1858 he was named a member of the French Academy, and in 1864 he was called to the prestigious Chair of Hebrew at the Collège de France, vacant since the dismissal of Ernest Renan under the pressure of the clerical party. The honor paid to Munk by non-Jews also had a wider impact by elevating the collective self-respect of French Jews.[6]

The Science of Judaism penetrated Jewish consciousness in France not only because of the efforts of these two scholars. In this respect, German-Jewish influence was important because of the publication, by Jewish and non-Jewish periodicals, of articles by men like Zunz, Frankel, Geiger, Sachs, Jost, and Graetz. Since the early 1850s Graetz's *History of the Jewish People* was of major importance in the shaping of French-Jewish consciousness, especially its third volume, *Sinai and Golgatha,* edited in 1867 with the assistance of Moses Hess and Gustave d'Eichthal. This volume, which dealt with the period of the Second Temple and the rise of Christianity, was considered an excellent rejoinder in the Christian-Jewish dispute that has been revived by Renan's book, *Life of Jesus* (1863). Renan denied any inner connection between ancient Jewish tradition and the new religious doctrine preached by Jesus, and presented the sequence of Judaism-Christianity as purely chronological. A Jewish reaction against this kind of Christocentric outlook was a necessity for Jewish self-esteem, and Graetz's work supplied arguments that fitted well into this context of the continuous public debate concerning the nature of historical continuity at a crucial stage of transition in the development of the world religions. The translation of *Sinai and Golgatha* as well as the remainder of Graetz's *History of the Jewish People* were intended to change the attitude of French Jewry toward their past so that they would view it not only as the spiritual heritage of a religious denomination, but as the history of a nation even after the destruction of the Second Temple and the worldwide dispersion of the Jews.

The Science of Judaism influenced even French Jewry's institutional evolution: The *Société littéraire pour la science du Judaisme* (1879) and the periodical *Revue des Études Juives* (1882) grew out of a continuous contact between French- and German-Jewish intellectuals.[7]

The two communities underwent a parallel process of modernization during the nineteenth century, but it is worthwhile to bear in mind that there were also some major divergences that historians have often neglected. The Revolution and the Napoleonic regime created a particular sociopolitical setting that differentiated French from German Jewry. We may perceive how far-reaching was the change brought about by the events between 1789 and 1815 when we observe the close cooperation between French- and German-Jewish community leaders only a few years before 1789. Cerf Berr, the leader and *shtadlan* of Alsacian Jewry, approached Mendelssohn in 1780, after the Jewish situation in Alsace had become critical, because of the unscrupulous machinations of the fanatical Jew-baiter François Hell. His tract, "Observations d'un Alsacien sur l'affaires présente des Juifs d'Alsace" (1779), represented Jews as an accursed and criminal people. Cerf Berr supplied Mendelssohn with material for a treatise advocating the Jews' claim for fair treatment by the state. Mendelssohn, in order to comply with the request of his Jewish brethren in Alsace, invited the ministerial counselor (*Kriegsrat*) C.W. Dohm to assist him in the preparation of the memoir, which would be submitted by Cerf Berr to the Council of State in 1780. The outcome was the publication, as late as 1784, of Louis XVI's *Lettres Patentes*. The royal measures were rather disappointing for the Jews, but they did at least abolish the body tax (*Leibzoll*). More significantly, the Jewish leaders in both countries cooperated in this affair. A Jew dwelling in the Berlin of Friedrich II could play a decisive role in the public debate on the status of the Jews in France.[8]

This cooperation itself reflected both traditional and innovative elements in Jewish cultural life. One bond was the well-established figure of Mendelssohn, not only as a man of letters and a member of the Berlin community, but also as an intercessor who was ready and able to intervene on behalf of fellow Jews even outside his local community. Just as he reacted to appeals addressed to him by community leaders in Altona, Königsberg, or Dresden (1769–1777), he wasted no time in responding to the call for help that had reached him from Alsace.

Second, the community still remained the major frame of reference for Jews and as such had many traits in common on both sides of the Rhine. True, it was a community of transition, as reflected in the radical shift in the attitude toward Jewish autonomy shown for example in Mendelssohn's objections on religious as well as civil grounds against the rabbis' right to impose the ban. Yet Jewish community life remained a sociocultural setting which Jews in Alsace had in common with Prussian Jews. A constant migration of men and ideas between the two communities was normal. Rabbis from abroad came to stay in French communities. One such was Jonathan Eibeschütz (1690–1764), who occupied the position of rabbi in Metz (1741) and left afterwards to settle in the German community of Altona-Hamburg-Wandsbeck (1750).

Mendelssohn, because of his Enlightenment conception of Judaism and his intervention of 1780, had great influence on the nature of the arguments chosen in the ensuing public debate in France. This debate evolved in three stages. First, four years before the French Revolution, when the Royal Society of Arts and Sciences in Metz announced a prize essay on the subject "Are there means of making the Jews happy and more useful in France?" Henri Grégoire clearly referred to Dohm and Mendelssohn. In 1787 Count Mirabeau, the advocate of equality who had come to know Mendelssohn and Dohm in Berlin, achieved prominence with his book *On Mendelssohn and Political Reform of the Jews.*

Second, this influence affected the legislative deliberations of the National Assembly during the French Revolution which led ultimately to the granting of citizenship to all Jews of France (1791). Jewish and non-Jewish champions of civil rights, Grégoire as well as Isaia Berr Bing, referred to concepts and ideas of Mendelssohn and the Berlin Haskalah.

Third, there was one term that permeated the public debate which was adopted by Furtado and the Jewish delegates at the Napoleonic assemblies (1806–1807): *régénération* or *civic betterment,* a term which had been introduced by C.W. Dohm in his book *Die bürgerliche Verbesserung der Juden* (1781). It appeared during the deliberations of the Sanhedrin, was sanctioned by the Sanhedrin's decisions, and included in the statutes of the Consistoire. During the public debate it underwent some modifications. Nevertheless, its use retained a discernible link with the enlightened outlook of the Berlin Haskalah, signifying modernization as encompassing all spheres of life, the socioeconomic, political, and the religious.

At the turn of the century there was not only a "German orientation" of French Jews, but for a limited time its opposite existed—a "French orientation" of German Jews, mainly in the areas of the struggle for civil rights and the reform of Judaism.

After 1789 the Jewish enlightened elite in Germany did not conceal its sympathy for the ideas of the French Revolution, viewing Napoleon as the messenger of its revolutionary heritage.[9] They greeted his "Jewish policy" with sincere good will, a sentiment articulated by Israel Jacobson, the Court Jew and intercessor of the Jewish community in Westphalia.

In 1805, before Napoleon summoned the Assembly of Notables to Paris, Jacobson had submitted to him a project for reorganization. It suggested that a Jewish council should be established which would be empowered to resolve all possible conflicts between the obligations of a Jew to his religion and to the state. This proposal was one stimulus for

Napoleon's convening of the Sanhedrin. Almost a year after the latter met, on 8 February 1808, the Westphalian Jewish Notables assembled under Jacobson's guidance to work out a sketch for a consistory, which was actually established on 31 March 1808. This sketch follows closely the French Consistory decree and in some matters copies it verbatim. One important difference was that this consistory allowed a layman like Jacobson to function as leader and to promote his program of *régénération*. His innovations were not far-reaching, but he tried to impose them on the none-too-willing communities throughout the Westphalian kingdom and was not satisfied with reforming religious services in the consistorial schools at Cassel and in the temple at Seesen.[10]

While before 1815 there were enough common elements in the respective sociopolitical contexts of German and French Jewry so that one could speak of a common pattern of modernization, the reaction after the Congress of Vienna abruptly modified the situation. In most German states Jews were deprived of their rights and returned to the status of second-class citizens. With this restoration of the previous situation the centralized community structure of Westphalia also disappeared. Henceforth the path of *régénération* in the two Jewish communities was largely different. The only reminder of Napoleon's rule and its impact on German-Jewish affairs was the decision of the first assembly of rabbis in Brunswick (1844) that explicitly sanctioned the decisions of the Paris Sanhedrin. The assembly, following a proposal by the Reform rabbi Ludwig Philippson, formed a special commission to examine the twelve questions put in 1807 to the seventy-one members of the Paris Sanhedrin. In light of German Jewry's particular reality, the Brunswick assembly adopted some minor modifications, but it preserved the core of the Sanhedrin decisions. Despite this event, 1815 was a turning-point, dissolving the "common sociopolitical setting" of the Jewish communities in the two countries. The development of the Reform movement in Germany provides evidence of this differentiation.

French Jewry, quite in contrast to its German counterpart, did not hasten to promote religious reform. During the nineteenth century there was no outstanding protagonist of Reform in France, neither rabbi nor layman. There were no Geigers, Holdheims, or Philippsons in France. Whatever change in religious ritual and observances took place was slow and slight. The consistorial rabbis convened in Paris only once during the whole century (1856) to articulate a policy of religious reform. The conference was called by the Grand Rabbi Ulmann, who was the most progressive and most inclined toward reform of the rabbis to have entered the Central Consistory. Nevertheless he made it clear in his preliminary outline of the agenda that the meeting should not be seen as a Sanhedrin and that no alteration to the law should be admitted beyond what could be justified by the halachah.[11] The conference's major aim was defined as increasing orderliness and dignity in the synagogues. The rabbis made every effort to prevent a breach, resolving that decisions would be taken according to a simple majority and that questions concerning their application would be held in abeyance. The assembly's deliberations confirmed Ulmann's moderate intentions. Many questions discussed in the rabbinical assemblies on the left bank of the Rhine were not even mentioned—questions such as the language of prayer, the revision of the prayer book, the question of the Messiah, the transfer of Shabbat services to Sunday, or circumcision. The decisions taken ultimately referred to marginal aspects of Reform;[12] the assembly decided to limit the number of *piyutim,* to organize synagogue services for the blessing of the newborn, to conduct the funeral services with more ceremonial, and to instruct rabbis and officiating ministers to wear a garb resembling that worn by Catholic clergy. It was also resolved to make greater use of the sermon in the synagogue, to reduce the length of services, to conduct them in a more dignified manner, and to introduce the ceremony of religious initiation, particularly for girls, whose religious instruction was to be inspected and approved. The assembly also called for the transfer of the rabbinical seminary to Paris. Regarding the controversy over the use of the organ in the synagogue, it was decided that its use on Shabbat and festivals was lawful, provided it was played by a non-Jew. Even this decision would be subject, however, to the authorization of the chief rabbi of the department concerned, at the request of the local rabbi. With the adoption of half-measures and the preservation of the independence of the local rabbi, a breach in the community was avoided. In the eyes of the consistorial leadership, unity had priority over a rapid transformation of religious observances and ceremonies.

Such radical reform attempts as were made in France remained a marginal phenomenon, as in the case of Olry Terquem's proposals. From the early 1820s Terquem wrote in favor of mixed marriages as a practical way of obeying the Sanhedrin's commandment "to love the Christians like brothers."[13] Between 1821 and 1837 he published "Nine letters" concerning radical Reform: he suggested the transfer of the Shabbat services to Sunday and the abrogation of some of the holidays and the traditional practice of circumcision. He attacked the Talmud and the observance of Halachah norms and advocated in its place the return to the Bible as the only source of Judaism.

The majority of the consistorial leadership clung to a moderate path of Reform. Even the periodical *Archives Israélites,*[14] which saw one of its roles as the awakening of public opinion to Reform, rejected Terquem's radicalism. No *Austrittsgemeinde* existed in France. The more conservative communities of Alsace-Lorraine lived alongside the Enlightened Jewish circles in Paris and other urban communities.

Only after almost a century of reform, something resembling a Reform Temple opened in France in 1907, founded by the small Union for Liberal Judaism. A Reform prayer book first appeared only in 1913. Hamburg's first Reform Temple had been inaugurated in 1818.

In 1872, L.R. Bischoffsheim, banker and community leader, wrote to Abraham Geiger deploring the backwardness of religious reform in France: "Many of the richest and most influential families do not visit the Synagogues. Their daughters marry Christian men and rich families' children receive no Jewish education, not even a scientific one. If this erosion continues, Judaism will be absorbed by Christianity. The only rescue might be religious reform!"[15] During the nineteenth century the majority of French Jewry rejected radical Reform. The reasons for this rejection, for the failure of Reform in France, are to be found in the particularly differentiated history of French Jewry in the nineteenth century.

After 1791, French Jewry traveled its particular road to modernization. The acquisition of civil rights in that year stimulated economic, social, and political integration. The Jewish elites, intellectuals as well as wealthy bourgeoisie, felt no obligation to prove that the Jewish religion was no obstacle to the adaptation and integration of Jews to a modern policy. After the abolition of the *décrêt infâme,* Jews were under no pressure to offer special expressions of loyalty to the state and its Christian culture. Neither the arguments of the right-wing clericals nor those of the radicals on the Left, contrasting adherence to Jewish religion and loyalty to the national state, perturbed the French-Jewish community leaders. Anti-Jewish circles were a minority when compared to the politically powerful moderate Center.

The French-Jewish pattern of modernization enabled French Jewry to resist the German-Jewish pattern. This resistance was buttressed by the original conception of Jewish politics created by French Jewry. German Jewry on the other hand was very reluctant to adopt a style of Jewish politics until the nineteenth century.

Twice during the nineteenth century the elite of French Jewry opted for independent Jewish action, while the elite of German Jewry abstained and at least twice even opposed such an initiative: (1) In 1840, on the occasion of the Damascus blood libel, the leaders of French Jewry used all the resources of political pressure offered by the existing political system in order to rescue Jews suffering for their Judaism in a world far removed from Paris. (2) In 1860, the founding of the Alliance Israélite

Universelle[16] formalized the willingness of French Jews to carry on Jewish politics in an organization bridging national boundaries. It was their publicly announced aim to help Jewish communities all over the world in their struggle for emancipation, honorable existence, and modernization, exploiting all possible means which the modern state put at their disposal for purposive political action.

In these two cases the German-Jewish elite reacted reluctantly, or even refused to join in international Jewish action of a political character. In 1840 Geiger wrote to his friend Derenbourg in Paris:

> As far as the Damascus blood libel is concerned, you are right; it is a quite honorable thing, when eminent people [Crémieux, Montefiore, Munk] manifest solidarity with persecuted brethren, but I for my part would spare my energies in order to promote a great Jewish achievement. In my eyes it is more important that Jews in Russia are admitted to become pharmacists or lawyers than that Jews in Asia or Africa are rescued.[17]

Ludwig Philippson mentioned quite different reasons from those of Geiger when he reacted negatively after French Jewry's second political act in 1860. The editor of the *Allgemeine Zeitung des Judentums* who had already given sufficient proof of his willingness to cooperate with Jewish communities all over the world on several occasions, made his position clear in a special article:

> To help Jews by intercessors is quite good, but you have to do it without political articulation, and any form of international organization must be prevented. Even the proper name "Alliance" must raise fear in the hearts of thousands of Christians who might be afraid of an organized secret power uniting the Jews all over the world.

Jewish politics in France were tied to a political conception of Judaism[18] which represented a clear deviation from that inspired by Mendelssohn. According to the new outlook, the Jewish heritage—the tradition transmitted by the Bible, the liberation from slavery in Egypt, the covenant between God and Israel, the Laws of Moses, the oral law of the Mishna and Talmud, the biblical as well as postbiblical history—all these elements of a holy religious tradition underwent a transmutation and acquired in modern French-Jewish consciousness a political significance which could serve as legitimation for political action in the Jewish present.

In conclusion, the question of the impact of German-Jewish developments on the modernization of French Jewry should be answered differently before and after 1789. German Jewry exercised a considerable impact before 1789, as long as the Jews on both sides of the Rhine lived in the common sociocultural setting of the traditional Jewish community. With the emancipation of French Jewry, the establishment of a centralized community system, the Consistoire, the impact of Reform on the life of German Jewry—this influence diminished steadily, to be replaced by the particular pattern of French-Jewish modernization. Even the flow of a certain German-Jewish influence through the Science of Judaism should not lead us to ignore the growing estrangement between the two Jewish communities, which reached its apogee in the wake of 1870.

Notes

1. F. Stern, *Gold and Iron: Bismarck, Bleichröder and the Building of the German Empire* (London: Allen & Unwin, 1977), pp. 6–7, 148–55.
2. L. Geiger, "A. Geigers Briefe an J. Derenbourg, 1833–1848," *Allgemeine Zeitung des Judentums (AZJ)* 60, no. 5 (1896).
3. D. McLellen, *Karl Marx: His Life and Thought* (New York: Harper & Row, 1977), pp. 62–79.
4. M. Schwab, *Salomon Munk, sa vie et ses oeuvres* (Paris: Leroux, 1900), pp. 22–56.
5. S. Cahen, *La Bible—l'Exode* (Paris, 1832); *La Bible—Les Nombres* (Paris, 1833), pp. 1–34.
6. M. Schwab, *Salomon Munk,* pp. 64–167.
7. E. Silberner, Letters of H. Graetz and M. Hess, in *Annali dell'Instituto Giangiacomo Feltrinelli* (Milano: Feltrinelli 1961).
8. A. Hertzberg, *The French Enlightenment and the Jews* (New York: Columbia University Press, 1969), chap. 10.
9. S. Ascher, *Ideen zur natürlichen Geschichte der Revolutionen* (Berlin, 1802); S. Ascher, *Napoleon oder über den Fortschritt der Regierung* (Berlin, 1808), pp. 81–93.
10. J.R. Marcus, *Israel Jacobson: The Founder of the Reform Movement in Judaism* (Cincinnati: Hebrew Union College Press, 1972), pp. 52–106.
11. S. Ulmann, *Lettre pastorale adressée aux fidèles du culte israélite au nom de la conférence des grands rabbins de France par son président le grand rabbin du Consistoire Central* (Paris, 1856).
12. *Compte rendu des résolutions formées par MM. les grand rabbins de France, réunis en conférence du 15 au 23 mai 1856* (Paris, 1856).
13. Tsarphati (O. Terquem), *Première lettre d'un Israélite français à ses coréligionnaires sur l'urgente nécessité de célébrer l'office en français le jour de dimanche* (Paris, 1821).
14. *Les Archives Israélites,* I (1840), pp. 1–5, 159–61, 518; II (1841), pp. 1–3, 237–41, 408, 468; III (1842), pp. 117, 637–39.
15. A. Geiger, *Nachgelassene Schriften* (Berlin, 1878), vol. 5, p. 345; letter from Bischoffsheim to Geiger, 7 September 1872.
16. M. Graetz, *From Periphery to Center* (Jerusalem, 1982), pp. 281–322.
17. *AZJ* 60, no. 24 (1896): 282.
18. M. Graetz, *From Periphery to Center,* pp. 154–85.

7

The Impact of German-Jewish Modernization on Dutch Jewry

Joseph Michman

Anyone who decides to investigate the influence Germany exercised on the Netherlands, and German Jewry on Dutch Jewry, should be forewarned that he is entering a field strewn with snares and pitfalls. For the Netherlands appear to have closer connections with Germany than any other non-German country. The Netherlands had been part of the German Holy Roman Empire;[1] the adjective *Dutch* (from *diets,* Dutch for *German*) reflects this historic relationship. William of Orange, the founder of the independent Dutch nation, proudly stated that he was "of German blood," at least in the words of the Dutch national anthem. Many a Dutch patriot felt the greatest difficulty singing these words during the German occupation in World War II, since both *German* and *blood* outraged his inner convictions.

Many Germans, on the other hand, interpreted such terms as proof—if any was needed—that the Netherlands formed a part of the German Reich. A mere accident of history had resulted in the separation of this German "border province" from the body to which it belonged by origin and because of the language and essential characteristics of its inhabitants.[2] The German nationalist Julius Langbehn went so far as to discern in these Lower Germans the vibrant root of the German Empire, and personalities like William of Orange and Rembrandt were in his eyes "the most beautiful flowers in the German garland."[3] No wonder National Socialist forerunners such as Wilhelm Marr[4] and Moeller van den Bruck[5] latched on to this theme, and no wonder that the Nazi authorities lost no time implementing this theory immediately upon their occupation of the Netherlands in World War II.[6] This conception of the Netherlands as a misplaced German border province influenced the German treatment of the Dutch Jews. The newly regained western province had to be cleansed of its Jewish inhabitants so that the Aryan population, no longer defiled by Jewish influences, could speedily be reintegrated as pure German within the German Reich. Because the Nazis viewed the Netherlands as German, they persecuted Dutch Jewry more severely than any other Jewish community in Western Europe.[7]

German Jews were also inclined to see the Netherlands as a German province, and the Dutch language as some kind of broad German no more or less intelligible than any other German dialect. This perception caused quite a few misunderstandings between German and Dutch Jews; it even cost Rabbi Jacob Rosenberg his chief rabbinical seat in Groningen after he had consistently denigrated the Dutch language.[8]

There were other reasons why German Jews tended to blur the boundaries between the Netherlands and Germany. Even the Ashkenazic Jews in Holland referred to themselves as "High-German" Jews, thus emphasizing that the founders of their community originated in southern Germany. Not that the various Ashkenazic congregations in the Netherlands were ever entirely German. They included many Jews from Alsace and, following the Chmielnicki pogroms and similar calamities, large numbers from Poland, Lithuania, Bohemia, and other countries, so that during the eighteenth century the original German element constituted only a small minority. But even the originally non-German Jews had German connections, often because of family ties but in many cases through commercial contacts. A lively trade was conducted with Hamburg, while the Leipzig Fair was a principal market for Dutch-Jewish merchants. The Netherlands were an important center of overseas trade, and in the latter half of the eighteenth century prominent Jewish commercial houses established branch offices in England and North America. We should also remember that in the eighteenth century the borders between Germany and the Netherlands were not as clearly defined as they are today. The eastern Dutch provinces of Groningen, Overijssel, Gelderland, and Limburg melted almost indistinguishably into western Germany. The Jews in these areas in particular were connected through close family and commercial ties with families in East Friesland, Münsterland, Westphalia, and especially, the Cleve area.

Despite the diverse and close economic cultural and religious contacts between Dutch Jews and their German cousins, significant differences did exist. I take the situation at the end of the eighteenth century as my reference point.

The Republic of the United Netherlands, as it was officially known, formed a national and cultural entity notwithstanding its federal character and the substantial independence of its provinces and cities. It opposed, and indeed had to oppose, the three great powers—France, Great Britain, and Germany—which surrounded and frequently threatened it. France's influence was due to the predominance of French language and culture among the well-to-do and the elite since the era of Burgundian rule in the fifteenth century. Great Britain's interest resulted from the intense rivalry between the two countries in shipping and commerce, particularly in their respective colonies. Germany took third place not because there were fewer Germans in the Netherlands than Frenchmen or Englishmen but simply because Germany was a relative latecomer. Politically Prussia began to play a role of some importance in the Netherlands only toward the end of the eighteenth century, as reflected in the intermarriage between the House of Orange and the Hohenzollerns. Culturally, however, classical and French influences were so strong in the Netherlands that an awareness of German culture developed slowly.

The Netherlands differed from all other European states in their complex constitutional arrangements. This complexity was reflected in the extremely confused legal and social status of the Jews in the Netherlands. The legal basis of Jewish presence in the Netherlands was a resolution passed in 1619 by the states of Holland and West Friesland which was subsequently adopted by the other provinces. By its terms each city or town could decide for itself whether it wanted to admit or exclude Jews or attach any conditions to their residence, with one significant restriction: it was forbidden to make the Jews wear any external signs that would set them apart from the general population. Understandably this resolution resulted in a multiplicity of particular regulations and arrangements that can be grouped in two broad categories: cities which admitted Jews and cities which did not. In the towns where Jews were admitted they nearly always lived an undisturbed and protected existence. While they were usually barred from the guilds, they found the authorities on their side whenever any trouble threatened from the general population. No pogrom or expulsion took place, nor do we have any information about Jews being molested as Jews.

The situation in Amsterdam deserves a closer look, because Amsterdam was the most powerful city in the entire country with the largest concentration of Jewish residents. It was Amsterdam that had forced through the resolution of 1619 in order to have a free hand in its dealings with the Jews. The burgomasters of this cosmopolitan port city, which already sheltered representatives of so many different nations, had no qualms about accepting members of the Jewish nation as well. In fact they hoped that the Portuguese-Jewish merchants would contribute to the city's continued economic expansion. It was thanks to the often wealthy Portuguese that the mainly destitute Ashkenazic Jews were admitted on the same conditions.

The Jews of Amsterdam were subject to certain economic restrictions. Not only were they barred from the guilds, but they were also forbidden after 1632 to own shops or taverns. However, the implementation of this decree was honored in the breach. For almost two centuries the civic authorities resisted any attempts to increase the number of restrictions. On the other hand the Jews enjoyed complete religious freedom, and in this respect their position was far superior to that of the Roman Catholics. Since Catholic worship was officially forbidden, the faithful were forced to conduct their services in churches hidden behind the façades of warehouses and in attics. The Jews were free to worship as they liked and even built three imposing synagogues which completely dominated their surroundings. This freedom of religion, and the consistently protective attitude of the authorities, gave the Jews a feeling of security and belonging. While lacking some of the privileges of the Protestant majority and suffering greater economic discrimination than the Catholics, the Jews did feel part of a pluriform society in which each group had its own rights and responsibilities and knew its place.

The demographic, economic, and legal structure of the Jewish community in the Netherlands differed from those of other Western European countries, Germany included. The Jews were not completely separate from the general community, but neither were they fully integrated. In 1800, the Jewish population of Amsterdam numbered between 20,000 and 25,000, making it one of the largest Jewish communities in the world. The Jews lived in fairly crowded conditions, several residential quarters were predominantly Jewish, and Jews formed a highly visible element in the city's everyday life. Amsterdam harbored a sizable Jewish proletariat, including quite a few rabble-rousers prone to riot at the drop of a hat. During the aborted Patriot Revolution of 1787 against the House of Orange, the *parnassim* had great difficulty preventing their Orangist subjects from joining the fray. I use the word *subjects* advisedly since the city fathers had delegated a large part of their authority over the members of the Jewish community to the *parnassim*. Apart from religious punishments such as the ban, they could impose prison terms or lodge complaints with the authorities who would invariably support the religious establishment. In Amsterdam the word *autonomy* was not merely a theoretical concept. The Jews lived within a large, separate but not segregated community in a city within a city, ruled—like all other cities in the Dutch Republic—by an oligarchy.

Oligarchic rule in the Jewish community reflected not only the general political arrangement but also the economic situation of Dutch Jews. It would be an illusion to think that Jewish poverty was restricted to the urban proletariate. All available records show that the majority of the

Jewish inhabitants of smaller towns and villages lived in conditions of poverty. However, their situation was quantitatively and qualitatively different from Amsterdam's. In the rural areas and provincial towns daily life was relatively cheap; there was always a way of scraping a few pennies together, and really indigent members of the community would depend on charitable contributions from their more affluent coreligionists.

In Amsterdam the situation was far more serious. Grave economic setbacks during the second half of the eighteenth century had dealt a heavy blow to both the Sephardic and the High-German communities, and many a wealthy family had been reduced to penury. The number of indigent Ashkenazic Jews on dole is estimated to have amounted to 17,000–18,000, and these had to be supported by a narrow upper layer of 3,000–4,000 more prosperous Jews. The necessary funds were provided by a charity fund (*kupath hazdakah*), which received its income from the sale of kosher meat. To ensure a steady replenishment of revenues, it was necessary to sell this meat at a high price and to prevent people from buying elsewhere. With the full support of the civil authorities, the *parnassim* took the most stringent measures to ensure that every Jewish family bought its meat exclusively at the communal slaughter-house.

These coercive measures could be justified by the community's enormous welfare expenses: in addition to relief payments, the poor were given clothing and food, including *matzoth* for Passover. The community also employed a small army of professional and clerical workers, among them physicians, midwives, nurses, pharmacists, and teachers. It also ran schools, a hospital, and at a later stage a workhouse. Charitable expenditures therefore constituted the largest item in the communal budget. This point, which historians have overlooked, cannot be stressed too much. The responsibility for the social and economic welfare of thousands of indigent Jews weighed heavily on the Amsterdam *kehillah* (community). This problem dominated the thoughts not only of the Jewish leadership, but also of the national and particularly the Amsterdam civic authorities when discussion began about Jewish emancipation. The perception of this social problem determined the difference between the emancipation of the Jews in the Netherlands on the one hand, and in France and Germany on the other.

Emancipation, the granting of civil equality to the Jewish inhabitants, was ratified by the National Assembly on 2 September 1796. It was a direct outcome of the conquest of the Republic of the United Netherlands and its replacement by the Batavian Republic as a French protectorate. The decision for emancipation was taken under heavy pressure from the French ambassador. The French representatives in the Netherlands and later the French occupation authorities, following French annexation, pursued the implementation of Jewish emancipation far more vigorously than was the case in France itself.

The situation the French faced in the Netherlands was very different from that in France. On the one hand, the unreconstructed traditional Christian religious establishment believed that Jews who professed a belief in their own Messiah could not possibly become equal citizens in a Christian state. On the other hand, the Dutch revolutionaries concluded that Jewish belief in a Messiah proved that the Jews supported a king and must hence be considered monarchists. But the opposition was not exclusively theological in nature. Merchants and shopkeepers feared the competition of thousands of Jewish peddlars and artisans who would threaten their livelihood if the guilds were dissolved and the Jews admitted to the professions of their choice. Fierce resistance also came from the Amsterdam burgomasters, who even sought legal aid in an effort to try and foil the acceptance of the emancipation decrees. The burgomasters' anti-Jewish sentiments are not surprising, for emancipation meant taking the care for the poor away from the *parnassim,* and the burgomasters were afraid to be saddled with the responsibility.[9]

Emancipation was a double-edged sword for the Jews as well. On the one hand it gave them equal rights, but on the other it put an end to their special autonomous form of government. It meant the annulment of the *takkanoth,* the regulations which empowered the *parnassim.* So the *parnassim* also organized a lobby, just as the burgomasters had done. The modernists (*maskilim*) were inclined to ascribe the negative attitude of the *parnassim* to a mere craving for power, and indeed the functionaries who lorded it over the *kehillah* cannot be entirely absolved on this score. But the *parnassim* also had factual arguments which would be wrong to neglect. They feared the erosion of the financial basis for relief of poverty. The justice of this argument did not become immediately apparent. While the state had proclaimed the legal equality of the Jews and the annulment of the *takkanoth,* in practice very little seemed to change.

From 1796 to 1808 the situation remained ambiguous and confused. Discrimination against the Jews survived, and the *parnassim* continued to exercise their authority. On the other hand, any Jew who rebelled against this discrimination, or who refused to obey the Jewish communal regulations, could turn to the authorities or to a court of law in the reasonable expectation of being vindicated. Obviously only a few were able to take this lengthy and often costly road. The authority of the *parnassim,* although weakened, remained sufficiently strong to be accepted by the mainstream of Dutch Jewry. The *maskilim* never converted more than a negligible minority, several dozen families consisting of a few hundred individuals, whereas the masses continued to cling with un-diminished fervor to the old regime.

This situation came to an end in 1808, when Louis Bonaparte, who had been proclaimed king of Holland, introduced an entirely new "church order" for the whole of his kingdom. Louis's Jewish policy was inspired by modernist Jewish advisers. It was largely patterned on the French consistorial legislation but omitted its anti-Jewish regulations to which Napoleon attached such great value. Unlike his brother, Louis possessed outspoken sympathy for the Jews and tried to do everything in his power to ameliorate their lot. He could not foresee that the new regulations would have the opposite effect. During Louis's reign (1806–1810) and the succeeding period of French annexation, the Netherlands became (1810–1813) impoverished and its Jewish inhabitants even more so. The implementation of the new regulations terminated the power of the *parnassim*. As a result the entire system of relief collapsed and the charitable revenues from the sale of meat dropped within four years to one-third of their former level. The price of emancipation was paid by the poor of Amsterdam. Hundreds of starving and sick indigents roamed the streets, ragged and destitute.[10]

The effects of the emancipation process determined the structure of the nineteenth-century Dutch-Jewish community: a thin upper layer of an affluent and educated elite, most of whom were gradually turning away from Jewish religious precepts, and a vast proletariat, the majority of whom remained faithful to their Torah and Jewish traditions until the third quarter of the nineteenth century. Outside Amsterdam the contrasts were less marked and the numbers involved fewer, but everywhere the prosperous were the exception, while the poor saw their already large numbers swelled by an influx of equally needy Jewish immigrants from Germany.

German-Jewish influence in the Netherlands should be evaluated in relation to the particular situation of the Dutch Jews as portrayed here. Demographic data about the German-Jewish influx have not yet been evaluated, but the German human input was clearly considerable, both as a result of immigration and through intermarriage. Genealogical investigation reveals many instances of a close intertwining of Dutch and German families. In the economic field no systematic study has yet been made of the Dutch Jews' commercial relations with Germany, but available information shows that these were very intensive.

These demographic and economic links provide the context for the discussion of the penetration of German-Jewish cultural influence.[11] From the third quarter of the eighteenth century German Haskalah (Enlighten-ment) ideas vied with the traditional French influence in the Netherlands.

The first connections were established by Naftali Herz Weisel, whose business affairs took him to Amsterdam, where he lived from 1755 till 1767.[12] Weisel befriended several Sephardic Amsterdam intellectuals, notably David Franco Mendes and Yitzhak Cohen Belinfante, whom he introduced to the works of Moses Mendelssohn. Their friendship continued after Weisel's departure for Copenhagen. A second admirer of Mendelssohn who took up residence in Holland was Naphtali Herz Ulman, who had been expelled from Mainz because of his heretical philosophical ideas.[13] In 1769 he published two treatises in Dutch. Shortly afterwards there followed the first Dutch translations of Mendelssohn's works.

Mendelssohn's first translators were non-Jewish scholars,[14] but this does not mean that his ideas found no adherents in Jewish circles as has been alleged by some Dutch-Jewish scholars.[15] On the contrary, Mendelssohn was highly regarded by the *maskilim* and later by official rabbinical circles until the end of the nineteenth century. Mendelssohn's close collaborator, Rabbi Solomon Dubno, visited Amsterdam already before 1787 and the prospectus for Mendelssohn's translation of the Bible, *Alim Literufah,* was printed in Amsterdam and signed by Dubno.[16] Dubno lived in Amsterdam the last quarter of his life (d. 1813) and influenced a group of younger people such as Sommerhausen, Mulder, and Lemans[17] who became the propagandists for the revival of Hebrew literature in the Netherlands. Dubno did not mix in Dutch politics but other emigrants are known to have been very active in this respect. David Friedrichsfeld, who maintained close relations with David Friedländer, published several polemical treatises refuting the accusations of the opponents of Jewish emancipation. Under the pseudonym Philanthropus, he contributed to the Yiddish pamphlets published by the Neie Kille (Adath Jesurun) against the Alte Kille.[18] Still another German Jew who deserves mention in this connection was Hirsch Sommerhausen, whose father had been the secretary of the Hague banker Boas.[19] Subsequently both father and son became teachers in Jewish schools in Amsterdam. Hirsch was an active Hebraist and one of the founders of Hanokh Lana'ar al pi darko, a group which initiated a Bible translation into Dutch in imitation of Mendelssohn's translation. They sought to combat the use of Yiddish among the Amsterdam proletariat.[20]

Another educational initiative was the founding in Groningen of a modern Jewish school, Tiph'eret Bachurim, by a follower of Mendelssohn, Dr. Heinrich Löwe.[21] This school was regarded as a model; it inspired the government officials who formulated the Law of 1817 on Jewish schools. The replacement of French by German influence may also be adduced from the development of a Jewish theatrical group in Amsterdam. It was founded in 1784 by J.H. Dessauer and called "Joods Hoogduits

Gezelschap." Its motto was *Industrie et Création* and *Amusement et Culture.* The group performed mainly operas translated from various languages including French, Italian, and German. But from 1796 onward almost all the performances were in German. Dessauer himself wrote a German play, "Mardochai und Esther, oder die geretteten Juden." After the French evacuation of the Netherlands in 1814 Dessauer's troups performed a German comedy in the reopened German playhouse, followed by a short play written by Dessauer, "Wir dürfen wieder spielen."[22]

That German Jews participated in the internal political argument is not remarkable, since most European intellectuals saw themselves as belonging to one brotherhood. It is striking, however, that German Jews were the only ones to disseminate the philosophical and religious ideas of the Enlightenment. The Dutch proponents, among them Hartog Bromet, Moses and Carel Asser, and Jonas Daniel Meyer were primarily interested in the Enlightenment's legal and social aspects. Religious publications such as those by Moses Cohen Belinfante and Sommerhausen were either translations from the German of treatises originally written in other languages or translations of German works. The sole more or less original Dutch contribution to the discussion concerned the bearing of arms on Saturday. But here too, the motive was practical. Jews had been serving in the army and navy of the Republic since the second half of the eighteenth century with the blessing of the chief rabbi of Amsterdam, the famous Rabbi Shaul. The revolutionary Jews demanded to be allowed to join the civil guard, but this demand was contested not only by the officers and men of the civil guard but also by the rabbinical authorities of Amsterdam. In a pamphlet, Hartog Bromet pointed out that the halachah did not forbid Jews to bear arms on *Shabbat,* referring to the blessing given by Rabbi Shaul as a solid precedent.[23] Moses Cohen Belinfante repeated these arguments in defense of the Jewish Arms Corps founded by King Louis Bonaparte in 1809.[24] Here too the discussion was not principally concerned with theoretical concepts, but with the pragmatic objective of full Jewish equality before the law. Non-Jews were exhorted to recognize the right of the Jews to join the militias, while Jews were shown that halachah permitted the bearing of arms.

Dutch Jews were not very interested in philosophical speculation, which was strictly a German polemic importation used by the modernists and decried by the traditionalists. Such arguments were adduced against N.H. Ulman's publications.[25] The followers of the old Amsterdam *kehillah* maintained that the rampant heretical notions were merely a consequence of German-Jewish immigration. Traditionalists viewed this alleged generosity toward impecunious German-Jewish immigrants as misplaced. The immigrants were seen as corrupting Dutch-Jewish youth through

German novels and philosophical treatises that undermined religion. Such accusations were levelled against the German Jews in the *Diskursen* of the Alte Kille.[26] Nearly a century and a half later, during the 1930s, the same argument was used against the Reform movement which was also dismissed as "import-non-Judaism."[27]

The establishment in 1797 of the secessionist congregation Adath Jesurun in Amsterdam should be considered against this background. This congregation has occasionally been called the first Reform congregation. In fact, the reforms were fairly superficial. Proponents of the breakaway congregation maintained that they simply selected the best from various liturgies, including part of the ritual of the Sephardic congregation in Amsterdam.[28] As their rabbi they chose a very Orthodox rabbi, Rabbi Israel Ger, who was acting as chief rabbi of the Ashkenazic congregation after the death of Rabbi Shaul (1790). He had been disappointed when the son of Rabbi Shaul, Rabbi Jakob Moshe, who was inferior to him as a talmudist, had been nominated chief rabbi of Amsterdam (1793).[29] The founders of Adath Jesurun could therefore argue plausibly that their motivations for its establishment were not religious.[30] This also facilitated its subsequent dissolution. The members were able to rejoin the old congregation, which had only to make a minor concession with respect to religious practice,[31] whereas the concessions in other areas were substantial. Anyone who sees the establishment of Adath Jesurun as an effort toward religious reform because it introduced minor changes in the service must conclude that it proved to be a nonstarter.

Subsequent developments showed that this religious conservatism was no mere coincidence, for religious reforms have never succeeded in the Netherlands. In the middle of the nineteenth century some Jewish journals advocated slight changes in order to enhance the decorum of the prayers in the synagogue. They attacked the rabbis who adhered strictly to the traditional service. The only serious effort to reform the liturgy was made at this time. The impetus again came from Germany. A group of Amsterdam notables invited a German rabbi, Dr. Isaac Chronik, a friend of Ludwig Philippson, to propagate the Reform ideology in the Netherlands (1856).[32] They founded an association, the Shoharei Deah, which organized lectures and composed a special liturgy. In no time tempers among Amsterdam Jewry rose to such a fever pitch that Dr. Chronik was assaulted by the masses and, fearing for his life, beat a hasty retreat to Germany. The Shoharei Deah then negotiated a compromise with the *kehillah* about the community's acceptance of liturgical reforms. Eventually, agreement was reached on the introduction of a choir, and this was the end of Shoharei Deah and the Reform movement in the Netherlands.[33]

However, Orthodoxy was also oriented toward Germany during the nineteenth century. Rotterdam, Groningen, Zwolle, and Maastricht imported their chief rabbi[34] from Germany; for several decades Amsterdam cast around for a German, preferably neo-Orthodox, chief rabbi of the type of Rabbi Jakob Ettlinger.[35] Promising students of the Amsterdam rabbinical seminary were sent to Germany—to Rabbi Selig Bamberger at Würzburg and to Rabbi Samson Raphael Hirsch at Emden—to absorb the spirit of neo-Orthodoxy and to learn its rhetoric.[36] As the century progressed, the spiritual authorities grew ever more dependent on Germany for rabbinical candidates capable of stemming the rising tide of secularization. Hirsch became a magical name within Dutch Orthodox circles. "And you, o youths, who founded a movement entirely in his spirit, yes, in a sense derived from, based upon the ideas which he succeeded in implanting into the young people around him. . . . May the memory of Hirsch's life always live among you," exhorted Chief Rabbi Tobias Tal in a commemorative address after Hirsch's death.[37]

It was apparently Heine who said that if ever the end of the world came in sight, he would move to Holland, since everything happened there thirty years later.[38] This possibly apocryphal but apt description characterizes the stagnation of the Netherlands during the second half of the nineteenth century. Hirsch's philosophy had a profound impact on Dutch Orthodoxy. Rabbi Tal belonged to a new breed of Dutch rabbis. His eulogy on Hirsch was addressed to an audience that included many persons who would eventually occupy prominent positions in the Dutch-Jewish community,[39] but Hirsch's ideas were not really implemented in the Dutch-Jewish community. On the one hand, it is quite understandable that the Netherlands did not produce an *Austrittsgemeinde*, in the absence of a visible Reform movement. However, Jewish synagogal and institutional boards accepted members who openly flouted the *mitzvoth*. Moreover, the position of the rabbis continued to be as subservient as before. These were Dutch and not Hirschian traditions. Only those Dutch Jews who were Dutch nationalists agreed with Hirsch's followers' violent repudiation of Jewish secularism. Dutch Orthodoxy had found Dutch Orthodoxy and Dutch nationalism quite compatible.

Only one religious figure explicitly confronted these issues, Holland's most famous chief rabbi, Dr. J.H. Dünner[40] (1833–1911). Dünner was born in Cracow and received his rabbinical training there. He then studied at the University of Bonn and received his doctorate in Heidelberg. In 1862 he was nominated rector of the seminary in Amsterdam and asked to reorganize it and raise its level. The Board of the seminary hoped that the nomination of an academically trained personality would prevent the seminary's incorporation into the theological faculty of one of the universities. It was Dünner's ambition to train a generation of Dutch-born rabbis and to check the import of German rabbis. Dünner even refused to recognize those Dutch Jews as rabbis who had been ordained by rabbinical authorities in other countries. His success was remarkable; from the beginning of the twentieth century onward most rabbinical vacancies in the Netherlands were filled by rabbis educated at the Amsterdam seminary. The program of *Dutchification* which had been initiated by the regime of King William I in 1814 was completed eighty years later by a Polish-born, German-educated rabbi.

Dünner's opposition to German rabbis did not derive from Dutch nationalist feelings. Dünner was a Jewish nationalist who insisted on introducing Jewish history into the curriculum of Jewish schools in the face of fierce rabbinical opposition.[41] Rather, he disapproved of the disunity in German Jewry and wanted to avert the danger of a division of Dutch Jewry along the lines of German Jewry: neo-Orthodoxy versus the Reform movement.[42] As an Orthodox Jew he despised Reform Judaism, but as a Jewish nationalist he condemned strongly the *Austrittsgemeinde.* Moreover, Dünner was one of the few rabbis in Western Europe who joined the Zionist movement early; his sermon supporting Zionism, delivered on *Rosh Hashana* 5699, was translated into German and distributed as a propaganda pamphlet. Yet Dünner did not succeed in instilling his conception of Judaism in his pupils. Almost all of them adhered to neo-Orthodoxy and later joined Agudath Jisrael. On the other hand, Dünner greatly influenced a group of young Jewish intellectuals who became the backbone of the Dutch Zionist organization at the beginning of the twentieth century.[43]

Neither Dünner nor Hirsch were Dutch Jews. Both of them show how from its inception Dutch Jewry, especially the Ashkenazim, depended for its ideologies on foreign sources, at first Eastern European and then German. But these imported ideas had to be adapted and transformed in practice in order to suit prevailing conditions in the Netherlands, where Jewish solidarity and Jewish social consciousness were conceived and articulated differently from elsewhere.

Notes

1. This was said by Maximilian I against the claim of the French (cited in *Die Niederlande im Umbruch der Zeiten,* ed. Max Freiherr du Prel [Würzburg, 1941], p. 11). Actually, Charles V was born in Flanders (Gent).
2. See K.D. Bracher, *The German Dictatorship* (New York: Penguin, 1973), p. 42.

3. See Fritz Stern, *The Politics of Cultural Despair* (New York: Doubleday, 1965), esp. pp. 190–96.
4. About Wilhelm Marr see M. Zimmermann, *Wilhelm Marr* (Jerusalem: Zalman Shazar Center, 1982) (Hebrew), pp. 69–70.
5. Van den Bruck called upon the Dutch to remain loyal to their German character and to strive to be included in *Gesamtdeutschland.* See Stern, p. 253.
6. This was the outspoken policy of the S.S. leadership. Gotlob Berger, a general of the SS, called the Dutch a people of German nationality. This also was the opinion of H.A. Rauter, Höherer S.S. and Polizeiführer in the Netherlands during the occupation, who wrote to Himmler that at least theoretically the Dutch were all *Volksdeutsche* (see N.C.K. In't Veld, *De SS en Nederland* ['s Gravenhage: Nijhoff, 1976], pp. 148–60, 817; K. Kwiet, *Rijkscommissariaat Nederland* [Baarn, 1969], p. 108).
7. This was the main reason why the Germans accelerated the deportation of the Jews from the Netherlands and completed it by the autumn of 1943.
8. Rabbi Jakob Rosenberg, formerly rabbi in Fulda, was chosen Chief Rabbi of Groningen on 17 September 1852. Of the three other rabbinic candidates, two—E. Loewenstamm of Fraustadt and Dr. L. Ettinger of Mannheim—were also German. Rosenberg refused to speak and preach in Dutch and was dismissed by the council of the *kehillah* on 31 December 1861. Nevertheless he remained in Groningen at least until 1866 and secured a Dutch passport. Much material about him can be found in the Institute of Microfilm of Hebrew Manuscripts in the Jewish National and University Library in Jerusalem.
9. See J. Michman, *Gotische Torens op een Corinthisch Gebouw* (Tijdschrift voor Geschiedenis, 1976), pp. 493–517.
10. See J. Michman, "The Conflicts between Orthodox and Enlightened Jews and the Governmental Decision of February 26, 1814," *Studia Rosenthaliana* 15 (1981): 20–36.
11. For comparison of the German and Dutch Haskalah see Frederique Hiegentlich, in J. Michman, ed., *Dutch Jewish History* (Jerusalem: Institute for the Research on Dutch Jewry, 1984), pp. 207–18.
12. On Weisel's stay in Amsterdam see J. Melkman, *David Franco Mendes* (Jerusalem: Massada, 1951), pp. 102–5.
13. See Z. Malachi, "N.H. Ulman, Maskil and Philosopher" (Hebrew), in *Studies on the History of Dutch Jewry,* ed. J. Michman, vol. 2 (Jerusalem: Institute for the Research on Dutch Jewry, 1979), pp. 77–88. His son Leon Jacob Ulman (1793–1856) belonged to the group of Dutch *maskilim.* He was a member of *Hanokh Lana'ar al pi Darko* (1808–1810), translated works of Mendelssohn and, like many of his fellow *maskilim,* was a mathematician and a physicist. He was a member of two societies: Mathesis Artium Genetrix and Tot Nut en Beschaving, which were founded by Jews.
14. The first translator was Rijklof Michael van Goens (1748–1810), a professor at the University of Utrecht. He was accused of insulting the Christian religion and forced to resign (1776). His friend Johannes Petsch translated other works of Mendelssohn. See a list of translations in S. Seeligmann, "Het geestelijk leven in de Hoogduitse Joodse Gemeente te 's Gravenhage," in D.S. van Zuiden, *De Hoogduitse Joden in 's Gravenhage,* Den Haag: Levisson, 1913, pp. 61–62. On the correspondence of van Goens with Mendelssohn

184 Toward Modernity: The European Jewish Model

see A. Altmann, *Moses Mendelssohn* (Philadelphia: Jewish Publication Society of America, 1973), pp. 245–46, 798–99.

15. S. Seeligmann argued that the influence of Mendelssohn on Dutch Jewry was very restricted (see "Moses Mendelssohn, invloed op de Nederlandse Joden," *Bijdragen en Mededelingen van het Genootschap voor Joodse Wetenschap in Nederland*, vol. 2 [Amsterdam, 1925], pp. 70–71) and this, too, was the opinion of J.S. da Silva Rosa ("Heeft Moses Mendelssohn invloed gehad op de Nederlandse Joden?" *De Vrijdagavond* 6, [1930]: 346–47). But all the writings of the Dutch *maskilim* are full of praise of him and accept his conception of Judaism at least theoretically. We cite here only one author: M. de Wulft, a teacher of Hebrew and Bible who attacked Dr. S.I. Mulder because he did not follow the Bible translation of Mendelssohn in his translation into Dutch: "By *him* [Mendelssohn] Israel should be helped. *He* should be the teacher of them all. *He* should give them the means to remove their misfortune, to advance their happiness" (M. de Wulft, *De zwakke en onbeduidende stem of billijke aanvraagaau den heer S.J. Mulder* [Amsterdam, 1827], p. 4). But Mendelssohn was revered even afterwards by rabbinical circles. See for example the appreciation of Mendelssohn in the *Handboek voor de Geschiedenis der Joden*, vol. 3 ([Amsterdam, 1873], pp. 498–99), written by D. Sluys and J. Hoofien, who may be regarded as representative of orthodoxy in the Netherlands.

16. In 1787 Rabbi Shaul, chief rabbi of Amsterdam, gave Dubno approbation after seeing him in Amsterdam; Rabbi Shaul knew Dubno from the time he officiated as rabbi in Dubno. (The approbation has been published in Gabriel Polak's *Ben-Gorni* [Amsterdam, 1851], pp. 46–48.) According to Mulder, Solomon Dubno lived in Amsterdam more than a quarter of a century; see S.I. Mulder, *Iets over de begraafplaatsen der Nederlandsch Israelitische Gemeente te Amsterdam* etc. (Amsterdam, 1851; off-print), p. 8. Solomon Dubno died in 1813, therefore he must have settled in Amsterdam before 1788.

17. The association for the study of Hebrew language and literature, Tongeleth, was founded in 1815. Likewise another association, Reshit Chochma, was founded in the same year; notwithstanding that the aim of this association was the study of rabbinical literature, its general meetings were held in Hebrew.

18. See D. Michman, "David Friedrichsfeld: A Fighter for Enlightenment and the Emancipation of the Jews" (Hebrew), in J. Michman, ed., *Studies on the History of Dutch Jewry*, vol. 1 (Jerusalem: Magnes, 1975), pp. 151–99.

19. On Sommerhausen as a Hebrew writer see my article in *Studies and Essays dedicated to K.D. Wormann* (Jerusalem: Magnes, 1976), pp. 72–80.

20. Documents about the translation of the Bible into Dutch are in J. Meijer, *Problematiek per Post* (Amsterdam, 1948), pp. 34–44.

21. For a detailed description of the curriculum of Tiferet Bachurim and its impact on the law of 1817 on Jewish education see D. Michman, "Jewish Education in the Early 19th Century," in J. Michman, ed., *Studies on the History of Dutch Jewry*, vol. 2 (Jerusalem: Magnes, 1979), pp. 108–12.

22. Jacob H. Dessauer was the founder, director, and dramaturgist of the theatrical company and head of its actors' studio for Jews. He was one of the founder members of the Felix Libertate association. An anonymous article about him appeared in *Oud-Holland* (1887, Amsterdam), pp. 194–99.

23. Harmannus Leonard Bromet (1724–1812) was the revered leader of the Felix Libertate group and for a short time a member of the Batavian National Assembly. He wrote two memoranda about the participation of the Jews in the Civil Guard: "Gelijkheid, Vrijheid, Broederschap, Aan onze waarde joodsche Medeburgers," Amsterdam, 22 March 1795, and "Tweede briev aan alle leden derselver societeit," Amsterdam, 26 March 1795. The *maskilim* argued that Jews had been soldiers in many places in the Republic (Zeeland, Utrecht, Rotterdam, The Hague) as well as Hamburg and the West-Indian colonies; see *Diskursen fun die Neie Kille,* no. 3.

24. M.C.B., *Aanmoediging aan de Hollandsche Israeliten tot het betreden van de voor hun geopende krijgsdienst* (Amsterdam, 1807).

25. S. Seeligmann quotes a treatise of Jacob Coppenhagen, *Bechi Naharoth* (Amsterdam, 1784): "A man came from somewhere, from Ulm, with the purpose to remove the Divine Providence," Seeligmann, p. 63.

26. *Diskursen fun die Alte Kille,* no. 16.

27. The first initiative to establish a liberal congregation in the Netherlands was taken by Dutch Jews. However, only after the influx of German refugees could two liberal congregations, in The Hague and Amsterdam, be founded. Not only the rabbis but also the lay leadership attacked the liberal Jews for importing a Judaism alien to the spirit of Dutch Jewry.

28. The religious aspects of Adath Jesurun cannot be dealt with here in detail. Suffice it to say that all the changes and innovations were of minor importance and some of them were merely imitations of Sephardic usages. The regulations of the congregation were published by D.M. Sluys: "Het reglement van Adath Jesurun (de "Neie Kehillo") te Amsterdam," *Nieuw Israelitisch Weekblad,* 12 and 19 June 1931. Most of them were destined to enhance the decorum in the synagogue. "We took the best of the usages of the two congregations," is said in the *Diskursen fun die Neie Kille,* no. 6. The chief rabbi of The Hague, J.A. Lehmans, criticized the new *minhagim,* introduced by Rabbi Israel Ger, the rabbi of Adath Jesurun. However, he did not reject them all out of hand, neither did he accuse Rabbi Israel Ger that his innovations undermined Jewish religion. See I. Maarsen, "Ma'amar Or Ha'emeth," *Otzar Hechajim,* no. 9 (Nisan 5693 [1933]):110–20; idem, "Een Haagse Opperrabijn over de 'Neie K'hilloh' (1797–1808)," *De Vrijdagavond* 8 (1931): 146–48; L. Fuks, "De Zweedse familie Graanboom, Een Hebreeuwse familiegeschiedenis," *Studia Rosenthaliana* 1 (1967): 85–106; and recently, J. Meijer, *Joodse Wetenschap in Nederland, een referaat buiten-de-orde* (Heemstede, 1982); J. Michman, "De stichting van het Opperconsistorie (1808)—een keerpunt in de geschiedenis van de Nederlandse Joden," *Studia Rosenthaliana* 18 (1984): pp. 41–60, 143–58.

29. Even the venomous *Diskursen fun die Alta Kille* recognized that R. Israel Ger had been a learned talmudist and seemed to be a pious man till he went over to Adath Jesurun. They accused him of being hypocritical because he joined the heretics. On the other hand the *Diskursen fun die Neie Kille* contained many jokes at the expense of Rabbi Jakob Moses Löwenstam, the chief rabbi of Amsterdam, who was nominated solely because his father and grandfather had been chief rabbis of Amsterdam.

30. In an address to King Louis Napoleon, M.S. Asser, C. Asser, H. de Lemon, and other founders of Adath Jesurun declared that their motives had not

been religious (Algemeen Rijksarchief, Staatssecretarie Lodewijk Napoleon; Inv. no. 324).

31. The only concession the old congregation had to make was the abolition of the blessing in the morning service: *shelo asani goy* ("that did not make me a Gentile").

32. Dr. Isaac Löw Chronik came in 1856 to Amsterdam, stayed later in Leiden and returned to Posen. At the recommendation of A. Geiger he was appointed rabbi in Chicago and there published a journal, *Zeichen der Zeit* (1869), but left Chicago in 1870.

33. See J. Coppenhagen, "De Reformbeweging in Nederland," *De Vrijdagavond* 6 (1930): 333–35, 344–46; G. Polak, *Hakarmel* (5620 [1860]): pp. 56–57, 147–48. The attitude of the Dutch Jews toward religious reform aroused the indignation of German Reform circles. See for example the tendentious and distorted description of Dutch Jewry by M. Philippson: "The unpleasant manner of the large majority of Dutch Jews accomplished the erection of a practically insurmountable barrier between Jews and Christians in independent Holland, in spite of the total political equality. The Christians regard Jewry as repugnant, a world with which they prefer to be in little personal contact." Martin Philippson, *Neueste Geschichte des Jüdischen Volkes* (Leipzig: Fock, 1910), p. 200.

34. The Royal Decree of 26 February 1814, appointed twelve main synagogues (*Hoofolsynagogues*) and each of them was entitled to nominate a chief rabbi (See J. Michman, *The Conflict*, pp. 33–34). But very often a chief rabbi officiated in more than one main synagogue. Moreover, in some main synagogues the office of chief rabbi remained vacant for long periods, e.g. Amsterdam (1838–1874), Groningen (1861–1889), and Rotterdam (1870–1885).

35. Samson Raphael Hirsch, too, was a candidate in Amsterdam. He paid a visit to Amsterdam in 1854 and conferred inter alia with Akiba Lehren. Two versions exist about this episode. Chief Rabbi Dr. J.H. Dünner suggested the name of S.R. Hirsch to Akiba Lehren, whereupon the latter told him about his talk with S.R. Hirsch. Akiba Lehren did not rate him an outstanding talmudist and therefore opposed his nomination. Hirsch on the other hand was very disappointed by his visit to Amsterdam; he complained about the low level of religious life and the lack of learning. See Benjamin de Vries, "The Influence of S.R. Hirsch on Dutch Jewry" (Hebrew), *Hazofeh,* 21 March 1947. Both versions may be true. On Hirsch's relations with Amsterdam see further J. Meijer, *Erfenis der Emancipatie* (Haarlem, 1963), pp. 60–63.

36. The two aspirant rabbis were J.M. Content and J. Hillesum. The correspondence regarding this episode has been published in J. Michman, ed., *Studies on the History of Dutch Jewry*, vol. 4 (Jerusalem: Magnes, 1984), pp. 45–66.

37. T. Tal, *Lezingen Mekor Chajim* (Amsterdam, 1892), p. 127. The lecture was translated into German and published by his son, Chief Rabbi Justus Tal: *Oberrabbiner T. Tal, Samson Raphael Hirsch* (Köln, 1914).

38. This saying is frequently cited but has not been found in the writings of H. Heine.

39. Sigmund Seeligmann (1873–1940), himself a German Jew by origin, wrote that the association Mekor Chajim was founded by a group of young men, most of them from Frankfurt am Main, who were fervent adherents of the "Trennungsgemeinde" (S. Seeligmann, *Opperabijn Onderwijzer in de lijst van zijn tijd, in de Joodse gemeenschap van Amsterdam* [Amsterdam, 1935], p.

5). Notwithstanding the fact that Seeligmann himself was, initially, one of the members of Mekor Chajim, this assumption is not substantiated by the official history of the association, written by its secretary, Rabbi L. Dünner, the eldest son of Chief Rabbi J.H. Dünner. He reports that the first members of the board were two Dutch Jews and one German Jew (see L. Dünner, "Kort overzicht van de geschiedenis der vereniging Mekor Chajim," Amsterdam, 7 June 1891, p. 4.). Seeligmann's attack on the ideology of Hirsch must be explained by his adherence to Zionism through the influence of Chief Rabbi Dr. J.H. Dünner, at whose insistence he apparently accepted the chairmanship of the Zionist organization in the Netherlands in 1904 (see M.H. van Kampen, "In Memoriam Sigmund Seeligmann," in *Menorah 5701,* ed. J. Melkman [Amsterdam, 1940], p. 148).

40. About Dünner see J. Melkman, "J.H. Dünner," *Menorah* (Amsterdam, 1940), pp. 125–33; B. de Vries, *Chidushe Harav Josef Zwi Dünner* (Jerusalem: Mossad Harav Kook, 1981), pp. 9–32; J. Meijer, *Rector en Raw,* vol. 1 (Heemstede, 1984).

41. Dünner received his *semicha* from Rabbi N.H. Dembitzer in Cracow. The activities and the scientific approach of Rabbi Dembitzer resemble in many respects those of Dünner. Dembitzer had a great interest in the history of the Jewish people, he was noted for his critical work in the field of talmudic and rabbinical literature. He supported the *yishuv* (the Jewish population in Israel before 1948) in Israel financially. Moreover, he had contacts with the Seminary in Breslau. Dünner, too, may be considered as belonging to the positivist historical school of Breslau. He published his first articles in Fraenkel's *Monatsschrift für Geschichte und Wissenschaft des Judentums.* A study of the relationship of Dünner with his teacher should be revealing.

42. In the course of time, Dünner became more and more opposed to the ideology of Hirsch. At first he appreciated the religious activities of Hirsch, but not his writings: he forbade the acquisition of Hirsch's books for the library of the Seminary because they were not scholarly enough. But the gap between him and the neo-Orthodox widened when Dünner joined the Zionist movement. See note 39 above, and the article by B. de Vries (note 40 above).

43. To this group, apart from Seeligmann, belonged E.S. Hen, who had translated the *Neunzehn Briefe* of Hirsch, Rabbi S.Ph. de Vries, and others. See S. Dasberg, *S.Ph. de Vries* (Lochem: de Tijdstroom, 1973), p. 46.

8

Trieste and Berlin: The Italian Role in the Cultural Politics of the Haskalah

Lois C. Dubin

Il Giudaismo italiano fu sempre ortodosso, e sempre più o meno illuminato. Non ebbe, come lo spagnuolo, il suo periodo di predominio d'una cultura esotica, e quindi di eterodossia; nè tampoco ebbe mai, come il settentrionale, un periodo di rozzezza e mancanza d'ogni civile cultura.
—S. D. Luzzatto (1848)[1]

Two striking features of modern Italian-Jewish history have been the rapid and extensive integration of Jews into state and society, and the relative ease with which Jews adjusted to life outside the ghetto. Many have noted that Italian Jews suffered fewer conflicts between tradition and modernity than most other European Jewries.[2] To contribute to our understanding of Jewish modernization in Italy, and its relation to the process elsewhere, especially in Germany, this essay focuses on the direct and articulate encounter between Italian Jews and two of the modernizing agents for Central European Jews—Enlightened absolutism and the Berlin Haskalah.[3] It examines the role played by Italian Jews in the cultural politics of Jewish Enlightenment in the late eighteenth century.

According to a central figure of the Jewish Enlightenment, Hartwig Wessely (Naftali Herz Weisel), the Italian role was key in the bitter controversies over educational reform engendered by his pamphlet *Divrei Shalom Ve'emet* (Words of peace and truth, 1782). Of them he wrote, "From the depths I cried out, [and] they heard my voice."[4] Italian Jews, both within and without the Habsburg realm, rallied to his cause. Why did Italian Jews respond to Wessely's cry, and how did they understand the cause of the Haskalah? Conversely, how did German *maskilim* perceive Italian Jews, and how did Italian Jewry become a kind of model for them? The interaction of Italian and German Jewries—how each functioned for the other as a reference point—illumines not only the spread of modernizing movements from German Jewry, but also some of the ways in which these movements drew sustenance from other centers and sources.

This essay does not attempt an overall analysis of Italian-Jewish modernization[5] nor a comprehensive treatment of all Italian Jews in the late eighteenth century. It is difficult to generalize about the widely varying statuses afforded Jews by the different states of northern and central Italy. The 30,000–35,000 Italian Jews, less than one-fifth of 1 percent of the total Italian population, lived in some eighty communities, ranging in size from as large as 5,000 or 6,000 to as small as a few dozen.[6] The disparity in conditions was great, from those in Leghorn and Trieste among the most favorable in all of Europe, to those in Rome, among the worst. Indeed one scholar has claimed that the "condition of the Jews of Italy in the second half of the eighteenth century is surely the most difficult to determine in all of Europe."[7]

A further reason for restriction of scope is that not all Italian Jewries were equally involved with Central European affairs. Our primary interest is necessarily those who were—the Jews of Habsburg northern Italy, i.e., of Trieste and neighboring Gorizia and Gradisca. These were the Jews to whom Wessely appealed and who in response spearheaded the Italian campaign on his behalf. Their horizons, like those of other Italian Jews in the eighteenth and nineteenth centuries, included Western Europe and the Mediterranean. But their location "on the German-Italian frontier" gave these northerners a special role, conduit between Central Europe and Italy.[8] Geographic proximity, direct Habsburg rule, economic and family ties brought them within the Central European orbit, while language and culture reinforced their extensive family and economic ties to Italian communities.[9] Thus, culturally Italian and politically Austrian, the Jews of Trieste and environs show in microcosm the interaction between Italian-Jewish traditions and realities, and Central European policies and ideologies.

In all three communities ghettos were founded late, Trieste in 1696–97, Gorizia in 1698, and Gradisca in 1769.[10] None really succeeded in segregating Jews from Christians. In Gorizia, for example, one-sixth of the city's population entered the ghetto daily to work in Jewish silk-manufacturing establishments. In Trieste, ghetto residence was not fully enforced from midcentury on: in 1753 wealthy Jews were permitted to live outside it, and by the time of its formal abolition in the 1780s, most Jews were no longer living in it. In 1782, there were 135 Jews in Gradisca;

in 1788, there were 270 Jews in Gorizia (4 percent of the population), and 670 Jews in Trieste.

Trieste's Jewish Community

The Triestine Jewish community grew dramatically, from 120 Jews in 1748 to 1,247 in 1802, doubling its percentage of the city's population from approximately 3 percent to 5–6 percent. The cause was Habsburg policy—declaration of Trieste as a free port in 1719 and the subsequent efforts to turn it into the empire's major port, the hub of Mediterranean and Central European commerce. These efforts included attractive terms for economically dynamic and religiously and ethnically diverse immigrants—Jews, Protestants, Greek Orthodox, Armenians. From the beginning, Jews were an integral part of Trieste's development into one of Europe's major commercial, financial, and shipping centers. The right to own real property was extended from privileged Jews to all Jews. The Jewish community's rights of organization and public worship were legally recognized. Jewish-Christian interaction was not limited to economic dealings, it included informal social and cultural contacts in coffee-house, theater, Masonic lodge, and literary society. The city's administration tried to foster what might be called "a neutral polity and society," in which religious considerations would not dominate. For example, when the Bishop tried to stop Trieste's very unusual Lenten season of opera and music, the civic authorities countered that "such popular entertainments . . . certainly exercized an attraction, especially in a Free Port filled with people of different nations and religions."[11] Thus Triestine Jewry was a formally recognized, rapidly growing immigrant community, playing an important economic and increasingly active cultural and social role in a dynamic, bourgeois, cosmopolitan entrepôt.

Enlightenment reached the Triestine community through a variety of channels, of which the Berlin Haskalah was only one. Enlightenment literature, particularly in Italian and French, was readily available, and at least some Jews were conversant with the ideas of the *Encyclopédie,* Voltaire, and Beccaria, to name but a few.[12] But the most important channel was that of governmental policy itself. Vienna tested many Enlightened Absolutist policies, including those concerning Jews, in northern Italy before implementing them elsewhere in the empire; in Trieste its experiments went furthest, partly because of the favorable attitude of local officials.[13] In fact, as we shall see, it was the Governor Count Zinzendorf who first urged contact between the local Jews and Berlin *maskilim.* Personal ties of a literary, economic, and family nature also connected northern Italian Jews to Vienna, to the Court, and leading

Jewish families. These, the Honigs and Arnsteins, were themselves patrons of the Berlin Haskalah and functioned at times as mediators between Trieste and Berlin *maskilim*.[14] Thus Vienna and Berlin in tandem were sources of Central European Enlightenment currents among the Jews of Trieste and environs.

The Toleranz Legislation and the Founding of the Scuola Pia Normale

Most Habsburg Jewries had their first experience of the policies of Enlightenment in Joseph II's *Toleranz* edicts of 1781–82, whose purpose was to "make Jews useful to the state." For the empire's Italian Jews, these edicts did not mark a radical departure. Indeed many of its provisions had been included in the 1779 Privilege of the Jews in Lombardy, and were long-standing realities for the Jews of Trieste, Gorizia, and Gradisca.[15] Compulsory ghetto residence, discriminatory signs, and the body tax had all been weakened or abolished earlier for Triestine-Jewish merchants. In all three places, Jews had long had the right to own real property without any of the qualifications of the *Toleranzpatent,* and were engaged in a variety of commercial and manufacturing activities. The Jews of Trieste were in fact concerned that their rights of property ownership, communal organization, public worship, and protection from forced baptism not be adversely affected by the new legislation. Eventually the Austrian authorities agreed that Triestine Jews should enjoy the best of both their old and their new statuses. One immediate result was that the post of managing deputy of the local exchange, the Borsa, was now open to Jews.

Nor was the cultural policy of the *Toleranz* legislation entirely new for Italian Jews. It mandated use of the local language in all official documents and compulsory primary education according to state standards, either in Christian "Normal-schools" or in Jewish ones to be established.[16] In Trieste as in other Italian-Jewish communities, many documents were already kept in Italian, and in its 1771 Statute, the empress had stipulated that Italian and German be taught. Jews later protested some of Vienna's Germanizing efforts, as did Triestine merchants generally, but their reason was their preference for Italian, not objection to the replacement of Hebrew by a Gentile language. As for the Normal-school system, Jews in this area had some contact with it in the late 1770s. In Gorizia the authorities had prompted Jews to engage a Christian teacher for "German, reading, writing, arithmetic, orthography, eloquence, geography, history of the country, urbanity"—an arrangement which lasted a few months.[17] In Trieste there were five Jewish students in

Christian Normal-schools by 1781, including two sons of the assistant rabbi.[18]

For the Jews of Trieste and environs, the 1781 Habsburg reform legislation was new in that it marked a concerted effort to establish state-supported Jewish elementary schools. Their responses were positive. To acclaim the policy and to set the entire issue of Jews, general education, and service to the state in proper perspective, the head of the Gradiscan community Elia Morpurgo wrote his *Discorso . . . Nel partecipare a quella Comunità la Clementissima Sovrana risoluzione 16. Maggio 1781,* in which he provided a very long list of what have often been called Jewish contributions to civilization.[19] In Gorizia and Gradisca Jewish schools were reorganized. And in Trieste the community drew up a plan in the winter of 1781-82 for the reform of its existing school. The plan was published under governmental auspices as *Regole per la direzione della Scuola Pia Normale sive Talmud Torà dell' Università degli Ebrei di Trieste,* and on 14 May 1782 (1 Sivan 5542) the new institution was opened with much pomp and ceremony.[20] Its approximately thirty-five students were divided into three grades for religious studies, and one elementary "Normal" class was started, with a more advanced one to follow later. One of the first schools in the empire to meet the new legislation's requirements, it was surely one of the most long-lived; despite all the intervening vicissitudes, it still functions today.

Two features distinguished the *Scuola Pia Normale sive Talmud Torà* of Trieste—its very combination of *pia* and *normale* studies, i.e., of Jewish and state curricula, under one roof, and the enthusiastic and sustained cooperation of the community's rabbinic and lay leadership.

Trieste was hailed at the time, especially by Wessely, for its unique combination of curricula. In Central Europe the two were usually kept separate: traditionalists strove to maintain control of autonomous religious schools (in Prague they made that their condition for permitting a Jewish Normal-school), while educational reformers concentrated almost exlusively on civic and vocational studies.[21] By contrast, compartmentalization was unnecessary in Trieste (1782) and Mantua (1788) when Jewish Normal classes were instituted.[22] The reason was simple: the basic principle of combined Jewish and general education was not new for Italian Jews. Their schools had traditionally taught some measure of general studies; in the eighteenth century this usually meant Italian and arithmetic.[23] We know little about the school that already existed in Trieste, but indications are that it too taught arithmetic, Italian, and German in addition to "sacred studies and good Hebrew letters."[24] For Triestine Jews, the novelty of the Normal-school was not its scope but rather state supervision and the emphasis on German.

The familiarity of the basic principle was one major reason for Trieste's enthusiastic implementation of the Josephine educational policy. The community's central figures, Rabbi Isaac Ben-Moses Formiggini and the lay leaders, worked together to set up the new school; there were no forces of opposition. Generally there may have been a somewhat freer attitude to innovation in this immigrant community than in older, more established ones.[25] In practical terms the Normal-school approach met the needs of the Triestine-Jewish community of merchants and entre-preneurs, making public and compulsory what private tutors offered. General education was a necessity for the young who were expected to be active participants in the life of the city. There was a political motive as well: ever-conscious of the need to maintain its favorable status, to show its worthiness as vanguard, this community was eager to cooperate with the government. The *Scuola Pia Normale* was intended to be a showcase of the entire community's dedication to the Habsburg ideals of Enlightenment.

Initial Contacts with Berlin and Wessely's Appeal for Help

During their months of organizing the new school, the Jews of Trieste made their first contact with Berlin about Enlightenment issues proper. The authorities had mandated morality as a separate subject in the new Jewish schools—"the most sound moral philosophy . . . according to the duties of every man, regardless of differences of religion"—and instructed Jews to compose new moral textbooks or to use appropriate ones already available such as those of the "well-known Mendelssohn in Berlin."[26] At the governor's behest, the Triestine-Jewish community, through its Sec-retary Joseph Gallico, wrote directly to Mendelssohn early in 1782. Neither that letter nor Mendelssohn's response is extant, but later cor-respondence indicates that he supplied them with information about his works and those of his colleague Wessely, and sent them the just-published pro-Josephine educational manifesto *Divrei Shalom Ve'emet*. The exact chronology is difficult to determine, but one fact emerges clearly: the Jews of Trieste had formulated their plan for the new *Scuola Pia Normale* before they received word from Berlin. Their plan was ready by 1 January 1782, and Mendelssohn's response seems to date from early April.[27] Thus Trieste had embarked on its own course of compliance with Vienna's policy and determined most of the details of implementation independently of the Berlin *maskilim*.

That suggestion of Governor Zinzendorf had momentous consequences, for (as we shall see) Trieste gained a place on the map of Jewish Enlightenment, and Wessely gained his staunchest allies in his struggle to modernize Jewish education in Central Europe.

Trieste's turn to Mendelssohn was especially timely for Wessely, in desperate straits because of the uproar his pamphlet caused in Central and Eastern Europe. Many rabbis fiercely condemned him for his contemptuous depiction of traditional talmudists and for the radical message implied by his work—that the "Torah of man" should take priority over the "Torah of God," i.e., the transmission of civic and vocational skills over religious tradition and values.[28] Chilling rumors reached him of excoriating sermons, book burnings, threats of bans and expulsion. For Wessely, news of Trieste's contact with Mendelssohn and the projected school confirmed the notion of acculturated Italian Jews he had indicated in his first pamphlet, and seemed to offer him a lifeline.[29] Without his own direct contact with Triestine Jews and without their permission, Wessely publicly invoked their support: he cast his second pamphlet *Rav Tuv Levet Yisrael* (Abundant goodness to the house of Israel), dated 24 April 1782, as a response to their purported letter to him endorsing his first pamphlet. In a private letter of May 7 to Trieste, Wessely begged their indulgence for taking this liberty. Pleading the greatest urgency in that letter and his subsequent one of June 28, Wessely appealed to Triestine Jews for an open declaration of support.[30]

Wessely implored Triestine Jews to wage a campaign on his behalf, to distribute his two pamphlets to other Italian communities such as Venice, Leghorn, Mantua, Pisa, Verona, and to canvass their "rabbis, judges, and sages" for written vindication of his name and approval of his cause to "remove the veil of ignorance" from all Israel.[31] Wessely was heartened by the expressions of goodwill he received from Trieste in mid-June, which included news of Elia Morpurgo's speedy translation of *Divrei Shalom Ve'emet* into Italian.[32] Wessely considered Italian Jews the ideal arbiters for the Jewish world at large, because he saw them as "great in Torah . . . crowned with worldly wisdom and manners," and endowed with broadmindedness and sound judgment.[33] Wessely, in his appeal employed flattery, promised honor and fame, and invoked the Jewish duties of mutual aid and unity. He even raised the specter of rescission of the new toleration if Jews were uncooperative. Cleverly, he addressed Triestine Jews both as bystanders who had not needed his message and for whom it was not at all controversial, and as participants whose fate was at stake because they were members of the entire House of Israel and subjects of the Habsburgs.[34]

The Italian Campaign

The entreaties from Berlin yielded a rich result: (1) active correspondence between the Italian headquarters (the Triestine community and

Gradiscan leader Elia Morpurgo) and Berlin (Mendelssohn and Wessely);[35] (2) letters of solicitation from headquarters to other communities in Italy, and beyond, even to Constantinople;[36] (3) responses—*pesakim, letters, poems*—from Trieste, Ferrara, Venice, Ancona, Reggio, Gorizia, and Modena, of which the prompt and positive reaction formed the basis of Wessely's third pamphlet, *Ein Mishpat* (Fountain of judgment), published in April 1784;[37] and (4) Morpurgo's publicistic outpouring of the next few years, during which he circulated his rambling polemic in support of Wessely, *Igeret Ogeret Ahavat Ha'adam Beasher Hu Adam* (A treatise treating of love of man *qua* man), had his above-mentioned *Discorso* and translation of *Divrei Shalom Ve'emet* published, and contributed to *Hame'asef* articles on education that combined Wesselian principles with Italian practise.[38]

The Italian campaign got off to a quick start. By early July 1782, Morpurgo's *Igeret Ogeret* and Rabbi Formiggini's approving *pesak* were ready for dispatch along with Wessely's two pamphlets. The letters of solicitation echoed some of Wessely's themes but also made a specific appeal to Italian Jews' cultural traditions: To fight against unjust persecution and for the legacy of Torah combined with worldly wisdom would help Italian Jews "recover their ancient valor, and become once again the great teachers of the Jewish world."[39]

Favorable judgments of Wessely's two pamphlets, the first as amended by the second, were rendered by seven rabbis—Formiggini of Trieste, Samuel Yedidiah Ben-Eleazar Norzi of Ferrara, Simhah (Simone) Ben-Abraham Calimani, Abraham Hayim Ben-Menahem Cracovia, and Abraham Ben-Isaac Pacifico, all of Venice, Hayim Abraham Israel of Ancona, and Israel Benjamin Bassan of Reggio.[40] They were all respected leaders, advanced in years, men who occupied positions of responsibility as *dayanim* and teachers. Some, such as Calimani and Bassan, were renowned among both Jews and Gentiles for their literary and scientific accomplishments. Their endorsements of Wessely ranged from the Venetians' enthusiastic to Hayim Abraham Israel's grudging one. Interestingly, he was the only respondent who was not Italian born and bred. Excluded from *Ein Mishpat* was the response of the distinguished halachist Ishmael Ben-Abraham Kohen of Modena, whose strictures on Wessely's first pamphlet were severe.[41]

The responses of *Ein Mishpat* show that the Italian rabbis took seriously the peace-making role Wessely thrust upon them. Seeking to give credit to each party to the controversy, they found merit on both sides; they favored the broader cultural horizons Wessely was trying to introduce among Ashkenazic Jews but shared the concern of his traditionalist opponents that Torah not lose pride of place. They upheld

Wessely's basic contention that because Torah and non-Torah wisdom are complementary, there is a legitimate and important place in Jewish education and culture for a wide range of linguistic, mathematical, moral, social, and physical sciences.[42] They concurred with his related demands for an ordered Jewish curriculum that would proceed from Scripture to Mishnah to Talmud, and for recognition of the principle of division of labor in Jewish society, i.e., that not all are talmudic scholars, and that therefore such expertise should not be the only goal of Jewish education.[43] But they disagreed with the precise details of Wessely's plan, above all with his initial formulation that the "Torah of man" be taught before the "Torah of God." As Rabbi Formiggini put it:

> Torah studies are the principle, since "from them the cornerstone, from them the support" [Zechariah 10:4] and the secure foundation for every edifice of knowledge and science. Delve into [the Torah] again and again "for all is contained within it" [Avot 5:22]. . . . In the first five years that our Sages designated [i.e., from ages five to ten, Avot 5:21], we ought not to confuse the children's minds with any other studies, "for their delight will be in the Torah of the Lord" [Psalms 1:2].[44]

Thus the Italians' overall message was that Torah ought to be supplemented, not supplanted. (Concern that Torah would be uprooted had caused Ishmael Kohen to be wary of Wessely's first pamphlet.)

Wessely's demands for general studies, an ordered curriculum, and division of labor were consonant with Italian Jewish educational practices. As stated above, some general studies had always been taught. Similarly, graded instruction based upon the sequence of Scripture, Mishnah, Talmud had long been the norm in Italy, as the Venetian rabbis indicated. And the corollary of division of labor—that Talmud is a subject for specialists— was implicit in the Italian-Jewish schools of the seventeenth and eighteenth centuries, for their aim was not to produce "scholars of the Law" (*talmidei hakhamim*), but rather "Jews knowledgeable in Torah and God-fearing."[45] Hence Hebrew grammar and Scripture, liturgy and ritual, ethics and Midrash were as important staples as halachah. Sometimes Talmud itself was reserved for only the oldest and brightest pupils. Generally, Italian-Jewish curricula were much less halachically oriented than the Ashkenazic.

Italians minimized their disagreements about details in order to strengthen what they considered to be Wessely's basic point—the complementarity of Torah and wisdom, of Judaism and general culture. Some of their arguments were standard: precedents of polymath Sages from King Solomon through the Sanhedrin to medieval luminaries, explications of rabbinic texts concerning wisdom and morality, and the religious and halachic utility of the sciences. In *Igeret Ogeret,* Morpurgo presented the argument of precedent most forcefully by reiterating the medieval claim that Jews were in fact the original masters of all the sciences, and that even Gentiles had acknowledged Jewish primacy.[46]

Some of the Italians' arguments were more distinctive. Rabbi Norzi provided a kabbalistic variation on the theme of wisdom and Torah when he stated on the authority of earlier kabbalists, Benjamin Kohen Vitale and Abraham Herrera among them, that the sciences and philosophy are compatible with "true Kabbalah."[47] The Venetians argued the case for a wide range of studies through an analysis of individual and societal human needs that was imbued with eighteenth-century notions of the state of nature and of the explosion of knowledge. The Venetians and Morpurgo highlighted both music and poetry as necessary disciplines, thus reflecting the prominent roles of these arts in Italian-Jewish culture.[48] One additional distinctive feature was revealed in Rabbi Bassan's disagreement with Wessely's strategy for introducing unfamiliar ideas and practises:

> Had it been possible in the early stages to advise R. Naftali [Weisel], I would have humbly told him not to write or publish a word, not even half a word, but [rather] only through his own speech to lend support to implementation [of innovations] in practise. . . . Only persistence of habit in them enlightens, so that people come to see the truth.

Rabbi Bassan was implying that practice and experience persuade better than theory or ideology. He was expressing the preference for pragmatic realism over ideological debate which was a point of pride among Italian Enlightenment figures generally, and a facet of the Italian temperament that became increasingly evident to both Italian and German Jews in their subsequent interaction.[49] The argument most revealing of Italian Jewish culture was that which concerned the prophylactic teaching of non-Jewish wisdom. The question for Italians was not whether, but how, non-Torah studies should be taught. What might be construed in other quarters as a dire threat was assumed as a reality, a fact of life by Rabbi Norzi; Jews do pursue the arts and sciences willy-nilly; therefore exclusion of them is not a practical or desirable option. The only choice is between proper and improper exposure:

> If only the sages of Israel would assume their responsibilities [Numbers 7:2], and teach students those sciences which are called external (*hizoniot*), then there would be no suspicion or questioning that they might cause confusion of mind or neglect of Torah, because they would show the straight path on which one cannot stumble. . . . So that everyone who [wants to]

approach the study of the sciences will not have to go knocking on the doors of people ignorant of the path of the Lord.[50]

Thus the teaching of non-Torah wisdom is not merely permissible; it is incumbent upon Jewish leaders to do so properly, for Jewish auspices obviate the need for recourse to less reliable teachers such as skeptics, heretics, or Gentiles. The underlying assumption was that non-Jewish culture in and of itself, if properly taught and integrated within a Jewish framework in which Torah remains paramount, need not be a threat to Jews or Judaism. Indeed, Morpurgo provided examples of how knowledge of Gentile cultures could enhance the appreciation of Judaism, i.e., help in the defense of Judaism.[51]

Thus the real question for Wessely's Italian defenders was method and parameters—how best to structure general studies in a Jewish curriculum. Legitimacy was not at issue; they argued that point for Wessely's opponents, not for themselves. With the exception of Hayim Abraham Israel, all displayed familiarity and ease with such studies. Morpurgo's references to Erasmus and Augustine, for example, showed his broad knowledge of Western literature.[52] Even Ishmael Kohen, Wessely's critic, considered proper knowledge of European languages indispensable for Torah scholars. Furthermore, his own Hebrew compositions revealed his acquaintance with contemporary Italian literature and ancient Greek mythology; the Sirens, Ulysses, and Parnassus were characters in one of his cantatas. In contrast, it is worth recalling Wessely's own strictures on the use of mythology in Hebrew literature.[53]

Ease and familiarity with non-Jewish realms—what we might call *acculturation*—was the basic premise of the Italian responses. Morpurgo stated it as a general social principle, the mutual adaptation of peoples living in close proximity.[54] In Italy, ghettos had reduced but never eliminated contact between Jew and Gentile. One factor was demography, the small size and isolation of many Jewish communities. Social adaptation was reflected in language and appearance. Jews generally spoke local Italian dialects and were taught to read and write Italian in Jewish schools. Though they might speak with particular intonation and accent, and among themselves use words of Hebrew origin, there was no significant linguistic barrier between Jews and Gentiles. At the beginning of the seventeenth century Leone Modena considered vernacular sermons commonplace, and bemoaned the decline of Hebrew among Italian Jews.[55] He also called attention to males' uncovered heads and clean-shaven faces. These widespread practices were not dismissed by authorities as deviations. His own picture shows a full beard but no head-covering, and pictures of a number of Italian rabbis of the seventeenth and eighteenth centuries, the distinguished halachists Samson Morpurgo and Ishmael Kohen among them, show fashionable hairstyles and few beards.[56]

Italian-Jewish acculturation was not simply a matter of social adaptation. It rested upon a positive evaluation of the high culture of Italian Gentiles. Long past Renaissance interaction, this fundamental appreciation continued to express itself in different ways: in the modicum of general studies always present in Jewish curricula, in the adoption of Italian literary forms in Hebrew literature, and in Jewish cultural norms which saw "Torah wisdom" and "all branches of knowledge" as integrally linked.[57] This cultural ideal, reinforced to a degree by Sephardic legacies, was personified in the Italian tradition of the rabbi-poet-doctor. These were leaders such as Samson Morpurgo, Shabbetai Marini, and Isaac Lampronti who were respected for their halachic mastery, university education, and literary prowess in both Hebrew and Italian, and often for their good relations with Gentile savants and authorities as well.[58]

For Italian Jews the ideal of cultural breadth was legitimately Jewish not only in theoretical or distant historical terms, but also in terms of their own more recent past. Supporters of Wessely and Enlightenment generally found role models not only in medieval giants such as Maimonides and Ibn Ezra, but also in Italian Jews from the generations immediately preceding them, their own rabbis and teachers such as Samson Morpurgo, Lampronti, Calimani, Bassan, David Nieto, Israel Gedaliah Cases, and Abraham Isaac Castello.[59] These instances may not have been as frequent in the ghetto period, i.e., the mid–sixteenth through eighteenth centuries, as earlier, and I do not wish to imply that the ideal of cultural breadth was universally held by Italian Jews during those centuries. Yet, however much horizons were narrowed, it is clear that this ideal retained its legitimacy and even some currency among Italian Jews.

The Italians rose to Wessely's defense because they considered his program compatible with their own experience and values, and with important strands of Jewish tradition through the ages. The factors of cultural openness and economic opportunity were present to varying degrees in all the communities. Not only in Trieste but also in Ferrara, Venice, Ancona, and Reggio there were constituencies likely to support modern education and greater integration with Gentile society, wealthy merchants whose lives and livelihoods were not confined to the ghetto.[60] What was unique to the Jews of Trieste and environs was the political pressure emanating from Vienna. Self-interest dictated that they organize resistance to Wessely's opponents, that they as vanguard urge reluctant Jews elsewhere in the empire to comply with the government's new policies, lest groundswells of Jewish opposition jeopardize their position, as Wessely had warned. Thus the Trieste-led public campaign to vindicate Wessely might serve multiple purposes—aid for Wessely himself, propagation of a worldly cultural ideal among other Jews, reinforcement of desirable trends at home, and indubitable proof to Vienna of their allegiance to the progressive ideals of the day.

Ambiguities of the Alliance: Convergence and Independence

With *Ein Mishpat,* Italian Jews emerged as Wessely's champions. They shared his goal that Jewish education facilitate the active participation of Jews in Gentile state and society. But Italian endorsement of *Divrei Shalom Ve'emet* was in fact qualified. For strategic and perhaps temperamental reasons, they did not emphasize their points of disagreement with Wessely, but close reading shows the measure of their distance from him. Their outlook was compatible with his but not identical to it, and their adoption of Berlin as a model was limited. In both theory and practice, the Italians diverged from the Berlin platform, displaying independence and a firm sense of their own traditions.

Let us examine more closely the core of Wessely's first pamphlet. He defined the "Torah of man" as the very essence of humanity—the unwritten code of behavior and body of knowledge concerning man and the world which is accessible through human reason and empirical observation, and shared by all societies.[61] He contraposed it to the "Torah of God," known only by divine revelation, and which prescribes laws and teachings for Jews alone. Significantly, he included even "fear of God," i.e., piety or spirituality, in the "Torah of man," presumably on the assumption that the human capacity for belief in God is universal. In Wessely's schema of Jewish education, the universal "Torah of man" should precede the specifically Jewish "Torah of God"; hence instruction in civility, the vernacular, and ethics, history and geography, mathematics and natural sciences should precede Hebrew and Jewish texts. Wessely's novelty lay in his attempt to separate an autonomous realm of human culture from the Torah, his designation of this realm by the somewhat strange term *torat ha'adam,*[62] and the radical dichotomy implied by his repeated juxtapositions of the two Torahs, human and divine. He asserted their complementarity, but the underlying logic was bifurcation of the two, and the priority of the human not only in time, but also in value. In Wessely's subsequent retractions he greatly reduced the scope and value of the "Torah of man" and brought down the very structure of two independent and juxtaposed realms. Perhaps he was sincere in his protestations that he had not intended such radically novel implications, but others grasped them as the thrust of *Divrei Shalom Ve'emet* and the Haskalah's educational message.

Wessely's Italian champions did not in fact accept that novel juxtaposition and transvaluation. All of them registered their concern that Torah remain primary (*ikar*) and other studies secondary (*tafel*). Most disagreed with Wessely's timetable for the introduction of non-Torah studies, stating that Italian practice was preferable. They shared Ishmael Kohen's fear that Wessely's changing the base from Torah to universal human culture meant upsetting the balance between core and periphery, "turning things upside down" with the inevitable consequence that "Torah will be forgotten in Israel."[63] And their conception of Torah did not match Wessely's initially circumscribed and dichotomous one. Theirs was an harmonistic integrative conception of Torah and wisdom, of religion and culture—in which God's Torah is the absolute value, the firm bedrock of education, and the all-embracing framework for every kind of knowledge.

Arguments from silence and by inference are sometimes problematic, but I think the Italians' reticence with regard to Wessely's very term *torat ha'adam* suggests their discomfort. It is possible of course that they did not consciously reject his term after a searching analysis. They may not have been aware of all its radical implications, but it is striking that they shied away from it, and used more familiar terms for the humanities and sciences such as *hokhmah* (wisdom), or its variants *hokhmot umuskalot* (the sciences and speculative disciplines) and *hokhmot hizoniot* (external studies).[64] Those who used the term, the Venetians and Morpurgo, did so in ways that implied no dichotomy or juxtaposition of two Torahs. Furthermore, Morpurgo specified its meaning as ethics or as its eighteenth-century subsets, the doctrines of tolerance and humanity. When Morpurgo translated *Divrei Shalom Ve'emet* into Italian, he hardly used the literal equivalent *la legge umana* (human law), preferring instead *la legge morale* (the moral law) and *la buona morale* (sound morality).[65] In any case, neither those who avoided the term nor those who modified its meaning can be considered exponents of Wessely's initially radical conception.

Nor did Wessely's transvaluation find expression in Trieste's *Scuola Pia Normale sive Talmud Torà*. There, too, the combination of Italian convergence and independence in relation to the Berlin Haskalah was evident in practice. As noted above, the formulation of the school's plan preceded Trieste's turn to Berlin. The framework outlined in the *Regole* of 1782 showed no fundamental discrepancy from other eighteenth-century Italian-Jewish schools, though its coverage of Hebrew texts was somewhat less intensive. Still, most of the long day was devoted to the *pia* curriculum—religious obligations and graded instruction in Hebrew and basic Jewish texts, including the Italian-Jewish staple of Aggadah. Only two hours per day were allotted to the German "Normal" teachers. (This was less than in Prague, where four hours per day were stipulated in summer time.) The standard textbooks of the state schools were to be used for the "Normal" subjects; later, a Haskalah favorite, Baruch Lindau's *Reshit Limudim* (The beginning of instruction, Berlin, 1788), was adopted for science.[66] The way in which the *Scuola Pia Normale* met the state's requirement of instruction in "philosophical morality" was perhaps emblematic: Trieste solicited help from Berlin, but in practice relied upon Italian Jewish resources. The school used as its modern ethical text Simhah Calimani's *Esame o sia Catechismo ad un giovane israelita istruito nella sua religione* (1782).[67] (Unlike later works of this genre, Calimani's catechism stressed the importance of the Oral Law and the observance of commandments.) In addition, the school continued the Italian-Jewish practice of the *accademia*, i.e., the public recital by students of ethical dramas or dialogues. The students were to expound "sound" and "natural morality" from the "purity of sacred biblical sources." One such event was reported by the city's official newspaper in glowing terms, and the text of the recital published by the government's press.[68]

Trieste's school met the criteria of Vienna and Berlin; it was in our parlance a Jewish day-school, combining Jewish and state curricula. But it would be a mistake to see this school solely or even primarily in terms of Central European initiatives, for it emerged from and continued the traditions of Italian Jewish education. Indeed, outside Trieste some Italians explicitly asserted the greater worth of Italian practices, notably with regard to curriculum and women as teachers for the very young.[69] Generally Italian Jews heard the Haskalah's education message as a supplement to their own traditions, not as a substitute or radical overhaul.

While Wessely's Italian supporters considered some of his suggestions worthwhile, they did not accept Berlin as an exclusive model for themselves, because they were too keenly aware of the differences in the cultural development of Ashkenazic and Italian Jews. Throughout the Italians' writings there was an unstated premise, an attitude to Ashkenazic culture that was ultimately condescending and patronizing. Morpurgo expressed it most pointedly when he contrasted Italian "eloquence" to Ashkenazic "stammering."[70] He acknowledged Ashkenazic excellence in halachah, Midrash, and kabbalah, but bemoaned their neglect of the fields now deemed important: Scripture and Hebrew language and letters, especially poetry. Ashkenazic Jews could hardly point the way when it came to Hebrew literature, European languages, and participation in Gentile culture; Sephardic and Italian Jews through the ages could do so much better. In Morpurgo's view, there were now reasons for hope. The means for cultural improvement were at hand—governmental policies, the mighty efforts of Mendelssohn and Wessely, and the steadily growing contribution of Ashkenazic authors to general science and literature.[71] Morpurgo hoped to encourage that trend with a German translation of his *Discorso,* whose message was Jewish honor through service to state and general culture. In addition he proposed to publish for Ashkenazic Jewry a remedial reading program, comprising medieval Sephardic poetic, philosophic, and ethical works in order to "teach . . . language, rhetoric, and ethics all at once in the manner of the ancient Romans and Greeks."[72]

Morpurgo employed an interesting and revealing tactic in his efforts to spur Ashkenazic Jewry forward: the expression of commonality and empathy. Invoking family ties and proximity—"on the German-Italian frontier . . . I too am a descendant of Ashkenaz"[73]—Morpurgo related that he had found egregious grammatical errors (stemming from faulty knowledge of both Hebrew and Italian) in the record-books of his own ancestors, Ashkenazic immigrants to northern Italy. Yet court officials in Vienna could hardly believe that Elia Morpurgo was a Jew because he spoke so correctly and elegantly![74] The implication was that German Jews, like northern Italian Jews before them, could progress; they too could master both Hebrew and the language of their surroundings. By way of commonality, Morpurgo was actually expressing an assumption of superiority, for he was in effect assuring Ashkenazic Jews that the gap between them and Italians could be bridged. But commonality served a second purpose for him—to prod Italian Jews themselves, for they too were not beyond reproach. To take advantage of the new opportunities all Jewries needed to improve themselves through conscious application of Enlightenment principles.[75] The significant point is that for Morpurgo and other Italian exponents of Enlightenment, Ashkenazic culture—and even the Berlin Haskalah—could not alone direct the way.

German Images of Italian Jews

Their public defense of Wessely made Italian, above all Triestine, Jews known as allies of the Haskalah. The storm around Wessely eventually calmed. While it is difficult to assess the precise impact of the Italian rabbis' intervention, Wessely and his colleagues acknowledged it as crucial.[76] No other Jewry had thus come to his aid. Wessely's notion of Italian Jews as acculturated was one of the reasons he had turned to them in the first place; in turn, their role in the *Divrei Shalom Ve'emet* controversy led to a reinforcement of that image. Mendelssohn, for one, thought the Venetians' *pesak* "very remarkable."[77] Other *maskilim* began to see Italian Jews in ever more positive, enlightened, and progressive terms.

Let us survey the elements upon which this image rested. Personal contacts developed beyond those of the 1770s discussed above. Most important was Herz Homberg, close associate of Mendelssohn and Wessely, who spent some five years, from late 1782, in Gorizia and Trieste as a teacher in the new Jewish schools.[78] In the regular correspondence between them, Mendelssohn highly recommended to Homberg his "worthy and noble-minded friend" Giuseppe Moise Luzzatto of Gorizia, not least for his knowledge of German and "taste for German philosophy."[79] The itinerant man of letters Samuel Romanelli sojourned a few years in Berlin and Vienna in the circles of *maskilim* and their patrons.[80] The *maskil* Rabbi Saul Lewin-Berlin visited northern Italy, drawn there according to one scholar by interest in Wessely's Italian supporters.[81] Elia Morpurgo corresponded with Mendelssohn, Wessely, and the *Me'asfim;* he suggested various projects for Italian-German cooperation in publishing, none of which came to fruition.[82] Overall, the Italian market for Haskalah publications in the 1780s was limited: Morpurgo was the only Italian subscriber to *Hame'asef,* and the *Biur* counted two, one anonymous from Trieste and one Dr. Salom of Padua.[83] *Hame'asef* did however publish works by Italians—Morpurgo's works on education, "Mikhtav Me'Elyahu" (Letter from Elija) and "Divrei Hokhmah Umusar" (Words of wisdom and ethics), and Dr. Ephraim Luzzatto's poetry.[84] It also carried reports of current events which *maskilim* interpreted as signs of Italian-Jewish political astuteness, i.e., commitment to the policies of Enlightenment. These were the campaign for Wessely, the establishment of modern schools in Trieste and Mantua, and approval by these two communities of the new Habsburg policy of military conscription in 1788.[85] Citing the Italians' greater adeptness in Gentile ways, Galician Jews had asked them for help in protesting to the emperor. To their surprise, both Italian communities viewed conscription favorably and urged compliance. Once again northern Italian Jews appeared as the vanguard of Habsburg Jewries.

The two most extensive portraits of Italian Jews were drawn by Wessely and Isaac Euchel. In *Divrei Shalom Ve'emet* Wessely presented Italian Jews in terms of his ideals. In the first pamphlet he mentioned their fluency in the language of their surroundings; in the second he stressed their synthesis of Jewish and general culture. Trying at one and the same time to flatter his Italian readers and to provide a model to other Jews, he addressed Triestine Jews thus:

> My words are unnecessary for you, you who from your youth have learned to speak the Italian and Spanish languages correctly, whose teachers are

undoubtedly eloquent, and are able to translate Hebrew expressions into the language people understand, thereby explaining to their students the clear meaning of the Torah and Prophets. And your customs have always been wise, in conformance with the norms of mutual tolerance and peaceful conduct among mankind. In addition, trade in your lands is with the large states of Europe, Asia, and Africa, and you get to hear of the customs of areas distant from you. All the communities of Israel in Italian lands have a similar advantage, and therefore many among you are experienced in civility, learned in rhetoric and poetry, and educated in ethical teachings based upon psychology. Moreover, all these qualities are found among the Torah scholars in your midst, the distinguished rabbis and great luminaries who have brightened the universe with their wisdom and teaching. Through the generations their compositions are filled with pleasantness, and their words are beautiful. Just as they include judgments and laws, so too do they include teachings of wisdom and civility.[86]

Wessely believed that maritime commerce, the high level of Italian culture and civilization, and the Sephardic component of the Italian-Jewish heritage had produced a Jewry which stood in sharp contrast to insular, unworldly Ashkenazic Jewry. Now he hoped that the Triestine school, the very expression of Italian-Jewish civic and cultural values, would serve as a model from which "the rest of our brethren the children of Israel . . . will learn, they too, to walk on the path which you [Trieste] have trod." Thus Wessely presented Italian Jews as the embodiment of the Haskalah's moral and cultural ideals.

Euchel further developed that characterization in his imaginary travelogue "Igrot Meshulam Ben-Uriah HaEshtamoi" (Letters of Meshulam son of Uriah the Eshtamoan), which appeared in *Hame'asef* in 1789–90. Euchel presented Livornese Jews of 1769 thus:

> The Jews in Leghorn live together in calm and security in fine homes amidst the nobles of the land, and their houses are stone-built and most of its people are merchants and notables. Most of them shave their beards and style their hair, there is no difference between their dress and that of the [other] inhabitants. They speak the language of the people correctly and eloquently like one of their orators. . . . Behold in this great city whose inhabitants number about 50,000, almost half [sic] are Jews. Most follow the Sefardic custom, and some among them are Germans and Poles, and they have splendid synagogues. They dwell peacefully and quietly, and they pursue every occupation and business their hearts desire. My heart gladdens and I am proud to see my brothers living securely amidst the Gentiles [literally, the captors] without foe or troublemaker.[87]

Social harmony depended of course not only on Jews but also on Gentiles, depicted as paragons in many respects, and most important, for their tolerance toward different religions and peoples. The traveler found Jewish culture flourishing, books and love of learning in abundance, and Hebrew poetry of superior quality, with Ephraim Luzzatto's deserving of special praise.

Euchel's portrait of Livornese Jews provided a social, economic, and cultural model for other Jewries. The ideals of Haskalah were realized here: peaceful coexistence unconstrained by ghetto walls, respected and productive economic activity, Jewish adaptation to Gentile mores along with continued Jewish cultural creativity. The implication was that the Italian example should both legitimate and encourage further Haskalah endeavor.

The image of Italian Jews as enlightened and progressive enjoyed currency among other German *maskilim*. *Hame'asef* published biographies of Jews associated with Italy, e.g. Joseph Delmedigo and Isaac Abarbanel.[88] Many *maskilim* acknowledged Italian preeminence in Hebrew language and letters, and printed works of past and present Italian authors, e.g. Emanuel of Rome, Abraham Farissol, Elijah Levita, Azariah de Rossi, Azariah Figo, Abraham Jaghel, Moses Hayim Luzzatto, Ephraim Luzzatto, and Samuel Romanelli.[89] Isaac Satanow in his introduction to *Mishlei Asaf* (Proverbs of Asaf) employed an Italian pseudonym—"Joseph Luzzatto of Italy"—in deploring the sorry state of Hebrew and calling for its revival.[90]

Some German *maskilim* went beyond culture and society to the sensitive realm of religion. They imputed to Italian Jews both a critical approach to religious tradition and a flexibility concerning religious law and ritual. Interest in Azariah de Rossi's *Meor Enayim* (Light of the eyes) and Saul Lewin-Berlin's claim of Italian provenance for the manuscript of *Besamim Rosh* (Incense of Spices), his collection of forged lenient responsa, may be seen in this light.[91] But the best example was a curious episode, which for the sake of convenience I call "the Florence Reform hoax." In 1796 European newspapers reported that a synod of Italian rabbis in Florence had sanctioned revolutionary changes in basic areas of Jewish law such as the Sabbath and *kashrut*. Italian rabbis issued heated denials in *Hame'asef* and in separate pamphlets, one published in Leghorn in Hebrew and a second in Hamburg in Hebrew and German.[92] However, the Tuscan Bishop Scipione de Ricci informed his inquirer, the Abbé Grégoire, that a synod had indeed taken place, though Italian rabbis had not sanctioned such reforms.[93] The whole episode remains murky. Even the origin of the story is uncertain. Some contemporaries suggested German rather than local Italian vintage. On that theory, the story was a concoction of German radicals who sought to further their own cause of religious reform by creating Italian Jews as a legitimizing precedent and spur. Whatever the origin of the story, what is striking is the plausibility north of the Alps of Italian Jews as religious radicals.

What could have contributed to this conception? Italian Jews' distinctive customs concerning beards and wine had aroused suspicion among some other Jews in the past.[94] Perhaps this was known to radical German *maskilim,* though their response would be approval, not censure. Perhaps they extrapolated from the one Italian in their midst who was known as a "scoffer of *mizvot,*" Romanelli.[95] But probably most significant was the Italian Jews' championing of Wessely and *Divrei Shalom Ve'emet.* That action—along with all the subsequent facts and fancies—may well have been interpreted as support for all so-called progressive causes. For radicals, religious reform was but a short step from Haskalah. Whether based on actual fact, wishful invention and projection, or misunderstanding of a different cultural tradition, the Florence Reform hoax shows the uses to which the progressive image of Italian Jews could be put.

Thus the support and legitimation which Italian Jews had provided for Wessely at a critical moment had helped foster among German *maskilim* an image of Italian Jews as acculturated, enlightened, politically adroit, and religiously flexible. Italian Jewry was as much a mirror as an independent entity for German *maskilim.* Italian Jews served them as a model—not as initiators of new ideals but rather as justification and actualization of their own German-bred goals of Haskalah. The *maskilim* derived inspiration from their closely related images of Italian and Sephardic traditions. Both seemed to offer confirmation of the possibility of Jews living harmoniously and creatively in Gentile societies. Drawing sustenance from both fact and fiction, German *maskilim* saw Italian Jewry as an ally in the struggle to modernize Jewish society and Judaism. In the aftermath of *Divrei Shalom Ve'emet* they were convinced of Italian convergence with their program.

Conclusions and Reflections

Italian Jewish responses to the cultural programs of Enlightened Absolutism and the Berlin Haskalah were generally favorable. When consulted by other Jewish communities about the issues of the day, Italian Jews of the Habsburg Empire, especially those of Trieste, exhibited a self-conscious sense of vanguard responsibility and spoke for the benefits of change. They championed Wessely's *Divrei Shalom Ve'emet* in order to help legitimate and spread his message, which they saw as a necessary corrective for Ashkenazic Jews. Proud to be allies of the celebrated Mendelssohn and Wessely, Triestine Jews in particular were gratified by their praise.

Yet Wessely's Italian allies were neither passive recipients nor imitators. They selected carefully from Berlin's wares, affirming values and methods that seemed familiar but rejecting that which struck them as radically new.[96] Their reservations did not stem from a narrow or obscurantist view of Jewish culture—none appreciated European languages and the arts, humanities, and sciences more than they—but rather from a different configuration of Judaism and general culture than the Haskalah's. For Italian Jews, neither Torah nor general culture had to yield in order for the other to have a place. Yet it was precisely that configuration of Judaism and general culture—their tradition of acculturation—which enabled Italians to find Wessely's message familiar and ultimately compatible with their own outlook.

Later, the drive for inclusion in the emerging Italian nation-state did not entail a Jewish debate about acculturation; its absence was in fact the distinguishing characteristic of Jewish modernization in Italy. Despite the ghetto, the Italians—in contrast to many other Jewries—had an ongoing tradition of cultural openness. And the continuity and vitality of that tradition were evident in the Italians' defense of Wessely. Indeed some of their arguments echoed themes which resonated through Italian-Jewish intellectual history. Rabbi Bassan's concern that general studies be taught under Jewish auspices was similar to the Provenzalis' rationale for a Jewish university in the 1550s, and Morpurgo's proposal to use non-Jewish culture to defend Judaism was reminiscent of Azariah de Rossi's approach.[97]

The Italian-Jewish tradition of accommodation of European culture was a decisive factor in the rabbis' legitimation of Wessely's program. It was a legacy at work among all respondents, even those from areas not affected by Enlightened absolutist policies. Thus, although Trieste was distinctive in many respects, it did share with other Italian Jews a potent cultural legacy.

That cultural legacy helped prepare Jews for integration, i.e., to make the transition out of the ghetto, which reduced the potential for conflict between tradition and modernity. Italian supporters of Haskalah were not a peripheral coterie of radical intellectuals but the rabbinic and communal elite. Their receptivity to Haskalah was predicated on its perceived familiarity, not its novelty. Their sense of cultural continuity, with their own and with medieval Sephardic traditions, permitted them to see harmony between old and new. Their willingness to mute differences and to find convergence between dissimilar positions, their disinterest in programmatic ideological statements, and their readiness to cooperate with lay leaders also contributed to an easing of tensions. In the long run, modernity had much less disruptive potential if invested with continuity and legitimacy by representatives of Jewish authority.[98]

The Italian alliance with Wessely enhanced the legitimacy of the Haskalah. That function revealed two-way traffic across the Alps, a reciprocal relationship between Italian and German Jews. Italy had a definite attraction for Berlin *maskilim*. In their efforts to revive Hebrew letters and create worldly and modern Jews, the Italian was one of the Jewish traditions from which they drew sustenance. *Maskilim* were aware of the Italian contribution to and transmission of Hebrew literature and Sephardic legacies.[99]

Italians and Germans saw each other as allies in the work of Jewish cultural modernization, but neither was an exclusive model for the other, and neither exerted a decisive transforming influence upon the other. Even in Trieste, where contact with Berlin Haskalah was greatest, governmental policies and Italian traditions were more important. German Haskalah was not Italian Jewry's ticket to European culture. The *Scuola Pia Normale* of Trieste, like the later *Collegio Rabbinico* of Padua, demonstrated the independent development of modern Jewish educational institutions in Italy.[100] Similarly, the Berlin Haskalah's vision of the future did not derive from Italian models; for German *maskilim,* the Italian image functioned primarily as post-facto legitimation. Neither was dependent on the other for setting its agenda, but once the convergence of their separate paths was recognized, each found reinforcement in perceived affinities and mutual admiration.

Not surprisingly, German *maskilim,* the supplicants in this encounter, emphasized convergence, while the Italians were more aware of the ambiguities of the alliance and the measure of their divergence. German modernizers continued to seek inspiration and legitimation from Italians until the Reform temple controversies of 1816–1820 put an end to their illusions.[101] But some contemporaries did perceive the differences between Italian and German approaches. In *Haorev* (He who lies in wait) of 1795, Baruch Jeitteles of Prague used Italian Jews to voice his critique of radical Berlin Haskalah. As a moderate alternative, he posed the Italian-Jewish synthesis of Enlightenment and tradition.[102] That view corresponded to the Italian-Jewish self-perception as enlightened moderates who could mediate between modernizers and traditionalists. This was their role in the *Divrei Shalom Ve'emet* controversy, and according to some of the Italian delegates, theirs once again at the Assembly of Notables and Sanhedrin in 1806-7. Indeed the record of those proceedings commended Italian rabbis for "their zeal, their talents, and their learning," noting that the "Rabbies [sic] of that country have been the first to give the example of literary and historical pursuits, connected with theological learning, and a profound knowledge of the Holy Writings."[103] Italians responded to later German-Jewish modernizing movements such as Reform and Wissenschaft as they had to Haskalah, with admiration for German aims and achievements, support for moderate progress, discomfort with radical novelty, and a keen sense of the distinctive contribution which their own tradition and temperament allowed them to make.[104]

Thus, in the Italian context, the Berlin Haskalah was somehow both familiar and novel. The Italians' was a complicated stance—a spirited but qualified defense of Haskalah. The ambiguities of the alliance suggest that there is no simple relation to be posited between the historical experience of Italian Jewry and Haskalah. While Italian Jews, past and present, served as models and advocates for the Haskalah in Central Europe, I think it misleading to see Italians historically as *maskilim avant la lettre*.[105] For that is to miss the difference in kind between Italian and German Jewries. Italian Jewry was on a different course, not just a different timetable. Neither in the sixteenth nor the eighteenth centuries were their terms of engagement with Gentile society those of Ashkenaz. Over a long period, cultural boundaries had been drawn differently in Italy. Even though Italian tradition had long accepted general culture as natural, and displayed certain tendencies critical of tradition itself, it had never deemed general culture of equal or greater worth than Judaism. And in their attempts to meet the new challenges of the eighteenth and nineteenth centuries, many prominent Italian Jewish thinkers tried to keep faith with that tradition.[106] If by the Haskalah movement we mean a group of intellectuals defining themselves in opposition to tradition and calling for radical cultural remaking, then we may agree with Assaf that Italian Jews—even in Trieste, where contact with Central European Haskalah was greatest—had no Haskalah movement, because they had no need of one.[107] There was Enlightenment in Italy, but no Haskalah.

These conclusions suggest that we should not view tradition, reaction, and adaptation monolithically. The case of Italian Jews shows that modernizing need not proceed by way of ideological pronouncement, that acculturation, Enlightenment, and Haskalah are not all synonymous, and that even in Central and Western Europe the paths of Jewish modernization were more varied than we have supposed.

Notes

This essay draws on my doctoral dissertation "Piety and Enlightenment: The Jews of Trieste in a Revolutionary Age, 1780–1820," written under the supervision of Professors Isadore Twersky and Yosef Yerushalmi. I thank them both for their support and guidance. I thank as well Benjamin Braude, Israel Bartal, Bernard

Cooperman, David Fishman, Hillel Kieval, Christine Korsgaard, Aron Rodrigue, and Sarah Stroumsa for their comments on earlier drafts of this essay. This research has been funded by the Harvard University Center for Jewish Studies, the Memorial Foundation for Jewish Culture, and the Social Sciences and Humanities Research Council of Canada. I am indebted to the staffs of the following institutions for their gracious assistance—the Central Archives for the History of the Jewish People (CAHJP), and the Jewish National and University Library of Jerusalem; the Comunità Israelitica (ACIT), Archivio di Stato (AST), and the Biblioteca Civica of Trieste; the Jewish Theological Seminary (JTS) of New York; and Harvard University Libraries. (These abbreviations are used in the following notes.)

1. "Italian Judaism was always orthodox and always more or less enlightened. It did not have, like the Spanish, a period of domination by a foreign culture, and therefore by heterodoxy; nor did it ever have, like the northern, a period of coarseness and lack of all civilized culture." Samuel David Luzzatto, *Il Giudaismo illustrato* (Padua, 1848), vol. 1, p. 29.
2. See the standard works of Attilio Milano, *Storia degli ebrei in Italia* (Turin: Einaudi, 1963); and Cecil Roth, *The History of the Jews of Italy* (Philadelphia: The Jewish Publication Society of America, 1946). For an overview of Italian Jewry in the modern period, with emphasis on social and economic factors, see the forthcoming study by Ariel Toaff, in Michael A. Meyer, ed., *The Age of Haskalah and Emancipation* (Hebrew), in the *History of the Jewish People* series (Jerusalem: Masada Press, forthcoming). I thank Professor Toaff for making his study available to me. On emancipation and integration see Renzo De Felice, "Per una storia del problema ebraico in Italia alla fine del XVIII secolo e all'inizio del XIX," *Movimento operaio* 7 (1955): 681–727; Salvatore Foà, *Gli ebrei nel Risorgimento italiano* (Assisi and Rome: Carucci, 1978); Guido Fubini, *La condizione giuridica dell'ebraismo italiano* (Florence: La nuova Italia, 1974); Marcel Grilli, "The Role of the Jews in Modern Italy," *Menorah Journal* 27 (1939): 260–80, and 28 (1940): 60–81, 172–97; Mario Rossi, "Emancipation of the Jews in Italy," *Jewish Social Studies* 15 (1953): 113–34; and most recently, Andrew Canepa, "Considerazioni sulla seconda emancipazione e le sue conseguenze," *La Rassegna Mensile di Israel* (henceforth *RMI*) 47 (1981): 47–89; idem, "Reflections on Antisemitism in Liberal Italy," *The Wiener Library Bulletin* 31 (1978): 104–11, and his other articles cited there. On relative absence of conflict see Raphael Mahler, *A History of Modern Jewry, 1780–1815* (New York: Schocken, 1971), vol. 1, p. 133; Simhah Assaf, *Mekorot Letoledot Hahinukh BeYisrael* (Sources for the history of Jewish education [Tel Aviv: Dvir, 1930]), vol. 2, pp. vi–vii; B. Dinaburg [Dinur], "B.Z. Rafael HaKohen Frizzi Vesifro 'Petah Enayim': Lidemutah shel HaHaskalah BeItalyah," (B. Frizzi and his book 'Petah Enayim': On the character of the Haskalah in Italy"), *Tarbiz* 20 (1949): 241–64, esp. p. 254; Umberto Cassuto, *Storia della letteratura ebraica postbiblica* (Florence: Casa editrice Israel, 1938), pp. 173–75; Isacco Garti, "Il carteggio Ascoli-Luzzatto conservato nella Biblioteca dell'Accademia dei Lincei," *Italia* 1 (1976): 70–88, esp. pp. 72, 77.
3. On this period see Nikolaus Vielmetti, "Die Gründergeschichte des Collegio Rabbinico in Padua," *Kairos* 12 (1970): 1–30, esp. pp. 1–15, and 13 (1971):

38–66. For relations and comparison of the two Jewries over time see Isaac
E. Barzilay, "The Italian and Berlin Haskalah: Parallels and Differences,"
Proceedings of the American Academy for Jewish Research 29 (1960): 17–54;
and Yomtov Ludwig Bato, "Italian Jewry," *Leo Baeck Institute Year Book,*
vol. 3 (New York, 1958), pp. 333–43.

4. Hartwig Wessely, *Mikhtav Shelishi: Divrei Shalom Ve'emet . . . Ein Mishpat*
("Letter no. three: Fountain of judgment" [Berlin, 1784]), p. 46b; see also
pp. 4b, 7b–8b, and note on p. 40a–b; and the beginning of his *Mikhtav
Revii: Rehovot* (Letter no. four: Broad places [Berlin, 1785]). His first two
letters, *Divrei Shalom Ve'emet* (henceforth *DSVE*) and *Mikhtav Sheni: Rav
Tuv Levet Yisrael* (Letter no. two: Abundant goodness to the house of Israel)
were first published in Berlin in 1782. All four were reprinted together in
Vienna (1826) and Warsaw (1886). Henceforth references to *Ein Mishpat*
are to the first edition, while those to the other three are to the second
edition (Vienna, 1826). On the controversy generally see, most recently,
Alexander Altmann, *Moses Mendelssohn* (Philadelphia: Jewish Publication
Society of America and the University of Alabama Press, 1973), pp. 474–89;
Jacob Katz, *Out of the Ghetto* (Cambridge: Harvard University Press, 1973),
pp. 57–79, 142–60; Moses S. Samet, "M. Mendelssohn, N. H. Weisel Verabanei
Doram" (Mendelssohn, Wessely, and the rabbis of their time), in A. Gilboa
et al., eds., *Mehkarim Betoledot Am Yisrael Ve'erez Yisrael Lezekher Zevi
Avneri* (Studies in the history of the Jewish people and the land of Israel
in memory of Zevi Avneri" [Haifa: Haifa University, 1970]), pp. 233–57.

5. Such an analysis would consider factors such as the demographic stability
of Italian Jews in this period, Italy's movement for national unification and
its pace of economic development, the role of Catholicism and religion in
Italian society and politics, and the legacies of Italy's advanced urban,
economic, and cultural development in medieval and early modern times.

6. De Felice, "Per una storia," p. 605.

7. The Jewish percentage in the northern half of the peninsula where Jews
were concentrated was obviously higher. See Alan Charles Harris, *La
demografia del ghetto in Italia (1516–1797 circa)* (Rome, 1967; published
by *RMI* with vol. 33, 1967), for estimates ranging from 0.6 percent to 9.4
percent in different locales. See most recently Roberto Bachi and Sergio
Della Pergola, "Gli ebrei italiani nel quadro della demografia della diaspora,"
Quaderni storici 19 (1984, = no. 55): 155–91.

8. "German-Italian frontier" comes at the end of Elia Morpurgo, *Igeret Ogeret
Ahavat Haadam Beasher Hu Adam* (Treatise treating of love of man *qua*
man), in *Devash Vehalav* (Honey and milk), *JTS* (1782), pp. 13b–32a, Adler
ms. 2492, microfilm no. 3687. On this manuscript and Morpurgo generally
see Isaac Rivkind, "Elia Morpurgo Mesaiyo shel Weisel Bemilhemet
HaHaskalah Leor Teudot Hadashot" (Elia Morpurgo, Wessely's ally in the
struggle for the Haskalah in light of new evidence), in *Studies in Jewish
Bibliography and Related Subjects in Memory of Abraham Solomon Freidus*
(New York: Alexander Kohut Memorial Foundation, 1929), Hebrew section,
pp. 138–59; also Paolo S. Colbi, "Elia Morpurgo capo della nazione ebraica
di Gradisca," *RMI* 46 (1980): 179–88; and Nikolaus Vielmetti, "Elia Morpurgo
di Gradisca protagonista dell'Illuminismo ebraico," in Pier Cesare Ioly-
Zorattini, ed., *Gli ebrei a Gorizia e a Trieste tra 'Ancien Régime' ed
Emancipazione.* Atti del Convegno di Gorizia, 13 giugno 1983 (Udine: Del

Bianco, 1984), pp. 41–46. On frontier see also B. Frizzi, *Giornale medico e letterario di Trieste* (Trieste, 1790), vol. 1, preface, where he stated his aim as the combining of the "solidity" of German scholarship with the "grace" of Italian. On this celebrated polymath see Dinaburg, "B.Z. Raphael Hakohen Frizzi"; and Daniele Nissim, "Modernità di vedute in un nostro illuminista: Benedetto Frizzi e le sue opere," *RMI* 34 (1968): 279–91. I intend to devote a separate study to him in the future. On Trieste's function generally as *Mitteleuropa*'s outpost in Italy see Angelo Ara and Claudio Magris, *Trieste. Un'identità di frontiera* (Turin: Einaudi, 1982).

9. Italian was the language of commerce and culture in Trieste, and of its Jews. Most Triestine Jews were of Italian origin, and communal records were kept in Italian. On the origins and economic activities of leading Jewish families see I. Zoller, *La Comunità israelitica di Trieste. Studio di demografia storia* (Ferrara, 1924), pp. 6, 10; and G. Cervani and L. Buda, *La comunità israelitica di Trieste nel secolo XVIII* (Udine: Del Bianco, 1973), pp. 90–128.

10. The following discussion is based on these works: Ioly Zorattini, ed. *Gli ebrei,* esp. the articles by Cervani, Altieri, and Del Bianco Cotrozzi; Orietta Altieri, *L'evoluzione socio-demografica della Comunità israelitica di Gorizia durante la dominazione absburgica 1778–1900,* unpublished Tesi di laurea, University of Udine, 1981-82 (I thank Dr. Altieri for making her study available to me); Giuseppe Bolaffio, "Sfogliando l'archivio della Comunità di Gorizia," *RMI* 23 (1957): 537–46, and 24 (1958): 20–40, 62–74, 132–41; Maddalena Del Bianco Cotrozzi, *La comunità ebraica di Gradisca d'Isonzo* (Udine: Del Bianco, 1983); Cervani and Buda, *La comunità;* Mario Stock, *Nel segno di Geremia. Storia della comunità israelitica di Trieste dal 1200* (Udine: Instituto per Enciclopaedia del Friuli-Venezia, Giulia, 1979); Liana De Antonellis Martini, *Portofranco e comunità etnico-religiose nella Trieste settecentesca* (Milan: Giuffré 1968). On Triestine Jewish culture in particular see Dinaburg, "B. Z. Raphael HaKohen Frizzi"; Vielmetti, "Die Gründergeschichte," and P. S. Colbi, "Tekufat Hazohar shel Hasifrut Haivrit Beir Trieste" (The golden age of Hebrew literature in Trieste"), *Sinai* 83 (1978): 70–79. Samuel David Luzzatto's two different, but overlapping autobiographies are a valuable source: "Toledot Shadal," *Hamagid,* 2–8 (1858–64), see Isaia Luzzatto, *Catalogo ragionato degli scritti sparsi di S.D. Luzzato* (Padua, 1881) for exact pages; and *Autobiografia . . .* (Padua, 1878). The second has appeared in a number of translated and excerpted editions, from "Selbstbiographie" tr. Isidor Busch, in *Jahrbuch für Israeliten* 6 (1847-48), pp. 95–116, to Moses A. Shulvass, ed. and tr., *Pirkei hayim* (New York: Talpiot, Yeshiva University, 1951).

11. Carlo L. Curiel, "Quaresime triestine del settecento," *La Porta Orientale* 2 (1932): 120–29. On the concept *neutral society* see Jacob Katz, *Tradition and Crisis* (New York: Schocken, 1971), and *Out of the Ghetto.*

12. See any of Frizzi's writings (listed in Nissim, "Modernità di vedute"), e.g. *Eloge de Monsieur Richard maître de langue française* (Trieste, 1791); and Elia Morpurgo, *Discorso pronunziato da Elia Morpurgo Capo della Nazione Ebrea di Gradisca. Nel partecipare a quella Comunità la Clementissima Sovrana risoluzione 16. Maggio 1781* (Gorizia, 1782).

13. Franco Valsecchi, *L'Assolutismo illuminato in Austria e in Lombardia,* 2 vols. (Bologna: Nicola Zanichelli, 1931–34); Giulio Cervani, *Riformismo*

settecentesco nella provincia mercantile del Litorale (Trieste e Fiume) (Rome, 1962; originally in *Fiume,* nos. 3–4 [1961]).

14. Rivkind, "Elia Morpurgo," pp. 147, 151; Morpurgo, *Discorso,* pp. 56–57, 74–75. From the 1790s, Vienna itself became an important center for Habsburg *maskilim.* See Reuven Fahn, *Kitvei Reuven Fahn* (Writings of R. F.), vol. 2: *Pirkei Haskalah* (Chapters of Haskalah [Stanislav: Hebrew University Press, 1937]); Salo Baron, "Letoledot HaHaskalah Vehahinukh BeVinah" (On the history of the Haskalah and education in Vienna), in Isaac Silberschlag and Yohanan Twersky, eds., *Sefer Touroff* (Touroff Festschrift [Boston: Teachers' Training Institutes, 1938]), pp. 167–83; G. Wolf, *Geschichte der Juden in Wien, 1156–1876,* (Vienna, 1876; rep. Vienna: Geyer, 1974).

15. For texts of legislation in Lombardy see Shlomo Simonsohn, *History of the Jews in the Duchy of Mantua* (Jerusalem: Kiryat Sefer, 1977), pp. 813–27. For Trieste see AST, "C.R. Governo in Trieste (1776–1809)," b. 83 and 219; CAHJP, "Archives of the Jewish Community of Mantua," microfilm HM 5188, f. 191. Also on Trieste see Ludwig Singer, "Neue Beiträge zur Geschichte der Toleranzpatente Josefs II," *B'nai B'rith Mitteilungen für Österreich* 34 (1934): 186–91, 233–37; De Antonellis Martini, *Portofranco;* Cervani and Buda, La comunità; and Maria Fausta Maternini Zotta, *L'ente comunitario ebraico. La legislazione negli ultimi due secoli* (Milan: Giuffre, 1983); these last two contain texts of laws and communal statutes. On the Josephine legislation in Italy generally see also Roth, *The History of the Jews in Italy,* pp. 422–24; Vittore Colorni, *Gli Ebrei nel sistema del diritto comune fino alla prima emancipazione* (Milan: Giuffre, 1956), pp. 66–72; and Josef Karniel, *Hamediniut Kelapei Hameutim Hadatiyim Bemamlekhet Habsburg Biyemei Joseph II, 1765–1790* (The Policy toward the religious minorities in the Habsburg monarchy in the time of Joseph II), unpublished Ph.D. diss., Tel Aviv University, 1980.

16. The Triestine versions of the edicts of May, October, and November 1781 concerning education are in AST, "C.R. Governo in Trieste (1776–1809)," b. 83. CAHJP has copies: Stern Collection, P 17/1241; and Archives of the Jewish Community of Mantua, microfilm HM 5187, f. 190 (the date 26 November 1782 on this copy is incorrect; the correct date is 26 November 1781). Mario Stock, "Giuseppe II d'Austria e l'emancipazione ebraica," *RMI* 39 (1973): 369–72, briefly summarizes the legislation.

17. Letter of 11 December 1775, CAHJP, Archives of the Jewish Community of Gorizia, IT/Go VI, p. 7.

18. AST, "C.R. Governo in Trieste (1776–1809)," b. 83 and 126; Luzzatto, *Autobiografia,* pp. 47–49.

19. Morpurgo, *Discorso.* Another work of Jewish apologetics written in the aftermath of the Josephine legislation was Benedetto Frizzi, *Difesa contro gli Attacchi Fatti alla Nazione Ebrea nel libro intitolato Della Influenza del Ghetto nello Stato* (Pavia, 1784; facsimile ed. Bologna: Forni, 1977); see also Simonsohn, *History of the Jews,* pp. 93–95.

20. *Regole* (Gorizia, 1782), and Colbi, "Elia Morpurgo," provide the date of the school's opening, about which there has been confusion (in Vittorio Castiglioni, *L'instituto scolastico della comunità israelitica di Trieste, 1786–1886* [Trieste, 1886]; Salvatore Sabbadini, *I primi passi della scuola ebraica triestina* [Trieste: Tipografia del L. Austriaco, 1916]; Cervani and Buda, *La comunità.* Colbi published recitations from the opening day's festivities in

Italian translation; I thank Dr. Nikolaus Vielmetti for sending me a copy of the Hebrew original. On the organizing of the school, see *Regole; AST,* "C.R. Governo in Trieste (1776–1809)," b. 67; ACIT #18, "Istruzione Scuole Pie Normale, 1782–1823."

21. For Wessely's praise see his fourth letter, *Rehovot* (see n. 4, above), p. 218. On Prague see Hillel Kieval's essay in this volume (chap. 4). On modern schools in Central Europe see also Mordechai Eliav, *Hahinukh Hayehudi Begermanyah Biyemei HaHaskalah Vehaemanzipazyah* (Jewish education in Germany in the period of Enlightenment and emancipation [Jerusalem: The Jewish Agency, 1960]), pp. 71–86, and Katz, *Out of the Ghetto,* pp. 124–31.

22. CAHJP, "Archives of the Jewish Community of Mantua," microfilms HM 5193, f. 217, and HM 5190, f. 220. On Mantuan education in the preceding decades see Simonsohn, *History of the Jews,* pp. 589–99.

23. *Enziklopedyah Hinukhit* (Educational encyclopedia [Jerusalem: Bialik Institute, 1964]), vol. 4, pp. 376–81, 406–9; Lelio Della Torre, *Scritti sparsi* (Padua: Prosperini, 1908), vol. 2, pp. 334–39; Assaf, *Mekorot,* vol. 2, pp. 121–213, for the seventeenth and eighteenth centuries.

24. *Regole,* p. 3; ACIT #18, "Istruzione Scuole Pie Normale 1782–1823," 28 April 1782, shows that the scripture, Maimonides (*Mishneh Torah*), Mishnah, and *Aggadah,* were among the "sacred studies" previously taught. On general studies see Castiglioni, *L'instituto scolastico,* p. 7, and Cervani and Buda, *La comunità,* p. 45.

25. Dinaburg, *B.Z. Rafael HaKohen.* On R. Formiggini see Mordecai Samuel Ghirondi and Hananel Neppi, *Toledot Gedolei Yisrael Ugeonei Italyah . . . [and] Zekher Zadikim Liverakhah* (History of the great Jewish scholars of Italy [Trieste, 1853]), pp. 169–71; Castiglioni, *L'instituto scolastico,* p. 10.

26. 26 November 1781, AST, "C.R. Governo in Trieste (1776–1809)," b. 83; CAHJP, "Archives of the Jewish Community of Mantua," microfilm HM 5187, f. 190.

27. *Regole,* pp. 4, 22; Moses Mendelssohn, *Gesammelte Schriften, Jubiläumsausgabe,* ed. Alexander Altmann (Stuttgart: Frommann, 1971), vol. 19, pp. 281–82. In this letter of 7 May 1782 (23 Iyar 5542), Mendelssohn refers to his letter to Trieste of one month earlier. See also Altmann, *Moses Mendelssohn,* pp. 477–82; Wessely, *Ein Mishpat,* pp. 7b–8b.

28. Katz, *Out of the Ghetto,* esp. pp. 65–68, 124–28, 151; Eliav, *Hahinukh Hayehudi,* pp. 39–51. Explicitly Wessely granted the "Torah of man" priority only in time, but the implied message—even if not wholly intended by Wessely—concerned value, and that was how it was generally understood. See second half of this chapter, under subheading "Ambiguities of the Alliance."

29. Wessely, *DSVE,* pp. 16–17; see also text below under subheading "German Images of Italian Jews."

30. The sequence of letters outlined by Wessely in *Ein Mishpat,* pp. 7b–8b (and in a later account based partially on it: Marco Tedeschi, *Due discorsi in morte . . . Samuel David Luzzatto . . .* [Trieste, 1866], pp. 16–23), is not clear. While it is possible that Wessely had received a direct letter from Trieste, it is more likely that he knew of Triestine reactions to *DSVE* through Gallico's correspondence with Mendelssohn. See Mendelssohn's letter of 7 May 1782 (23 Iyar 5542), published in part by Isaac Samuel Reggio, *Kerem*

Hemed 1 (1833): 5–7, esp. p. 7, and completed by Rivkind, "Elia Morpurgo," p. 153, n. 2. 28 June 1782 (16 Tamuz 5542) letter in Rivkind, pp. 150–55.

31. Rivkind, "Elia Morpurgo," pp. 153, n. 2; 154.

32. Wessely's letter of 28 June was in response to Gallico's letter of late May, which is not extant (cf. Tedeschi, *Due discorsi*, p. 19). The translation with notes—which Morpurgo claimed to have completed in three days (*Igeret*, p. 14a)—appeared as *Traduzione di Elia Morpurgo de' Discorsi ebraici di tolleranza e felicità diretti da Naftali Herz Weisel agli ebrei dimoranti ne' domini dell'Augustissimo Imperadore Giuseppe II, il Giusto* (Gorizia, 1783).

33. Rivkind, "Elia Morpurgo," p. 153, n. 2; see also text below under subheading "German Images of Italian Jews."

34. See also *Rav Tuv*, pp. 25–26; *Ein Mishpat*, p. 4b; Morpurgo, *Igeret*, p. 21b; Rivkind, "Elia Morpurgo," pp. 144, 149–50, 157–58.

35. Extant letters, in addition to those cited above in n. 27 and n. 30: Morpurgo to Mendelssohn, 8 May 1782 (24 Iyar 5542), in Rivkind, "Elia Morpurgo," pp. 147–49 (also in Mendelssohn, *Gesammelte Schriften*, vol. 14, pp. 285–86); Morpurgo to Wessely, 11 August 1782 (1 Elul 5542), in Rivkind, "Elia Morpurgo," pp. 155–56; R. Formiggini to Wessely, n.d., apparently summer 1783, *Ein Mishpat*, pp. 42a–43a; Wessely to Morpurgo, 17 January 1786 (18 Shevat 5546), in M. Letteris, *Mikhtevei Ivrit* (Hebrew letters [Vienna, 1862]), pp. 120–22. Wessely complained of a hiatus in the Northern Italian correspondence; the reason is unknown. Two other channels of communication are: Morpurgo's correspondence with the *Me'asfim* (see nn. 38, 72); and the correspondence between Mendelssohn and Herz Homberg. Homberg was a teacher in Gorizia and Trieste (1782–1787). For Mendelssohn's letters between 4 October 1782 and 6 September 1785, see his *Gesammelte Schriften*, vol. 13, pp. 82–300. We have little evidence about the role of Homberg in the Italian campaign from his arrival in Gorizia in the autumn of 1782. Though he married and made some friends in the area, the authorities were aware that here, as elsewhere, he made enemies too. See Vielmetti, "Elia Morpurgo," pp. 44–45; Fahn, *Kitvei*, p. 155; Luzzatto, *Autobiografia*, pp. 21, 47–49; Wolf, *Geschichte*, p. 124.

36. Extant are: Morpurgo to Rabbi Israel Benjamin Bassan of Reggio, 30 May 1782 (17 Sivan 5542), in Rivkind, "Elia Morpurgo," pp. 149–50; Morpurgo to Rabbi Abraham Isaac Castello of Leghorn, 14 August 1782 (4 Elul 5542), ibid., pp. 157–58; and Morpurgo to Rabbi Jacob Danon of Constantinople, 22 January 1784 (28 Tevet 5544), ibid., pp. 158–59. See Tedeschi, *Due discorsi*, pp. 19–21, for a possible paraphrase of the letters sent by Triestine leaders.

37. Excerpts of *Ein Mishpat*, are in Assaf, *Mekorot*, vol. 2, pp. 213–18. On the possibility of other Italian answers, see Rivkind, "Elia Morpurgo," pp. 143, 145, 153n.3; one extant is that of Rabbi Ishmael Kohen (Laudadio Sacerdote), *Sheelot Uteshuvot Zera Emet* (Leghorn, 1796), vol. 2: *Yoreh deah*, no. 107 (also in Assaf, *Mekorot*, vol. 2, pp. 219–21). As for the conspicuous absence of Leghorn and Mantua we can only speculate about lost, late, or lukewarm answers, or failure to respond. I do not think that Rabbi Castello's poem against wealthy libertines and sceptics, which some have linked to the *maskilim* and educational reforms, solves the riddle; see Abraham Barukh Piperno, *Kol Ugav* (Voice of the pipe, [Leghorn, 1846]), pp. 28a–29b, 78b–80b,

81b–82b; Ghirondi and Neppi, (*Toledot,* pp. 16–22; Assaf, *Mekorot,* vol. 2, p. 277.

38. See nn. 8, 12, 32, above. Morpurgo began *Discorso* in 1781 and completed it by 8 May 1782, translated *DSVE* in May 1782, and completed *Igeret* by 2 July 1782 (20 Tamuz 5542). To *Hame'asef:* "Divrei Hokhmah Umusar" (Words of wisdom and ethics, written in 1783), *Hame'asef* 3 (1785–86): 131–37, 147–56, 164–76; and "Mikhtav MeElyahu" (Letter from Elia, written February 1784), *Hame'asef* 3 (1785–86): 66–78. The fullest edition of "Mikhtav" is in Assaf, *Mekorot,* vol. 2, pp. 222–33.

39. Tedeschi, *Due discorsi,* p. 20. Unfortunately it is not clear whether this is a paraphrase of eighteenth-century documents or imaginative reconstruction.

40. For expressed dissatisfaction with the first see Rabbi Bassan, *Ein Mishpat,* 40a–b. On Rabbi Formiggini see n. 25, above. R. Norzi (Norsa) was the father of one of the Triestine school directors; Ghirondi and Neppi, *Toledot,* p. 277 refer to him as Rabbi Borgo (Borghi). On Rabbi Calimani see Ghirondi and Neppi, pp. 345–47; Benedetto Frizzi, *Elogio dei rabbini Simone Calimani e Giacobbe Saravale* (Trieste, 1791, published as pp. 37–70 with *Elogio del rabbino Abram Abenezra*); Hayim Schirmann, *LeToledot Hashirah Vehadramah Haivrit* (Studies in the history of Hebrew poetry and drama [Jerusalem: Bialik Institute, 1979]), vol. 2, pp. 194–216. On Rabbi Cracovia see Ghirondi and Neppi, p. 42. On Rabbi Pacifico see Ghirondi and Neppi, p. 33. On Rabbi Hayim Abraham (b. Moses) Israel see Ghirondi and Neppi, p. 115; Abraham Yaari, *Sheluhei Erez Yisrael* (Emissaries of the Land of Israel [Jerusalem: Mosad Harav Kook, 1977]), pp. 129, 398–400. Born in Jerusalem, he lived in many places in the Eastern Mediterranean before settling in Italy in 1766, at the age of fifty-eight. On Rabbi Israel Benjamin (b. Isaiah) Bassan see Ghirondi and Neppi, p. 153; Benedetto Frizzi, *Elogio del rabbino Israele Beniamino Bassano* (Ferrara or Trieste[?], 1791); Piperno, *Kol Ugav,* esp. pp. 84b–85a; Giuliano Tamani, "Cinque lettere inedite di Binjamin Bassani a G.B. De Rossi," *RMI* 33 (1967): 429–41.

41. Kohen, *Sheelot,* vol. 2. On R. Kohen, see Giuseppe Cammeo, *Per il centenario della morte ʳdi Rabbi Ismanhèl Coen Zedek . . .* (Udine: Domenico del Bianco, 1911); Baruch Mevorah, *Napoleon Utekufato* (Napoleon and his era [Jerusalem: Bialik Institute, 1968]), pp. 103–20.

42. I use the terms *non-Torah wisdom, non-Torah studies,* and *general studies* in order to avoid the term *secular studies,* which I think prejudices the issue.

43. On ordered curriculum see Venetians, *Ein Mishpat,* p. 23a–b; on division of labor see Rabbi Formiggini and Venetians, *Ein Mishpat,* pp. 11a–b, 33a–b.

44. *Ein Mishpat,* p. 12a.

45. *Enziklopedyah,* vol. 4, pp. 407–8, 410; also Della Torre, *Scritti sparsi,* vol. 2, p. 336, and Simonsohn, *History of the Jews in the Duchy of Mantua,* p. 598. Some Italian communities such as Leghorn, Ancona, and Modena did teach Halakhah earlier and more intensively, a fact reflected in Rabbi Israel's and Rabbi Kohen's *Pesakim* on *DSVE.* On the question of the effects of the proscription of the Talmud see Robert Bonfil, *Harabanut BeItalyah Bitekufat Harenesans* (The rabbinate in renaissance Italy [Jerusalem: Magnes Press, 1979]), pp. 22–23, 171, 182.

46. Morpurgo, *Igeret,* pp. 17b–18a, including citation of the classic passage in *Pesahim,* p. 94b, and *Discorso,* esp. pp. 36, 75–82; cf. Maimonides, *Guide of the Perplexed,* I:71, and Judah Halevi, *Kuzari,* I:63, II:66.

47. *Ein Mishpat,* p. 14a–b. On Benjamin Kohen Vitale (called R. Benjamin Bassan of Reggio in *Ein Mishpat*), see Ghirondi and Neppi, *Toledot,* p. 55.

48. *Ein Mishpat,* pp. 28a–29a; Morpurgo, *Igeret,* pp. 19b–20a (Rivkind, "Elia Morpurgo," p. 140); Morpurgo, "Mikhtav," in Assaf, *Mekorot,* vol. 2, p. 226. See also Schirmann, *Letoledot Hashirah,* vol. 2, pp. 44–94, 194–96, esp. n. 2; and Dan Pagis, *Hidush Umasoret Beshirat Hahol Haivrit. Sefarad VeItalyah* (Change and tradition in the secular poetry of Spain and Italy [Jerusalem: Ketev, 1976]).

49. *Ein Mishpat,* p. 40b; I. S. Reggio, "Petihat," *Bikurei Haitim, 5591* 11 (1830): 3–5; *Israelitische Annalen* 1 (1839): 79–80, 157; Eric W. Cochrane, *Tradition and Enlightenment in the Tuscan Academies, 1690–1800* (Chicago: University of Chicago Press, 1961), pp. 239, 248; Valsecchi, *L'Assolutismo,* vol. 2, pt. 1: *La Politica interna,* pp. 119–21.

50. *Ein Mishpat,* p. 17a. Cf. the Provenzalis' 1564 plan to found a Jewish university, Assaf, *Mekorot,* vol. 2, pp. 115–20, and Simonsohn, *History of the Jews,* p. 583; and Riccardo Di Segni, "Due contratti di Rabbini Medici di Ancona del 1692 e 1752," *Annuario di Studi Ebraici, 1969–70, 1971–72* (Rome, 1971), pp. 97–104, where teaching Latin is the rabbi's duty.

51. Morpurgo, *Discorso,* pp. 54–55; idem, "Divrei," pp. 174–76.

52. Morpurgo, "Mikhtav," in Assaf, *Mekorot,* vol. 2, p. 225; idem, *Igeret,* p. 18a; idem, *Discorso,* p. 54.

53. On Rabbi Ishmael Kohen see Schirmann, *Letoledot Hashirah,* vol. 2, pp. 73–74; on Wessely, *Nahal Habesor* (Stream of tidings), pp. 7–8, bound with *Hame'asef* 1 (1783–84). I thank Dr. Israel Bartal for bringing Wessely's strictures to my attention.

54. Morpurgo, *Igeret,* pp. 14b–15a; see also idem, "Divrei," pp. 167–69.

55. Leone Modena, *Historia de riti hebraici* (Venice, 1638), vol. 2, pt. 1, in *RMI* 7 (1932–33): 383–84. See also Della Torre, *Scritti sparsi,* vol. 2, pp. 238–45, 334–39; and R. Bonfil, "Ahat Miderashotav Haitalkiot shel R. Mordekhai Dato" (Una predica in volgare di R. Mordekhai Dato), *Italia* 1 (1976): 1–32 (Hebrew section).

56. Modena, ibid., pp. 312–13. For pictures see: Modena and Morpurgo in Roth, *The History of the Jews of Italy,* 401–2; Kohen in Cammeo, *Per il centenario;* also Shabbetai Marini and Abraham Cohen in Meir Benayahu, "Rabbi Avraham HaCohen MeZante Velahakat Harofim Hameshorerim BePadova" (Rabbi Abraham Cohen of Zante and the Padua group of doctors-poets), *Hasifrut* 7 (1978, = no. 26): 108–40; Moses Gentili (Hefez), in *Encyclopedia Judaica,* vol. 7, p. 414; Abraham Reggio of Gorizia in Giuseppe Bolaffio, "Abram Vita Reggio," *RMI* 23 (1957): 204–17; Rafael Nathan Tedesco in I. Zoller, "Il Principe archivescovo Sigismundo Hohenwart ed il suo atteggiamento verso l'ebraismo," *La Porta Orientale* 3 (1933): 16–33. (Tedesco was a teacher and then Rabbi in Trieste in the 1780s and 1790s, see Ghirondi and Neppi, *Toledot,* 274–76.)

57. Cecil Roth, *The Jews in the Renaissance* (Philadelphia: Jewish Publication Society of America, 1959); Moses A. Shulvass, *The Jews in the World of the Renaissance* (Leiden: Brill, 1973). For recent reappraisals see Robert Bonfil, "The Historian's Perception of the Jews of the Italian Renaissance:

Towards a Reappraisal," *Revue des Études juives* 143 (1984): 59–82; David B. Ruderman, *The World of a Renaissance Jew: The Life and Thought of Abraham ben Mordecai Farissol* (Cincinnati: Hebrew Union College Press, 1981), pp. 144–48; Yosef Hayim Yerushalmi, *Zakhor: Jewish History and Jewish Memory* (Philadelphia and Seattle: Jewish Pub. Society of America & Univ. of Washington Press, 1982), pp. 53–75, esp. p. 60; Arthur M. Lesley, "Hebrew Humanism in Italy," *Prooftexts* 2 (1982): 163–77. On literature see Pagis, *Hidush;* on cultural norms see R. Formiggini and the Venetians, *Ein Mishpat,* pp. 11a–b, 34b.

58. Benayahu, "Rabbi Avraham"; Edgardo Morpurgo and Abdelkader Modena, *Medici e chirurghi ebrei dottorati e licenziati nell'Università di Padova dal 1617 al 1816,* ed. Aldo Luzzatto et al. (Bologna: Forni 1967), pp. 41, 55–57, 62–63; Ghirondi and Neppi, *Toledot,* pp. 62–63, 131–37. For proud invocations of this tradition see Morpurgo, *Discorso,* pp. 85–90; and I.S. Reggio, "Devarim Ahadim: Bet Limud Harabanim beir Padova" (A few words about the rabbinical college in Padua), *Bikurei Haitim, 5591* 11 (1830): 5–10.

59. Morpurgo, *Discorso;* Frizzi, *Difesa,* esp. pp. 80–82; on Frizzi's elegies of Rabbis Calimani, Bassan, and Saraval see note 40, above; on Saraval and Cases see Dinaburg, "B.Z. Raphael HaKohen Frizzi," pp. 244, 248–50, and Simonsohn, *History of the Jews,* pp. 700–701, 733–34; later, see Lelio Della Torre, *Cinque discorsi* (Padua, 1834), pp. 34–35, and I.S. Reggio's explicit statement in his anonymously published, *Riflessioni d'un Israelita del Regno Illirico Sopra un Articolo del Decreto di S.M.I.R.A. in date 4 Febbrajo 1820 . . . futuri rabbini* (Venice, 1822), pp. 4–5; "Ma senza ricorrere a' tempi remoti ne abbiamo più recenti esempi nella nostra Italia."

60. Toaff, (forthcoming, see n. 2, above); in the meantime, Gino Luzzatto, "Sulla condizione economica degli ebrei veneziani nel secolo XVIII," *RMI* 16, no. 7–8 (1950, = *Scritti in onore di Riccardo Bachi*), pp. 161–72; R. B. Bachi, "Sekirah al Hakalkalah Hayehudit BeItalyah Erev Tekufat Napoleon" (A sketch of Jewish economic activity in Italy on the eve of the Napoleonic era), *Zion* 12 (1946–47): 66–73; Werther Angelini, *Gli ebrei di Ferrara nel Settecento. I Coen e altri mercanti nel rapporto con le pubbliche autorità* (Urbino: Argalia, 1973).

61. Wessely, *DSVE,* ch. 1. His second and fourth pamphlets were filled with retractions, e.g., *Rav Tuv,* pp. 31–32, 37–38.

62. 2 Samuel 7:19. Its meaning has perplexed commentators. Wessely's usage seems unlike previous ones.

63. *Zera Emet,* vol. 2, no. 107, using the phrase from *Baba Batra,* p. 16a. *Ein Mishpat:* R. Formiggini, pp. 10a–11a, 12a–b; R. Norzi, p. 17a–b; Venetians, 33a; R. Israel, pp. 36b–37a.

64. *Ein Mishpat:* R. Formiggini, pp. 10a–b, 12b; R. Norzi, p. 14a–b, R. Israel, p. 36a; Gallico, in Hezekiah David Bolaffio, *Ben Zekunim* (Filius senectutis, [Leghorn, 1793]), p. 78a.

65. *Ein Mishpat:* Venetians, pp. 21a–b, 25a, 34a–b; Triestine school directors, p. 45a–b (cf. Colbi, "Elia Morpurgo," pp. 187–88). Morpurgo: *Igeret,* p. 14b, 22b; Letter to Mendelssohn, in Rivkind, "Elia Morpurgo," p. 158; Morpurgo, "Divrei," p. 168; idem, "Mikhtav," in Assaf, *Toledot,* vol. 2, pp. 223, 229; idem, *Traduzione,* pp. 6–12, 15–16. See also Morpurgo, "Divrei," *Hame'asef* 3 (1785–86): 75, and Assaf, *Toledot,* pp. 229–30, for Morpurgo's citation of the Italian use of the term *Studia humanitatis* for studies such as German,

arithmetic, grammar, history, and geography; appropriately he then revised it to *Scuole Normale* (Normal classes); however, even *Studia humanitatis* did not necessarily have dichotomous connotations (Paul Oskar Kristeller, *Renaissance Thought,* [New York: Harper & Row, 1961], pp. 9–11, 74–75, 110–11).

66. *Regole,* pp. 17–21, and *Regolamento per le scuole pie normali degli ebrei in Trieste* (Trieste, 1797), ch. 27; on Prague see Hillel Kieval's chapter in this volume.

67. *Esame* (Gorizia, 1782; Trieste, 1784; Verona, 1821), was dedicated to the directors of the Triestine school, 4 June 1782; Vielmetti, "Die Gründerge-schichte," pp. 11–12. The other recent work used was Moses Hayim Luzzatto's *Mesilat Yesharim* (Path of the upright).

68. *Regole,* p. 20, and Raffaele Nathan Tedesco, *Indagine di qual sia tra i morali mali il peggiore. Accademico gareggiamento scolastico* (Trieste, 1786), p. 3; L'Osservatore Triestino, 18 March 1786, pp. 144–45 (excerpts in Castiglioni, *L'instituto scolastico,* pp. 12–13, and in Oscar De Incontrera, "Vita triestina del Settecento nelle cronache de 'L'Osservatore Triestino,'" *La Porta Orientale* 24 (1954): 82–83; on *accademia* in Italian Jewish schools generally see Schirmann, *LeToledot Hashirah,* vol. 2, pp. 74–80.

69. Rabbi Ishmael Kohen, *Zera Emet,* vol. 2, no. 107; *Ein Mishpat:* R. Formiggini and R. Israel; Morpurgo, "Mikhtav," in Assaf, *Mekorot,* vol. 2, pp. 228–29. Even Morpurgo did not recommend studies such as mathematics or history before the age of ten.

70. *Igeret,* pp. 15a–b, 16a, 17b, 19b. For earlier Italian views of Ashkenazic cultural deficiencies see Israel Zinberg, *A History of Jewish Literature,* vol. 4: *Italian Jewry in the Renaissance Era,* tr. and ed. Bernard Martin (Cincinnati and New York: Hebrew Union College Press & Press of Case Western Reserve University, 1974), pp. 44, 157.

71. Morpurgo: *Discorso,* pp. 57, 71, 95, and appendix *Opere di celebri ebrei moderni; Traduzione,* p. 13, n. a; *Igeret,* pp. 22b, 23b; "Mikhtav," in Assaf, *Mekorot,* vol. 2, pp. 223–34; also Rabbi Bassan, *Ein Mishpat,* p. 41b, and Frizzi, *Difesia,* p. 81.

72. Morpurgo, Letter to Mendelssohn, in Rivkind, "Elia Morpurgo," pp. 147–49; idem, *Igeret,* pp. 18a, 19a–20a, 27a–b. See also Rivkind, p. 141, and p. 148, n. 1, on Morpurgo's announcement in *Hame'asef* 1 (1783–84): 31–32, 45–46, of his plans to publish an anthology; *Hame'asef* 1 (1783–84): 15, on Lampronti's *Pahad Yizhak* (Fear of Isaac). For a plan which did materialize see Elia Sarker Ex-Morpurgo, *Esame del Mondo* (Trieste, 1796), a translation of Yedaiah Bedersi's *Behinat Olam.*

73. *Igeret,* pp. 23a, 32b.

74. Ibid., pp. 17b, 22b–23a.

75. Enlightenment concerns are reflected throughout Morpurgo's and Frizzi's works (see n. 8, belov). For some of Morpurgo's specific criticisms see his *Igeret,* pp. 16a, 17a, 30b–31a.

76. See n. 4 above; also *Hame'asef* 1 (1783–84): 158–60, for announcement of *Ein Mishpat;* Aaron Wolfsohn-Halle, in *Hame'asef* 7 (1794–97): p. 291; David Friedrichsfeld in *Hame'asef* 8 (1808–9): p. 266.

77. Wessely, *Rehovot,* p. 218; Mendelssohn, *Gesammelte Schriften,* vol. 13, p. 95.

78. See n. 35, above.

79. Mendelssohn, *Gesammelte Schriften,* vol. 13, pp. 180, 186; see also pp. 94–95, 113, 179.
80. Schirmann, *LeToledot Hashirah,* vol. 2, pp. 239–301; and Samuel Romanelli, *Ketavim Nivharim,* ed. Hayim Schirmann (Selected works [Jerusalem: Bialik Institute, 1968]).
81. Moses Samet, "R. Shaul Berlin Ukhetavav" (R. Saul Berlin and his works), *Kiryat Sefer* 43 (1968): 429–41.
82. See references to *Hame'asef* in n. 72, above; Wessely to Morpurgo, in "Letteris"; on Morpurgo's association with a Gorizian printer see Marino De Grassi, "La stampa ebraica e di autori ebrei a Gorizia nell'Ottocento nei fondi della Biblioteca dei Musei Provinciali," in Ioly Zorattini, ed., *Gli ebrei,* pp. 133–34.
83. *Hame'asef* 3 (1785–86): 64; Mendelssohn, *Gesammelte Schriften,* vol. 14, p. 382; Wessely to Morpurgo, in "Letteris." On Dr. Salom's literary and political activities see Morpurgo and Modena, *Medici,* pp. 101–2. However, over the next two decades Italian translations of German-Jewish works began to appear, see Mendelssohn's *Gerusalemme* (Trieste, 1790), and *Fedone* (Venice, 1806), and Dohm's *Riforma politica degli Ebrei* (Mantua, 1807).
84. Ephraim Luzzatto's poetry, in *Hame'asef* 2 (1784–85): 49–51, 177–78; *Hame'asef* 3 (1785–86): 112–113. On Ephraim Luzzatto and his brother Isaac (also praised in *Hame'asef* 1 [1783–84]: 160), see Schirmann, *Letoledot Hashirah,* vol. 2, pp. 217–35.
85. On the campaign and schools, *Hame'asef* 1 (1783–84): 158–60, 161–65, 177–81; *Hame'asef* 5 (1788–89): 255–56. On conscription, *Hame'asef* 4 (1787–88): 386–88; Simonsohn, *History of the Jews,* p. 475; CAHJP, "Archives of the Jewish Community of Mantua," microfilm HM 5193, f. 216. For citation of Trieste's response by a group of Bohemian Jews, see G. Wolf, "Die Militärpflicht der Juden," *Ben Chananja* 5 (1862): 61–63.
86. *Rav Tuv,* pp. 25–26, 55; see also n. 29.
87. *Hame'asef* 6 (1789–90): 173–74; the letters from Leghorn are on pp. 171–76, 245–49; the others are on pp. 38–50, 80–85. On Livornese Jews—4,327 in 1784—see Carlo Mangio, "La communauté juive de Livourne face à la Révolution Française," in Bernhard Blumenkranz and Albert Soboul, eds., *Les Juifs et la Révolution Française* (Toulouse: Eduard Privat, 1976), pp. 191–210; Lucia Frattarelli Fischer, "Proprietà e insediamento ebraici a Livorno dalla fine del Cinquecento alla seconda metà del Settecento," *Quaderni storici* 18 (1983, = no. 54): 879–96; and Alfredo Toaff, "Vita artistico-letterario degli Ebrei a Livorno nel '700," *RMI* 8 (1933): 370–78.
88. *Hame'asef* 1 (1783–84): 124–27, 140–44 on Delmedigo; ibid., pp. 38–42, 57–61, on Abarbanel.
89. See nn. 84, 87 above; Moritz Steinschneider, "Hebräische Drucke in Deutschland (Berlin, 1762–1800)," *Zeitschrift für die Geschichte der Juden in Deutschland* 5 (1891): 154–86; *Hame'asef:* 2 (1784–85): 28–31, 5 (1788–89): 282–88, 8 (1808–9): 233, 9 (1809–10): 75–80; Ruderman, *The World of,* pp. 165–66; *Bikurei Haitim, 5592* 12 (1831): 182–83; I. Tishbi, "Darkhei Hafazatam shel Kitvei Kabbalah LeRamhal Bepolin UveLitah" (The spreading of Ramhal's kabbalistic writings in Poland and Lithuania), *Kiryat Sefer* 45 (1969–70): 127–54, esp. pp. 151–52.
90. *Mishlei Asaf* (Berlin, 1789), vol. 1.
91. *Sefer Sheelot Uteshuvot Besamim Rosh* (Berlin, 1793), introduction.

92. Katz, *Out of the Ghetto,* pp. 136–37; *Hame'asef* 7 (1794–97): 271–73; *Mikhtevei Harabanim Hamuvhakim . . . Bearei Italyah* (Leghorn, 1796; also with German, *Getreue Uebersetzung . . . Briefe der Herren Ober-Rabbinen und Aeltesten* [Hamburg, 1796]).

93. Maurice Vaussard, *Correspondance Scipione de' Ricci—Henri Grégoire* (Florence and Paris: Didier, 1963), pp. 15, 20.

94. Isaac Rivkind, "Teshuvat Harav Yehudah Aryeh Modena al Gilui Harosh" (Responsum of R. Judah Aryeh Modena on bareheadedness), in *Louis Ginzberg Jubilee Volume* (New York: American Academy for Jewish Research, 1945), pp. 401–23, Hebrew section; Gerson Cohen, "Letoledot Hapulmus al Setam-Yenam BeItalyah Umekorotav" (On the history of the controversy over Gentiles' wine), *Sinai* 77 (1975): 62–90, 74–75 on beards. (I thank Talya Fishman for bringing this article to my attention.)

95. Dinaburg, "B.Z. Raphael HaKohen Frizzi," p. 251.

96. Cf. the observations on Italian receptivity to Enlightenment in Giorgio Candeloro, *Storia dell'Italia moderna* (Milan: Feltrinelli, 1956), vol. 1, pp. 74–75; and Cochrane, *Tradition and Enlightenment,* pp. 232–40, 247–48.

97. See n. 50 above; Robert Bonfil, "Some Reflections on the Place of Azariah de Rossi's *Meor Enayim* in the Cultural Milieu of Italian Renaissance Jewry," in Bernard Dov Cooperman, ed., *Jewish Thought in the Sixteenth Century* (Cambridge: Harvard University Press, 1983), pp. 23–48, esp. pp. 38–43, nn. 81, 87.

98. However there were limits to harmonization. In the late 1780s Frizzi's criticisms in print of Jewish society made him *persona non grata* in Mantua; hence, his move to Trieste. See Dinaburg, "B.Z. Raphael HaKohen Frizzi," p. 249; and Simonsohn, *The History of the Jews,* p. 711.

99. Isaiah Sonne, *Hayahadut Haitalkit: Demutah Umekomah Betoledot Am Yisrael* (Italian Jewry: Its character and place in Jewish history. [Jerusalem: Ben Zwi Institute, 1961]), p. 25; Schirmann, *LeToledot Hashirah,* vol. 2, p. 232; Cassuto, *Storia,* pp. 135–42, 173; Dante Lattes, "La letteratura ebraica nel periodo illuministico (Da M. H. Luzzatto ad Abraham Mapu)," *RMI* 7 (1932): 143–66; F. Lachower, *Toledot Hasifrut Haivrit Hahadashah* (The history of modern Hebrew literature [Tel Aviv: Dvir, 1963]), vol. 1, pp. 1–49.

100. Vielmetti, *Die Gründergeschichte;* Barzilay, "The Italian," p. 52; Salo W. Baron, *A Social and Religious History of the Jews* (New York: Columbia University Press, 1937), vol. 2, p. 207.

101. *Hame'asef* 8 (1808–9): 286; *Sulamith,* I (1806–7), pt. 1, pp. 327–28, pt. 2, pp. 372, 380–81, II (1808–9), pp. 145–51. The role of Italian Jews in the politics of the early reform deserves further treatment; I plan to publish such a study in the future.

102. Ruth Kestenberg-Gladstein, *Neuere Geschichte der Juden in den böhmischen Ländern* (Tübingen: Mohr, 1969), vol. 1, pp. 135–39.

103. Andrea Balletti, ed., *Gli Ebrei e gli Estense. Col l'aggiunta di Il Tempio Maggiore Israelitica e Lettere del Rabbino Maggiore Jacob Israele Carmi* (Reggio Emilia, 1930; facsimile ed. Bologna: Forni, 1969), *Lettere,* esp. pp. 22, 27–28, 76, for one of the Italian delegate's views; for the record, see Diogene Tama, *Transactions of the Parisian Sanhedrim [sic], or Acts of the Assembly of Israelitish Deputies of France and Italy,* tr. and ed. F. D. Kirwan (London, 1807), p. 266. See also Simon Schwarzfuchs, *Napoleon, the Jews*

and the Sanhedrin (London: Routledge & Kegan Paul, 1979); and Sergio I. Sierra, "Aspetti del' opinione pubblica ebraica in Italia sul Sinedrio napoleonico," in E. M. Artom et al., eds., *Miscellanea di studi in memoria di Dario Disegni* (Turin, 1969), pp. 239–53.

104. S. D. Luzzatto's views may be the most vociferous and well known, but others also wished to moderate German influences, e.g. Luzzatto, *Epistolario italiano, francese, latino* (Padua, 1890), vol. 1, pp. 357–77, 520–21; I.S. Reggio, *HaTorah Vehafilosofya* (Torah and philosophy [Vienna, 1827]), pp. 144–45; Lelio Cantoni, in I. Luzzatto, *Catologo*, pp. 398–400, 403–4; Paolo Colbi, "Gli Ebrei italiani alla vigilia del Risorgimento (leggendo la 'Rivista Israelitica' annate 1845–47)," *RMI* 29 (1963): pp. 438–45, esp. p. 441.

105. Bonfil, pp. 180–81. For different views see Baron, *A Social*, vol. 2, pp. 205–12; Barzilay, "The Italian."

106. Cassuto, *Storia*, pp. 173–75; Robert Bonfil, "Un filone shadaliano in E. S. Artom," *RMI* 32 (1966): 167–75; Ariel Toaff, "Ancora sul filone shadaliano in E. S. Artom," *RMI* 32 (1966): 322–25. See also José Faur, "Sephardim in the Nineteenth Century: New Directions and Old Values," *Proceedings of the American Academy for Jewish Research* 44 (1977): 29–52, much of which is about Elia Benamozegh of Leghorn.

107. Assaf, *Mekorot*, vol. 2, Introduction, pp. vi–vii.

9

The Englishness of Jewish Modernity in England

Todd M. Endelman

The entry of European Jews into the social, cultural, and political life of the states in which they lived was a complex historical movement. The journey from tradition to modernity—that is, the acquisition of civil equality, abandonment of ancient rituals and beliefs, adoption of non-Jewish values and patterns of behavior, and absorption into new spheres of activity—embraced Jews living in the most diverse social and political circumstances, rich and poor alike. Thus, the character and pace of modernization among European Jews in the period 1770–1870 varied from state to state and sometimes, within each state, from region to region and from one social stratum to the next. In general, these variations derived from larger differences in the transformation of the various European states in the eighteenth and nineteenth centuries. Jewish acculturation, integration, and emancipation advanced—or in some cases lagged—roughly in step with the fundamental changes occurring in the surrounding societies as they left behind the traditional ways of the old regime.

Despite the diversity of Jewish experiences during the break up of the old order, most Jewish historians until recently looked to the German-Jewish experience as the paradigm for the transformation of European Jewry and to Moses Mendelssohn, the *maskilim,* the pioneers of Reform, and the practitioners of Wissenschaft des Judentums as the key actors in this development. The theme of this volume—the impact of German-Jewish modernization on Jewries outside Germany—certainly reflects this Germanocentric orientation. Yet from the perspective of both English history and, indeed, the histories of any of the liberal states in the West, this emphasis appears problematic, for by any of the criteria historians normally invoke in discussing the transformation of Europe in this period, the German states were hardly in the vanguard of change. The Prussia of Moses Mendelssohn and David Friedlander was a social and economic backwater, lagging far behind France, Holland, and Britain in those developments characteristic of the modernization process. It lacked an entrepreneurially minded, politically conscious bourgeoisie, representative political institutions, the infrastructure for industrial take-off, and a liberal capitalist ethos.

The course of Jewish modernization in Central Europe reflected the "backward" nature of the states in that region. German Jews faced formidable obstacles to their incorporation into state and society, and the self-consciously modern programs they developed to transform Jewish life were rooted in a belief that their exclusion from the Gentile world was due to their outmoded habits and customs. The schemes of the *maskilim* reflect the absence of toleration and integration, the failure of widespread German-Jewish rapprochement. They do not betoken the path-breaking role of German Jewry in forging new links with Gentile society but its inability to achieve those links in a natural, informal way. What Karl Marx wrote in 1844 about the relationship between German social theory and the actual history of the German people applies equally well to the situation of German Jewry: "Just as the nations of the ancient world lived their prehistory in the imagination, in mythology, so we Germans have lived our post-history in thought, in *philosophy*. We are the *philosophical* contemporaries of the present day without being its historical contemporaries. . . . In politics, the Germans have *thought* what other nations have *done*. . . . The abstraction and presumption of its philosophy were in step with the partial and stunted character of their reality."[1] Or, to paraphrase Marx—and to put the matter crudely— German Jews were thinking what Jews elsewhere, and in England in particular, were already doing.

The ideological programs created by the Haskalah and later by Reform Judaism had little impact on the course of Anglo-Jewish history, primarily because they were inappropriate to the English context. In England, acculturation and integration were well advanced before the 1770s,[2] the decade usually designated as the turning point in the modernization of German Jewry. Spontaneously and naturally, without recourse to ideo-logical programs, wealthy Ashkenazim in England had begun abandoning the marks of Jewish identity by midcentury. Men shaved their beards and gave up wearing the long caftanlike coat typical of Central European Jewry. Women no longer covered their heads nor dressed demurely, preferring instead the fashionable low-cut gowns of the time that exposed ample amounts of flesh. Jews adopted a style of life not noticeably different from that of other wealthy Englishmen. They attended the theater and the opera, gossiped and played cards in the coffee houses of the City, had their portraits painted by the best artists of the period, lost money at the faro tables in St. James's Square, threw lavish parties and entertainments, took the waters at Bath, and acquired country homes. (When the Palestinian rabbi Haim Yosef Azulai visited London in the spring of 1755 to collect funds for the Hebron yeshivah, he found that all the wealthy Jews had left the metropolis for their country estates.) Jewish bankers and brokers also adopted a code of sexual behavior radically freer than that permitted by Jewish law, indulging themselves with open abandon in high-class brothels and with expensively maintained mistresses. They also displayed great laxity in the observance of *kashrut* and Sabbath and in attendance at synagogue. Among the Sephardim, these trends were even more marked since many of their families had been immersed in the social and cultural life of the non-Jewish world prior to their settlement in England.

A similar process of acculturation occurred among the Jewish poor, although perhaps not at quite such an early date. The street hawkers and old-clothes men of Anglo-Jewry took to many of the patterns of urban life of the social class to which they belonged, including irreligiosity, criminal activity, sexual promiscuity, street violence, and prize fighting. Their assimilation of a lower-class life-style, like the adoption of upper-class mores by prosperous Jews, proceeded apace uninfluenced by events in or doctrines from Germany. For Anglo-Jewish acculturation at all social levels was well under way before the appearance of the first publicistic writings of the Berlin Haskalah (e.g. Naphtali Herz Wessely's *Divrei Shalom Ve'emet,* 1782) and before the creation of the first institutions to normalize the Jewish situation (e.g. the Berlin *Freischule,* 1781).

The integration of English Jews into Gentile circles also commenced before 1770. At all levels of society, and from very early in the eighteenth century, small groups of anglicized Jews began to forge social relationships with their non-Jewish peers. Highly acculturated Sephardic brokers, ensconced in their Thames-side homes to the west of London, entered into the social life of the neighborhood's fashionable set. Well-to-do Sephardim were admitted to masonic lodges as early as the 1730s; some with scientific interests were elected Fellows of the Royal Society. Wealthy Ashkenazim appeared in upper-class Christian circles at a later date than their Sephardic predecessors, due to their later arrival in England and their previous isolation from broader social and cultural currents. Still, there were a few Ashkenazic families—the Franks and the Harts being the most notable examples—who moved quite easily into the social life of the English countryside around midcentury. At the lower end of the social scale, intimate and sustained socializing between Jews and Gentiles was far more pronounced than among elite circles. The Jewish poor and petit bourgeoisie of London lived on close physical terms with their non-Jewish neighbors, lodging in the same narrow streets and crowded courts, frequently in the same buildings. They sought entertainment and diversion in the streets, the public houses, the theaters, and the open spaces of the City and the East End, where they mixed with non-Jews in an atmosphere not governed by the rigid conventions of upper-class socializing.

Clearly, then, the transformation of English Jewry in its initial stages was an autochthonous development, the outcome of indigenous conditions rather than foreign trends. After all, German Jewry in the middle of the eighteenth century was still overwhelmingly traditional in its outlook and behavior, at least according to the standard accounts of this period, and could not have served as a model for Jews elsewhere. What then of later developments? Did Jews in late-Georgian or Victorian England seek to emulate the trailblazers of Berlin, Hamburg, and Frankfurt? Did the Haskalah, the Wissenschaft des Judentums, or Reform Judaism influence the development of Anglo-Jewish history from the 1770s on?

In the case of the Haskalah, the earliest of these attempts to reshape traditional life and thought, the evidence that German thinkers and publicists exerted a critical influence on Anglo-Jewry is slim. Cecil Roth's essay "The Haskalah in England,"[3] which treats the Haskalah largely as a literary phenomenon rather than as a movement for social change, reveals only three instances of direct contact between German *maskilim* and English Jews. The first of these came in 1781, when Moses Mendelssohn corresponded with Robert Lowth, Bishop of London, and used Joseph Hart Myers, physician to the Sephardic synagogue in London, as his intermediary. In the second instance, when Benjamin Goldsmid, later one of the outstanding financiers in London during the revolutionary and Napoleonic wars, traveled in Germany in the late 1770s, he had some contact with *maskilim* there. And third, when Michael Josephs was a young man, prior to his emigration to London, where he achieved prominence as a communal reformer and Hebraist, he spent five or six years in Berlin, during which time he came under Mendelssohn's influence. There is no reason to believe that these few direct contacts had any significant impact on the modernization of Anglo-Jewry. Indeed, most of the figures whom Roth discusses were not communal leaders but Hebrew scholars who had some familiarity with secular topics and wrote in a modernized Hebrew style, frequently on themes of general cultural interest. However, their concern with the revitalization of Hebrew and their familiarity with non-Jewish literature do not add up to a Haskalah movement. They did not create institutions to modernize Judaism or

Jewish life or compose tracts to rouse their fellow Jews out of their traditional ways. Most important, these individuals did not constitute a cohesive circle of intellectuals committed to the transformation of the fundamental structure of Judaism.

The break with traditional practices that was so characteristic of Anglo-Jewry in the late-Georgian period occurred largely without recourse to ideological justification. Most English Jews adopted the habits of Englishmen because they wanted to feel at home there. They quietly abandoned the ways of traditional Judaism whose practices set them apart from other men and interfered with their pursuit of pleasure and success. Very few felt it was necessary to change the public character of Jewish worship or the fundamental beliefs of Judaism in order to gain respect and acceptance outside their own community. Instead, they maintained a nominal allegiance to Orthodox ways and simply ignored those beliefs and practices that were an obstacle to worldly aims.

There were, it is true, a handful of anglicized Jews who became militant opponents and public critics of traditional Judaism in the late-Georgian period, but they did not constitute a cohesive group and had no apparent influence on the conduct of communal affairs. The most articulate critic among them was, oddly enough, Isaac D'Israeli, father of the future prime minister, who quit the Sephardic synagogue in 1817 and had his children baptized soon thereafter. In his novel *Vaurien* (1797), in an essay on Mendelssohn (1798), and in *The Genius of Judaism* (1833), he developed a critique of traditional Jewish life similar to that of the radical *maskilim* in Germany. D'Israeli explicitly rejected the authority of rabbinic law, which he characterized as obsolete and arbitrary, and called for a radical reform of traditional Jewish education, which he blamed for the Jews' intellectual inferiority, aesthetic degeneracy, and physical temerity. He urged Jews to reject every "anti-social principle" in their culture that set them apart from non-Jews, so that they might fuse socially and politically with their fellow citizens. But like other radical opponents of Orthodoxy in England, D'Israeli was too much the outsider to have any influence on the community and his attacks thus evoked no known response.[4]

In the late-Georgian period there was also a small group of moderate reformers who hoped to revive and modernize Jewish life. Unlike their German counterparts, they did not set out to make sweeping changes in Jewish tradition, nor did they develop any systematic intellectual framework for their dissent from Orthodoxy. As a group, they commented more frequently on the necessity of expanding the intellectual perspective of Anglo-Jewry than they did on the necessity of changing this belief or that custom. In particular, they rejected the idea that the study of rabbinic texts should be the foundation of Jewish learning while other subjects remained peripheral. The printer Levy Alexander and the engraver Solomon Bennett, for example, criticized Anglo-Jewry for its indifference to secular letters—Alexander described his fellow English Jews as "abject slaves of prejudice and obstinacy"—while praising German Jewry for their intellectual enlightenment.[5] Yet the only sphere of communal life in which these critics acted as agents for modernization was education of the poor, and even here it is difficult to say whether their ideas were decisive. The merchants and brokers who governed the community's schools also shared their objections to traditional Jewish education, although their concerns were more pragmatic.[6]

Even if we assume that these moderate nontraditionalists influenced the London notables in the establishment of modern Jewish schools, the extent of their indebtedness to currents emanating from Germany still remains to be measured. Some of their writing does suggest a familiarity with the Berlin Haskalah. They frequently celebrated Mendelssohn as the great symbol of Jewish Enlightenment and progress in the modern era, and in 1825 Moses Samuel published a biography of Mendelssohn, praising his work to revive the Jewish people in the most extravagant terms. However, while hailing the achievements of the German *maskilim,* these English reformers rarely said anything specific about their redefinition of Judaism and Jewish identity. This would seem to suggest that they were more concerned with the social consequences of Enlightenment (that is, with proving to the non-Jewish world that Jews were capable of becoming Europeans) than with the intellectual reconciliation of Judaism and European culture. If true, this would also explain why they treated the German *maskilim* as a homogeneous coterie and ignored or remained ignorant of the profound differences among the radicals, the moderates, and Mendelssohn himself. Indeed, these Anglo-Jewish moderates could never have accepted the ideas of such German radicals as David Friedländer and Lazarus Ben-David. That they treated them in this indiscriminate way may mean that they knew little of their work at first hand and were relying instead on secondary accounts and reports.

The absence of a coherent ideology of social and religious transformation in the origins of Jewish modernity in England is symptomatic of the unintellectual character of Anglo-Jewish history in general. By comparison with the German-Jewish middle class, well-to-do English Jews in the eighteenth and nineteenth centuries were ill educated and intellectually unsophisticated. They took little interest in the intellectual life of the country nor did they make any significant contribution to either English letters or Jewish scholarship. The Jewish salons of Berlin and Vienna had no counterparts in London. Similarly, it would be impossible to find an Anglo-Jewish equivalent for either Heinrich Heine or Karl Marx. Very few Jewish youth attended university before the end of the nineteenth century, although there were universities in Britain (Oxford and Cambridge aside) that admitted professing Jews.[7] This indifference to the world of ideas stemmed primarily from the character of Jewish integration into English society rather than, presumably, from any innate lack of intelligence. The path to acceptance by the English ruling class was relatively straightforward: the amassing of an enormous fortune, the purchase of a country home, generous contributions to Jewish and Gentile charities, lavish entertaining, and the acquisition of genteel manners and deportment. A university education played no role in certifying Jews as acceptable, nor did a mastery of European literature or thought, especially since the upper-class circles to which upwardly mobile Jews sought admission had little enthusiasm for clever intellectuals. Thus, in transforming themselves into English gentlemen and ladies, Jews did not have recourse to ideological thinking either to justify in their own eyes the changes they were making or to convince non-Jews of their willingness and ability to reconcile their Jewishness with the demands of active citizenship. Like the aristocratic and gentry circles which they sought to emulate, they shunned theoretical systems and philosophical abstractions, preferring instead an empirical, piecemeal approach to gaining acceptance in the larger society.

This is nowhere more evident than in Anglo-Jewish efforts to reform the character of Jewish worship. The commercial and financial magnates who controlled the institutional life of the community and who spearheaded efforts to make Judaism conform more closely to dominant English patterns were primarily motivated by social considerations. In altering traditional practices in the worship service, they strove to make their service more decorous rather than more rational, more genteel rather than more theologically correct. Nor surprisingly, rabbis and scholars, who were few and far between in England before the late nineteenth century, played a negligible role in shaping the course of reform. The situation in Germany was, of course, far different.

The earliest move to dignify Jewish worship in England came in the mid-eighteenth century, when the Great Synagogue ordered its *hazzan* to wear canonicals, that is, a long black robe with a pair of white ribbons hanging at the front of the neck. After this innovation no further efforts to make Anglo-Jewish worship more genteel occurred until the 1820s, when some of the London congregations introduced (or attempted to introduce) minor reforms such as limiting the number of *misheberachs,* hiring *hazzanim* who could chant the liturgy in a straightforward rather than florid style, prohibiting children from interrupting the reading of the Scroll of Esther on Purim with noisemakers, and slightly abridging the singing of some of the psalms on the Sabbath. Some of the reforms were designed to make attendance at synagogue more attractive to congregants who no longer understood Hebrew and who were impatient with the length of the traditional service. But most of them, particularly those initiated by the Ashkenazic congregations, were of a cosmetic character, undertaken within the context of traditional Judaism. They were concerned with the external appearance of Jewish worship, not with the internal content of Jewish prayer. None of these reforms was of a radical nature. There were no attempts, as in Germany, to tamper with references to the restoration of the Davidic kingdom or the coming of the Messiah, since English Jews, whose legal disabilities were few, did not face pressure to renounce their belief in a distinctive Jewish fate in the messianic age.[8]

After 1840, however, religious reform in England was a less quiet and modest affair. The creation of a Reform congregation in London that year (the West London Synagogue of British Jews) by a handful of wealthy Ashkenazim and Sephardim who seceded from their respective synagogues provoked considerable communal disharmony, at least initially. Historians have offered two interpretations of this secessionist movement, in neither case finding any significant influence from currents in Germany. The older view, which was most fully developed by Albert M. Hyamson, sees the breakaway largely as the outcome of an internal split within the Sephardic congregation.[9] According to this interpretation, progressive-minded Sephardim took the initiative in founding the Reform group when the privileged members of the congregation refused to sanction the establishment of a branch synagogue in the West End, nearer their homes than the existing synagogue in Bevis Marks, and with it a service conducted in a more decorous manner. The revisionist view, argued by Robert Liberles, shifts the focus from Sephardim to Ashkenazim as the chief actors in the secessionist venture and places the entire affair in a much broader context.[10] According to Liberles, the financier Isaac Lyon Goldsmid, a militant spokesman for full emancipation, was the major figure in the establishment of the Reform synagogue. Goldsmid, who was dissatisfied with the cautious attitude of the Board of Deputies in seeking emancipation, saw the proposed congregation as an alternative institutional platform from which to campaign for full access to political office. Thus, Liberles views the reforms initiated by the secessionists as efforts to promote emancipation, seeing in particular in the elimination of the second day of festivals a significant attempt to facilitate Jewish entry into government life.

The older interpretation is clearly inadequate, for it accords no importance to Goldsmid and his family, who were instrumental in the creation of the new synagogue, as Liberles has clearly shown. On the other hand, the argument that the rise of the Reform movement in England was primarily precipitated by political objectives seriously underestimates the role of social ambitions and hopes in the secession movement. Undoubtedly, as Liberles asserts, the goal of emancipation contributed to the Goldsmids' desire to create a new institution, but they and their Sephardic associates were also motivated by social objectives, i.e., winning respect and acceptance outside the Jewish community. Indeed, Goldsmid's interest in synagogue reforms predated the first campaign for emancipation by almost a decade. Throughout the 1820s, before Jewish emancipation had appeared on anyone's political agenda, Goldsmid actively worked to make the service at the Great Synagogue more genteel and decorous.[11] These early attempts at reform had no political overtones whatsoever; they sought to make the service conform more closely to Anglican notions of reverence and solemnity. Goldsmid and his coadjutors were aware of Christian opinion about the indecorous character of Jewish worship and were eager to make the public face of Judaism more respectable, since they themselves aspired to gentility and had absorbed many of the standards of the English upper class.[12]

Social motives such as these were still at work in the early 1840s—among both Sephardim and Ashkenazim—when the breakaway occurred. In fact, the social benefits of Reform may have been paramount in the minds of the former, since there is no evidence of intense Sephardic interest in pursuing parliamentary emancipation.[13] The character of the reforms instituted at the new synagogue further confirms this interpretation. The changes made there did not reflect any politically inspired goal to make Judaism less offensive or more attractive to the Tory politicians who were the principal impediment to the relief of Jewish disabilities. Rather, they reflected the bibliocentric, or neo-Karaite ideas of D.W. Marks—first minister to the congregation and compiler of its prayerbook—and the social needs of the founding members, who shared Marks's views to a large extent.[14] Nothing of a nationalist or particularist nature was eliminated. Prayer in Hebrew was retained as were specific prayers for the coming of the Messiah, the return to Zion, and the restoration of the Temple cult. Most of the reforms were of a moderate cosmetic nature: *shaharit* (the morning prayer) began at a later hour, *aliyyot* and *mesheberachs* were abolished, the *mussaf amidah* was shortened, and an English sermon was introduced. The one substantial break with tradition was the abolition of the second day of all festivals. This innovation may have been the outcome of Goldsmid's desire to permit

Jews to participate more easily in political life, or it may reflect Marks's antirabbinic outlook, which led him to devalue customs without biblical authority—or perhaps both. In any case, it was the only radical reform to be implemented.

Even if the example of the Hamburg temple inspired Isaac Lyon Goldsmid to establish a Reform congregation in London, as is sometimes claimed,[15] it was the idea of establishing an independent congregation and not the specific character of the reforms undertaken there that motivated him, for the ideology of German Reform cannot be traced in any of the changes introduced by him and his associates. Indeed, there is a virtual consensus among historians that the establishment of the West London Synagogue of British Jews did not involve any radical doctrinal reformulation of Judaism or any wholesale repudiation of traditional practice.[16]

The independence of the English Reform movement from developments in Germany can also be seen in the growth of a second Reform congregation, which was founded in Manchester in 1856. Two distinct currents led to the establishment of this synagogue. First, local pride and self-confidence created pressure for a greater degree of independence from the authority of the Board of Deputies and the Chief Rabbinate, both of which were under the control of the London plutocracy. Second, some of the wealthiest Jews in Manchester were of German birth and had abandoned traditional belief and practice before their arrival in England. Many of them became Unitarians, others remained unaffiliated, and still others desired a Judaism more dignified and decorous, shorn of customs they considered superstitious. This latter group spearheaded the creation of the Manchester Synagogue of British Jews; twenty-nine of the forty-six founder members were of German birth, and sixteen of these were from large cities in which religious modernism was at its strongest.[17] This evidence would seem to invalidate the claim that German influence on Anglo-Jewish modernization was slight. In fact, Bill Williams argues in his history of Manchester Jewry that Reform there primarily represented "the impact of currents of thought emanating from Germany." In his view, it was "a foreign import which subsequently gained adherents from local causes."[18]

Williams's conclusion is undoubtedly correct if he means that the *idea* of modernizing Judaism—rather than any specific ideology of Reform or set of doctrinal and liturgical innovations—was a German import, or that the success of Reform in Germany inspired German Jews in Manchester to undertake their own improvements. But he is decidedly wrong if he means that the Manchester reformers looked to Germany for guidance in matters of doctrine and liturgy. The model that the

Manchester group emulated was the West London Synagogue of British Jews; they adopted its prayer book and its form of public worship. The German-born Tobias Theodores, whom Williams treats as the ideologue of the Reform movement in Manchester, appears to have been ignorant of the historicist developmental framework of German Reform. Moreover, neither he nor any of the other founders showed any interest in denationalizing Judaism. What they wanted, above all, was freedom from central control and flexibility in shaping a service that had become, in their judgment, unseemly and undignified.[19] Thus, by comparison with its ostensible counterpart in Germany, Reform Judaism in England was a rather tepid affair.

The appeal of Reform in England was very limited. Only three Reform congregations were founded in the nineteenth century, in London, in Manchester, and in Bradford, established in 1873. Few English Jews, certainly no more than 10 percent, were attracted to Reform Judaism at any time before World War II;[20] Reform's failure to make headway was not due to any widespread commitment to traditional standards of personal observance. Most English Jews were not orthodox by the standards of continental Orthodoxy at the time or of British Orthodoxy today.[21] Despite this they did not flock to Reform Judaism, in part because they did not feel any compelling need to alter the public face of Judaism, namely its theology and worship service. Political pressure to make Judaism acceptable to the Christian majority was very weak. English Jews did not feel that Judaism was on trial or that they had to prove their loyalty to the nation by abandoning their ethnic particularism. In addition, well-to-do Jews were reluctant to tamper with established patterns of public observance because of the high status that the ruling class attached to religious tradition in general. The conservative nature of Orthodoxy, however nominal the attachment of the Anglo-Jewish bourgeoisie to it, paralleled the conservative nature of the Church of England, while the liberal character of Reform paralleled that of Nonconformity, which did not enjoy the social standing of Anglicanism. Most wealthy English Jews valued religious tradition simply because it was venerable and established. The United Synagogue and the Chief Rabbinate enjoyed their support because they could claim to be the Jewish equivalents of the Church of England and the Archbishop of Canterbury.[22] The barrister Arthur Cohen, president of the Board of Deputies from 1874 to 1894, although not an observant Jew himself, dismissed Reform Judaism with the comment, "I don't believe in reforms in ritual brought about by merchants and City men."[23] The London *Jewish Chronicle,* which was the mouthpiece of progressive upper-middle-class Jewry, consistently denounced the Reform movement in Germany. Marcus Bresslau, a frequent contributor to the paper, branded the reformers as "infidels, who have thrown off the burden of all religion, who discard the oral law and adopt only a few of the written laws which suit their convenience."[24]

Despite the absence of much enthusiasm for Reform Judaism, there was widespread interest among London congregations in the introduction of cosmetic reforms in the mode of worship. From the 1840s on, as a result of pressure from the wealthy Jews who dominated communal affairs, Chief Rabbi Nathan Adler sanctioned a number of changes designed to enhance the tone of the worship service. For example, he banned very young children from attending services; he forbade congregants to chatter, gossip, or leave their places during services; he ended the public sale of *mitzvot* and limited the announcement of monetary offerings during services; and he encouraged the introduction of all-male choirs. The most radical innovation sanctioned by Adler was the institution of a divided Sabbath and festival morning service to accommodate West End Jews who did not want to attend services that customarily began at 8:00 or 8:30 in the morning. Adler ruled that the early service—*shaharit*—might be held from 8:30 until 9:30 and then a second service—*kriyyat ha'Torah* and *mussaf*—might follow from 11:00 until 1:00.[25]

If there was any ideological underpinning to the religious thinking of the communal notables who demanded reforms such as these, it was an amorphous belief in the primacy of biblically ordained obligations over rabbinically instituted ones.[26] This bibliocentric orientation, which was undoubtedly influenced by the pervasive bibliocentricity of English culture, was less a crystallized doctrine than a vague, shapeless tendency. With few exceptions, most Anglo-Jewish notables felt that the Bible was the primary source of divine wisdom and law and that all its ceremonial requirements were binding, while the interpretive body of rabbinic traditions was not fully incumbent on modern Jews. In general they did not openly reject the Oral Law but rather downplayed its significance, asserting usually that while the rabbis of antiquity were wise and holy men, their enactments were not eternally binding and some might have to change to meet altered circumstances. They also believed that religious change—by which they meant essentially alterations in public worship— could be obtained if sanctioned by the established ecclesiastical authority, i.e., the chief rabbi, for in their eyes he had the power to make reforms by virtue of his position alone, regardless of the halachic status of the changes. They thus invested him with power that no traditional rabbinic scholar would have claimed. They did so because they saw the chief rabbi as a Jewish archbishop of sorts rather than as an halachic authority.

The fundamental reason for the failure of German-Jewish patterns to be duplicated in England was the radically different political and social circumstances in which English Jews lived. In comparison to Central Europe there was little violent antipathy to Jews in England, although substantial prejudice and insensitivity still colored daily relations. Jews were viewed by many as the traditional enemies of Christianity, as cheats and sharpers, as aliens and outsiders. Within elite social circles there was also resistance to accepting Jews as intimate acquaintances. In addition, caricaturists, novelists, and dramatists frequently employed unflattering stereotypes of Jews in their work. Charles Dickens's Fagin is the best-known example of this tendency.[27] But these offensive portraits, like the anti-Jewish images in the popular mind and the social snobbery of the aristocracy and gentry, lacked political resonance. They did not erupt into an anti-Jewish campaign, with one exception—the Jew Bill agitation of 1753, and even here there is some debate about how these events are to be evaluated[28]—nor did they bespeak a widespread desire to turn back the tide of Jewish integration. Anti-Semitism before 1880 or so remained outside the realm of political life, and so British Jews by and large were spared the constant display of virulent public anti-Semitism as well as the occasional anti-Jewish riots that so disturbed the equilibrium of German Jews. In short, the Jewish presence in England was not problematical in the way it was in Central Europe.

The weakness of public antipathy to Jews stemmed from a variety of historical and political circumstances. First, the absence of an organized Jewish community in England between 1290 and 1656 weakened the cumulative impact of centuries of Christian hostility, although it did not eliminate it altogether. For three and a half centuries, inherited anti-Jewish feelings, lacking concrete issues on which they could be focused, had found expression almost solely in literature;[29] as a consequence, hostility to Jews was not as deeply ingrained or as sharply defined as elsewhere.

Second, English Protestantism possessed an active philo-Semitic strain generally absent on the Continent. Although philo-Semitism sought the eventual conversion of the Jews, in the short run it worked to better their status. And if it is impossible to state with any precision how this tradition made life easier for Jews before the campaign for emancipation, it is also equally hard to believe that it was without impact. In negative terms it meant that there was a large body of religious thought that did not identify Jewry as the embodiment of evil. From 1830 on the influence of philo-Semitism was more immediately apparent: some of the most active proponents of emancipation were philo-Semites who desired the integration of Jews into English society as a prelude to their conversion.[30]

Third, England was a more religiously diverse nation than Germany and became increasingly more so between 1770 and 1870. Jews were only one of several religious minorities and not necessarily the most despised of the lot. Political considerations prevented the Established Church and the ruling class from attempting to impose religious uniformity. The English were learning to be tolerant because they had no other choice. As Voltaire remarked in his *Philosophical Letters,* "If there were only one religion in England, one would have to be afraid of despotism; if there were two, they would cut each others' throats; but there are thirty, and they live happily in peace."[31] Voltaire, of course, exaggerated the harmony growing out of England's religious diversity. Relations between Anglicans and Nonconformists, on one level, and Protestants and Catholics, on another, were frequently embittered and fractious. In fact, many of the great political battles of the nineteenth century had distinctly religious overtones, with Anglicans and Nonconformists doing battle not only on church matters but on economic and social issues as well. Nevertheless, the inability of any one religious group to achieve dominance meant that the sphere of religious toleration was greater than elsewhere in Europe. Interestingly, the most vitriolic religious bombast and rant were directed not at Jews but at Catholics, hatred of whom was in some respects the English equivalent of German hatred for Jews. Catholics suffered from their identification with the Catholic powers of Europe, England's traditional enemies; with the Catholic rebels in Ireland, who were threatening Britain's hold there; and with the papacy in Rome, whose claims to authority and demands for allegiance were supranational. For Protestants, popery was more than a disagreeable religion; it was associated with the arbitrary exercise of power and other allegedly un-English traits. Thus, in the period 1770–1870, Catholics were much more likely than Jews to be cast as the agents of the Anti-Christ and the enemies of sacred English institutions.[32] Like Blacks in the American South and Japanese and Chinese on the Pacific Coast, they served as alternative objects of contempt, deflecting hostility that might otherwise have been directed at Jews.

Fourth, the English ruling class was less hostile to finance and commerce, the traditional areas of Jewish occupational concentration, than its counterparts in the German states. No great odium was attached to banking and brokerage, nor were Jews uniquely associated in the public mind with these fields. (In fact, their contribution to Britain's phenomenal economic expansion between 1750 and 1850 was minimal.[33]) The aristocracy and gentry, Britain's ruling elite in the eighteenth and nineteenth centuries, were not unfriendly to industrial and mercantile expansion. English society as a whole, David Landes has written, demonstrated "an exceptional sensitivity and responsiveness to pecuniary opportunity. This was a people fascinated by wealth and commerce, collectively and individually."[34] Anticapitalist anti-Semitism, which imagines the Jews to be the bearers of modern capitalism and hence the corrupters of traditional society, was confined largely to those groups fighting a rearguard action against the new order: Tory paternalists, romantic radicals, High Church country parsons, backwater gentry. These enemies of modernity were not a powerful party; they did not determine state policy or mold public opinion as was the case in Germany.[35]

Fifth, the emergence of powerful imperialist sentiments in the Victorian period precluded the development of xenophobic feelings that might otherwise have been expressed in an assertive nationalism with anti-Semitic overtones. The acquisition of a great empire in Africa and Asia allowed the English to define their sense of national character in opposition to the colonized peoples over whom they ruled, rather than a "foreign" minority at home. Their feelings of superiority emerged from their domination of non-White people, whom they considered backward and inferior, slaves of ignorance, superstition, and magic. At the same time, imperial military campaigns satisfied the more brutal and aggressive instincts of the British by providing them with a violent bloody spectacle in which they could vent their emotions—from a distance, and without actual personal involvement. As J.A. Hobson noted, jingoism allowed "the lust of the spectator, unpurged by any personal effort, risk, or sacrifice" to gloat "over the perils, pains, and slaughter of fellow-men whom he does not know, but whose destruction he desires in a blind and artifically stimulated passion of hatred and revenge."[36] With such an outlet abroad there was little energy left for an assertive, anti-Semitic nationalism at home.

The absence of strong, broadly based opposition to the entry of Jews into English society can be seen in the course of emancipation there.[37] In the first place, the term *emancipation* in the context of English history refers to the removal of a much narrower and less significant range of disabilities than in Germany. Jews born in England after the readmission of 1656 became subjects of the Crown and were entitled to most of the rights of other Englishmen who were also not communicants of the Established Church. This second-class citizenship was not especially grievous: essentially it meant that Jews could not hold elective office or take degrees at Oxford and Cambridge, disabilities from which Nonconformists and Roman Catholics also suffered before their own emancipation. Unlike the German states, Britain had no statutes that spelled out what was permitted and what forbidden to Jews. There were no laws, for example, specifically barring Jews from particular occupations, certain cities, restricting the size of Jewish settlements, or regulating the management of communal organizations. In short, the Jews of England, prior to their emancipation, were not rightless aliens who had to fight for the fundamental rights of citizenship. The few obstacles of a legal character to full integration affected only the Jewish upper-middle class; they were of no consequence to the great bulk of Jews living in England since they in no way interfered with their ability to earn a living, raise a family, or enjoy their leisure.

Before 1829 the leaders of Anglo-Jewry made no attempt to gain full political emancipation, for they had little interest in entering government service, studying at the ancient universities, or gaining admission to the Inns of Court. They were content to achieve success in commerce and finance. In the wake of the Catholic Emancipation Act of 1829, which allowed Catholics to sit in Parliament and hold public office (but did not permit them to take degrees at Oxford and Cambridge), a small circle of very wealthy Jews began to press the government to remove similar disabilities affecting Jews. These men viewed their second-class political status largely as a stain on their honor, as a stigma marking them off from other propertied Englishmen.[38] As Isaac Lyon Goldsmid told the prime minister, Sir Robert Peel, in 1845, the Jews "desired to be placed on an equality in point of civil privileges with other persons dissenting from the established church not so much on account of the hardship of being excluded from particular stations of trust or honour, as on account of the far greater hardship of having a degrading stigma fastened upon us by the laws of our country."[39] Initially, only a handful of Jewish notables supported the emancipation campaign, but over the years, as the community became more prosperous and more immersed in English life, the movement drew increasing support so that when Lionel de Rothschild took his seat in the House of Commons in 1858 it was widely regarded as a triumph for Anglo-Jewry as a whole.

Emancipation came to the Jews of England in a piecemeal fashion between 1830 and 1871. There was no single legislative campaign to remove in one fell swoop all the civil disabilities from which Jews suffered. Some fell by the wayside without legislative action. For example, in 1833 Jews became eligible to practice as barristers when the benchers of Lincoln's Inn decided that Francis Henry Goldsmid, the first Jew to present himself for admission to the Bar, might take the requisite oath in a manner acceptable to his conscience, i.e., omitting the Christological phrase in the oath. Similarly, in 1830 Jews gained the right to be admitted freemen of the City of London, which meant that they might operate retail shops within the City's boundaries, when the Court of Common Council ruled that they could subscribe the oaths in a manner acceptable to them. In other instances legislation was necessary. In 1835, for example, Parliament enfranchised all Jews who were otherwise qualified to vote in elections; in 1845 it permitted Jews elected to municipal office to take the oaths in a form acceptable to them; in 1871 it abolished all religious tests for matriculation and graduates at Oxford and Cambridge, a measure that simultaneously benefited Nonconformists, Catholics, and Jews alike.

In many cases legislative action followed and confirmed what had already been accomplished in practice. Jews had been voting in municipal and parliamentary elections and holding local offices for at least a decade before Parliament officially affirmed their right to do so. David Salomons and Lionel de Rothschild were each elected several times to the House of Commons (although never seated) before Parliament decided, in 1858, that each House should determine the manner for swearing in its own members, a decision that broke the impasse between Commons and Lords over Rothschild's right to take his seat. Thus, as was so frequently the case in the history of emancipation in England, the question of Jewish participation in political life was not decided in the abstract but rather on empirical grounds.

Although emancipation was not completed until 1871, it would be a mistake to view its delay as evidence of widespread resistance to the entry of Jews into new spheres of activity. The timing of emancipation depended, in the first place, on Jewish initiative, and, as noted above, Jews did not begin to press for the removal of the few civil disabilities affecting them until the middle decades of the nineteenth century. In most instances they succeeded in gaining what they wanted without too great a struggle. Only one issue provoked noticeable opposition: the right of Jews to sit in the House of Commons. But even in this instance the Commons, which of course represented a far-broader spectrum of public opinion than the Lords, voted to accept Jews as members as early as 1833 but was prevented by the Upper House from actually doing so until 1858.

Opposition to seating Jews in the Commons was led primarily by High Churchmen and diehard evangelicals, who resented the political circumstances that had forced them to grant Catholics and Nonconformists their rights and who were further angered by the increasing intervention of the state in church matters. After Catholic emancipation they were loath to consider any further dilution in the religious character of the state, and they accordingly blocked the entry of Jews into Parliament for almost three decades. Their opposition, however, was not representative of any widespread resistance to Jewish integration. Emancipation did not become a major issue in Victorian politics. Although it inspired dozens of pamphlets and editorials, it was not a divisive or explosive question, as it was in Germany. As Lord Ashley noted in 1853, "The popular voice, to take it in the full extent of the term, is neither upon one side or the other. There is, upon the whole, a general apathy upon the question. Where any feeling is entertained in its regard, that feeling is deep and serious; but that feeling has not, however, pervaded the whole mass of the community."[40]

Because the course of emancipation in England was relatively smooth— at least by comparison with Germany—most Jews there felt little pressure to renounce traditional beliefs. A few very wealthy Jews who were active in the establishment of the London Reform congregation may have been willing to pay a price for the removal of their civil disabilities, but they were hardly typical.[41] Most never felt called on to sacrifice their beliefs. As Abraham Gilam has persuasively demonstrated, emancipation in England was unique in modern Jewish history: it was not conditional. Parliament did not expect Jews to reform any of their beliefs or practices as a prerequisite to full political equality; in fact, Parliament had little interest in what Jews thought or prayed or how they acted in their shops and synagogues. In Gilam's words, "Their Jewishness was taken for granted, whether compatible with the modern concept of nationality or not." To be sure, there were pressures to make Jews conform more closely to English standards of gentility, but they were social rather than political— a condition that reflected the relative weakness of the British state. In contrast to Germany, intellectuals and politicans did not look to the state to revitalize society, to reform its degenerate and wayward elements and prepare them for active citizenship. The social arena and the marketplace, to which Jews already had access before they applied for parliamentary emancipation, took precedence over those areas under the tutelage of the state. Thus, in England the social emancipation of the Jews preceded their legal emancipation by a half-century or more.

The emancipation experience of Anglo-Jewry reflected the liberal character of state and society in England, just as its patterns of acculturation and integration derived from social and political conditions there and not currents of thought emanating from Central Europe. That local conditions shaped Anglo-Jewish life more than ideological trends origi- nating in regions with very different social and political systems is hardly a revolutionary conclusion. And yet it is a conclusion whose implications have not yet been absorbed into historical writing about the origins of Jewish modernity in the West, where the tendency still is to measure change in light of German-Jewish standards. If the Anglo-Jewish experience was not indebted to German currents because of the significant differences between the two host countries, then does it not follow that wherever Jews lived in conditions substantially different from those in Berlin or Frankfurt their entry into the majority society would have taken a course shaped by local conditions? If so, the question of the impact of the

German Haskalah and the Reform movement on other Western Jewries may not be the most fruitful question to ask in exploring the transformation of all European Jewry in the eighteenth and nineteenth centuries. As a heuristic device it is valuable, but not when it obscures the impress of native currents and structures. The individuality of historical phenomena can too easily be sacrificed in the pursuit of a common pattern of Jewish modernization. Because there was no uniform road to Jewish immersion in secular culture and the modern state, no single historical model can adequately describe the passage from tradition to modernity for all segments of European Jewry.

Notes

1. Karl Marx, "Contribution to the Critique of Hegel's Philosophy of Right: Introduction," in *Karl Marx: Early Writings,* trans. and ed. T.B. Bottomore (New York: McGraw-Hill, 1964), pp. 49, 51.
2. The following discussion is based on Todd M. Endelman, *The Jews of Georgian England, 1714-1830: Tradition and Change in a Liberal Society* (Philadelphia: Jewish Publication Society, 1979), chs. 4, 5, 6, 8.
3. Cecil Roth, "The Haskalah in England," in *Essays Presented to Chief Rabbi Israel Brodie on the Occasion of his Seventieth Birthday,* ed. H.J. Zimmels et al., 2 vols. (London: The Soncino Press, 1967), vol. 1, pp. 365-76.
4. Endelman, *The Jews of Georgian England,* pp. 149-54.
5. Ibid., pp. 154-59.
6. Ibid., ch. 7.
7. Cecil Roth, "The Vicissitudes of the First Oxford Jewish Graduate," *The Oxford Magazine* 3, new ser. (1962-63):230-32; idem, "The Jews in the English Universities," *Miscellanies of the Jewish Historical Society of England* 4 (1942):102-15; Raphael Loewe, "The Evolution of Jewish Student Feeding Arrangements in Oxford and Cambridge," in *Studies in the Cultural Life of the Jews in England,* ed. Dov Noy and Issachar Ben-Ami, Hebrew University Folklore Research Center Studies 5 (Jerusalem: The Hebrew University Press, 1975), pp. 165-84.
8. Endelman, *The Jews of Georgian England,* pp. 160-64.
9. Albert M. Hyamson, *The Sephardim of England: A History of the Spanish and Portuguese Jewish Community, 1492-1951* (London: Methuen, 1951), ch. 15. See also James Picciotto, *Sketches of Anglo-Jewish History,* rev. and ed. Israel Finestein (London: The Soncino Press, 1956), ch. 50, and Cecil Roth, *The Great Synagogue, London, 1690-1940* (London: Goldston & Son, 1950), pp. 253-54.
10. Robert Liberles, "The Origins of the Jewish Reform Movement in England," *AJS Review* 1 (1976):121-50. See also John M. Shaftesley, "Religious Controversies," in *A Century of Anglo-Jewish Life, 1870-1970: Lectures to Commemorate the Centenary of the United Synagogue,* ed. Salmond S. Levin (London: United Synagogue, n.d.), pp. 93-95.
11. Roth, *The Great Synagogue,* pp. 252-53; Endelman, *The Jews of Georgian England,* p. 161.

12. Liberles agrees that some of the reforms introduced at the West London Synagogue of British Jews were "a response to the criticial views of the British public." "The Origins of the Jewish Reform Movement in England," pp. 139–41.
13. Two recent accounts of the emancipation struggle clearly establish that Ashkenazim spearheaded Anglo-Jewish efforts to gain parliamentary relief, although in several instances Sephardim, e.g. J.G. Henriques and Moses Mocatta (both members of the Reform congregation), participated in delegations calling on parliamentary leaders. Moses Montefiore's conservative approach to emancipation may have been typical of the Sephardic community as a whole. See M.C.N. Salbstein, *The Emancipation of the Jews in Britain: The Question of the Admission of the Jews to Parliament, 1828–1860* (Rutherford, N.J.: Fairleigh Dickinson University Press, 1982), and Abraham Gilam, *The Emancipation of the Jews in England, 1830–1860* (New York: Garland, 1982).
14. For the prevalence of neo-Karaite views in Victorian Anglo-Jewry see Steven Singer, "Orthodox Judaism in Early Victorian England, 1840–1858," Ph.D. diss. (Yeshiva University, 1981), pp. 52–79, and Jakob J. Petuchowski, "Karaite Tendencies in an Early Reform Haggadah: A Study in Comparative Liturgy," *Hebrew Union College Annual* 31 (1960):223–49.
15. E.g., Shaftesley, "Religious Controversies," pp. 94–95.
16. Petuchowski, "Karaite Tendencies," pp. 223–24; Singer, "Orthodox Judaism in Early Victorian England," pp. 63–65; Salbstein, *The Emancipation of the Jews,* pp. 93–94; Liberles, "The Origins of the Jewish Reform Movement in England," pp. 135–37, 141–42, 148; Stephen Sharot, "Reform and Liberal Judaism in London: 1840–1940," *Jewish Social Studies* 41 (1979):212.
17. Bill Williams, *The Making of Manchester Jewry, 1740–1875* (Manchester: Manchester University Press, 1976), p. 260.
18. Ibid., pp. 259–60. Williams also claims, without evidence, that Reform elsewhere in England was probably due to German developments as well.
19. Ibid., pp. 247–63.
20. Sharot, "Reform and Liberal Judaism in London," p. 222.
21. For patterns of religious observance in the Victorian period see Singer, "Orthodox Judaism in Early Victorian London," ch. 6.
22. For a brief discussion of how the alleged virtues of establishment shaped the development of the United Synagogue see Israel Finestein, "The Lay Leadership of the United Synagogue since 1870," in *A Century of Anglo-Jewish Life,* p. 32. Anglo-Jewish devotion to the ideal of establishment also shaped relations between the Board of Deputies and the Reform synagogue in the mid-nineteenth century. See Gilam, *The Emancipation of the Jews in England,* pp. 42–43.
23. Lucy Cohen, *Arthur Cohen: A Memoir by His Daughter for His Descendants* (London: Bickers & Son, 1919), p. 24.
24. *Hebrew Observer,* 4 March 1853. For similar condemnations of the Reform movement in Germany see the *Jewish Chronicle,* 17 October 1845, 29 June 1855, 30 January 1857.
25. Singer, "Orthodox Judaism in Early Victorian London," pp. 143–65.
26. Ibid., pp. 52–79.
27. There is a large literature on the image of Jews in nineteenth-century English fiction and drama. The most recent account is Anne Aresty Naman, *The Jew*

in the Victorian Novel: Some Relationships between Prejudice and Art (New York: AMS Press, 1980). Interestingly, Dickens softened the references to Fagin's Jewishness when he revised and corrected *Oliver Twist* for the edition of his works published by Chapman and Hall in 1867-68. Apparently, Dickens had been made aware of the offense his Fagin had given Jews and sought to mitigate the anti-Jewish tone of the novel. Similarly, it has been argued that Riah, the "good" Jew in *Our Mutual Friend* (1864-65), was also an attempt to make amends for the pain caused by Fagin. I know of no similar gesture made by a German author. See Mark Gelber, "Teaching 'Literary Anti-Semitism': Dickens' *Oliver Twist* and Freytag's *Soll und Haben*," *Comparative Literature Studies* 16 (1979):1–11, and Harry Stone, "Dickens and the Jews," *Victorian Studies* 2 (1959):223–53.

28. For different interpretations of the Jew Bill agitation see Thomas W. Perry, *Public Opinion, Propaganda, and Politics in Eighteenth-Century England: A Study of the Jew Bill of 1753* (Cambridge, Mass.: Harvard University Press, 1962); Endelman, *The Jews of Georgian England*, pp. 59–60, 89–91; Jacob Katz, "The Term 'Jewish Emancipation': Its Origin and Historical Impact," in *Emancipation and Assimilation: Studies in Modern Jewish History* (Westmead, Farnborough, Hants.: Gregg International, 1972), pp. 29–30.

29. Bernard Glassman, *Anti-Semitic Stereotypes without Jews: Images of the Jews in England, 1290–1700* (Detroit: Wayne State University Press, 1975).

30. Endelman, *The Jews of Georgian England*, ch. 2; Mel Scult, *Millennial Expectations and Jewish Liberties: A Study of the Efforts to Convert the Jews in Britain up to the Mid-Nineteenth Century* (Leiden: Brill, 1978); David S. Katz, *Philo-Semitism and the Readmission of the Jews to England, 1603–1655* (Oxford: Clarendon Press, 1982).

31. Francois Marie Arouet de Voltaire, *Lettres Philosophiques,* ed. Gustave Lanson, 3rd ed., 2 vols. (Paris: Librairie Hachette, 1924), vol. 1, p. 74.

32. G.F.A. Best, "Popular Protestantism in Victorian Britain," in *Ideas and Institutions of Victorian Britain: Essays in Honour of George Kitson Clark,* ed. Robert Robson (New York: Barnes & Noble, 1967), pp. 115–42; E.R. Norman, *Anti-Catholicism in Victorian England* (New York: Barnes & Noble, 1968); Walter L. Arnstein, *Protestant versus Catholic in Mid-Victorian England: Mr. Newdegate and the Nuns* (Columbia: University of Missouri Press, 1982).

33. Harold Pollins, *Economic History of the Jews in England* (Rutherford, N.J.: Fairleigh Dickinson University Press, 1982), chs. 2, 5, 6; Todd M. Endelman, "L'activité economique des Juifs anglais," *Dix-Huitieme Siecle* 13 (1981): pp. 113–26.

34. David S. Landes, *The Unbound Prometheus: Technological Change and Industrial Development in Western Europe from 1750 to the Present* (Cambridge: Cambridge University Press, 1969), p. 66.

35. Endelman, *The Jews of Georgian England*, pp. 97–105.

36. J.A. Hobson, *Imperialism: A Study,* (Ann Arbor: University of Michigan Press, 1965), p. 215.

37. The best accounts of the course of emancipation are Gilam, *The Emancipation of the Jews in England,* and Salbstein, *The Emancipation of the Jews in Britain.* The legal status of Jews in England is described at length in H.S.Q. Henriques, *The Jews and the English Law* (London: J. Jacobs, 1908).

38. Endelman, *The Jews of Georgian England*, pp. 276–81.

39. Quoted in Gilam, *The Emancipation of the Jews in England,* p. 15.

40. Quoted in Salbstein, *The Emancipation of the Jews in Britain,* p. 235. For further evidence of public apathy regarding Jewish emancipation, see the other observations of politicians cited by Salbstein, pp. 234–35.
41. See, e.g., Francis Henry Goldsmid's remarks on the national character of the Jews in *The Arguments Advanced against the Enfranchisement of the Jews, considered in a Series of Letters* (London, 1831), pp. 13–17.

10

German-Jewish Identity in Nineteenth-Century America

Michael A. Meyer

One of Simon Dubnow's principal contributions to Jewish historiography was his conception of shifting hegemonic centers, each for a time exercising a dominant influence on Jewries in other parts of the world. Such centers spiritually strengthened those younger or weaker Jewish communities that were dependent on them. Yet in the course of time and for a variety of historical reasons, some of these initially peripheral settlements themselves made successful bids for hegemony. Thus, according to Dubnow, Spanish Jewry gained independence from the Oriental Gaonate in the tenth century, and five hundred years later the mantle of leadership fell upon the German-Polish Jews. In the twentieth century, Dubnow looked toward a joint hegemony shared by Jews in the European-American Diaspora and in the Land of Israel.[1]

Whatever the shortcomings of Dubnow's grand scheme, when applied to the entire course of Jewish history the notion of an inchoate Jewry looking to an established, intellectually productive one for inspiration and guidance, then gradually—or fitfully—breaking away to assert its own primacy is suggestive for specific instances. It can, for example, be usefully applied to the relation of the American-Jewish community to its German-Jewish origins during the nineteenth century.[2] From the beginning of large-scale Jewish immigration from Germany to the United States in the 1830s until the demographic submergence of German Jewry in America beneath the flood tide of East European immigration at the end of the century, there was a discernible tension between forces making for preservation of the German-Jewish heritage as represented by Jews still in Germany, and those that pressed in the direction of greater spiritual independence. While German Jewry could and did serve as a model of modernization, especially in matters of religion, acculturation in the United States worked mostly in the opposite direction: toward an assertion of independence from the German matrix. Although for a period of time German Judaism was venerated almost without qualification, by the last decades of the nineteenth century its hegemony was under severe attack even by those German Jews in America who owed it the most. The purpose of this essay is to trace this conflict of forces as it appeared in the realms of culture and religion and to explain the eventual disavowal of German Judaism as a model for American Jewry.

Unlike its European antecedents, American Jewry did not undergo a multidimensional process of modernization. Only about 2,000 Jews were living in the British colonies when the colonists successfully gained their independence. The United States enshrined in its constitution the political equality for members of all religious groups for which European Jews were still struggling, in part by giving evidence of their modernity. Moreover, American Jewry was not forced into a narrow economic structure, nor did it possess the comprehensive corporate structure of its European counterparts or an authoritative rabbinate of the old style. From the start, American Jews were integrated into the general socio-political life to a degree that was only partially achieved in Central Europe even after a long process of modernization. Only in the spheres of culture and religion can one speak meaningfully of a process of Jewish modernization as opposed simply to the universal processes whereby all immigrants adapted to American life.

Between 1825 and 1875 the Jewish population in the United States grew from about 15,000 to about 250,000. The vast majority of the immigrants in that period came from Germany, initially from the villages and small towns in Bavaria and other southern states, later also from northern Germany. They emigrated because of legislative restrictions limiting Jewish marriages and choice of occupation, but their main motive was economic self-improvement. Few came at any time solely because of the attraction of American political ideals. Those who could stay usually remained. Particularly in the first half of the nineteenth century, the German-Jewish immigrants were mostly young, male, and poor, ill-educated Jewishly, and with little if any secular culture. Modernized German Jews began to come to America only in the 1850s and then again after the Civil War. All but a few intellectuals spurned emigration at any time. Many of the early migrants moved to small towns in the American South and Midwest, peddling inexpensive items and maintaining in America those rural patterns of life with which they had been familiar in Germany.[3] The rapid urbanization of Jews in Germany only after midcentury was paralleled by the German-Jewish experience in America.

Most of the early German immigrants had little time for matters either Jewish or German. They struggled to make a living and to improve their economic lot wherever possible. Their occupational situation required their gaining a basic knowledge of the English language, considerable freedom from ritual constraints, and full devotion to the great American enterprise of "making money." But while Americanization was the key to economic success, it was also pursued out of a sense of gratitude for what the new land offered. Supporting oneself in America was not easy, and some succumbed to the hardship, but there were no artificial barriers to advancement for those who combined skill or intelligence with hard work. In their initial drive to establish themselves economically, the early immigrants rarely looked back upon Germany with any nostalgia. They had never really identified as Germans either politically or culturally. Most spoke and wrote only Judeo-German (Yiddish), not the German of Moses Mendelssohn, and were unacquainted with the classics of German literature. Germany primarily represented for them the restrictiveness which they had been pressed to flee; positively, the old country meant little more than the landscape of their childhood.

Leaving Bavaria or Württemberg also meant leaving behind the pervasive religious atmosphere of its Jewish communities. Judaism in America was represented by the well-established Sephardim whose congregations those German Jews interested in religion initially joined, in preference to transplanting their own rite. Although there were considerable numbers of German Jews in America already in the eighteenth century, the first successful Ashkenazic congregations were not established until the 1820s.[4] And even after the foundation of German synagogues, the trend to association with the more Americanized, prestigious, and dignified Sephardic congregations continued in some German-Jewish circles well into the nineteenth century. It is noteworthy that one of the principal Americanizers of German Jewry in the United States, Isaac Leeser, though himself born in Westphalia, served a Sephardic congregation, Mikveh Israel in Philadelphia. Yet the Ashkenazic members were often treated as pariahs by the Sephardim and regarded with some contempt by more German-conscious Jews. Rabbi David Einhorn used to call them "Portugiesen aus Schnotzebach."[5] As long as the German Jews were neither themselves Americanized nor brought with them any significant modern cultural baggage from Germany, the Sephardic elite presented the best example of what a modern American Jewry should be like. But as German Jews appeared in the United States in ever-greater numbers, as those who came had increasingly undergone modernization in Germany, and as the earlier immigrants from Germany found more time for culture and religion, a specific German-Jewish identity in America began to emerge.

As early as 1807, a member of the Bleichröder family, then resident in New York, had written that Jewish immigrants in America were considerably more cultured than those who were born in the country.[6] Although this purported correlation between newness to the American scene and a higher cultural level may not have held in the succeeding decades, it was generally still true by the 1850s. As larger numbers of acculturated German Jews came to the United States, the process of Americanization slowed considerably. Germany ceased to be merely a land of origins and its Judaism no longer seemed inappropriate to the American context. For more than a generation after midcentury, American Jews of German origin looked across the ocean for direction and inspiration.

The more favorable attitude of American Jews to things German was influenced by the rising respect accorded German culture in the United States. Jews constituted only a small portion of the 5.5 million Germans in America according to the census of 1850. By the 1860s it was widely felt that Germany had much to offer America and even that the mission of its emigrants was to conquer the New World for German values.[7] While not all cities became as Germanized as Milwaukee, Cincinnati, or St. Louis, the German immigrants sought minimally to preserve certain elements of their old life in the New World. The most obvious attribute of their cultural origins was the German language. Immigrant churches in America fostered the mother tongue, as did a variety of social, fraternal, and philanthropic societies. German-language newspapers flourished. Thus, while earlier Yiddish-speaking Jews had no support in the American context for retaining their language—and as a result Americanized very rapidly—German-speaking Jews were part of a larger language group which encouraged their endeavors to preserve the German heritage.[8]

Still in the 1840s Jewish parents usually did not attempt to teach their children German. When Rabbi Max Lilienthal served in New York during that period, he was forced against his will to give confirmation instruction in English.[9] In the next two decades, however, a considerable proportion of the Jewish immigrants made determined efforts to pass on the German language—and hence German culture—to their children. In 1856, on a visit to Easton, Pennsylvania, Isaac Leeser complained that there, as elsewhere, parents in the Jewish school insisted on having German as the vehicle of instruction. Three years later Rabbi Bernhard Felsenthal of Chicago estimated that 90 percent of the present Jewish generation in America either knew only German or knew it better than English. Despite assimilatory pressures, German Jewry in America had considerable success in maintaining the German language. As late as 1874, the *Deutschamerikanisches Conversationslexicon* pointed out that German predominated in the majority of some 400 Jewish communities in the United States. And even a decade later, Rabbi Isaac Mayer Wise noted that in a number of congregations English-speaking children still had to learn their catechism in German, and the German language was taught in the Sabbath schools "as if it were a part of Judaism."[10]

While English usually had to be used in business, German was retained in the sanctuary of the home as the language of the family. Women immigrants especially continued to read and speak mostly German. To a high degree it became the language of the synagogue. Congregational records were kept in German, in one case—Rodeph Shalom of Philadelphia—after they had been written in English for a number of years.[11] More important, and for a longer period of time, German served as the language of sermons and portions of the liturgy. Orthodox congregations no less than Reform ones wanted preachers who could deliver religious discourses of the type that were familiar to them from Germany. But for some Reform leaders the use of German in the synagogue was not merely a concession to familiar structures and expressions, not simply a passing phase in the process of Americanization. Felsenthal noted that the younger generation should learn German because the German people were still the leading cultural influence in the world "and we bow our heads in reverence before its spirit . . . we American-German Jews." The German tongue, it seems, was thought essential for modern spirituality even in America. Germany, said Rabbi David Einhorn, was the "land of thinkers, presently the foremost land of culture and, above all the land of Mendelssohn, the birthplace of Jewish Reform. . . . Now if you remove the German spirit or—what amounts to the same thing, the German language—you have torn away the native soil and the lovely flower must wither." Without the German language, Einhorn believed, the Reform movement was nothing but a shiny veneer. It was a manikin without heart or soul; neither proud temples nor magnificent chorales could breathe any life into it. Hanns Reissner was right when he claimed that for the first generation of Jewish immigrants to America and beyond, German became nothing less than a "sacred language."[12]

The retention of the German language was facilitated by the usually favorable relations between Jewish and Gentile immigrants. The Christians who took the initiative to leave Germany were less likely to have harbored anti-Jewish prejudices than those who remained, and once they arrived most of them readily accepted the American value of social equality. When Jews with German professional training reached America, having fled German discrimination, they were, ironically, hailed as representatives of superior German university training. With few exceptions, Gentiles welcomed Jews into German cultural societies whose counterparts in Germany would have most likely excluded them. In San Francisco in 1852, a Jew headed a cultural and social club that included the most distinguished Germans of the city. German Jews could feel like insiders in these groups while they still remained outsiders in America.[13]

Educated Americans gave considerable attention to German-Jewish writers, encouraging Jews to take pride in their former compatriots. Emerson, a great fancier of German literature, had also read Moses Mendelssohn; Heine was repeatedly translated into English by Americans, his poetry and essays frequently discussed. American periodicals mentioned the popular German-Jewish novelist Berthold Auerbach more often than any German author except Goethe; and for a time Auerbach was possibly more widely known in America than any German writer.[14] Jews and non-Jews came together in celebration of their common cultural heritage. Thus it occurred that German Jews in America continued the modernization process begun in Germany within an imported German context, thereby paradoxically slowing down their assimilation to modern America.

Even Jews who had not attained a formal education while still in the old country sought to make up for it once they had established themselves economically in America. They created their own literary societies and listened to lectures in German on diverse topics. In Philadelphia, a Gabriel Riesser society was in existence for many years.[15] Religious leaders established German-language Jewish newspapers and German sections in those which were published in English. Isaac Mayer Wise's popular *Die Deborah* endured for nearly half a century, from 1855 to 1902. A new Jewish intellectual journal, *Der Zeitgeist,* was established in Milwaukee as late as 1880.

German Jews in America broadened the framework of organized Jewish life, which for the Sephardim had been centered strictly upon the synagogue. They formed a panoply of independent fraternal and charitable associations, perhaps patterned in part upon such long-standing German-Jewish models as the *Gesellschaft der Freunde* and the *hevrot* of the German communities. Yet the manner of raising funds—dinners, charity balls, lotteries, and the like—was strictly American.[16] The most significant early association founded by German Jews in America was B'nai B'rith, which originated in New York in 1843 and was apparently modeled upon Freemasonry. By 1851 there were eleven B'nai B'rith lodges, all but two conducting their transactions in German. Unlike the synagogue, which in the 1850s was already dividing traditionalists from reformers, and which left out those German Jews who had become wholly indifferent to religion, B'nai B'rith could include all German Jews within a framework which was secular without being secularist. Indeed, it has recently been suggested that B'nai B'rith in America initially served the function of a "secular synagogue."[17] As such, it enshrined and perpetuated the culture and mores of German Jewry. Like the German-language synagogue, B'nai B'rith thus served as a brake upon assimilation by creating a unique amalgam of peculiar Jewish symbolism and transplanted German values. Yet the German element does not seem to have lasted as long in B'nai B'rith as it did in the synagogue. By 1855, the order had already changed its official language from German to English.

One of the reasons that German Jews looked to their old homeland for inspiration was that they had not yet produced in America the equivalent of a Heine or a Riesser. In the nineteenth century, Jews in America remained outside the cultural establishment to a greater degree than in Germany. Despite discrimination, a number of Jews in the old country had gained professorial chairs by the 1880s. There were notable Jewish philosophers, writers, poets, artists. But here in America, lamented an anonymous writer in a German-Jewish periodical, Jews "have contributed nothing either in art or in science." They had failed to produce men of the political stature of an Eduard Lasker or the literary merit of a Berthold Auerbach because the German spirit had insufficiently penetrated American Jewry, which, alas, was too much concerned in outer show and too little in inner content.[18] For this writer, and for others, Germany signified the life of the spirit while America meant chasing after the almighty dollar.

As American Jews admired their German brethren for contributing so richly to general culture, so too they esteemed their work as modern scholars of Judaism and bearers of Jewish religion and culture. Abraham Geiger's *Jüdische Zeitschrift für Wissenschaft und Leben* had its readers and contributors in America as did Ludwig Philippson's *Allgemeine Zeitung des Judentums,* the more traditional *Israelitische Wochenschrift,* and Samson Raphael Hirsch's neo-Orthodox *Jeschurun.* American rabbis praised and depended upon the work of Leopold Zunz and his fellow workers in the vineyard of Wissenschaft des Judentums. By comparison, American-Jewish culture remained weak and immature. In 1878 Bernhard Felsenthal protested that American Jewry could not yet be expected to produce significant scholarship on its own. A few years earlier, in 1866, he had written that American rabbis could only be trained in Germany, preferably in Berlin, where they could study with Zunz, Steinschneider, and other teachers at the Ephraim'sche Lehranstalt.[19] In the 1870s, the Hochschule für die Wissenschaft des Judentums drew students from America, including Felix Adler, who shortly thereafter left the Jewish fold to found the Ethical Culture movement, and Emil G. Hirsch, who became a prominent Reform rabbi in Chicago. A decade later, Bernard Drachman, subsequently a teacher at the Jewish Theological Seminary in New York, and Morris Jastrow, who became a professor of Semitics at the University of Pennsylvania, were the first American-born Jews to study at the Breslau Jüdisch-Theologisches Seminar.

For the sake of the younger generation, which was not fully at home in the German language, American Jews began translating into English major works of German-Jewish thought and scholarship. Among the most active translators were the most Americanizing of the Jewish leaders in the United States, Isaac Leeser and Isaac Mayer Wise. Leeser, who also did English translations of the Hebrew Bible and prayerbook, produced an English version of Mendelssohn's *Jerusalem* in 1852. In rapid succession, Wise contributed to the *Asmonean* English excerpts from the writings of Zunz, Geiger, Frankel, Rapoport, Luzzatto, Krochmal, Holdheim, Jost, and Graetz. Others produced similar gleanings for English-language Jewish periodicals. In 1865, Geiger's *Judaism and Its History* appeared in New York, and all three works published by the predecessor to the present Jewish Publication Society during its 3-year existence from 1872 to 1875 were translations from the German. The first major project of the society's later successor in name and task was a slightly abridged translation of Graetz's multivolumed history, which appeared between 1891 and 1898.[20] In terms of Jewish culture and scholarship, up to the last decades of the century American Jews appreciatively accepted the hegemony of German Jewry.

German Judaism served as the model in the sphere of religion almost to the same degree as in the sphere of culture. American-Jewish leadership was not closed to specifically American influence, but until it gathered strength, until it recognized that American Jewry was destined to overshadow its nineteenth-century German source, it ascribed religious authority to the German thinkers who had sought to create postghetto Jewish ideologies and to the innovations which had modernized the German synagogue. This was especially true for the reformers, but not for them alone. The traditionalist Isaac Leeser, for example, greatly admired the Berlin rabbi Michael Sachs, whose position on the religious spectrum he represented in America, and both he and those who shared his religious views have been regarded as American exponents of Zacharias Frankel's positivist-historical Judaism.[21] When American Jews sought to adapt their religious institutions to the modern world, they looked to the German example as a guide. The extent to which their religious leaders minimized or maximized the German connection seems to have depended largely on how deep their own German experience had been.

Neither Leeser nor Wise had German university training or much direct acquaintance with the intellectual ferment in German Jewry during the first half of the century. Most of those who were especially tied to Germany—like Rabbis David Einhorn, Samuel Adler, and Samuel Hirsch—had both. Upon arrival they set out to make American Judaism a true copy of the German original. Only gradually did they begin to claim that the copy possessed a lovelier form and a rosier future than the model upon which it was fashioned.

Much has been written about the first efforts at religious reform in the United States which took place in Charleston, South Carolina, beginning in 1824. It seems evident that those members of Beth Elohim, a Sephardic congregation who sought to introduce decorum, an English sermon, a few prayers in the English language, and somewhat later an organ, were motivated by specifically American influences, especially by Protestantism in the city. Yet even at the beginning they expressed their awareness of religious reform in Holland and Germany. And when Gustav Poznanski, who had lived in Bremen and Hamburg, became preacher and reader of the congregation in 1836, he brought with him the spirit of the Hamburg Reform temple, which had embodied Sephardic elements in its pronunciation of Hebrew, in the melodies used for the liturgy, and in the formulation of certain prayers. Some of the English hymns, published by the congregation in 1842, were adapted from the Hamburg temple's *Gesangbuch,* and the memorial service on the Day of Atonement was taken from its prayerbook. A little later Beth Elohim introduced the confirmation ceremony, based on the ritual formulated by Rabbi Leopold Stein of Frankfurt.[22]

For modernizing Ashkenazic Jewish congregations in America, the Hamburg temple ritual served as the chief model. A native of Hamburg living in Baltimore helped to found the first specifically Reform congregation in America, Har Sinai, in 1842. He was commissioned to present to the members a description of the temple's prayerbook, which had just appeared in a revised edition amidst great controversy. It was thereupon adopted and apparently used until David Einhorn introduced his own prayerbook in 1856.[23]

Temple Emanu-El of New York, which held its first service in 1845, did not begin its rapid process of reforms until more than a decade later. Yet from the beginning its choir sang chorales from Munich and Vienna while members listened to sermons in German, at first by Ludwig Merzbacher from Fürth and later by Samuel Adler. Not until 1868 did the congregation elect a second professional preacher whose task was to address the congregation in English. Without doubt the introduction of reforms did reflect, as Leon Jick has argued, the upward social mobility of the congregation. But it is worth noting that David Einhorn attributed the slow progress of Reform at Temple Emanu-El to the disproportionate influence of the small "aristocratic Portuguese element" in the congregation, that element which was the most established in American society. Moreover, the reforms which were eventually introduced were nearly all precedented in Germany, the leadership was well aware of German examples, and despite increasing wealth, the ambience of Temple Emanu-El and similar congregations in New York and elsewhere remained more German than American for decades.[24] If Reform was motivated solely by the desire for rapid Americanization, its Germanic character remains inexplicable.

Increasingly the German congregations in America were led by men who had been influenced by the modern rabbinate in Germany. In Baltimore and Cincinnati there were former students of Leopold Stein, in New York, men who had been instructed as children by Samuel Adler and David Einhorn. Not surprisingly, the wealthier German synagogues in America soon sought to obtain leading figures from Germany as their rabbis. Abraham Geiger twice refused offers; Leopold Zunz, a contributor to the first German-language American-Jewish periodical, *Israels Herold,* was considering a position in New York as early as 1833. Others did come, at first mostly less well-known individuals (except Max Lilienthal), and then more prominent names after midcentury. German speakers continued to dominate the American rabbinate as late as 1872, when an editorial in the *New York Herald* took note of how few men were capable of delivering sermons in English.[25]

The outstanding Germanizer among nineteenth-century rabbis in America was David Einhorn, who, beginning in 1855, successively occupied pulpits in Baltimore, Philadelphia, and New York. His influence through his prayerbook *Olat Tamid,* his intellectual journal *Sinai,* and through the perpetuation of his ideas by his similarly inclined sons-in-law Emil G. Hirsch and Kaufmann Kohler, was ultimately more decisive for Reform Judaism in America than the less radical ideas of Isaac Mayer Wise. While Wise, the proponent of Americanization, was by far the more popular and practically effective leader, it was Einhorn's philosophy that dominated the Reform movement in America from the 1870s until the 1930s. In an article he published in *Sinai* in 1859, Einhorn wrote: "German research and knowledge constitute the source of the Jewish Reform idea, and *German* Jewry possesses the mission to gain life and currency for this idea upon American soil." Without it, American Jews might well give up their ceremonial laws and their old costumes, but they would do so out of accommodation, not within a principled system that affirmed a modernized Judaism even as it rejected outdated forms.

Only German Jews, nurtured on German-Jewish religious thought, could have any conception of Judaism's historical development or its universal character. At least for the present, Einhorn believed the Reform idea still required the German umbilical cord; it was too young in America, too much in ferment to divest itself of its original German shell. Only after the German-Jewish heritage would be fully absorbed could American Jewry seek to be more independent, to substitute the English language for the German, and to embark on its own course. In all but one important respect Einhorn was very American: he spoke out from the pulpit on controversial issues such as slavery, a venture rarely if ever undertaken by rabbis in Germany in the nineteenth century.[26] Although Einhorn's devotion to the spiritual heritage of the German nation remained undiminished to his final sermon in 1879, his respect for Jewish thinkers in Germany, especially for those who called themselves "Reformers," had begun to decline precipitously a decade earlier. By the 1870s it was not only the Americanizers, but Einhorn and other Germanists among the radical Reformers who were seriously questioning whether Philippson, Geiger, and other German Reformers could still serve as guides for the Jewish religion in America. A revolt was under way, and even Einhorn became a part of it.

As the radical Reformers' views on German Jewry soured, they drew nearer to those of that most enthusiastically American among the American-Jewish Reformers, Isaac Mayer Wise. Bereft of all nostalgia for Europe, Wise did not identify himself actively as a German Jew or encourage others to do so. He consistently took pride in his coreligionists' capacity to acculturate rapidly in America, leaving behind foreign attachments while clinging all the more fervently to their inherited identity as Jews. Modernization, in Wise's writing, was associated with America, not Germany. In the United States Jews faced new challenges which Wise believed they had not encountered abroad. Forced to respond to a throng of propagandizing missionaries and to raucous atheists, the "thoughtless ceremonial Jew" was transformed into the "thinking and enlightened Israelite."

As early as the 1850s, American Jewry had already shown its mettle. In 1855, the Cleveland Conference brought together a handful of moderate Reformers and traditionalists to affirm their belief in the divine origin of the Bible and in the Talmud as its authoritative expositor. Wise, who was a participant, immediately insisted that this conference had done more than the German rabbinical assemblics of the 1840s and the current meetings in Giessen and Wiesbaden. It had defined principles, not just dealt with specific practices. Moreover, the American meeting had done more good than "the dry historical investigations of [Zacharias] Frankel's school. The latter, however much we appreciate their scientific labor, entirely neglect the wants of the time; writing the biographies of the old Talmudists, they forget the questions of the day and the disunion and disharmony that tears the congregations asunder." As synagogues became more German in the early 1860s, Wise struggled against the trend. Sarcastically he wrote: "The Alexandrine Hebrews had a Greek ritual, the Babylonians adopted the Chaldean, and the American Israelites, in the midst of an English speaking community, should be German. They call that reform, we call it retrogression." Yet in those years, even Wise was forced to preach in German in his Cincinnati congregation at least every other week.[27]

For Wise, Europe represented above all oppression. He felt no loyalty whatever to the Austrian Empire of his origins.[28] In America Jews preached upon occasion from Christian pulpits; in 1860 Rabbi Morris Raphall had opened a session of Congress with a prayer. The equivalent in Germany would be hard to imagine. What contemporary German culture offered, Wise held in the 1870s, was not religious idealism, but such enemies of religion as materialism and Darwinism. America, by contrast, had given the Jews liberty. Here they were free to participate in its great and manifest destiny; here Jewish religious values could find a fertile soil. The Jewish leadership in Germany, Wise believed, had failed to appreciate the virtues either of America or of its Jewry. Men like Ludwig Philippson used every occasion to put it in its place. They could not grasp "the significance of American Jewry for all Israel."[29]

Wise's assessment of the critical attitude shared by the Jewish leadership in Germany was no exaggeration. Ludwig Philippson expected that the men he recommended for American pulpits and teaching positions would continue to write appreciative letters. When they did not, he accused some of "gross ingratitude" and claimed that others were "purposely seeking to estrange Jews there completely from German Judaism." According to Philippson, American Jewry could lay no claim to significant religious creativity. Its entire religious development was "either brought along or imported from Germany." To argue otherwise was an "absurd presumption." It was the daughter raising herself above her mother to whom she owed everything; it was the self-flattery of insisting "we savages are after all better men."[30]

Zacharias Frankel's position was not as possessive nor as crudely stated, but in its own way it was even more devastating. In an article in his *Monatsschrift,* Frankel related a few facts about the Jewish settlement in America, but then noted—still in 1863—that American Jewry really had no right to claim that it possessed a history at all. Frankel held in common with his colleague, Heinrich Graetz, that Jewish history in its proper sense consists of endurance in the face of suffering on the one hand and of spiritual creativity on the other. But American Jewry had never had to struggle for its survival and it had not as yet produced a significant religious or scientific literature. Thus American Jews would simply have to recognize that they had yet to enter Jewish history. Not surprisingly, when Graetz published volume eleven of his *Geschichte der Juden* in 1870, he devoted only a solitary sentence and a half to the Jews of America. Even in the later English edition Graetz included no more than a single paragraph on the subject.[31]

One of the most favorably disposed toward American Judaism within the German-Jewish religious leadership was Abraham Geiger. This inclination was especially marked at the end of Geiger's life, after he had taught American students at the *Hochschule* in Berlin. Geiger encouraged his friend, David Einhorn, in the difficult task of transplanting the German spirit to the tumultuous American environment, submitted material to his periodical *Sinai,* and directed Kaufmann Kohler to the United States as the land of promise for progressive Judaism. While Geiger believed that American Jewry still lacked maturity, he could appreciate its hopeful freshness and even admit that perhaps German Jews were like the biblical Reubenites who reached their patrimony first, aided their brethren, but did not themselves settle in the promised land.[32] It was only when the American rabbis dared to challenge his wisdom that Geiger became defensive, or rather a bit aggressive.

In preparation for the Leipzig Synod held in the summer of 1869, Geiger had composed a list of theses on liturgy and marriage laws which he wanted that assembly to consider.[33] Later the same year, eleven American Reform rabbis gathered in Philadelphia in order to deal collectively with religious issues and especially with questions of marriage law.[34] The participants included all the major American Reformers, ranging from the most radical to relative moderates like Wise and Moses Mielziner. One of them, Kaufmann Kohler, had just arrived from Germany and had been present at the Leipzig Synod.[35] The Philadelphia deliberations were conducted in German and references were made to Leipzig and to Geiger's theses. A series of resolutions, ranging from the theological to the practical, was adopted and speedily became known in America and in Europe. On a number of points the resolutions deviated from Geiger's theses, to his very great displeasure. In the tone of a father castigating his wayward sons, the veteran German Reformer now chastised the Philadelphia gathering for straying from the proper path. The conference "must give up all petty jealousy toward the old homeland," he wrote in his *Zeitschrift.* "It should rather recognize spiritual depth as it is nurtured in Germany and participate in it, utilizing without conceit the greater freedom in practical matters given them by their circumstances."[36] With all his sympathy for American Jewry, Geiger could not yet reconcile himself to German Jewry being located on the periphery rather than at the center of religious modernization, or to his views being ignored or contradicted by his colleagues in America. Perhaps he also recognized that the Philadelphia Conference, for all its German character, was an assertion of intellectual independence.

Even more striking than Geiger's parental expression of rejection was the overreaction to it by his spiritual son, David Einhorn. In an article in the *Jewish Times,* Einhorn accused Geiger of believing that the Torah was only to be found *me'ever layam* (beyond the ocean), of taking the position *im aini kan mi kan* (if I am not here, who is), and in effect holding the Philadelphia rabbis to account for not declaring *"in Geiger Alles, ausser ihm Nichts!"* Aside from the psychodynamic tension of the situation there were of course general and specific points of significant difference between the two men. Einhorn leveled the most substantive general charge against Geiger when in the same article he called him, not favorably, a *ba'al teshuvah*.[37] Geiger, as well as others of the early Reform leaders in Germany, had made their peace with the exigencies of united Jewish communities embracing liberal as well as conservative elements. Unlike Samuel Holdheim who, as Jakob Petuchowski has shown, was in some respects more of an antecedent for Einhorn than was Geiger,[38] other Reformers in Germany had not stuck by their principles; the movement had succumbed to concession and compromise. Hence, it could no longer claim to be on the leading edge of religious development. In America, with its religious voluntarism and lack of communal constraints, religious reform was freer to take its destined course. And in fact, just as the Reform movement in Germany was becoming more conservative, its offspring in America was becoming ever more radical in theory and practice. Ironically, Wise was now closer in spirit to German Reform than was Einhorn.

The most significant single difference between Geiger and the American Reform rabbis concerned the position of women, an issue determined by the disparity of cultural values between the two countries. The Philadelphia Conference had voted to allow a bride to respond to the wedding formula recited by her husband by uttering the same words given only a change of gender. This institution of reciprocal vows, combined with an exchange of rings, did not find favor in Geiger's eyes. While he was willing to recognize the wife's equality with her husband, he insisted that the two would always occupy a different position in society, that the husband would "always remain master of the house" and would have the determinative say. The husband should, therefore, speak for both while "the chaste bride, who has already more whispered than audibly spoken her 'yes' should not have to speak and act publicly, but rather attend the words of her husband with a soulful look as she eagerly stretches out her finger so that the ring can be placed upon it. For the future as well," Geiger concludes, "the husband will be the one who gives, the wife the one who receives."[39] For all of his Germanism, Einhorn was by now sufficiently Americanized to brand such talk the worst romanticism. Though he claimed that women's equality was a prophetic, and hence not originally an American notion, Einhorn lived in an environment where women—for all the disabilities they still suffered—were treated more as equals than in Germany. The Jewish traveler I.J. Benjamin had been struck and offended by the Women's Rights movement which he encountered in the United States in 1860.[40] While in nineteenth-century Germany even Liberal congregations seated men and women separately, in America the "family pew" had spread to nearly all the larger synagogues, including very conservative ones; and one looks in vain in nineteenth-century Germany for an equivalent of the American Rebecca Gratz, founder of the modern Jewish Sunday school.

During the 1870s and 1880s, even in those circles which had heretofore been most worshipful of their German antecedents, there now arose a chorus of criticism for Germany and German Jewry, together with praise for America and its Jews. The case of Rabbi Bernhard Felsenthal of Chicago is illustrative. No one except perhaps Einhorn had been more fervent a devotee of German culture and more attached to German Jewry than Felsenthal, who had written in 1866:

> With regard to the assertion that we should emancipate ourselves from German Jewry and proclaim our independence, we say: Alas, for us if we were now to free ourselves from German Judaism and its influences! As in the Middle Ages the sun of Jewish scholarship shone loftily and marvellously in Spain. . . . That sun now stands in the German heavens and from there sends its beneficent light to all Jews and Jewish communities among the modern cultured nations. Germany has replaced Sefarad.[41]

Felsenthal argued that without the influence of German Jewry American Judaism would "either sink into an ossified orthodoxy or into nihilistic, raw and presumptuous bar-room wisdom." Both would be of a strictly American variety. The Orthodoxy would more likely be a kind of hysterical Methodism, a benightedly strict Calvinistic puritanism, or an ostentatious High Church display than a Torah-true Judaism in accord with Talmud and *poskim*. For the nihilists, Thomas Paine would serve as the model.[42] In short, Felsenthal believed that American Jewry—across the religious spectrum—still required a subservient relationship to German Judaism lest it assimilate the worst characteristics of American religion and philosophy.

In succeeding decades, however, Felsenthal's views changed almost completely. He came to believe that America had as much idealism as Germany, and without the attendant sickly romanticism. He even went so far as to claim that the American environment had been a blessing for Judaism; it had not had to suffer governmental interference because of the American separation between church and state, and thus had been able to develop freely on its own. In fact, Americanization represented the real test of Jewish modernity. Could it survive in an open cultural context without state authority for community taxation as was the case in Germany? It was a challenge which American Jewry had met very well. In "idealistic" Germany, Felsenthal now writes with sarcasm, Jews did not make the same sacrifices to establish Jewish institutions that were being made in America. Moreover, American Judaism was more tolerant of diverse religious expressions. In contrast to the situation in Germany, American Jewry held no elections of a centralized *Gemeinde* which could factionalize the communities. Each of the three branches recognized the right of the others to practice Judaism differently.[43] Perhaps it is no mere coincidence that as Felsenthal was becoming more of an American, he was also becoming a fervent Zionist. Although Zionism during the 1890s was just as much a minority viewpoint in the United States as it was in Germany, to Felsenthal the pluralistic American milieu must have seemed more capable of tolerating a Jewish national movement than the more conformist political atmosphere of Germany.

During the 1880s it became much more difficult for American Jews to speak favorably of the German state. While some had welcomed Prussia's liberalism in the 1860s and celebrated its victory over France in 1871, Germany was now seen as a land whose purported spirituality had failed to curb a vicious outbreak of anti-Semitism. Rabbi Jacob Voorsanger of San Francisco protested that the language of the German anti-Semite Adolf Stöcker had no place in the American synagogue.[44] As for the Jews of Germany, by American-Jewish lights they had not risen sufficiently to the occasion. Adolf Moses, the rabbi of Mobile, Alabama, severely castigated the philosopher Hermann Cohen, when, in response to the anti-Semitism of Heinrich von Treitschke, he expressed the hope that Judaism would eventually dissolve into German Protestantism and that the Jews would one day lose the physical characteristics that set them apart. However profound Cohen's philosophy, his supine response showed that an attack on his Jewishness could turn an otherwise clear mind to confusion. American Jews, said this radical Reformer, were proud of their racial characteristics and did not intend to give up their separate religious identity for the sake of national unity.[45]

From the perspective of German Jews in America, the lessons to be learned from the Jews of Germany were now mostly negative ones. For the radical Reformers, German Judaism had settled into stagnation, into a "murky swamp," as Kaufmann Kohler put it. The living spirit of Judaism had fled Germany, he believed, the "prophetic spirit that once called forth Reform has been exhausted." Although the founding fathers had failed in their own land, what they had sought to build could be created in America. While some of the Germanizing American rabbis continued to look askance at Isaac Mayer Wise's organizational efforts, sooner or later they had to recognize his accomplishments: a Union of American Hebrew Congregations in 1873 and the first successful American seminary, the Hebrew Union College, which he founded in 1875. Eleven years later, Conservative Jews in America also established their own theological seminary. It remained now only to assert the new hegemony. Adolf Moses put it with typical American hyperbole in 1882: "From America salvation will go forth, in this land (and not in Germany) will the religion of Israel celebrate its greatest triumphs." Or, as Kaufmann Kohler believed, Judaism in the new world will reinvigorate Judaism in the old. American Jewry had learned from Germany; now it was ready to teach.[46]

If the Philadelphia Conference in 1869 symbolized the rabbinic turn toward independence in religious matters, the successful completion of the *Jewish Encyclopedia* in 1906 marked the coming of age of American-Jewish scholarship. German Jewry had failed to produce a collective monument of equivalent stature. Now its best scholars contributed to an American project whose editorial board was entirely composed of Jews resident in the United States. Although almost all the American writers—who wrote many of the most significant articles—had been trained in Wissenschaft des Judentums abroad, they were pursuing their discipline in America.[47]

It is ironic that just as the mantle of modern Jewish religious and intellectual leadership was passing from Germany to America, German Jews in the United States found themselves inundated by an influx of their brethren from Eastern Europe. It is equally ironic that this influx of East European Jews was largely responsible for sustaining the remnants of a separate German-Jewish identity in America for another generation and more. Still not a part of the American establishment, but for the most part ever-more peripherally Jewish, the wealthier New York families now stressed their German ancestry far more than their Oriental heritage.[48] Eager to remain separate from the newcomers, even as they sought to promote their welfare, the *yahudim* segregated themselves both socially and religiously on the basis of their German origins, thus braking somewhat an otherwise accelerating pace of Americanization.[49] For their part, East European Jews in America—whether devoutly Orthodox or secular Yiddishists—possessed their own Old World loyalties. Thus it was not until after the Holocaust that hegemony within the Jewish people would finally pass incontrovertibly to American Jewry, and to the state of Israel.

Notes

1. Simon Dubnow, *Nationalism and History,* ed. Koppel S. Pinson (Philadelphia: Jewish Publication Society of America, 1958), pp. 272, 348.
2. A most valuable tool for the exploration of this subject has been Rudolf Glanz, *The German Jew in America: An Annotated Bibliography* (Cincinnati: Hebrew Union College Press, 1969).
3. Bertram W. Korn, *Eventful Years and Experiences* (Cincinnati: American Jewish Archives, 1954), pp. 1–26; Bernard D. Weinryb, "The German Jewish Immigrants to America," in Eric E. Hirshler, ed., *Jews from Germany in the United States* (New York: Farrar, Straus, 1955), pp. 113–26; Rudolf Glanz, *Studies in Judaica Americana* (New York: Ktav, 1970), pp. 188–89, 192; Leon Jick, *The Americanization of the Synagogue, 1820–1870* (Hanover, New Hampshire: Published for Brandeis University Press by the University Press of New England, 1976), pp. 39, 137, 175.
4. Jick, *The Americanization of the Synagogue,* pp. 20–26.
5. *Deutsch-Amerikanische Skizzen für jüdische Auswanderer und Nichtauswanderer* (Leipzig, 1857), pp. 47–50; Emil G. Hirsch, "Hüben and Drüben," *The Jewish Reformer,* 5 February 1886, p. 11; Max J. Kohler, "The German-Jewish Migration to America," *Publications of the American Jewish Historical Society* (New York: PAJHS, 1909), pp. 9, 87–105.
6. *Hame'asef* 8 (1809): 13–14, German supplement.
7. Emil Lehmann, *Die deutsche Auswanderung* (Berlin, 1861), pp. 81, 102–3.
8. Glanz, *Studies in Judaica Americana,* p. 12; Hyman B. Grinstein, *The Rise of the Jewish Community of New York, 1654–1860* (Philadelphia: The Jewish Publication Society of America, 1945), pp. 207–9.
9. Glanz, *Studies in Judaica Americana,* p. 70; *Allgemeine Zeitung des Judenthums* (*AZJ*) 11 (1847):145.
10. Jacob R. Marcus, *Memoirs of American Jews, 1775–1865,* vol. 2 (Philadelphia: The Jewish Publication Society of America, 1955), p. 87; Bernhard Felsenthal, *Kol Kore Bamidbar: Über jüdische Reform* (Chicago, 1859), p. 24; Glanz, *Studies in Judaica Americana,* pp. 99, 138–39, 222; Bernhard Felsenthal, *Jüdisches Schulwesen in Amerika* (Chicago, 1866), pp. 10–11; Isaac M. Wise, "Judaism in America," *American Jews' Annual* 1 (1884-85):44.
11. Jick, *The Americanization of the Synagogue,* pp. 21, 222; H.G. Reissner, "The German-American Jews, 1800–1850," *Leo Baeck Institute Year Book* (*LBIYB*) X (1965), pp. 93–94.
12. Felsenthal, *Kol Kore Bamidbar,* p. 24; David Einhorn, *Ausgewählte Predigten und Reden,* ed. Kaufmann Kohler (New York, 1880), p. 90; Reissner "The German-American Jews," p. 92.

13. Glanz, *Studies in Judaica Americana,* pp. 98–100, 214, 237–39; Reissner, "The German-American Jews," p. 65–68, 94–97; I.J. Benjamin, *Three Years in America, 1859–1862,* vol. 1 (Philadelphia: Jewish Publication Society of America, 1956), p. 241; Weinryb, "The German Jewish Immigrants," p. 124; Glanz (pp. 144–45) also notes some instances of discrimination.

14. Henry A. Pochman, *German Culture in America* (Madison: University of Wisconsin Press, 1957), pp. 143, 172, 338–39, 346, 684–85.

15. *Die Deborah* 5 (1859–60): 62; Grinstein, *Jewish Community of New York,* p. 202; Albert M. Friedenberg, "American Jews and the German Revolutionary Movements of 1848–1849," *PAJHS* 17 (1909):205.

16. Kohler, "The German-Jewish Migration to America," p. 103; Glanz, *Studies in Judaica Americana,* p. 157.

17. Deborah Dash Moore, *B'nai B'rith and the Challenge of Ethnic Leadership* (Albany: State University of New York Press, 1981), pp. 1–34. See also *Deutsch-Amerikanische Skizzen,* pp. 89–108; Reissner, "The German-American Jews," pp. 98–100.

18. "Americanisirtes Judenthum," *Der Zeitgeist* 1 (1880):237.

19. Adolf Kober, "Jewish Religious Life in America as Reflected in the Felsenthal Collection," *PAJHS* 45 (1955–56):100, 125; Felsenthal, *Jüdisches Schulwesen,* pp. 30–34.

20. Bertram W. Korn, *German-Jewish Intellectual Influence on American Jewish Life, 1824–1972* (Syracuse: Syracuse University, 1972), pp. 8, 13, 21.

21. *The Occident* 20 (1862):369; Moshe Davis, *The Emergence of Conservative Judaism* (Philadelphia: Jewish Publication Society of America, 1965). Yet the German influence on those men who founded the Conservative movement in America seems to have been considerably less. For example, as Davis notes (p. 109), they did not have the same commitment to the German language. It is interesting that of the nineteen leaders of the "Historical School" in America whom he singles out for special biographical treatment (pp. 329–66), only seven—just slightly more than a third—came from Germany. Four were from Hungary and three were Sephardim. This difference of origins may have been at least one factor in the split between Conservatives and Reformers during the 1880s. It should also be noted that Lance Sussman, who is currently completing a doctoral dissertation on Isaac Leeser at the Hebrew Union College, has been able to argue persuasively that Leeser's Judaism is better defined as an immutable doctrinal Orthodoxy than as a historically conditioned development.

22. Maurice Mayer, "Geschichte des religiösen Umschwunges unter den Israeliten Nordamerikas," *Sinai* 1 (1856):101–7, 171–81; *Hymns Written for the Service of the Hebrew Congregation Beth Elohim, Charleston, S.C.* (Charleston, 1842); Lou H. Silbermann, *American Impact: Judaism in the United States in the Early Nineteenth Century* (Syracuse: Syracuse University, 1964); Jick, *The Americanization of the Synagogue,* pp. 12–13, 55–56, 81–86; Bernard Martin, "The Americanization of Reform Judaism," *Journal of Reform Judaism* (Winter 1980):35–36.

23. Wise, "Judaism in America," p. 42; Mayer, "Geschichte des religiösen Umschwunges," pp. 198–200.

24. *AZJ* 11 (1847):22; *Sinai* 4 (1859):161–69; Mayer, "Geschichte des religiösen Umschwunges," pp. 202–3; *The New Era* 4 (1894):121–32; Grinstein, *Jewish Community of New York,* pp. 353–71; idem, "Reforms at Temple Emanuel

of New York," *Historia Judaica (HJ)* 6 (1944):163–74; Jick, *The American-ization of the Synagogue,* pp. 88–96.

25. *The Jewish Reformer,* 29 January 1886, p. 11; Korn, *German-Jewish Intellectual Influences,* p. 18; Guido Kisch, "Israels Herold: The First Jewish Weekly in New York," *HJ* 2 (1940):75–76; Morris U. Schappes, *A Documentary History of the Jews in the United States, 1654–1875,* 3 ed. (New York: Schocken, 1971), pp. 554–57. At Emanu-El, German was maintained until 1879, See Martin, "The Americanization of Reform Judaism," p. 38. Rodeph Shalom of Philadelphia alternated the language of sermons until close to 1894. See Henry S. Morais, *The Jews of Philadelphia* (Philadelphia, 1894), p. 76. According to Robert Kahn ("Liberalism as Reflected in Jewish Preaching in the English Language in the Mid-Nineteenth Century" [Hebrew Union College DHL dissertation, 1949], p. 53), only in the late 1860s did the German sermon become the exception.

26. *Sinai* 4 (1859):161–62; Einhorn, *Ausgewählte Predigten,* pp. 90, 185; Bernhard N. Cohn, "Early German Preaching in America," *HJ* 15 (1953): pp. 101–2.

27. *Die Deborah* 1 (1855–56):313; *American Israelite* 2 (1855): 137; 8 (1862):324.

28. Jacob R. Marcus, *The Americanization of Isaac Mayer Wise* (Cincinnati: Privately printed, 1931), pp. 8–12.

29. *Die Deborah* 2 (1856–57):340; Joseph Gutmann, "Watchman on an American Rhine," *American Jewish Archives* 10 (1958):135–44. David Einhorn, despite his Germanism, shared some of Wise's messianic hopefulness regarding America. See Gershon Greenberg, "The Significance of America in David Einhorn's Conception of History," *American Jewish Historical Quarterly* 63 (1973), pp. 160–84.

30. *AZJ* 29 (1865):405–7; 44 (1880):435.

31. Zacharias Frankel, "Zur Geschichte der Juden Amerikas," in *Monatsschrift für Geschichte und Wissenschaft des Judenthums* 12 (1863):366–67; Heinrich Graetz, *Geschichte der Juden,* vol. 11 (Leipzig, 1870), p. 231; idem, *History of the Jews,* vol. 5 (London, 1892), pp. 749–50. By contrast the earlier historian, Isaac Marcus Jost, showed a relatively high degree of interest in American Jewry. Although he too noted that "there cannot yet be a history of the American Jews" because their communities were still too atomized, he devoted a special section of sixteen pages to them. He listed all of the communities and institutions known to him as well as Jews who had held political offices, and he devoted special attention to Mordecai Manuel Noah's Ararat project for a Jewish colony on the Niagara River. See Isaac Marcus Jost, *Geschichte der Israeliten,* vol. 10 (Berlin,[2] 1847), pp. 221–36.

32. *Jüdische Zeitschrift für Wissenschaft und Leben (JZWL)* 2 (1863):66–67; 11 (1875):224–25.

33. *JZWL* 7 (1869):161–67.

34. *Protokolle der Rabbiner-Conferenz abgehalten zu Philadelphia, 3–6 November 1869* (New York, 1870). An English translation of the proceedings was published by Sefton D. Temkin as *The New World of Reform* (Bridgeport: Connecticut Hartmore House, 1971).

35. Later Kohler noted: "The broadness of view and independence of thought, which characterized all the deliberations, formed a striking contrast to what I had heard and witnessed at the Leipzig Synod." See his *Personal Reminiscences of My Early Life* (Cincinnati, 1918), p. 12. On the Leipzig and Augsburg synods, see Michael A. Meyer, "The Jewish Synods in Germany

in the Second Half of the Nineteenth Century" (Hebrew), *Studies in the History of the Jewish People and the Land of Israel* 3 (1974):239–74.

36. *JZWL* 8 (1870):21–22.
37. *The Jewish Times* 2 (1870–71): pp. 107, 187–88.
38. Jakob J. Petuchowski, "Abraham Geiger and Samuel Holdheim: Their Differences in Germany and Repercussions in America," *LBIYB* 22 (1977):149–59. Petuchowski shows that Einhorn had already been critical of Geiger on a previous occasion.
39. *JZWL* 8 (1970): p. 12.
40. I.J. Benjamin, *Three Years in America*, vol. 1, p. 34.
41. Bernhard Felsenthal, *Jüdisches Schulwesen in Amerika*, pp. 36–37.
42. Ibid.
43. *Die Deborah*, 19 July 1894, pp. 5–6.
44. *The Occident* 20 (1862):363–66; *The Jewish Times* 3 (1871–72):76; *Der Zeitgeist* 3 (1882):220.
45. Adolf Moses, *Prof. Dr. Hermann Cohen in Marburg und sein Bekenntniss in der Judenfrage. Eine Reminiszenz und Kritik* (Milwaukee, 1880).
46. *Der Zeitgeist* 1 (1880):268–69; 3 (1882):10, 249; *The Jewish Reformer*, 29 January 1886, p. 12.
47. Korn, *German-Jewish Intellectual Influences*, pp. 9–10.
48. Stephen Birmingham, *"Our Crowd": The Great Jewish Families of New York* (New York: Harper & Row, 1967), pp. 148–49.
49. Kaufmann Kohler no doubt spoke for many German Jews in America when, as late as 1910, he extolled the German people's deeper sense of history, their science, philosophy, and biblical criticism, while condemning only their tendency toward a racial definition of German identity. See *Tägliches Cincinnatier Volksblatt*, 23 February 1910, p. 5. The influence of German Judaism reappeared in the twentieth century with the transplantation of Samson Raphael Hirsch's neo-Orthodoxy and the discovery of the German-Jewish thinkers Hermann Cohen, Leo Baeck, Franz Rosenzweig, and Martin Buber. For this twentieth-century German-Jewish influence see Korn, *German-Jewish influences*, pp. 14–15, and Martin, "The Americanization of Reform Judaism," pp. 50–55.

About the Contributors

Israel Bartal is widely known as a leading expert in the field of East European Jewish literature and history. He has been a senior lecturer and visiting professor in Israel and North America, and his publications include the results of studies of the Jewish community in Palestine during the eighteenth and nineteenth centuries.

Lois C. Dubin is completing her Ph.D. at Harvard University in the field of Jewish history and literature. She currently lectures in religious studies, and is Horace W. Goldsmith Fellow in Judaic Studies, Yale University.

Todd M. Endelman is currently professor of history at the University of Michigan. His publications include *The Jews of Georgian England, 1714–1830* (1979) and articles on Jewish themes in several major journals.

Emanuel Etkes is professor of modern Jewish history at the Hebrew University of Jerusalem, specializing in the social and intellectual history of Eastern European Jewry. He has published a monograph on Rabbi Israel Salanter and the beginning of the Musar Movement, and various articles on Hassidism, Jewish Enlightenment, and Eastern European Orthodoxy.

Michael Graetz is Avraham Harman Associate Professor of modern Jewish history at the Hebrew University of Jerusalem, and head of the University's Department of Jewish history. He is also a member of the Senate of the Lessing Academy, Wolfenbüttel, Federal Republic of Germany. He is editor of the Hebräische Beiträge zur Wissenschaft des Judentums, and is author of *Jewish Entrepreneurship during the Nineteenth Century* (1986) and *From Periphery to Center,* on the nineteenth century history of French Jewry (1982).

Jacob Katz is professor of history at the Hebrew University of Jerusalem. He is author of *Out of the Ghetto: The Social Background of Jewish Emancipation; Jews and Freemasons in Europe; From Prejudice to Destruction: Anti-Semitism;* and *Exclusiveness and Tolerance: Studies in Jewish-Gentile Relations in Medieval and Modern Times.*

Hillel J. Kieval is currently assistant professor of history and international studies, and chairman of the Jewish Studies Program at the University of Washington, Seattle. He is the author of many books and articles, including *Transforming the Castle: National Conflict and Jewish Culture in Bohemia, 1870–1918* (1986).

Michael A. Meyer is professor of Jewish history at the Hebrew Union College, Jewish Institute of Religion, Cincinnati, Ohio. His publications include *German Political Pressure and Jewish Religious Response in the Nineteenth Century* (1981); and *Ideas of Jewish History* (1974). He is currently working on a comprehensive history of the Reform Movement in modern Judaism.

Joseph Michman is a research fellow at the Hebrew University of Jerusalem, and chairman of the executive board of the Institute for Research on Dutch Jewry. He is the author of many books and articles on Jewish studies.

Michael Silber is an instructor at the Department of History of the Jewish People, the Hebrew University of Jerusalem.

Robert S. Wistrich is currently associate professor of modern European and Jewish history at the Hebrew University of Jerusalem. His many publications include *Hitler's Apocalypse: Jews and the Nazi Legacy* (1986) and *Who's Who in Nazi Germany* (1982).

Index

Absolutism, 34, 35, 37, 43, 49
Academische Verein Kadimah, 57, 68n58, 68n59
Acculturation. *See* Culture; Social integration
Adler, Felix, 253–54
Adler, Rabbi Nathan, 236
Adler, Samuel, 255, 256
Adler, Victor, 66n40
Alexander, Levy, 230
Altmann, Alexander, 55, 56
American Jewry: anti-Semitism and, 251; associations of, 252–53; culture/scholarship and, 253–54, 263; German influence on, 4, 247–48, 250–55, 256–58, 259–60, 261–64; immigration and, 248–49; rabbinical education and, 253–54; rabbinical leadership and, 259–60; religious reform and, 254–57, 260; social integration and, 3, 248, 251–52; women and, 260–61
Anti-Semitism: in Austria, 58; in Central Europe, 74–75, 76; in England, 237–39; in Galicia, 37; in the Netherlands, 171–72, 176–77; in Prague, 76–77; in Vienna, 46, 53, 57, 58, 59, 60–61, 62, 63, 69n66; in the United States, 251
Arnstein, Fanny von, 46
Ashkenazic Jews: American Jewry and, 249, 255; in England, 226, 227, 232, 233, 244n13; homogeneity of, 10; in Italy, 203–4, 206, 208; in the Netherlands, 172, 173, 175
Asser, Carel, 179
Asser, Moses, 179
Auerbach, Berthold, 252
Auto-emancipation, 56–57
Azulai, Rabbi Haim Yosef, 227

Beit Hamidrash (journal), 55, 67n44
B'nai B'rith, 252–53

Bach, Joseph, 123
Bamberger, Rabbi Selig, 181
Banet, Mordechai, 114
Barukh of Shklov, Rabbi, 20, 21, 22, 25, 26
Bassan, Rabbi Israel Benjamin, 198, 200, 209
Baumgarten, Emmanuel, 70n74
Beer, Peter, 94, 96, 97, 104n74, 107, 110
Belinfante, Moses Cohen, 179
Belinfante, Yitzhak Cohen, 178
Ben-David, Lazarus, 230
Ben-Eliahu, Yosef, 17, 25
Ben-Sarah, Rabbi Leib, 33–34
Benjamin, I. J., 261
Bennett, Solomon, 230
Bernays, Haham, 48
Berr, Cerf, 163
Bezeredy, Istvan, 141
Bible, 14, 18, 19, 236
Biedermann, Hermann, 120
Biedermann, Michael Lazar, 46–47, 64n11, 119–20, 121, 122, 149n49
Bing, Isaia Berr, 164
Biographies, 18
Birnbaum, Nathan, 57, 58, 68n60
Bischoffsheim, L. R., 167
Bleichroder, Gerson, 159
Bloch, Rabbi Joseph Samuel, 60–62, 63, 70n74
Bohemia. *See* Prague, Haskalah movement in
Boskowitz, Rabbi Wolf, 113, 114, 115
Briesach, Isaac, 120
Breisach, Salomon, 120, 122
Breisach, Wolf, 120, 121, 150n57
Bresslau, Marcus, 235
Brill, Rabbi Azriel, 114
Bromet, Harmannus Leonard, 185n23
Bromet, Hartog, 179
Bureaucracy in Galicia, 37–38, 40

Haim of Volozhin, Rabbi, 18
Halachah, 14, 16, 18, 23–24, 179, 197
Halberstam, Elazar, 28
Halevi, Rabbi Yehuda, 20
Hame'asef (journal), 18, 19, 54, 82, 85, 102n31, 107, 196, 205, 206, 207
Hapsburg monarchy: educational reform and, 89–90; Galician Haskalah movement and, 33–36, 37, 40–41, 111–12; Hungarian Haskalah movement and, 7, 110–12, 122, 133; Prague Haskalah movement and, 74–81, 83, 89–92, 98–99, 105n94; reforms of, 43, 89–90; Trieste Haskalah movement and, 191, 192–94. *See also Toleranzpatent*
Harzfeld, Leopold, 120
Haschachar (journal), 55, 57
Haskalah movement: characteristics of, 14–15, 72–73; definition of, 13–15; education and, 3; *Halachah* and, 14; Hebrew language and, 14–15; opponents of, 73; social integration and, 15; Talmud and, 14; theology of, 14; Torah and, 14. *See also* name of nation/city, e.g. Russia, Vienna
Hassidism, 9, 10, 24, 28, 36, 38
Hazaddik, Joseph, 99n3
Hebrew language, 14–15, 55, 68n50, 197
Hell, François, 163
Herrera, Abraham, 198
Hess, Moses, 162
Hildesheimer, Rabbi Esriel, 127
Hirsch, Emil G., 254, 256
Hirsch, Rabbi Samson Raphael, 160, 181, 182, 186n35, 187n42, 253, 255
Hobson, J. A., 239
Hock, Simon, 97
Holdheim, Samuel, 125, 138, 260
Homberg, Herz, 38, 94, 95, 97, 112, 205, 217n35
Horowitz, Rabbi Pinchas Halevi, 10, 99n3, 114
Horwitz, Lazar, 54, 67n44
Human intellect, importance of, 23
Humanism, 15, 21, 55, 56–58. *See also* Enlightenment, Western
Hungary, Haskalah movement in: conservatism of, 124–26; education and, 110–12, 115, 121, 132–33, 145n21, 146n27, 146n29, 148n37; emancipation

and, 136–40; Enlightenment and, 109; German influence on, 7–8, 107–10, 112–13, 117–20, 122–24, 125, 134–36, 142–43; Hapsburg monarchy and, 7, 110–12, 122, 133; harmonizing aspect of, 115; idealism and, 135; ideology and, 129–30, 134–35, 142–43; liberalism and, 136, 138, 140, 141; nationalism and, 136; Neology and, 124, 129–30, 134–35, 142; orthodoxy and, 129; politics and, 136–40, 142; Prague's influence on, 115–17; publishing and, 107–8, 127–29, 139, 144n5; rabbinical education and, 126, 135; rabbinical leadership and, 112–15, 124, 125, 127; radicals and, 138; Revolution of 1848 and, 125–26, 137–40; social context of, 108–10; social integration and, 109–10, 139–40, 141–42; traditional observance and, 133–34; Vienna's influence on, 117–20; yeshivot and, 114–15
Hurwitz, Eliah, 113
Hyamson, Albert M., 232

Ibn-Gabirol, Shlomo, 162
Ibn-Paquda, Rabbi Bahya, 20
Ibn-Tibbon, Rabbi Yehuda, 19
Idealism and Hungarian Haskalah movement, 135
Ideology: in England, 229, 230–31, 234, 236; Hungarian Haskalah movement and, 129–30, 134–35, 142–43; Italian/Trieste Haskalah movement and, 191, 192–94; Russian Haskalah movement and, 26–28
Immigration/migration: American Jewry and, 248–49; of Czech Jews to Vienna, 69n64; French Haskalah movement and, 161, 163–64; in the Netherlands, 179–80
Israel, Hayim Abraham, 199
Italy/Trieste, Haskalah movement in: Ashkenazic Jews and, 203–4, 206, 208; culture and, 196, 199–200, 201–2, 203–4, 209–10, 211; definition of, 211; demography and, 190–91; education and, 93, 189, 192–94, 202–3, 210; Enlightenment and, 191, 194, 204, 210–11; German influence on, 5, 191–92, 194–211; Hapsburg monarchy and, 191,